D1329899

UNITED STATES
WELFARE
POLICY

MORAL TRADITIONS SERIES
James F. Keenan, SJ, series editor

UNITED STATES
WELFARE
POLICY

A Catholic Response

THOMAS J. MASSARO, SJ

GEORGETOWN UNIVERSITY PRESS
Washington, D.C.

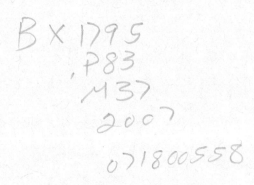

As of January 1, 2007, 13-digit ISBN numbers have replaced the 10-digit system.

13-digit 10-digit

Paperback: 978-1-58901-156-4   Paperback: 1-58901-156-2

Cloth: 978-1-58901-155-7   Cloth: 1-58901-155-4

Georgetown University Press, Washington, D.C.

Library of Congress Cataloging-in-Publication Data

Massaro, Thomas, 1961–
United States welfare policy : a Catholic response /
Thomas J. Massaro.
     p.   cm.—(Moral traditions series)
Includes bibliographical references and index.
   ISBN-13: 978-1-58901-155-7 (hardcover : alk. paper)
   ISBN-10: 1-58901-155-4 (hardcover : alk. paper)
   ISBN-13: 978-1-58901-156-4 (pbk. : alk. paper)
   ISBN-10: 1-58901-156-2 (pbk. : alk. paper)
1. Public welfare—Religious aspects—Catholic Church.
2. Public welfare—United States. 3. United States—Social policy.
4. Catholic Church—Doctrines. I. Title.
BX1795.P83M37 2007
261.8′325820973—dc22   2006031178

⊗ This book is printed on acid-free paper meeting the requirements of the American National Standard for Permanence in Paper for Printed Library Materials.

14 13 12 11 10 09 08 07   9 8 7 6 5 4 3 2
First printing

Printed in the United States of America

Contents

PREFACE

Practically every author would prefer to begin a preface like this one by describing how the volume grew out of the author's hopes or aspirations—fervent desires for a better understanding of a given field of inquiry or for a better future for society or similar optimistic goals.

I cannot, in all honesty, open on such a sanguine note. Rather, this book grows out of my sense of frustration, on two counts.

First, our nation's social policies fail to reflect the full range of our values as Americans. The rhetoric surrounding the welfare reform of 1996 and the repeated attempts to reauthorize that legislation since 2002 reveal a disturbing gap between the laws we have enacted as a nation and the ethical values we profess as a people. To be sure, the dominant discourse of recent debates over welfare policy did reflect a certain subset of the values Americans tend to hold dear: our legitimate concern about limiting fiscal outlays, encouraging personal responsibility, and enforcing a work ethic. As a result, an open-ended federal entitlement for low-income families was replaced with capped block grants to states. A number of recently enacted social policies also reaffirm our strong work ethic, commitment to honesty, and high regard for stable and independent family life. This is why our newest policies seek to transform welfare into a work-based system of temporary support for low-income families; they reflect an eagerness to separate out those who truly need welfare from those who, with less claim to legitimate need, would take advantage of the system to obtain handouts. But very few features of welfare policy today correspond to another set of our noble national aspirations. These include our collective desires to help the truly needy, to reduce poverty through concerted public action, and to support children who are unfortunate enough to be born into single-parent families whose adult members display significant barriers to employment. Public opinion surveys consistently indicate that the American public thinks our nation is doing too little to help lift poor families above the poverty line. While it is true that an overwhelming majority of Americans repeatedly registers its suspicion of a welfare system that has historically been hampered by a variety of unintended consequences and perverse incentives, we also give ample evidence of understanding the importance of providing the support necessary to make work a realistic route to financial independence, capable of lifting families out of lives of grinding poverty.[1] The options enacted in recent federal and state policies regarding low-income families reflect only a fraction of the social priorities we affirm.

A second source of frustration associated with the topic of this book is the relative silence of ethicists whom we might hope would take up the task of analyzing recent public policy from a normative perspective. Although there has long been a tacit division of labor between ethical theorists and the more practical type of moralist, recent events in both foreign policy and domestic social policy have rendered this convention more objectionable, even disturbing. America's most distinguished ethicists generally write books about theories, often quibbling over fine points of scholarly concern that remain at a high level of abstraction. As if hesitant to apply theories to real-life situations, these highly respected ethicists too seldom get around to engaging concrete social and political issues. In the desire to stay on familiar ground where they are the undisputed experts, professional ethicists generally avoid the arduous task of doing the painstaking homework and venturing forth on the shifting sands of the policy debates of the moment. There are, of course, many scholarly books and articles on public policy, but these are with rare exceptions written from outside the guild of ethicists and generally proceed from a strictly political, sociological, or historical point of view. As a result, most commentators on public policy exhibit perceptible discomfort when venturing into the territory of the ethical. It is infinitely easier to describe policy options and legacies of political history than to draw well-informed judgments on what is right or wrong about a presidential initiative or a legislative package being considered in Congress.

What, then, are we left with? Much of what now passes for policy analysis consists of an unsatisfying blend of policy history and a reporting of statistics that attempts to measure social well-being in the relatively simplistic ways adopted by those who are derisively called number crunchers and bean counters.[2] While such literature is surely relevant and often quite helpful in providing necessary pieces of the ethical puzzle, it leaves us far short of the goal of rendering serious normative judgments. A full engagement of the ethics of public policy must not sidestep deeper and more contentious questions about the shape and meaning of the good life. What types of policy are truly in the public interest as it is most broadly conceived? Is it possible to identify a core of common nonnegotiable social values, and so to overcome the seeming paralysis of ethical reflection in pluralistic social settings? If we dare to hope that such a constructive project is possible, surely the basic survival needs of millions of innocent children will emerge among those items that deserve protection and special concern as overriding moral priorities.

This book employs Catholic social teaching as its key ethical perspective from which to view contemporary American social welfare policies. Over the past century, Catholic social thought has emerged as an important tradition of reflection on the meaning of life in human society and an influential articulation of political, social, and economic values. I do not expect everyone to find all of its claims and commitments satisfying or consistent with their own deepest convictions about the meaning of justice in society. However, Catholic social teaching does display numerous remarkable features that are likely to attract support from many quarters. It proposes a coherent set of priorities for social existence and, in keeping with its desire to address audiences beyond the Catholic faithful, leaves wide leeway for those differences of opinion that inevitably emerge among people of good will. In a spirit of dialogue, it invites its hearers to apply its principles to the complex challenges of modern economic and political systems. The Church's social documents, authored by recent popes, councils, and bodies of bishops, offer a distinctive point of reference for measuring U.S. social policy against the standards of a system of religiously grounded values. In employing Catholic social teaching, the framework of ethical thought that I happen to know best, by no means do I intend to preclude the contributions of other ethical orientations in future policy debates. Rather, I hope precisely to encourage dialogue and to invite further engagement with those who would comment on vital policy issues from any perspective of their choosing— from whatever point on the political spectrum and from whatever philosophical or religious perspective they consider their home.

This volume is a work of religious social ethics. Social ethics is by nature an interdisciplinary field, acting as a crossroads for readers with a great variety of interests and backgrounds. I assume on the part of my readers no previous knowledge of either of the universes of discourse I enter, either theology or policy analysis. I have attempted to balance what will be of interest for those looking for a primarily theological analysis of a key policy issue with what will interest readers more concerned about the formation and administration of social policy itself. Above all, I have attempted not to overburden the reader with excessive detail regarding debates that at times seem interminable. I frequently employ endnotes to substantiate my analysis with evidence that might otherwise break the flow of arguments made in the text itself.

I have attempted to document as fully as possible the claims and unavoidable generalizations I make in each chapter, but readers should be aware of a dilemma that creeps up in works like this one that seek to comment on rapidly changing policy developments. As in many works involving current events, certain sacrifices had to be made in the interest of timely publication. This manuscript was completed in July 2006, shortly after Congress had once again abandoned hope for a definitive reauthorization of the 1996 welfare law. After putting off the task of a thorough reauthorization for nearly four years since the initial expiration of the law on September 30, 2002, Congress during early 2006 extended existing welfare arrangements by rolling provisions for program funding into the 2006 budget reconciliation bill. Now that the welfare system can continue by law until September 2010 without substantial changes, the federal government appears to be further than ever from reaching agreement on a comprehensive revision of the 1996 law. The current juncture thus provides a convenient stopping point for surveying recent trends in social policy. Further, the desire to publish timely analysis of policy measures often conflicts with the desire to support with suitable evidence the effects of recent changes in a comprehensive way. A more satisfying version of this book would supply somewhat richer documentation regarding even more recently measured results of welfare reform since 1996. I would like to be able to cite such sources as Census Bureau data collected after 2004, more recent welfare reports from all fifty states, and many other independent studies that are being prepared as this volume goes to print. No one has a God's-eye view of the results of welfare reform, but I do sometimes envy those who, five or more years from now, will have before their eyes the full range of data on, for example, the success of welfare-to-work programs covering the entire pivotal period 1996–2006 and beyond.

This work was supported by several people and institutions that have earned my deep gratitude. Much of the initial research and drafting took place during a sabbatical year (2002–2003) awarded to me by the Weston Jesuit School of Theology. A generous Faculty Fellowship grant from the Lilly Endowment Theological Research Grants program (administered by the Association of Theological Schools) funded half of my research sabbatical. I thank the editors at Georgetown University Press for their excellent assistance and patience. Although I have thoroughly reworked and updated all the analysis, certain sections of chapters 1 to 4 borrow from my 1998 work, *Catholic Social Teaching and United States Welfare Reform,* and I thank The Liturgical Press for facilitating my use of materials from that out-of-print volume. I would also like to thank my friends at the Leonard Neale House Jesuit Community in Washington, D.C., for hosting me so graciously during the months when my research activities cluttered their basement rooms with unsightly stacks of books and papers.

I dedicate this book to the faculty and staff of the Weston Jesuit School of Theology in Cambridge, Massachusetts. Nobody, anywhere, has ever enjoyed more wonderful friends and colleagues.

NOTES

1. Among the best sources of data and analysis of public opinion on welfare are the following: Martin Gilens, *Why Americans Hate Welfare: Race, Media, and the Politics of Antipoverty Policy* (Chicago: University of Chicago Press, 1999); John E. Tropman, *Does America Hate the Poor? The Other American Dilemma* (Westport, CT: Praeger Publishers, 1998); R. Kent Weaver and William T. Dickens, eds., *Looking Before We Leap: Social Science and Welfare Reform* (Washington, DC: Brookings Institution, 1995), esp. chap. 4, "Public Opinion on Welfare Reform."

2. Those phrases conjure up images of Jeremy Bentham, who invented a metric called "utiles" to compare social outcomes of discrete decisions. This father of utilitarianism is quite susceptible to parody but has surely been among the most influential figures in the modern field of philosophical ethics. Indeed, it might be

said that the default position of contemporary ethics is still a brand of utilitarianism (focused on maximizing the greatest good of the greatest number based on consultation of individual personal preferences and calculations regarding their interaction) that threatens to ignore such justice concerns as the rights of the minority. The common-sense orientation of utilitarianism risks sacrificing the interests and even dire needs of people who are unpopular or who somehow come to be outvoted or overlooked entirely. Although not to be dismissed out of hand, ethicists since at least as far back as the 1971 publication of John Rawls's *A Theory of Justice* (Cambridge, MA: Harvard University Press, 1971) have generally agreed that something more complex than standard versions of utilitarianism is needed. See, for example, Ralph D. Ellis, *Ethical Foundations for Policy Analysis* (Washington, DC: Georgetown University Press, 1998).

INTRODUCTION

On August 22, 1996, President Bill Clinton signed into law the Personal Responsibility and Work Opportunity Reconciliation Act (PRWORA), which drastically changed the nature of our nation's welfare system. The law abolished the major federal cash assistance program, Aid to Families with Dependent Children (AFDC), and replaced it with the Temporary Assistance for Needy Families (TANF) program. The new system offered cash assistance to low-income families on a far more restricted basis. Benefits were conditioned on stricter work requirements and, for the first time ever, were subject to time limits. Reflecting welfare reform's fundamental agenda of devolution to enhanced state and local control, the federal contribution now consists of capped block grants to the states. By revoking the former income entitlement, one that dated from the days of the New Deal, the U.S. government embarked on what was intended to be a six-year experiment regarding the funding and administration of welfare. These new arrangements for public assistance for our nation's poorest families are markedly different from the welfare system that had operated for the previous sixty years.

As of this writing in July 2006, our nation still awaits a thorough review and definitive reauthorization of the 1996 welfare law, which technically expired September 30, 2002. Although the House of Representatives has repeatedly passed versions of updated welfare arrangements as favored by President George W. Bush, the Senate has held up final action on new welfare legislation. Neither the 107th Congress nor the 108th Congress, each featuring narrow Republican majorities, has been able to break the logjam on welfare. The result has been a series of stopgap measures and funding extensions that have retained welfare essentially in its present form since September 2002 and will likely do so until September 2010. In effect, the six-year trial period of welfare reform and the TANF system it established has been more than doubled.

Despite the uncertainties associated with each election cycle, it is possible to make an educated guess about the shape of future welfare arrangements, based mainly on the proposals that have worked their way partially through Congress so far. The president joins most members of Congress in an eagerness to make permanent the major welfare measures in effect since 1996. Only a handful of moderate Republican senators have prevented this desire from being incorporated into a definitive reauthorization law. Indeed, the few changes that in recent years came closest to adoption as amendments to the current law would have had the effect of restricting welfare even further. Work participation quotas would have risen from 50 to 70 percent of recipients, required work hours would have been expanded, and exemptions for new mothers possibly curtailed. Holding up these proposals have been a series of demands by Democrats and moderate Republicans, some of them on the Senate Finance Committee that must authorize any new welfare bill, for such concessions as enhanced federal subsidies for child care in exchange for support for these more restrictive measures. The stalemate is reminiscent of what took place in the previous round of welfare reform, as President Clinton's signing of PRWORA in 1996 was the long-delayed closing act of years of public debate and congressional wrangling, featuring two earlier vetoes on the part of Clinton himself of proposed welfare bills. Media coverage of these developments reveals that, at both these junctures of the ongoing saga of federal welfare policy, nerves have been rubbed raw on this issue. The protracted delays and lingering air of contentiousness surrounding both rounds of debates reflect the general history of welfare, a policy upon which Americans experience deep value conflicts, a recurring and tortuous inability to reach consensus, and a proclivity toward acrimonious public discourse.

There has indeed been a sharp divide between those who have consistently opposed the sweeping revision of our welfare laws and those who have supported these new policy directions. Liberals, who form the core of the opposition to PRWORA and its reauthorization, generally view this historic repudiation of the federal government's sixty-year commitment to low-income families as a colossal mistake. The "mean season" of ugly rhetoric demonizing welfare recipients that produced the 1996 law during the Newt Gingrich–led 104th Congress continues to be a nightmare of bad memories for progressives. Yet even those on the left find themselves reluctantly admitting that the measures, however flawed, brought about substantial progress for many poor families, at least during the first five years of their enactment. They attribute most of the successes in transitions from welfare to work to the strong economy of 1996–2001, years that stand out as among the most exceptionally prosperous in American history.

For supporters of the PRWORA legislation, particularly those on the right-hand side of the political spectrum, welfare reform was generally viewed as a glorious success in social policy. They point with satisfaction to the astonishing reduction of welfare caseloads, which fell 60 percent nationwide, from an all-time high of fourteen million people in 1994 to only six million by September 2001. Yet the glee of sponsoring an experiment that succeeded was mitigated by haunting suspicions that the gains were fragile and that efforts at reauthorization proceeded on increasingly shaky grounds. The new work-based welfare system had not fully been tested by the conditions of a recession, and the uptick in the welfare rolls during 2002 loomed as an alarming omen, coming as it did at the very moment that Congress was considering a Bush proposal to increase work requirements significantly during the attempted reauthorization process. While utter disaster for millions of poor single parents and their children never struck, it is clear that the past decade has presented significant new challenges to this hard-pressed population. The most recent report on the outcomes experienced by single parents in the state of Wisconsin, a welfare pioneer usually looked to as a showcase of success, confirms these fears. This major University of Chicago study released in May 2006 documents how poorly low-income families have fared in the age of welfare reform, as many such families are experiencing "profound difficulty balancing the demands of work and parenting."[1] Not only are earnings and income well below the levels hoped for by welfare reform advocates, but as many as 16 percent of such families in this Wisconsin study saw a child removed from their homes by social service agencies because of evidence of abuse or neglect.[2] Deep anxiety about the future sustainability of work-based welfare programs prevents even the most ardent cheerleaders for TANF from a full-throated celebration of their accomplishments.

This volume explores not only the politics and outcomes of welfare reform, but also the normative significance of recent changes in American social policy. The moral analysis contained here will proceed according to the insights developed in Catholic social thought, a religious framework that supplies rich ethical resources for making judgments about the means and ends of public policies. The relevance of Catholic social teaching to U.S. policy is not exhausted by the realization that the Roman Catholic Church comprises the single largest religious community in the United States. A careful examination of Catholic social thought reveals a tradition of reflection featuring a methodology that in no way precludes nonadherents from employing its analytic framework as well as its conclusions.

By proceeding along lines that invoke the findings of reason and empirical observation rather than with an overriding emphasis on revelation, Catholic social teaching exhibits a proclivity to be open-ended and accessible to all people of good will in a way that is particularly well-suited to a pluralistic society like the United States. As such, this tradition of social thought exercises a double voice. On the one hand, it is a highly useful instrument for a religious community seeking to serve society as a public church actively engaged in advocacy for a distinctive vision of social justice. On the other hand, it emerges as a uniquely useful set of tools readily employed by a more general audience of policy analysts concerned about values such as equity and in support of an agenda of advancing the well-being of the poor and expanding economic opportunities for the most vulnerable members of society.[3]

The genre of this volume is religious social ethics addressing issues of public policy. One hard-won lesson that comes from long experience is that any expectation of translating religiously grounded values directly into public policy is bound to meet with frustration. So many past attempts to link the two in a facile way have proven to be unworkable or unsustainable, if not ultimately counterproductive. Our nation's experiment with the prohibition of alcohol in the early decades of the twentieth century demonstrated as much, to cite just one attempt to legislate morality in a ham-fisted way. Yet the impulse to bring religious values into the public arena is an authentic and deeply felt one. Indeed, it might well be argued that true adherence to the fullness of the gospel demands that Christians attempt nothing less than this. The task of religious social ethics may thus accurately be described as an attempt to act on this imperative by means of connecting the dots, in other words, highlighting the application of religiously grounded principles to social issues in concrete and practical ways. Since the connections between everyday issues like welfare reform and the contents of religious faith are far from obvious to many observers, bringing a religious message to bear upon contemporary social and political issues invokes a distinctive set of challenges indeed.

These general observations are especially true of the present work, which involves linking controversial policy developments of recent years with the insights of a venerable religious tradition regarding the meaning of social justice. These two worlds—of contemporary public policy debates on one hand, and religiously grounded claims about social justice on the other—require some explicit bridging, and this book seeks to accomplish this important task in a way that is satisfactory and illuminating for both sides of the equation. Because such efforts can prove to be quite arduous and even risky, perhaps the analogies of bridging and connecting the dots should give way to the analogy of juggling, the art of deftly keeping several fragile objects in the air at the same time. The juggling act attempted in this volume unfolds in a series of chapters that introduce the raw material for ethical judgments regarding policies that can be assessed more thoroughly once we have reviewed the relevant moral resources.

The payoff at the end of this work depends upon the grounding contained in earlier chapters. Two chapters introduce the contents of Catholic social thought as it is relates to welfare policy. Chapter 1 is a general review of those themes in universal Catholic social teaching that apply to social policy, and chapter 4 examines how the Catholic Church in the United States has applied these insights to social policy in recent decades, especially at the time of the welfare reform of the mid-1990s. The remaining chapters (2, 3, 5, and 6) consist primarily of policy history and analysis. They seek to explain the unfolding developments and rationale behind changes in the direction of welfare policy in recent decades, focusing of course on the events that led to the landmark welfare overhaul of 1996 and the attempted reauthorization of that law since 2002. The second half of chapter 6 draws on all the preceding materials in identifying and evaluating pivotal ethical concerns regarding current welfare policy. This analysis allows the drawing up of a number of recommendations for improvement in social welfare policy. It is the author's hope and expectation that the reader will find enough continuity between the earlier accounts of both Catholic social teaching and the development of U.S. welfare policy to agree that the final conclusions and moral judgments are adequately grounded in what precedes them.

Our national experiment since 1996 with a new style of welfare arrangements has been neither a resounding success nor an utter disaster. An objective assessment of the performance of the TANF system so far would have to include attention to both the accomplishments and shortcomings of welfare reform. On one hand are the numerous success stories, instances where families moved into financial independence after years of languishing on public relief, often motivated by the get-tough policies mandated by new federal law and implemented by states. On the other hand, it is impossible to ignore substantial causes for concern about how poor families are faring under the new welfare laws that subject them to sanctions, time limits, and work requirements. Even the partial data available to researchers confirm that many vulnerable families have indeed suffered from the loss of benefits, restrictions on eligibility, and a heightened level of income insecurity unprecedented since the Great Depression. By altering the social contract that undergirded the previous six decades of American social policy, the latest rounds of welfare reform signal a major policy departure that merits close analysis.

It is beyond the scope of this book definitively to resolve the debate about the legacy of the welfare reform of 1996. However, this volume does seek to call attention to the need to move beyond the generalizations that all too often characterize the claims of those who comment on welfare policy. Facile claims about the ability of low-income, single-parent families to transition into the job market on reasonable terms require closer investigation than they customarily receive in the media and public discourse. Those who claim that the former welfare entitlement needlessly perpetuated dependency usually overestimate the ability of such families to achieve financial independence. Conversely, those who lament the abolition of the entitlement are often guilty of exaggerating the barriers to employment faced by single mothers with young children. A key relevant insight is that each family faces its own distinctive set of challenges regarding work, child care, and overall stability. The best policies are those that exhibit the greatest flexibility regarding expectations and timelines for progress toward independence. Coming up short, then, are any proposed analytic frameworks that fail to disaggregate the welfare caseload to account for the many types of families with differing needs and varying resources and assets.

One realistic response to the complexity of this subject matter is to acknowledge the existence of a large and open-ended research agenda that summons social scientists and policy analysts to arduous future work on welfare and poverty. It is absolutely crucial that all parties encourage an accurate and comprehensive contextualization of welfare policy within the life of our nation and its families. For example, we should constantly ask: How exactly do various types of families interact with the welfare system, as they cycle on and off public assistance according to income fluctuations? Precisely which policies, programs, and administrative arrangements would strike the right balance of fostering healthy independence while not requiring a given family to accomplish goals that lie beyond its abilities? How may public policy challenge families to do their best without placing them in impossible situations? The most comprehensive assessments will locate the state and federal components of TANF within the patchwork of other means-tested programs, some of which (particularly health care programs like Medicaid) dwarf TANF, the major cash benefit welfare program and the one that receives the most attention. Another vital item in a constructive research agenda involves identifying the distinctive features of poor families according to relevant social indicators, including factors of health, education, and family composition. Further, achieving an accurate measure of the success of welfare reform in any state or jurisdiction will depend upon detailed knowledge of the process of implementation. Such items as the exercise of discretion on the part of caseworkers and the variable way that on the books regulations are enforced (e.g., whether sanctions and allowable exemptions from program rules are administered according to the letter of the law) demand careful study before conclusions about program effectiveness should be drawn.

Welfare continues to be among the most contested terrain in all of American politics. It remains a daunting task to forge a consensus on a social welfare policy that closely matches most or all of the values held in common by the American populace. Perhaps no single set of poor relief arrangements is capable of balancing all the values we as a nation hold dear. For example, there appears to be a permanent and unavoidable tension between two clusters of such values: those regarding personal responsibility (of each person for his or her family's well-being); and those regarding social responsibility (exercised by governments and other agents of the common good on behalf of the most vulnerable members of society). Certainly we wish social policy neither to coddle people so that they lose all incentive to develop themselves by their own initiative nor to place people in impossible situations, lacking both the means for advancement and the security of a safety net. Perhaps it is the distinctive potential contribution of religious traditions such as Catholic social teaching to help clarify in the minds of the American populace the relevant set of values and to offer hope that these values might shape more satisfactory social policies in the future.

Sadly, despite the occasional rhetoric and aspirations of would-be welfare reformers, the topic of welfare reform in the United States seldom evokes the sentiment of hope anymore. In reviewing the recent history of welfare policy as presented in this volume, we must face the fact that, collectively, we have squandered many opportunities to adopt social policies that truly advance the well-being of the poorest families in our midst. As a nation, we have so far neither made adequate commitments of resources to invest in their lives nor paid adequate attention to the conditions that reinforce their plight and limit their horizons. We nevertheless may dare to hope that future welfare arrangements, built on more accurate assessments of the characteristics and needs of low-income families, may truly represent the best of our national efforts and possibilities for collective action to improve the lives of poor parents and children in our midst.

NOTES

1. Erik Eckholm, "For the Neediest of the Needy, Welfare Reforms Still Fall Short, Study Says," *New York Times,* May 15, 2006, A19.
2. Ibid. The longitudinal study was conducted by the Chapin Hall Center for Children at the University of Chicago. Its primary coauthors are Dr. Mark E. Courtney, director of the Center, and researcher Amy Dworsky. The fortunes of 1,075 single parents in Wisconsin were tracked over several years to document the study's conclusions regarding work-force participation, employment and earnings, poverty rates, and outcomes for children over time. The text of the report is available at www.chapinhall.org (accessed June 24, 2006). The findings of earlier studies on the same topic will be treated in chapters 5 and 6 below.
3. For insightful treatment of related issues regarding the authority and implicit ecclesiology of Catholic social teaching, especially regarding its distinctive style of cultural engagement in a situation of pluralism, see Richard R. Gaillardetz, "The Ecclesiological Foundations of Modern Catholic Social Teaching," in *Modern Catholic Social Teaching: Commentaries and Interpretations,* ed. Kenneth R. Himes, O.F.M. et al., 72–98 (Washington, DC: Georgetown University Press, 2005).

Catholic Social Teaching: General Approaches to Social Policy

Modern Catholic social teaching is one outstanding expression of the ongoing attempt of Christians in every age to advance the dialogue between the gospel and the culture in which they find themselves. In key documents emerging from recent popes, councils, and groupings of bishops, the Catholic Church has boldly addressed the needs of our age for a serious consideration of the requirements of justice. Starting with the publication of Pope Leo XIII's encyclical letter, *Rerum novarum* (Of New Things), in 1891, Church leaders have contributed to an evolving body of teaching on economic, political, cultural, and social matters.

Among all the writings that might be termed Catholic social teaching, the easiest to identify are a set of approximately a dozen documents emanating from Vatican sources. Most of these fit within the genre of the papal social encyclical, substantial writings that take the form of a letter intended to circulate widely among the faithful, and indeed among all persons of good will. However, at least one document from the Second Vatican Council of 1962–1965 (The Pastoral Constitution of the Church in the Modern World, or *Gaudium et spes*) and one document from the 1971 Synod of Bishops (*Justitia in mundo* [Justice in the World]) also focus squarely on social issues and are thus considered key parts of the social teaching of the universal Catholic Church.[1] Table 1.1 at the end of this chapter lists the year of publication, title (usually in the original Latin), and source of each of the Church documents referred to in the chapter.

VEHICLES OF CATHOLIC SOCIAL TEACHING

There are, of course, other Catholic sources of wisdom about life in human society than the official social teaching documents described above. Much credit should also be given to a parallel track of unofficial Catholic social teaching that has shaped the moral imagination of generations of Catholics and contributed to effective leadership for social change. The words of courageous labor leaders influenced by their Christian faith (Lech Walesa comes immediately to mind), the example of charitable service by saintly people (Dorothy Day and Mother Teresa, among others), the efforts of countless local leaders of Christian communities working for peace and justice in its many forms—all are eloquent expressions of Catholic social teaching in the broadest sense. It might well be argued that without these local applications and enactments of commitments to social justice, the words of popes and bishops would be largely wasted efforts, without influence in a world hungry for justice.[2]

At an intermediate level, between officially promulgated Vatican social teaching and these local expressions of work for justice, lie diverse efforts on the part of bishops. Individual bishops in their dioceses, as well as regional and national episcopal conferences and similar ad hoc groupings of bishops, frequently address issues of political and economic justice of relevance to their own localities, regions, and nations. Very often a bishop or group of bishops will apply the broad themes found in Vatican documents to local needs and situations of injustice. For example, in the United States alone, recent decades have witnessed the publication of dozens of pastoral letters on diverse matters of social concern. The black bishops joined their voices to publish a 1984 letter on racism, the Appalachian bishops in 1975 addressed the economic situation of their region, the bishops of the northwestern states took up the protection of the Columbia River in a 2001 letter, and the bishops of the southeastern states taught about worker justice in the poultry industry of their region.[3] Numerous examples of similar teaching documents could be cited on the part of individual bishops and even statewide conferences of bishops who seek to inform or influence legislation in state capitals.

The most public attention, of course, has focused on national groupings of Catholic bishops. There are 108 such episcopal conferences throughout the world. In the United States this body of over 200 bishops representing the entire country has changed its name several times (for decades it was called the National Catholic Welfare Conference and then the National Conference of Catholic Bishops, or NCCB) and in 2001 settled on the title United States Conference of Catholic Bishops (USCCB). Besides holding semiannual deliberative meetings, the Bishops' Conference maintains a professional staff in Washington, D.C., with several departments dedicated to the task of promoting social justice and applying Catholic social teaching to issues of the day. As we shall see in chapter 4, the Bishops' Conference has been quite active in recent years in advocating for a version of welfare reform that would uphold the multiple values expressed in the Catholic social tradition.

THE METHODOLOGY OF CATHOLIC SOCIAL TEACHING: THREE CAVEATS

Before proceeding further, we should note three caveats about how to make proper use of Catholic social teaching. First, the tradition of social teaching must be distinguished somewhat from other types of Church pronouncements on matters of theological doctrine. When Church leaders address the faithful with teachings about the proper organization of economic life or the pursuit of values such as political justice, they do not intend to bind the consciences of believers in quite the same way as they do when they teach on subjects involving the inner core of explicitly theological dogma, such as the nature of the Holy Trinity or the presence of Christ in the sacraments. On matters where theological perspectives are only one part of a larger picture and where the expertise of Church officials is limited, the content of Church teachings is perhaps best described as consisting of a set of prudential judgments. While some underlying truths that ground the teachings might well be considered to lie within the core of the Christian faith, the actual applications and policy recommendations that flow from these commitments admit of a certain amount of fluidity and even uncertainty.

For example, when the Church insists on the principle that the rights of persons of all races must be equally respected, it is offering a perspective that cannot be denied without refusing a core principle of Christian theology, namely the equal dignity of all humans. However, if a pope or bishop were to recommend, within the context of a social teaching document, a specific program to redress inequality (such as affirmative action admissions and hiring policies or busing school children to alleviate the effects of residential segregation by race), there is room for a legitimate diversity of opinions about the wisdom of such applications of the underlying theological principles. Distinguishing between those areas where disagreement is allowable and those that require assent of all the faithful follows upon recognizing the existence of a hierarchy of truths. The message is that loyal Catholics are called to take the Church's social teachings seriously, but not to confuse them with solemn pronouncements on matters of doctrine that are closer to the core of their faith. Indeed, the moral guidance proposed on subjects pertaining to social justice is explicitly offered by the Church to all persons of good will regardless of their religious affiliation. It would be inconsistent to tie the practical recommendations within these documents too closely to membership in good standing in the Catholic Church. Room for respectful disagreement is part of the proper understanding of the import of Catholic social teaching.

A second caveat pertains to the related issue of specificity and detail. It is important to distinguish between the role of universal social teachings, which generally come from Vatican sources, and local applications of universal principles, such as the moral exhortations and social analysis contained within the pastoral letters issued by national episcopal conferences

or regional and statewide conferences of bishops. A helpful encapsulation
of this insight is contained in the 1971 document, *Octogesima adveniens* (A
Call to Action), where Pope Paul VI declares:

> In the face of such widely varying situations it is difficult for us to utter a uni-
> fied message and to put forward a solution which has universal validity. Such
> is not our ambition, nor is it our mission. It is up to the Christian communi-
> ties to analyze with objectivity the situation which is proper to their own
> country, to shed on it the light of the Gospel's unalterable words and to draw
> principles of reflection, norms of judgment and directives for action from the
> social teachings of the church.[4]

The words of Paul VI indicate a necessary division of labor and a sensitivity to local context. A universal authority can speak in general terms about
values and principles, but no moral teacher can expect to offer guidance that
is directly applicable in the vast array of cultural and social settings around
the world. Serious discernment about the implications of universal Catholic
social teaching must be taken up by those most familiar with local contexts.
For example, in societies sharply divided by tribalism, racism, or vast inequalities in wealth, bold measures toward reconciliation, redistribution,
and redress of inequitable concentrations of resources may recommend
themselves as necessary steps toward alleviating gross injustice. In such settings, Catholic social teaching may constitute a courageous voice in support
of land reform, taxation that is more progressive, or the forging of a new
social contract to support social justice. In other societies, where human
rights are widely respected and inequalities are smaller, Catholic moral
teaching will not need to exert such a strong voice and may settle for issu-
ing less challenging calls for modest amounts of social change. In the interest of matching the message to the context, Catholic social teaching operates
on two or more levels, eager to differentiate messages with universal import
from those that apply only to a local situation.

The third caveat pertains to the precise method of employing the documents of Catholic social teaching to argue a given position or to substantiate an argument. Anyone familiar with the central problematics of biblical
interpretation will appreciate the challenges in this regard. Like the scrip-
tures, the tradition of Church social teachings is rich, long, and complex.
Attempts to point to isolated texts to establish simple conclusions run the
risk of trampling roughshod over fine nuances in the development and understanding of the tradition. The most responsible hermeneutic will insist
upon viewing the tradition in its entirety, with a reluctance to jump to conclusions without a thorough weighing of the entire sweep and trajectory of
the tradition of thought. Nevertheless, the temptation to engage in proof-
texting remains strong. Even accomplished scholars sometimes fall into the
trap of inordinate reliance upon a single fragment of a papal social encyclical that seems to support a preferred position on a given issue.

One quite egregious attempt to "steal" the heft of the tradition for a particular position was on display in a debate in the early 1990s. When Pope John Paul II published *Centesimus annus* (The Hundredth Year) in 1991, many eyes soon fell on number 48 of the text of that encyclical. Here, the pope noted the existence of "malfunctions and defects in the social assistance state," that is, excesses in the administration of welfare state programs that sometimes "lead to a loss of human energies and an inordinate increase of public agencies, which are dominated more by bureaucratic ways of thinking than by concern for serving their clients, and which are accompanied by an enormous increase in spending."[5] Of course, it is hardly breaking news that government programs have a tendency to become bloated and out of touch with the needs of their intended beneficiaries. Vigilance against such abuses is an important and widely recognized task of public officials. Yet some right-wing commentators on Catholic social teaching isolated these few clauses from their context in order to launch an argument that Catholic social teaching supports their agenda for sharp reductions in the size and scope of government antipoverty programs.[6] These voices attempted to convey the impression that John Paul II could be counted as an ally of a very conservative and partisan political position that proposes strictly market solutions to social problems and, specifically regarding welfare programs, favors the elimination or privatization of most social services.

Even a cursory examination of the facts will reveal to any objective observer that this conclusion is patently false. The sentences in dispute appear in a section of the document labeled "State and Culture" that expends considerable effort defending the legitimate role of governments to intervene in the economy to relieve poverty and advance the common good. Just eight paragraphs earlier, John Paul II submits: "It is the task of the state to provide for the defense and preservation of common goods such as the natural and human environments, which cannot be safeguarded simply by market forces."[7] Further, this encyclical caps a century of Catholic social documents that frequently go to extraordinary lengths to champion the principle that prudent but substantial government interventions in the economy are not only allowable but often represent a moral obligation. Catholic social teaching has indeed developed a nuanced position on the appropriateness of national (as opposed to local and private) responses to human needs, but it is hardly an uncritical cheerleader for a small-government agenda. What lessons can be discerned in this episode? The debate over the significance of this section of *Centesimus annus* is emblematic of the contested nature of Catholic social teaching, subject as it is to a variety of interpretations. It is also a valuable reminder of the wisdom of maintaining a complexified hermeneutic in drawing conclusions from texts such as these.

Respecting the three caveats outlined above will contribute to the responsible pursuit of the task at hand. The remainder of this chapter identifies those aspects of Catholic social teaching most relevant to the topic of welfare policies. The body of documents that form the Catholic social tradition as a whole is quite wide ranging, encompassing themes such as human rights, international peace, religious freedom, the sacredness of human labor, and the dignity of family life. In one sense, all of these themes are part of a unified network of moral values and social concern, a rich tapestry that resists unraveling. But in another sense, it is possible to identify distinct strands of this tradition so that we may follow the key threads to their implications for social organization in general and welfare policy in particular.

THE CENTRAL VISION OF CATHOLIC SOCIAL TEACHING

When a new document of Catholic social teaching is published, a majority of the attention it receives invariably focuses on the positions it stakes out on controversial topics. This was true, for example, of the U.S. bishops' letter, *Economic Justice for All,* released in 1986. Media coverage of this pastoral letter zeroed in on the contrast between the recommendations the bishops were making for our nation's economic life and the actual policies the Reagan administration was enacting at that very moment. While no one is surprised that the spice of controversy comes to dominate public discourse, it is usually helpful to delve a bit below the surface on such matters. In order to understand the underlying rationale for the conclusions and policy recommendations of Catholic social documents, we shall first examine the core theological and philosophical commitments implicit in this tradition of reflection. Upon this bedrock of fundamental beliefs lies a set of priorities and principles that shape the analysis of social reality that typifies Church statements on all such matters in recent decades. Implicit in the investigation below is the thesis that Catholic social teaching does indeed flow out of a unified and coherent vision of the origin and nature of human life in society. Without a thorough understanding of this underlying vision, the specific conclusions endorsed by those who apply Catholic thought to specific issues are destined to remain quite opaque.

The tradition of Catholic social thought consistently and most deliberately attempts to hold in careful balance the goods of the individual and of human society. We start, then, with brief sections describing how Catholic social teaching treats these two poles: the individual and the community. These initial observations set the table for investigations of more specific topics that move us closer to our eventual goal of evaluating the adequacy of contemporary welfare policy.

The Dignity of the Human Person and Human Rights
An overarching concern of Catholic social teaching is the consistent defense of the dignity and well-being of each individual. Any inventory of themes in that teaching must begin with its high regard for the value and transcendent worth of each person.

The notion that human beings have great worth is hardly a novel or controversial claim. However, Catholic social teaching documents address the topic of human dignity in a distinctive way, one that is firmly embedded in a comprehensive view of the origin, nature, and destiny of the human person. A passage from *Sollicitudo rei socialis* (On Social Concern), a 1987 encyclical of John Paul II, reveals some of the typical affirmations of the Catholic tradition in this regard:

> There exist in the human person sufficient qualities and energies, a fundamental "goodness" (cf. Gen. 1:31), because he is in the image of the Creator, placed under the redemptive influence of Christ, who united himself in some fashion with every man, and because the efficacious action of the Holy Spirit "fills the earth." (Ws 1:7)[8]

According to this comprehensive cosmological vision, the creation narrative in the first chapters of Genesis is a key warrant for human dignity. Each person is created in the image of God, and so in some way reflects the goodness of the Creator. Even the power of sin in no way cancels out this bestowal of dignity. Our status as children of God somehow sets us apart from the rest of the created order. Unique among God's creatures, humans are called into a personal relationship with their Lord. As the Vatican II document *Gaudium et spes* (Pastoral Constitution of the Church in the Modern World) asserts: "An outstanding cause of human dignity lies in man's call to communion with God. From the very circumstances of his origin, man is already invited to converse with God."[9] The special status of the human person is not merely a function of origins. We are sustained by the Holy Spirit throughout our lives and destined for eternal life with God.

From these theological affirmations flow ethical imperatives. Reverence for human persons is a reflection of the reverence due to God. By according human dignity such a central place in its social philosophy, Catholic social teaching suggests a number of commitments and priorities that introduce normative elements into political and economic life. Such an initial commitment to promote human dignity, while by no means settling all relevant questions about policy strategies and trade-offs with other values, does favor those social arrangements that promote universal human well-being in the most direct ways. If we wish to protect human dignity, we must also pursue an allocation of resources that allows all people an opportunity to live in a manner commensurate with their innate worth. Social institutions should be organized so that a decent minimum (or, in the words of *Gaudium et spes,* the "absolute essentials" of life) is available to all.[10] Provisions for other human goods beyond subsistence, such as a measure of equity and equal participation, may be considered further ramifications of a commitment to human dignity. The promotion of human dignity emerges, then, as a key criterion for authentic social development. Of particular import for the remainder of our study is the conclusion that we may judge social policies by how well they advance respect for the personal dignity of each and the accomplishment of universal human well-being.

One way of speaking about these priorities is to turn to the discourse of human rights. The triumph of human rights as a key framework for measuring ethical progress was surely one of the greatest accomplishments of the international community in the twentieth century. International covenants such as the Universal Declaration of Human Rights (approved by the United Nations General Assembly in 1948) affirm that human persons deserve certain types of treatment, such as immunity from various types of harms and opportunities for physical, social, and intellectual advancement. International organizations such as Amnesty International and Human Rights Watch display great courage in exposing violations of human rights and struggling to advance those rights around the globe. Beginning especially with Pope John XXIII's 1963 social encyclical, *Pacem in terris* (Peace on Earth), Catholic social teaching has joined the worldwide consensus regarding human rights. In that encyclical, Pope John offered a rather comprehensive listing of the many types of human rights (including political, civil, economic, cultural, and social) and referred to these rights as "universal and inviolable."[11] Catholic scholars have offered profound subsequent reflection on the place of human rights within the Church's social teaching.[12]

The differences between the Catholic and secular versions of human rights discourse may be subtle, but they are important to recognize. While their actual listing of positive rights and immunities may appear to be nearly identical, the two traditions of reflection part ways on the issue of the grounding of these rights. Secular rights theories display the shortcoming of not growing out of a shared comprehensive vision of reality. In the interest of attracting the widest possible support, they remain deliberately thin with respect to underlying philosophical commitments. As a result, they offer only limited guidance in approaching difficult questions, such as how to resolve seemingly intractable conflicts of rights. The use of rights talk in Catholic circles, on the other hand, is situated within a more comprehensive, and therefore potentially more satisfying, portrayal of the world. This picture has room not only for the individual human person, but also for the web of relationships that surrounds each of us, including our links to God, other persons, the natural environment, voluntary associations, and wider human communities. Within this broader context, recognizing human rights is less a matter of accommodating conflicting claims to scarce goods and more a matter of balancing rights and corresponding duties within a community of common interests. Because they exist within a rather thick construal of social reality, human rights in Catholic thought do not devolve into mere weapons that contending parties wield against one another to bolster their case for desired goods or outcomes. Rather, a Catholic approach to rights displays the advantage of situating rights within a framework of carefully delineated social priorities that, at least ideally, are shared by all participants in society. Instead of being isolated claims against others in an atmosphere of competitive individualism, rights emerge as benchmarks to measure the attainment of shared values regarding the flourishing of all members of society.

Everything Catholic social teaching might say about human rights is derived from its moral anthropology, that is, its understanding of the nature of human personhood and the ethical implications that flow from it. Perhaps the most important element at play here is the Catholic affirmation of human transcendence. Each human has inestimable value. We are more than the sum of our possessions and accomplishments. Human life has a distinctive character such that human subjecthood resists quantification or reductionism, whether economic, behavioral, or scientific in nature.[13] As possessors of free will and rational intelligence, human persons transcend the environment they inhabit and the physical conditions they face. Although this principle is grounded in fundamental elements of Christian cosmology, it holds potentially quite concrete implications for social policy. The moral obligation to protect the dignity of the human person implies a respect for the freedom of human agency and an insistence that persons not be pigeonholed in ways that compromise their innate worth. Public policies and programs that treat human behavior in a mechanistic or deterministic way, reducing social development merely to a material progress that does not account for free will and spiritual values, is objectionable as an offense against our transcendent nature.

The Social Dimension: Solidarity, Common Good, Participation

Unless we balance the picture of personal dignity and human rights developed above with the Catholic tradition's high regard for the communal dimensions of life, we might receive the false impression that Catholic social teaching is merely a sophisticated version of individualism. Nothing could be further from the truth. In Catholic social philosophy, rights come paired with duties, and the expectation of reciprocity—returning service to the community in exchange for the benefits we receive—is an integral part of the Catholic social vision.

The single word that best summarizes the values behind this communal aspect of human life is solidarity. The Catholic documents that employ the theme of solidarity treat it as both an internal attitude and an objective, observable praxis.[14] Solidarity emerges as a social norm that allows us to judge institutions and policies in terms of how effectively they bring diverse people together in a closer bond of friendship and communion. If a given practice, policy, or structure fails to advance cooperation and partnership, but instead increases social distance and diminishes the achievement of true human community, then it is subject to the judgment that it must be altered in order to contribute to greater human flourishing.

By according solidarity such a prominent place in its social ethic, Catholic teaching supplements its vision of the dignity of persons with an emphasis on the relationships among all individuals. In order to be morally good in the fullest sense, these relationships must be characterized by mutual concern for the well-being of others and by a willingness to make necessary sacrifices for the common good of the human community as a whole. This attention on the part of Catholic social theory to the health of the ties binding humans together is at considerable variance with the market-based theories featured in classical and neoclassical economics. These approaches eclipse altruism, other-regard, and human bondedness with an almost exclusive focus on material benefit and self-interest. By contrast, Catholic social teaching emphasizes human interdependence and social cooperation as not only normative values but also as empirical facts that constitute important features of our common human nature.

Human community is the locus where human dignity is recognized, realized, and protected. Recent documents of Catholic social teaching link the theme of solidarity in provocative ways to other components of Christian faith and practice. They invoke the communal dimensions of events in the history of the people of Israel and the life of Jesus, the Eucharistic meal shared as a sacrament, and even the inner life of the Trinity of divine persons.[15] The underlying theological vision suggests something profound: that all humans share bonds of identity and even of common destiny that should inspire us to acts of selflessness in the pursuit of justice and mutual well-being.

The term "common good" refers to a notion that is related to solidarity but enjoys an even longer and more substantial heritage in Western philosophical thought. The Christian tradition of reflection on common good borrows from the pagan philosopher Aristotle, whose insights into human social existence were incorporated into the theological vision of St. Thomas Aquinas in the thirteenth century. According to the anthropology of Aristotle, the human person is by nature a social animal, a being of the polis. Every person is a part of the polis, and the goal of the polis is the common good.[16] All laws and social relations are measured by how they advance the common good. Aquinas was careful to distinguish the earthly progress that is associated with the common good from the spiritual progress that is the ultimate goal of every human. The former he called *felicitas* (happiness) and the latter *beatitudo* (blessedness). These natural and supernatural goods are not to be confused, but the parallel tracks do bear some relation to each other. The legislation adopted by wise rulers will help all citizens to greater perfection in every way.[17] Furthermore, the common good is a substantive notion; it is not merely the conglomeration of private interests or preferences, but an objective and identifiable set of conditions that advances the flourishing of humanity.

The modern Catholic social theory that inherits this tradition of reflection is noteworthy for its organic view of society. All the parts of society are interconnected, and the growth or diminishment of one affects all the others. No one can, in all honesty, aspire to go it alone. At the very least, we depend upon one another inasmuch as we are linked as members of a common political society under the leadership of civic authorities. Modern Catholic social teaching is among the most consistent carriers of these themes. In *Mater et magistra* (Christianity and Social Progress), a 1961 social encyclical of Pope John XXIII, the common good is defined as embracing "the sum total of those conditions of social living whereby men are enabled more fully and more readily to achieve their own perfection."[18] While this formulation is quite vague, it has come to be interpreted in later documents in terms of protecting such values as freedom, equality, human rights, and standards of social justice—values that recognize the importance of both individuals and the various types of groupings to which they belong. The organic view of society calls us not to sacrifice the interests of individuals to collectives in some crass way, but to balance very carefully the overlapping concerns and values that foster the protection and flourishing of all.

In an individualistic age such as ours, it is increasingly easy to overlook the insight that the good of each person is bound up with the good of the community. Economic and political life often seem to be narrowing their focus to include only private benefits, jettisoning much of the public-spiritedness of former eras to the demands of special interests and the tyranny of the bottom line. The challenge of accelerating pluralism and the seeming breakdown of all vestiges of social consensus lead many to interpret the common good in much more modest ways, if not to relegate it entirely to irrelevance. The theologian David Hollenbach, in a particularly important recent work on the topic, notes how the theme of common good has come to be eclipsed in public life, but dares to call for its revitalization both in Christian thought and in public discourse in general, for there are numerous serious social problems that other dominant values (such as economic efficiency and a superficial brand of tolerance) simply cannot handle.[19]

The path of least resistance is to follow the logic of self-interest alone. In the field of social policy, this entails a sharply reduced effort to improve the lives of the least fortunate members of society. It means deliberate inattention to those elements of our social systems—quality education, broad access to credit and health care, fair zoning regulations, equitable legal and immigration procedures—that represent conditions of social living that might contribute to the flourishing of families currently deprived of adequate opportunities. If asked, most affluent members of society would claim (with seeming accuracy, at least on the surface of things) that they have no direct stake or interest in improvements in social services or income maintenance that support the poorest members of society. The common good is one of those resources of Catholic social thought that might prompt a rethinking of entrenched positions, so that even those who currently enjoy more than an average share of the benefits of social well-being might consider making deeper sacrifices for the social progress of others, including future generations.

A practice closely related to the value of pursuing the common good is broad participation in social deliberations. Promoting the common good is not merely a matter of ensuring broad distribution of benefits and equity in outcomes. The organic vision of society proposed by Catholic social teaching implies that all members of society, that is, all the parts of a properly unified social body, enjoy fair opportunities to make their mark on the process of social decision making. The theme of participation has been rising in importance in Catholic social ethics in recent decades as the legitimate aspirations of many long-neglected social groups have come to the fore.[20] Some of these are ethnic minorities; others are people marginalized from the cultural mainstream by poverty or other sources of social isolation. Perhaps the most significant such demographic grouping consists of the women of the world. Although women comprise slightly over half the human population, a variety of cultural, economic, and political forces have conspired to diminish their opportunities for full participation in social institutions, such as education and the professions. Redressing this gross injustice is one of the central struggles of our age. Both Catholic social teaching and the social policies of nation-states around the world will be judged by how well they measure up to this key challenge in the decades ahead.

The task of offering definitive measurements of levels of participation resists easy accomplishment. Challenges will surely arise regarding any observer's assessment of how much participation has been achieved by a given social group. Much less is universal agreement likely on any proposal regarding what level of participation is adequate for the minimum achievement of justice. But the very nature of participation suggests that its accomplishment is a function of real opportunities to contribute to key social processes. Progress toward fuller participation is a matter of overcoming barriers that prevent long-oppressed groups from playing their full and rightful role in the entire range of activities and institutions of social life.

POSITIONS REGARDING TWO KEY INSTITUTIONS

Two observations about the route to full participation are helpful in introducing this section of our investigation of the tradition of Catholic social teaching as it relates to social policy. First, the ordinary way that people participate in the economic life of society is through their labor, which both depends upon and makes possible the ownership of property. Second, the ordinary way that people participate in the political life of society is through democratic processes that influence government structures and policies. The next topics to examine, accordingly, are private property and the role of the state. A synopsis of how Catholic social teaching understands these two crucial institutions will shed further light on the significance of government policies that seek to address poverty and invite broader social participation.

Private Property
At several places where they take up questions of distributive justice and the proper arrangement of social institutions, the documents of Catholic social

teaching recapitulate an ongoing debate within the history of Christian thought about the nature of property ownership. This debate begins with a shared core of beliefs but soon proceeds to areas of potential dispute. All Christian reflection on the holding of material goods derives from the biblically based doctrine of creation, which includes the conviction that God created the material world for the benefit of all and bestows dominion over all creation to humankind as a whole. Christian positions about the possession and use of property are thus shaped by central beliefs about the divine order. These include such notions as God's permanent lordship over all creation, the intention of God that the material world serve the needs of all, and the importance of a moral stewardship that demands responsible use of all resources intended to sustain life universally.

In the patristic era (the earliest centuries of the fledgling Christian church), these themes were cited in polemics against avarice, in exhortations for detachment and charity, and in frequent but imprecise attempts to describe the obligations of distributive justice.[21] The scholastic era brought attempts at a more systematic treatment of the topic of property, as Christian thinkers began to employ several important distinctions. Among these were distinctions between: (1) the use of possessions and their ultimate ownership; and (2) God's original intention for creation (the absolute natural law) and prudent reliance on those institutions suited for a world marred by sin (operating under the relative natural law, which governs human behavior after the fall). The key question to be settled, of course, remained the same in the thirteenth century (when property meant primarily land) as in the twenty-first (when property is increasingly a matter of less tangible assets such as information, technical expertise, and the human capital of job skills). What type of ownership arrangements can be justified using Christian theological arguments?

A key text that sets the stage for modern Catholic social teaching on property appears in the *Summa Theologiae* of Thomas Aquinas. When Aquinas addresses the topic "Of Theft and Robbery," he pulls together many strands of the prior biblical, philosophical, and theological traditions to mount a series of subtle arguments regarding the ways humans may properly procure, dispense, and utilize material goods.[22] By presenting ownership as a complex bundle of rights and responsibilities, Aquinas affords later thinkers the opportunity to develop a much sharper analysis of property issues. Aquinas sets the frame for modern Catholic approaches to property by introducing a dialectic between two sets of concerns that accord to the institution of private property its dual character, as individual and as social dimensions. On the one hand, the concern for the common, which derives from God's original intention that the goods of creation serve the sustenance needs of all, imprints the use of material things with a social stamp. As Aquinas declares: "With regard . . . to their use . . . man ought to possess external things, not as his own, but as common, so that he is ready to communicate them to others in their need."[23] Here Aquinas cites scriptural and patristic sources that condemn the coexistence of great wealth and dire poverty as he builds up a case to justify a social obligation for the sharing of earthly goods. If sharing does not take place voluntarily, in situations of extreme need such as the threat of starvation, theft by the poor from the surplus of the rich may be defensible.

On the other hand, Aquinas judges that it is not only morally lawful but necessary for people to have exclusive control over other aspects (besides use) of property. This is so for the most practical of reasons in this fallen world, where human sinfulness is expressed in such mundane forms as inattentiveness, slovenliness, and greed. "There would be confusion if everyone had to look after any one thing indeterminately," as when goods are shared by imperfect beings who tend to be overeager to benefit from the contribution of others, but slothful about doing their own share of work.[24] Therefore, "human affairs are conducted in a more orderly fashion if each man is charged with taking care of some particular thing."[25] The individual character of material possessions, which we recognize in the institution of private property, is strictly instrumental, since it is primarily a concession to human sinfulness.[26] However, for a fallen world, private ownership is defensible as a prudent arrangement. Indeed, it emerges as the only practical way for most people to meet their needs for material sustenance, to provide for their future, and thus to insure that God's common gifts of creation are used for their intended purpose.

The documents of modern Catholic social teaching move back and forth between the poles of this dialectic of social and individual concerns. Because they are historically conditioned by the political atmosphere in which they were written, their analysis of the role of private property in society undergoes significant variation as context changes. Of all these documents, Pope Leo XIII's 1891 encyclical, *Rerum novarum,* the very first of the genre, differs the most from the others in its treatment of property. This encyclical was primarily concerned to counter the appeal among Catholic workers in Europe of a form of socialism that sought to eliminate private ownership of the means of production. In its desire to bolster the case for the necessity of retaining the practice of private ownership, *Rerum novarum* neglected the Thomistic claim that private property is necessary primarily as a concession to sin. Joining his voice to those of previous commentators, moral theologian Charles Curran recounts several ways in which Leo XIII either misinterpreted or drew only selectively from Aquinas's position on property, dominion, and natural law in this encyclical.[27] As a result, *Rerum novarum* portrays property as a demand of the natural law in the strict sense, an interpretation that leads the document to downplay the social character of property ownership.

The very next social encyclical in chronological order, Pius XI's 1931 letter, *Quadragesimo anno* (After Forty Years), is more authentically Thomistic in its treatment of property. It strikes a felicitous balance between the individual and social aspects of material goods, a balance that is retained in subsequent documents of Catholic social teaching. It seeks to relativize the property rights it affirms by warning of

> a double danger to be avoided. On the one hand, if the social and public aspects of ownership be denied or minimized, the logical consequence is "individualism," as it is called; on the other hand, the rejection or diminution of its private and individual character necessarily leads to some form of "collectivism."[28]

The "twofold character of ownership, which we have termed individual and social," becomes the overarching framework for all the subsequent efforts of Catholic social teaching to offer moral guidelines for the proper use of wealth.[29] The social dimension of property creates an obligation to measure all uses of material goods in terms of the common good. This criterion constrains individuals in their economic decisions and governments in their policies. The notion of the universal destination of material goods (a Christian belief about the divinely mandated order) thus serves as the ethical basis for a number of moral imperatives with profound implications for economic structures, including public policies regarding the poorest members of society and convictions about what is owed to them.

Quadragesimo anno emphasizes that these injunctions sometimes justify economic interventions on the part of government: "When civil authority adjusts ownership to meet the needs of the public good . . . it effectively prevents the possession of private property, intended by nature's Author in his wisdom for the sustaining of human life, from creating intolerable burdens."[30] Later documents frequently reaffirm this principle that ownership needs to be adjusted so that property serves the livelihood of those in greatest need.[31] Yet true to their character, subsequent Vatican social teaching documents refrain from prescribing detailed courses of action. It is beyond the scope of papal social teaching to recommend measures that would specify legislative strategies for such actions as curtailing monopolies, regulating markets, providing poor relief, or writing tax codes. When Church leaders feel the need to address such specific policy directions, it most frequently falls to local or national conferences of bishops to apply universal principles to their particular political and economic contexts.

Nevertheless, documents from Rome frequently venture to denounce the extreme positions on property: collectivism for its refusal to recognize the private dimension of property; and extreme laissez-faire liberalism, featuring nearly absolute ownership rights, for its refusal to recognize the social dimensions of property.[32] The insistence of Catholic social teaching that private property be neither abolished nor given free rein serves as testimony to the proposition that such "isms" as liberalism and collectivism never constitute anything more than half-truths. Such ideologies are at best partial insights into the human condition that require correction and supplementation from other perspectives.

The Role of the State

A passage from *Sollicitudo rei socialis,* the 1987 encyclical of Pope John Paul II, serves as a helpful conceptual bridge from the topic of private property to a consideration of the role and responsibility of the state as it is portrayed in Catholic social teaching:

> The goods of this world are originally meant for all. The right to private property is valid and necessary, but it does not nullify the value of this principle. Private property is, in fact, under a "social mortgage," which means that it has an intrinsically social function, based upon and justified precisely by the principle of the universal destination of goods. . . . The motivating concern for the poor must be translated at all levels into concrete actions, until it decisively attains a series of necessary reforms.[33]

Not all of the morally mandated reforms called for are likely to occur through voluntary efforts. Other measures necessary for the enactment of economic justice and the protection of the poor require the active involvement of the instrumentality of the state. Governments legitimately execute the powers of regulating economic activity when they act in the public interest through such measures as collecting taxes, instituting environmental and safety regulations, preventing monopolies, and providing public services and infrastructure improvements.

The most frequent objection to such economic interventions is the complaint that they require coercive force to be effective. Unlike libertarianism and similar schools of thought that are highly averse to government action, Catholic social teaching recognizes a number of potential justifications for such interventions. This comfort with assigning social tasks to government rests on the Aristotelian-Thomistic tradition of reflection that defines the state as a natural institution for humans as social beings. Catholic social theory follows Aristotle and Aquinas in identifying a package of social goods the accomplishment of which requires an active role for civil authorities. The twentieth-century philosopher and heir to this tradition, Jacques Maritain, offers the definition: "The state is a part which specializes in the interests of the whole" and its particular concerns are "with the maintenance of law, the promotion of the common welfare and public order, and the administration of public affairs."[34]

This by no means implies that governments enjoy a carte blanche in extending their control over economic affairs. Since freedom and human rights are prominent among the goods it seeks to protect, Catholic social teaching is aware of an implicit cost accompanying every such intervention. Decisions to employ government power to accomplish a goal must be the result of a careful weighing of pros and cons. Coercive action beyond what is required to accomplish defensible social objectives is an offense against prudence and cannot be justified. In his writings on public policy, the American Jesuit John Courtney Murray often repeats the adage: "as much freedom as possible, as much government as necessary."[35] Ultimately, all restrictions on the freedom of any members of society are justified by the goal of increasing the freedom of all. Resort to the coercive apparatus of the state is a self-limiting principle, since, to quote Murray once again, "constraint must be for the sake of freedom."[36]

An illuminating example of how this principle has been applied to justice issues in American economic life involves the work of Monsignor John A. Ryan, a most important figure in American Catholic Church life in the first half of the twentieth century. As the major interpreter of Leo XIII's *Rerum novarum* in the American context, Ryan was a proponent of an activist, though limited, government, one whose policies should be oriented toward creating favorable conditions for the attainment of distributive justice. Among his many writings, Ryan's most ambitious work describes his proposal for an economic system that would insure that fair shares of output would reach the four key sectors that contribute to production: capitalists, laborers, landowners, and business managers.[37]

Ryan challenges the conventional titles to wealth as incomplete. Ordinarily, people stake their claims to income based on effort, productivity, sacrifice, inheritance, gift, purchase, first occupancy—in short, any mode of contribution to the production process. However, Ryan calls attention to an additional good that is at stake in economic transactions: the goal of preserving lives threatened by utter destitution. In order to safeguard the minimum requirements for leading a reasonably adequate human existence, Ryan proposes the "criterion of need" to supplement the conventional bases of claims to goods.[38] Inspired by *Rerum novarum*'s claim that God intends material creation to serve the needs of all, Ryan concludes that each person is owed access to enough of the goods of the earth to support his or her life. Since this access is conditioned upon and becomes actually valid through the expenditure of labor, then those "who are in present control of the opportunities of the earth are obliged to permit reasonable access to these opportunities by those who are willing to work."[39]

The bottom line of Ryan's analysis is the idea with which his name is most frequently associated: the right of workers to "a living wage." In advocating this notion, Ryan's work leaves a rich fourfold legacy still appreciated by social ethicists today. First, Ryan models for future generations of theologians how a general principle from a papal encyclical can be applied to a local or national context. *Rerum novarum* had called for "a family wage," but had left unspecified what this might entail. Ryan does the legwork necessary to spell out the precise ramifications of Pope Leo's challenge within the context of the U.S. economy of his day. Ryan devotes a major portion of his book-length defense of the living wage to documenting such details as regional costs of living and sample family budgets, itemized to provide for reasonable expenses, in the interest of determining with some precision a satisfactory wage level.[40]

Second, in challenging on ethical grounds the Malthusian "iron law of wages" that was the conventional wisdom in American economic thought of his time, Ryan supplied some of the impetus for a religion-labor alliance that would play an important role in subsequent U.S. labor history. The very principle of collective bargaining rests on the assumption that not every free exchange is automatically a fair exchange. Ryan makes this point in his indictment of the "starvation wages" that result from an economic regime of laissez-faire, one that too readily trusts the complexities of social justice to the invisible hand of supposedly free market determination.[41] In order to foster fairer outcomes, the bargaining position of labor would be improved by reforming the procedures and the very ground rules governing labor markets. Ryan detected an imbalance in the power equilibrium within the world of American industrial relations of a century ago. He sought to address these injustices by supporting the growth of organized labor as a key force capable of checking the wage-setting prerogatives of employers who preferred to pay subliving wages.

Third, Ryan advanced Catholic thought about the role of government in achieving vital protections for workers in the new industrialized social order. Whereas *Rerum novarum* had argued for the notion of the family wage but had shied away from specifically advocating legislation to enact it, Ryan leaves no uncertainty about the proper course of action. He asserts: "The state has both the right and the duty to compel all employers to pay a living wage."[42] This is part of the legitimate function of the state in promoting the general well-being of society. Ryan portrays the achievement of a living wage as a demand of justice, not of charity alone.[43] He goes so far as to introduce the language of rights ("the laborer's claim to a Living Wage is of the nature of a right") in an effort to move the argument away from the arena of convention (fixed "just wages" had been a practice in medieval guilds and elsewhere, as Ryan notes) or charitable activity and into the legal-juridical sphere.[44] Voluntary compliance on the part of employers is not an adequate basis to insure that justice is done. Legislation mandating the enactment of wage scales adequate for a decent livelihood for workers is imperative and obligatory, not optional. Ryan cites the early achievement of minimum wage legislation in other nations such as Australia and New Zealand as a potential model for a U.S. initiative.[45]

Fourth, Ryan demonstrates an adherence to a key principle mentioned above, namely, the guideline that government intervention should remain as small and noncoercive as possible while still able to achieve its goals. Indeed, in proposing reforms to remove what he saw as the major defects of the industrial system of his day, Ryan frequently employs the phrase "an ethical minimum."[46] Ryan surely was referring not just to a "minimum" in the literal pay scale, but also in the more general sense of the lowest level of intervention in the free economy that is still consistent with the protection of the basic rights of workers. Instituting a minimum wage does not require a great deal of bureaucracy or intrusive government meddling in the affairs of employers. It is more a matter of oversight than of burdensome interference with the management of private enterprises.

The pragmatic side of John Ryan led him to make a number of concessions to actual economic conditions that might alter how we apply such principles of justice as the ethical minimum in wage scales. Already noted above is Ryan's commitment to adapting the standards for what constitutes a reasonable family budget to the conventions of adequacy in a given time and location. In fact, he even limits the scope of his living wage proposal to those industries and sectors profitable enough to support such a minimum wage level.[47] In thus exempting some employers from the actual obligation to pay a living wage (at least in the short run), Ryan cites a general principle that is applied in several other places in his work: the notion that "no one is morally bound to do the impossible."[48] In order to serve as practical guidelines, our notions regarding moral obligation must link the "ought" with the "can." The discourse of absolute positive rights is at variance with this pragmatic consideration and so is not an idiom favored within Catholic social teaching.

Ryan demonstrates a consistent sensitivity to this concern for holding together "ought" and "can." He nuances his use of the notion of rights, holding that even "inviolable moral claims" are not absolute in extent.[49] Ryan considers several important instances where rights are limited by the conditions in which they might be attained. For example, a nation experiencing absolute scarcity simply cannot enact or enforce the standard of a decent minimum (in the form of a living wage or any other distributive mechanism) to protect workers from poverty if that poverty is already an unavoidable general condition.[50] Similarly, the prima facie obligation of each person to engage in enough productive work to avoid poverty is suspended when a worker is placed in a position (such as in a slack labor market) where "conditions for which he is in no wise responsible, and which take no account of his human dignity" prevent that worker from escaping destitution.[51] Such a worker cannot be considered morally culpable for the resulting condition of poverty experienced by his or her family. Neither workers nor employers can be held morally responsible unless they have the freedom and opportunity to fulfill their obligations. Once again, "ought" implies "can."

Ryan's work reveals much about the patterns of thought by which Catholic social teaching addresses the role of government. His writings in the early decades of the twentieth century not only apply the message of *Rerum novarum* to the American context but also anticipate the content of future encyclicals. The remainder of this section addresses three concerns that arise in the work of Ryan as well as in the documents of Catholic social teaching regarding the activities of public authorities. These concerns are limitations upon the scope of government, alternatives to government intervention, and methods for adjusting our notions of proper governmental responsibility to the changing demands of new eras.

First, we have already noted some of the implications within the work of John Ryan of the Catholic position on the limited nature of the state. Since the state is not the ultimate source of rights, legislation does not create rights but merely recognizes them.[52] Proper government action fosters the achievement of those universal entitlements that flow from the innate dignity of each person. As *Rerum novarum* argues, "man is older than the state," so our "recourse to the State" is always instrumental.[53] Reliance on state action must always be for limited purposes that require specification and justification. Pope Paul VI's 1967 encyclical, *Populorum progressio* (On the Development of Peoples), clarifies the conditions under which government programs are justified: "Every program has in the last analysis no other raison d'etre than the service of man." This task includes the goal of "free[ing] man from various types of servitude" and "render[ing] the world a more human place in which to live."[54] Modest attempts at the regulation of wages, such as the adoption of living wage legislation, serve the humanization of the economy by helping to insure that property will be used to fulfill its appropriate end: the service of human livelihood.

Second, we have already noted Ryan's aversion to excessive governmental interventions. It is important to emphasize that Ryan turns to government primarily as a last resort, only when the operations and interactions of the four private economic sectors he identifies fail to produce just outcomes. Note that Ryan published his major works well before the 1931 encyclical *Quadragesimo anno* coined the term "subsidiarity." In introducing this awkward but eminently useful term (referred to not as a theological truth but rather as "a principle of social philosophy"), Pope Pius XI advises:

> One should not withdraw from individuals and commit to the community what they can accomplish by their own enterprise and industry. So, too, it is an injustice and at the same time a great evil and a disturbance of right order to transfer to the larger and higher collectivity functions which can be performed and provided for by lesser and subordinate bodies. . . . The State authorities should leave to other bodies the care and expediting of business and activities of lesser moment.[55]

Unlike other notions central to Catholic social teaching, subsidiarity is not linked to specific roots in scripture or natural law. It is perhaps best characterized, in the words of John Coleman, as "neither a theological nor even really a philosophical principle, but a piece of congealed historical wisdom . . . affirm[ing] the importance of social pluralism and intermediate groups."[56] Subsidiarity is a principle of government action that seeks to strike a balance between statism, on the maximal end, and anarchy, on the minimal end. It recommends only as much centralization as is necessary for human flourishing, but as little as is possible while pursuing legitimate goals. Governments should not usurp the functions appropriate to other levels of activity, but there nevertheless remain important tasks that only government can accomplish.

Implicit in the invocation of the principle of subsidiarity is a distinction between state and society, with the imperative that the latter never be absorbed into the former. The distinction is a crucial one in efforts to ward off potential totalitarian tendencies. Government is only one aspect of the larger entity we call society. Responsibilities for social functions are assigned on a prudential basis. Government intervention beyond its normal sphere of competence is necessitated only when lesser bodies (the vast array of social groupings that includes voluntary associations, corporations, nonprofit organizations, and other "mediating structures") cannot complete their own tasks without assistance.[57] The encyclical *Quadragesimo anno* employs a series of verbs to describe the actions of government in social coordination: "directing, supervising, encouraging, restraining as circumstances suggest or necessity demands."[58] Each of these descriptive words supports the core meaning of subsidiarity: that the state plays its proper role when its actions constitute assistance (in Latin, *subsidium*) to, rather than replacement of, the efforts of individuals and voluntary groupings within society.

Of course, merely to invoke the principle of subsidiarity does not settle very much. Even if all parties agree on the validity of this principle, rival interpretations quickly emerge. Precise judgments about proper courses of action always depend on detailed knowledge of the concrete situation in which subsidiarity is applied. In recent welfare debates, subsidiarity has been invoked in numerous arguments about the potential role of charitable organizations (including faith-based organizations) to deliver social services. As we shall see in the next chapter, the trading of charges and countercharges about the proper role of public vis-à-vis private agencies often reveals far more about the ideologies of the participants in that debate than it does about the actual merits of the principle of subsidiarity and its appropriate application to the case at hand.

Third, John Ryan's analysis raises important concerns regarding how and whether it is possible to adjust the lessons of Catholic social teaching on the role of government to new issues that arise with the advent of new historical eras with novel economic realities. Ryan's work (as well as the papal encyclical *Rerum novarum* that it sought to interpret and apply) was part of a broader effort among theologians, concerned Christians, and social scientists to update their thinking in light of the demands of a new era of large-scale industrialization. This vast economic upheaval had transformed the social and political order of the West over the course of a few generations, raising new and profound questions about social relationships and political responsibilities. Ryan viewed the notion of the living wage as a novel application of the Church's social commitment necessitated by these new challenges:

> Now, the simple and sufficient reason why this general right of the laborer takes the special form of a right to a Living Wage, is that in the present industrial organization of society, there is no other way in which the right can be realized. He cannot find a part of his livelihood outside of his wages because

there are no unappropriated goods within his reach. . . . He can effectively realize his natural right of access to the goods of the earth only through the
medium of wages.[59]

A more recent example of economic and social upheavals that demanded
a similarly striking metamorphosis in Catholic social teaching unfolded during the 1960s. Church documents published during that decade of rapid
change testify to a major adjustment in the way Church leaders approached
the topics of private property and the responsibility of public authorities for
distributive justice in a radically transformed economic context. Pope John
XXIII's 1961 encyclical, *Mater et magistra,* set this process in motion when
it highlighted the existence within political economy of the trend it dubbed
"socialization." This term is not to be confused with an identical term from
the field of developmental psychology, nor with its cognate, "socialism." It
is a shorthand way of saying "the increase in social relationships."[60] After
surveying trends of modernization in many fields (technology, economics,
politics, etc.), Pope John notes:

> One of the principal characteristics of our time is the multiplication of social
> relationships, that is, a daily more complex interdependence of citizens. . . .
> These developments in social living are at once both a symptom and a cause
> of the growing interventions of public authorities in matters which, since they
> pertain to the more intimate aspects of personal life, are of serious moment
> and not without dangers.[61]

This new interdependence is neither good nor bad in itself. However, the
response on the part of government that it evokes is subject to judgment by
the ethical criteria surveyed above (e.g., how well it respects the simultaneous goals of individual dignity and the common good). Indiscriminate na-
tionalization of industry, as one example of a common policy response of
that era, is an overreaction to the new facts of interdependence. A total refusal of public authorities to sponsor programs to address the legitimate
needs of citizens (for income security, protection of rights, etc.) amidst potentially overwhelming economic forces beyond their control constitutes a
serious abdication of responsibility.

In addressing the challenges presented by these changed conditions within
nations and in the international arena, *Mater et magistra* explicitly reaf-
firms the institution of private ownership, but also adds a new nuance to the
tradition's insistence on the social function of property.[62] The encyclical
notes that, given the present circumstances, social responsibility must now
be carried out along a dual track of public and private initiatives. The enhanced interventions of government agencies must not be considered as replacing private, voluntary, and charitable efforts to share wealth and to
enact concern for the less fortunate. The existence of a new sector of public
property does not absolve the owners of large shares of private property

from the moral obligations incumbent upon them to exercise regard for the indigent.[63]

All the subsequent documents of Catholic social teaching build upon this analysis of what John XXIII called "new aspects of the social question"[64] in defining and describing the role of government in this new era. For example, just four years after the publication of *Mater et magistra*, Vatican II's *Gaudium et spes* recommended that public authorities meet their new responsibilities by adopting new objectives and directing renewed efforts toward "providing employment and sufficient income for the people of today and of the future."[65] With its characteristic optimism, this document makes the judgment that "socialization, while certainly not without its dangers, brings with it many advantages with respect to consolidating and increasing the qualities of the human person, and safeguarding his rights."[66]

These same concerns persist in the encyclicals of Pope Paul VI. *Populorum progressio* addresses several aspects of the trend toward greater economic interdependence. Systematic solutions, such as greater coordination of international aid, are necessary responses to the need for a humane development. To these ends, there is a legitimate and growing role for public authorities, who alone have the ability to coordinate true development, so long as they avoid the temptation of "complete collectivization or of arbitrary planning."[67] Paul VI's subsequent apostolic letter conducts a doleful survey of those categories of people who are harmed by the new interdependence, including among their numbers "the victims of situations of injustice" such as refugees and those marginalized by "racial discrimination" and "industrial change."[68] This survey leads to the conclusion that "there is a need to establish a greater justice in the sharing of goods, both within national communities and on the international level."[69] While this document contains an especially strong denunciation of secular ideological utopias, from Marxism to liberal ideology, it nevertheless finds numerous warrants for public authorities to play a constructive role in creating favorable conditions for the flourishing of humanity within the new situation of increased interdependence.[70]

The social encyclicals of John Paul II complexify the Catholic approach to the challenge of socialization. These three documents introduce some new and helpful terms to describe the political implications of increased economic interdependence. The 1981 encyclical *Laborem exercens* (On Human Work) notes how, amidst the increased complexity of social relations, the state has assumed the function of an "indirect employer" with responsibility for various aspects of the labor process:

> The concept of indirect employer includes both persons and institutions . . . and the principles of conduct which are laid down by these persons and institutions and which determine the whole socioeconomic system or are its results. . . . The indirect employer substantially determines one or other facet of the labor relationship. . . . This is not to absolve the direct employer from his

own responsibility, but only to draw attention to the whole network of influences that condition his conduct. . . . The concept of indirect employer is applicable to every society and in the first place to the state. For it is the state which must conduct a just labor policy.[71]

When *Laborem exercens* affirms that "the role of the agents included under the title of indirect employer is to act against unemployment," it is restating a key message of earlier encyclicals: the regulation of conditions of employment is part of the legitimate responsibility of government.[72] As forces beyond our planning capability speed the process of socialization, it is incumbent upon public authorities to play their proper role in executing policies that serve workers.

John Paul II can offer only quite indistinct criteria for measuring how adequately governments respond to the phenomenon of socialization. *Laborem exercens* advises:

> This group in authority may carry out its task satisfactorily from the point of view of the priority of labor, but it may also carry it out badly by . . . offending basic human rights. We may speak of socializing only when the subject character of society is ensured, that is to say, when on the basis of his work each person is fully entitled to consider himself a part-owner of the great workbench at which he is working with everyone else.[73]

A regime of indiscriminate collectivization does not measure up to these criteria, since it fails to protect human rights and to reward hard work by "associating labor with the ownership of capital."[74] On the other hand, a regime of unfettered liberal capitalism, as John Paul II claims in a passage from *Sollicitudo rei socialis* cited above, "fails to honor the truth that private property is under a 'social mortgage.'"[75]

While government authority can easily be misused in these and numerous other ways, it nevertheless serves a vital and positive moral function. John Paul II demonstrates an insightful appreciation of the ways in which the irreplaceable tasks of government change from age to age when he includes this observation in the 1991 encyclical *Centesimus annus*:

> It is the task of the state to provide for the defense and preservation of common goods such as the natural and human environments, which cannot be safeguarded simply by market forces. Just as in the time of primitive capitalism the state had the duty of defending the basic rights of workers, so now, with the new capitalism, the state and all of society have the duty of defending those collective goods which, among others, constitute the essential framework for the legitimate pursuit of personal goods on the part of each individual.[76]

In the age of advanced socialization we inhabit, public authorities are assigned the care of the overall social ecology. Elected lawmakers and appointed officials are entrusted with the task of protecting those elements of the common good that would fall through the cracks if market forces were not thus supplemented. Catholic social teaching continues to affirm that the preservation of collective goods is the proper responsibility of government today. While some commentators accuse it of veering toward excessive statism, this tradition of reflection continually updates its core commitment to advocating a healthy view of government—as a necessary and natural part of a well-ordered human community that serves the entire society as the indispensable agent of the common good.

THREE PRINCIPLES FOR SOCIAL POLICY

This chapter has opened up a window on Catholic social teaching, revealing key elements within this tradition of reflection that are most relevant for conducting an ethical evaluation of social welfare policies. Most of these insights are of the deep background variety. What Catholic teaching says about the social character of property or the way subsidiarity influences perceptions of governmental interventions emerges as a basic building block of public policy positions, but admittedly is hardly of immediate assistance in policy analysis.

Ethical reflection usually proceeds by means of delineating and applying relevant principles. By drawing up general statements of normative significance, ethicists describe and advance their arguments about moral values and about which courses of action best accomplish them. In chapter 4 we will investigate the moral principles and propositions actually articulated by the U.S. Catholic bishops as they have addressed the topic of welfare reform in recent years. But it will also be helpful to distill a few even more general principles drawn from Catholic social teaching and applicable to social policy. This concluding section of chapter 1 identifies three such broad principles and briefly describes the significance of each.

Social Membership Must Be Universal
We have already seen (in our survey of such themes as human dignity and solidarity) how Catholic social teaching articulates its commitment to the common Christian theme of universalism. We are all children of God, precious to our Creator. The overcoming of divisions among people is not only desirable, but reflects God's intentions for the world. No people, regardless of their natural endowments or even their culpable failure to achieve high levels of skill or income, lie outside of God's care and saving intention for the world.[77] The inclusiveness of God's love, in creating, sustaining, and offering redemption to all people without exception, serves as a proper model for human activity. A social unity that transcends all artificial division emerges, then, as a constituent part of the common good, as a key condition for the flourishing of each person and of the community as a whole.

But in acknowledging the Catholic theological theme of universal membership, we in no way surrender our ability to recognize social complexities and competing values. One area where such complications arise involves the relationship between worldwide human society and the discrete bounded national entities that seek to protect their rightful sovereignty and to control membership within their frontiers. Policies on immigration and the policing of borders are thus most relevant to the question of social membership. It would be blatantly unrealistic to expect the citizens of a given affluent nation to make an open-ended commitment to expend all their resources for the benefit of the needy worldwide community, as laudable as such imagined efforts would be. Also among the most enduring of these issues is the complex interplay of equality and inequality. Although Catholic social teaching has generally been a prophetic voice for a more equitable distribution of wealth, it also recognizes the folly of opposing all differences of outcome. In countering late-nineteenth-century socialist calls for radical egalitarianism, *Rerum novarum* warned:

> Humanity must remain as it is. It is impossible to reduce human society to a level. The socialists may do their utmost, but all striving against nature is in vain. There naturally exist among mankind innumerable differences of the most important kind. People differ in capability, in diligence, in health and in strength; and unequal fortune is a necessary result of inequality of condition.[78]

As the twentieth century witnessed an even more sharply exacerbated gap between the rich and poor, Catholic leaders found existing inequalities harder and harder to justify. Much of the growing gulf dividing the human race into affluent and destitute portions appeared to be due not to the free play of natural forces, arbitrary as they might be, but to a more pernicious set of dynamics. The life chances of the largest segment of humanity increasingly appeared to be systematically impeded by structures of massive injustice. Aspirations for mobility toward a better life were being frustrated by political and economic systems dominated by elites who, deliberately or not, thwarted the potential social progress of the poor. Conditions faced by the poor grew more dire, as the very lives of millions were threatened by disease, famine, war, and loss of their land and livelihood. As Church officials grew in awareness of these disturbing trends, the documents of Catholic social teaching spoke out more forcefully against growing inequality. The Second Vatican Council's 1965 document, *Gaudium et spes,* laments:

> While an enormous mass of people still lacks the absolute necessities of life, some, even in less advanced countries, live sumptuously or squander wealth. Luxury and misery rub shoulders. While the few enjoy very great freedom of choice, the many are deprived of almost all possibility of acting on their own initiative and responsibility, and often subsist in living and working conditions unworthy of human beings.[79]

Populorum progressio reflects these same weighty concerns in expressing a longing for

> a world where every man, no matter what his race, religion or nationality, can live a fully human life, freed from servitude imposed on him by other men or by natural forces over which he has not sufficient control; a world where freedom is not an empty word and where the poor man Lazarus can sit down at the same table with the rich man.[80]

Many further selections from recent Catholic social teaching documents could be cited to demonstrate the tradition's growing concern about threats to social unity and universal membership. Moreover, this is one area where papal encyclicals appear stronger on moral exhortation (urging a change of heart or a renewed commitment to concern for the destitute) than on concrete suggestions for structural change or public policy. While Vatican social thought surely cannot be expected to serve as a comprehensive resource for policy strategies, it has come to emphasize one relevant and potentially crucial theme: widespread social participation. The section earlier in this chapter on common good and solidarity highlighted the call to full participation as an increasingly prominent element of recent Catholic social documents. Enhanced participation emerges as a remedy for forms of marginalization that undercut human dignity and unfairly isolate certain demographic groups from the mainstream of society.[81]

Although it is hard to pin down precisely what makes someone a fully recognized agent in society, there are several undisputed hallmarks of social membership. In contemporary Western societies, the ability to vote and to earn income are key signs that someone is a full participant in the political and economic life of society.[82] To deny someone reasonable opportunities to obtain these goods constitutes an offense against the principle of universal membership. Focusing for now on economic participation in society, the Catholic perspective on these issues would seem to emphasize the responsibility of public authorities to enhance employment opportunities as a key aspect of public policy. Indeed, the documents of Catholic social teaching fully affirm the desirability of government intervention to supplement the private sector in expanding job opportunities. *Gaudium et spes,* for example, states: "It is the duty of society . . . in keeping with its proper role, to help its citizens find opportunities for adequate employment."[83]

But what about those situations where this path is blocked—when the conditions in job markets or other barriers to employment (such as the existence of full-time family obligations) make the holding of a job impossible or inordinately burdensome for a given individual or a segment of the population? Such situations that restrict the ability of potential workers to engage in ordinary methods of earning income necessitate reliance upon what economists call second-best solutions. These are fallback options that preserve as many of the relevant values as possible. Not all the benefits of paid employment (financial self-sufficiency, participation in the workplace) can be achieved in such cases. Nevertheless, from an ethical perspective, it is essential to preserve those crucial goods that can be safeguarded: the life, security, and dignity of the persons affected as well as their dependent children. When public authorities act systematically to protect citizens from economic insecurity, they are providing what is often termed a "safety net." The goal of this type of public assistance is to guarantee a dignified minimum of material support to people affected by unemployment due to age, illness, family situation, or economic conditions beyond their control.

Kenneth Boulding notes that "virtually all societies, once they attain a certain stage of development, accept some responsibility for the social minimum below which their members should not be allowed to fall."[84] Catholic social teaching supports this form of income maintenance that protects, in words crafted by the U.S. bishops, "the right to security in the event of sickness, unemployment, and old age . . . with benefits sufficient to provide individuals and their families with a standard of living in keeping with human dignity."[85] John Paul II includes this related claim within his treatment of the responsibilities that accrue to governments as "indirect employers" in this era of interdependence and socialization:

> The obligation to provide unemployment benefits, that is to say, the duty to make suitable grants indispensable for the subsistence of unemployed workers and their families, is a duty springing from the fundamental principle of the moral order in this sphere, namely the principle of the common use of goods or, to put it in another still simpler way, the right to life and subsistence.[86]

One subcategory of these unemployment benefits is the form of income maintenance that in common American parlance has come to be called welfare. These are transfer payments and in-kind benefits targeted toward low-income families with no other means of subsistence. Unlike Social Security benefits, the provision of such transfers is based upon a means test rather than upon a contributory principle that assumes at least one member of a given family has a history of regular participation in the workforce. That these measures have the character of second-best solutions is a truth conveyed by this qualification offered by the Brookings Institution economist Robert Reischauer: "The welfare system exists largely as a last resort, one that picks up the pieces when other systems and institutions fail. Failure in the educational system, in marriages and families, and in labor markets are the major systemic causes of welfare dependency."[87]

People receiving welfare benefits have by and large fallen through the cracks in the economic structure of modern societies. Receiving these benefits by no means assures such families access to the mainstream of society, but it offers them at least part of what they need to survive. Depending upon the policies of the particular states they inhabit, these families are eligible for cash and in-kind benefits that provide them with anywhere from reasonably modest material comfort at the upper end of the welfare scale to a very bare minimum existence at the lower end, where public assistance must be supplemented with some other sources of income in order to keep these families from hunger, homelessness, and utter destitution. By supplying an income floor that safeguards the lives and health of members of very poor families, this assistance serves as a precondition for more substantial progress toward full social participation. A comprehensive solution to the problems of poor families would include sweeping reforms of social systems (especially changes in education and employment opportunities) and perhaps changes in the affected individuals themselves (to prepare them and their families better to take advantage of whatever economic opportunities do become available). As administered within present institutional structures, welfare is a necessary Band-Aid, not the full structural remedy required to address the problem of the marginalization of poor families.

There is a remarkable overlap between the moral justification for social provision found within Catholic social teaching and the conceptual framework of what is usually called the welfare state or the social assistance state. The historical project of the secular welfare state hinges on the assumption by public authorities of responsibility for establishing favorable conditions for national economic performance, including healthy rates of growth, employment, and inflation as well as a measure of economic security for all citizens. In a mature welfare state, key goods are decommodified and access to life's necessities is guaranteed to all citizens on an entitlement basis. Social insurance covers the exigencies of life in industrial society, including the possibility of illness, the chance of job-related injuries, the need for retirement benefits, and other situations causing fluctuations in earnings levels across the life cycle. In short, a fully developed welfare state is committed to providing citizens with a full panoply of social and economic rights to complement the political and civil rights that are essential parts of full citizenship.[88]

Welfare states take many historical forms, depending on their context.[89] Some welfare states, while still a long way from fully socialist regimes that would control productive capital, represent rather ambitious attempts to engage in significant levels of economic planning, where government plays a relatively large role in providing economic security, often by socializing much of the national income. Contemporary U.S. policies, for their part, consist of rather modest efforts to provide safety nets for only the very poorest families. American welfare programs generally provide categorical and means-tested benefits rather than universal benefits. This limits the progress that can be made toward true social inclusion, for a dynamic of stigmatization threatens to accompany all such targeted benefits. Recipients of means-tested benefits in the United States suffer from being singled out by their need, so the ability of these social programs to decrease the social distance between the poor and those in the mainstream is seriously questioned.

Several related hard questions remain for later in our study of U.S. welfare policy: Do our national policies treat recipients as unwelcome intruders in a prosperous land? Do recipients receive the message that they are "surplus people" whose fate is of little importance to others? Is resentment over unequal social contributions a crucial subtext of U.S. social policies? The answers to these questions contain both empirical and normative implications for policymakers and analysts.

Make a Preferential Option for the Poor

The previous principle involved the recognition of the full social membership of the least advantaged, specifically those who need public assistance. The principle examined in this section calls attention not to the question of belonging, that is, the status of the poor, but to the more routine treatment they receive in society. We shift our focus from the threat of utter abandonment to the call for marginal adjustments in the distribution of social burdens and benefits.

The phrase "preferential option for the poor" has the advantage of being explicitly mentioned in documents of the Catholic Church, albeit only in recent decades. Rooted in Latin American liberation theology, it first appeared in the 1979 documents of the Conference of Latin American Bishops held in Puebla, Mexico.[90] However, since this theme has conceptual roots in scripture, in both Old and New Testaments, it is not surprising to find references to nearly identical notions in previous documents of Catholic social teaching. In his 1971 letter, *Octogesima adveniens*, Pope Paul VI offers a paraphrase, "preferential respect due to the poor," and calls for "the most fortunate [to] renounce some of their rights so as to place their goods more generously at the service of others."[91] The opening sentences of *Gaudium et spes* famously identify the Church with the concerns of the poor, but this document's subsequent calls for the attainment of justice, including the reduction of economic inequality, contain only faint echoes of the phrase "option for the poor."[92]

Although the phrase served as something of a lightning rod for controversy and serious misunderstanding during his pontificate, John Paul II referred to an option for the poor in two of his three social encyclicals. *Sollicitudo rei socialis* lists among the "characteristic themes and guidelines" recommended by the tradition of Catholic social teaching "the option or love of preference for the poor." This priority is immediately linked to concrete actions that give it flesh:

> This is an option, or a special form of primacy in the exercise of Christian charity, to which the whole tradition of the Church bears witness. It affects the life of each Christian inasmuch as he or she seeks to imitate the life of Christ, but it applies equally to our social responsibilities and hence to our manner of living, and to the logical decisions to be made concerning the ownership and use of goods.[93]

Early in the 1991 anniversary encyclical *Centesimus annus,* John Paul II interprets *Rerum novarum*'s call to improve the conditions of workers a century earlier as a manifestation of the preferential option for the poor long before the phrase was coined. Recognizing that the Church was engaged in advocacy for the poor throughout the centuries, John Paul notes, provides "an excellent testimony to the continuity within the church of the so-called 'preferential option for the poor'" and to "the church's constant concern for and dedication to categories of people who are especially beloved to Jesus Christ."[94]

Putting aside the potential charge of anachronism, we find in these citations key elements that afford a constructive use of the concept of option for the poor. Even without the benefit of further theological analysis, we can say the following about this principle and its application to social policy. First, although it is something of a neologism, the option for the poor has deep roots in scripture and the historical praxis of the Church, an institution that has continually expressed a special dedication to the needs of the most marginalized members of society.[95] Second, in describing God's special relationship with the disadvantaged, the option for the poor establishes an ethical imperative for all the faithful to do likewise. As individuals and as participants in numerous social organizations, we are called to reorient the priorities of every social agent and institution so that they serve the least fortunate. Third, the preferential option is not intended as an adversarial slogan that endorses class conflict, but rather proposes a particular type of social unity, one that emphasizes a widening of concern and an overcoming of the forces of exclusion.[96] Fourth, the option for the poor exerts a potent tug of conscience on all who recognize the legitimacy of its demands. This motivates them to view social reality from the perspective of the poor and to measure their actions in new ways. At the very least, it rules out certain courses of action such as utter apathy toward the poor and a destructive brand of social Darwinism favoring the view that society's "losers" somehow deserve their plight.

It is, however, easier to say what the option for the poor rules out than to determine precisely what it supports or even obliges in conscience. Regarding social policy in particular, it would be hard to specify any particular courses of action as absolutely required by an option for the poor. Surely this principle leads its adherents to favor those outcomes that are most advantageous to those with the lowest incomes, but little is settled by this generalization. Forging consensus on precisely what conditions contribute to the well-being of the least fortunate has proven elusive in recent debates over welfare reform. For some observers, generous benefit levels are key measures of a policy committed to the well-being of the poor. Others fear that indiscriminate handouts unaccompanied by reciprocal responsibilities (such as work requirements) are actually detrimental to the social standing of the poor, even if their material income rises in the short term.

Interpreting the ramifications of a preferential option for the poor remains, in the end, a matter of prudential judgment. People of good will might well disagree on the answers to questions like the following: What forms of government and private-sector efforts are likely to be most effective in opening up the greatest opportunities? What is the best combination of direct transfer payments, indirect work supports, and even punitive disincentives against undesirable behavior? Our answers are likely to depend upon both empirical data and moral principles. Ideally, the empirical and the moral will not be in conflict. Rather, the recommendations of social science and those of ethical analysis will hopefully work creatively in concert to steer us toward enlightened and effective policies to produce mutual benefit for all.

Do Not Place People in Impossible Situations

This final principle has already received attention in the course of our examination of the role of the state. As creatures with physical needs, human beings exhibit a fragility that responsible public policy must take into account. It is not only immoral, but also constitutes bad policy, to deprive people of opportunities for honorable means of subsistence, for to do so diminishes their personal freedom and renders them less than full and active participants in society. Wise policy, then, offers people a minimum measure of security, a buffer separating them from the most dire want. In the absence of such provisions, even seemingly free markets for goods and labor become potentially coercive loci of desperate exchanges. Protecting the dignity of people includes shielding them from the exploitation that accompanies being forced into "trades of last resort."[97]

As seen above, John Ryan's argument in defense of the living wage was premised upon a philosophical commitment, namely the insistence that "ought implies can." People must not be asked to do the impossible, in this case, to provide for the physical needs of themselves and their dependents without adequate opportunities to discharge these duties. If work is not available, or if existing job opportunities are not adequate to support a decent existence, then the industrial economy is laying upon people burdens they cannot endure. These considerations led Ryan to argue that "human needs constitute the primary title of claim to material goods,"[98] and this ensemble of social concerns spurred him to support public policies to alleviate this burden. In the practical order, as Ryan was well aware, the criterion of human need is never more than a partial standard, for it becomes impractical unless combined with other titles to goods: distribution according to effort, sacrifice, contribution, and so on. Nevertheless, as we turn our attention in the coming chapters to the plight of those whose potential work contributions are quite limited (and in any case are not highly valued by society), we will be considering a segment of the population for whom distribution by need plays a vitally important role in making possible the pursuit of the full range of social goods, including the preservation of life itself.

Table 1.1

Documents of the Catholic Church Cited in Chapter 1

YEAR	TITLE	SOURCE
1891	*Rerum novarum*	Pope Leo XIII
1931	*Quadragesimo anno*	Pope Pius XI
1961	*Mater et magistra*	Pope John XXIII
1963	*Pacem in terris*	Pope John XXIII
1965	*Gaudium et spes*	Second Vatican Council
1967	*Populorum progressio*	Pope Paul VI
1971	*Octogesima adveniens*	Pope Paul VI
1971	*Justitia in mundo*	Synod of Bishops
1979	*Redemptor hominis*	Pope John Paul II
1981	*Laborem exercens*	Pope John Paul II
1986	*Economic Justice for All*	U.S. Bishops
1987	*Sollicitudo rei socialis*	Pope John Paul II
1991	*Centesimus annus*	Pope John Paul II

Note on format for citations: Catholic social teaching documents normally contain standard section numbers, so these will be listed after the title of the document for purposes of citation. The original versions of Vatican documents appear in Latin, so the Latin titles will be retained to avoid confusion. Unless otherwise noted, the Vatican documents cited all appear in David J. O'Brien and Thomas A. Shannon, eds., *Catholic Social Thought: The Documentary Heritage* (Maryknoll, NY: Orbis Books, 1992).

NOTES

1. The full English texts of all twelve Vatican documents that fall into this category are found in David J. O'Brien and Thomas A. Shannon, eds., *Catholic Social Thought: The Documentary Heritage* (Maryknoll, NY: Orbis Books, 1992). This volume also includes the U.S. bishops' 1986 pastoral letter, *Economic Justice for All.*

2. Marvin L. Krier Mich, *Catholic Social Teaching and Movements* (Mystic, CT: Twenty-Third Publications, 1998), contains especially rich and insightful testimony to the concrete expressions of Catholic social teaching in organized movements for social change, such as struggles for worker justice, peace, and human rights.

3. U.S. Black Catholic Bishops, "What We Have Seen and Heard." The letter was originally published in 1984 and appears in Thomas J. Massaro, SJ, and Thomas A. Shannon, eds., *American Catholic Social Teaching* (Collegeville, MN: Liturgical Press, 2002); Catholic Bishops of Appalachia, "This Land Is Home to Me: A Pastoral Letter on Poverty and Powerlessness in Appalachia." The full text of this pastoral letter appears in *American Catholic Social Teaching*, ed. Massaro and Shannon. A second letter updating the economic and ecological concerns of the bishops of the same region bears the title *At Home in the Web of Life* (Webster

Springs, WV Catholic Committee of Appalachia, 1995); "The Columbia River Watershed: Caring for Creation and the Common Good," *Origins* 30, no. 38 (8 March 2001): 609–19; *Voices and Choices: A Pastoral Message on Justice in the Workplace from the Catholic Bishops of the South* (Cincinnati, OH: St. Anthony Messenger Press, 2000) was released 15 November 2000. The statement, in both English and Spanish, was produced by the Catholic Committee of the South and, in addition to the print version, is available at www.poultry-pastoral.org.

4. *Octogesima adveniens*, 4.

5. *Centesimus annus*, 48.

6. Typical of this school of opinion is George Weigel, "The Virtues of Freedom: *Centesimus Annus*," in *Building the Free Society: Democracy, Capitalism and Catholic Social Teaching*, ed. George Weigel and Robert Royal (Grand Rapids, MI: William B. Eerdmans Press, 1993), 207–23.

7. *Centesimus annus*, 40.

8. *Sollicitudo rei socialis*, 47. The use of noninclusive language in official English translations of Vatican documents is unfortunate, but most scholars agree that replacing masculinist renderings with gender-neutral versions risks introducing inaccuracies and anachronisms.

9. *Gaudium et spes*, 19.

10. Ibid., 69.

11. *Pacem in terris*, 9.

12. See, for example, David Hollenbach, SJ, *Claims in Conflict: Retrieving and Renewing the Catholic Human Rights Tradition* (New York: Paulist Press, 1979); Mary Ann Glendon, *Rights Talk: The Impoverishment of Political Discourse* (New York: Macmillan Company, 1991).

13. Pope John Paul II is especially firm in his rejection of the various types of reductionism. See, for example, nos. 12–13 of his 1981 social encyclical, *Laborem exercens*. In the course of arguing for "the priority of labor," John Paul II denounces materialist ways of thinking that reduce humans to the same level as "things."

14. See *Rerum novarum*, 21; *Mater et magistra*, 219; *Gaudium et spes*, 32; *Sollicitudo rei socialis*, 38–40, 45; *Centesimus annus*, 10.

15. *Gaudium et spes*, 32, 38; *Sollicitudo rei socialis*, 40.

16. Aristotle, *Politics*, 1.2.

17. Among the places where Thomas Aquinas treats these elements of his social theory is his Treatise on Law contained in his *Summa Theologiae*, I–II, q. 90–96.

18. *Mater et magistra*, 65.

19. David Hollenbach, SJ, *The Common Good and Christian Ethics* (New York: Cambridge University Press, 2002), 9, xiii.

20. See, for example, *Economic Justice for All*, the 1986 Pastoral Letter of the U.S. bishops, which lifts up participation as a key measure of social progress. The full text appears in *Catholic Social Thought*, ed. O'Brien and Shannon. See esp. no. 77.

21. One excellent source of texts (primarily from Clement, Basil the Great, Ambrose, John Chrysostom, and Augustine) and commentary upon them is Charles Avila, *Ownership: Early Christian Teaching* (Maryknoll, NY: Orbis Books, 1983).

22. Thomas Aquinas, *Summa Theologiae*, II-II, q. 66. The passage is usually remembered for its seemingly surprising conclusion that, under certain circumstances, theft may be permissible.

23. Ibid., a. 2.
24. Ibid.
25. Ibid.
26. In fact, all three of Aquinas's justifications for private holdings in this text may be interpreted as measures of prudence in response to the existence of sin in the world.
27. Charles E. Curran, *Directions in Catholic Social Ethics* (Notre Dame, IN: University of Notre Dame Press, 1985), 23–27.
28. *Quadragesimo anno,* 46.
29. Ibid., 49.
30. Ibid.
31. See *Gaudium et spes,* 70; *Populorum progressio,* 66; *Sollicitudo rei socialis,* 31.
32. Here, in contrast to the way the term is employed in common U.S. political parlance, "liberalism" refers to economic approaches that emphasize free markets unimpeded by regulations. This is the meaning of liberalism as it is treated in most papal social encyclicals. See, for example, *Quadragesimo anno,* 54.
33. *Sollicitudo rei socialis,* 42–43.
34. Jacques Maritain, *Man and the State* (Chicago: University of Chicago Press, 1951), 12.
35. John Courtney Murray, SJ, "Leo XIII: Two Concepts of Government," *Theological Studies* 14 (1953): 559.
36. John Courtney Murray, SJ, *We Hold These Truths: Catholic Reflections on the American Proposition* (New York: Sheed and Ward, 1960), 160.
37. John A. Ryan, *Distributive Justice: The Rights and Wrongs of Our Present Distribution of Wealth* (New York: Macmillan Company, 1925).
38. Ibid., 304.
39. Ibid., 359.
40. John A. Ryan, *A Living Wage: Its Ethical and Economic Aspects* (New York: Macmillan Company, 1912), 128.
41. Ryan challenges these simple assumptions of Adam Smith and his heirs, among other places, in ibid., 12–19.
42. *Rerum novarum,* 34, argues that just wages should be enforced by private "societies or boards." The state may at most "be asked for approval and protection," but should not be the primary agent of this reform "in order to supersede undue interference on the part of the State"; Ryan, *A Living Wage,* 301.
43. Ibid., 10–22.
44. Ibid., 43, 23.
45. Ibid., 315.
46. Ibid., "Author's Preface," viii and passim.
47. Ryan, *Distributive Justice,* 366–70; Ryan, *A Living Wage,* 249.
48. Ryan, *A Living Wage,* 249.
49. Ibid., 45.
50. Ibid., 79.
51. Ibid., 244.
52. Ryan addresses this point in *A Living Wage,* 55–66. Here he takes issue with positivistic notions of the origin of rights in social groupings. He identifies Hegel as a proponent of such dangerous views, views that, Ryan fears, threaten to deify the state and to violate individual dignity.
53. *Rerum novarum,* 6.

54. *Populorum progressio,* 34.
55. *Quadragesimo anno,* 79–80.
56. John Coleman SJ, "Development of Church Social Teaching," in *Readings in Moral Theology No. 5: Official Catholic Social Teaching,* ed. Charles E. Curran and Richard A. McCormick SJ (New York: Paulist Press, 1986), 183.
57. This phrase was popularized by the work of Richard John Neuhaus and Peter Berger in the 1980s. Two hundred years earlier, Edmund Burke described the same phenomena as the "little platoons" of society.
58. *Quadragesimo anno,* 80.
59. Ryan, *A Living Wage,* 100.
60. The original Latin phrase is *socialium rationum incrementa,* although the official Italian, French, and German versions use cognates of "socialization." For a detailed discussion of the origins of this term and its subsequent translation, see Donal Dorr, *Option for the Poor: A Hundred Years of Catholic Social Teaching* (Maryknoll, NY: Orbis Books, 1992), 132–35.
61. *Mater et magistra,* 59–60.
62. Ibid., 109.
63. Ibid., 116–21.
64. This phrase serves as the title of part 3 (nos. 123–211) of *Mater et magistra.*
65. *Gaudium et spes,* 70.
66. Ibid., 25.
67. *Populorum progressio,* 33.
68. *Octogesima adveniens,* 15–16.
69. Ibid., 43.
70. Ibid., 26–35, 18, 46–47.
71. *Laborem exercens,* 17.
72. Ibid., 18.
73. Ibid., 14.
74. Ibid.
75. *Sollicitudo rei socialis,* 42.
76. *Centesimus annus,* 40.
77. 1 Tim. 2:4.
78. *Rerum novarum,* 14.
79. *Gaudium et spes,* 63.
80. *Populorum progressio,* 47. In many writings and addresses, Pope John Paul II also displays a fondness for citing the story of the beggar Lazarus and the rich man, found in Luke 16: 19–31. See, for example, *Sollicitudo rei socialis,* 33; *Redemptor hominis,* 16. The latter appears in *Origins* 8, no. 40 (March 22, 1979): 625–44.
81. See, for example, *Gaudium et spes,* 65 and 73; *Centesimus annus,* 52.
82. These two goods are singled out by Judith Shklar in *American Citizenship: The Quest for Inclusion* (Cambridge, MA: Harvard University Press, 1991), 15.
83. *Gaudium et spes,* 67. See also *Laborem exercens,* 18; *Centesimus annus,* 52; U.S. Bishops, *Economic Justice for All,* 80 (which discusses the right to employment) and 150 (which calls for guaranteeing full employment).
84. Kenneth E. Boulding, "The Boundaries of Social Policy," *Social Work* 12, no. 1 (1967): 6.
85. U.S. Bishops, *Economic Justice for All,* 80.
86. *Laborem exercens,* 18.

87. Robert D. Reischauer, "The Welfare Reform Legislation: Directions for the Future," in *Welfare Policy for the 1990s,* ed. Phoebe H. Cottingham and David T. Ellwood (Cambridge, MA: Harvard University Press, 1989), 19.

88. The idea of social and economic rights that accompany citizenship is associated with the great British theorist of the welfare state T. H. Marshall. See his essay, "Citizenship and Social Class," reprinted in *Citizenship and Social Class,* ed. Tom Bottomore (London: Pluto Press, 1992).

89. For a comprehensive analysis of the origins of welfare state policies in the Western democracies, see Alexander Hicks, *Social Democracy and Welfare Capitalism: A Century of Income Security Politics* (Ithaca, NY: Cornell University Press, 1999).

90. Puebla Final Document, part 4, chap.1. Reprinted in *Puebla and Beyond: Documentation and Commentary,* ed. John Eagleson and Philip Scharper (Maryknoll, NY: Orbis Books, 1979).

91. *Octogesima adveniens,* 23.

92. *Gaudium et spes,* 1, opens with this clarion call: "The joys and the hopes, the griefs and the anxieties of the men of this age, especially those who are poor or in any way afflicted, these too are the joys and hopes, the griefs and anxieties of the followers of Christ."

93. *Sollicitudo rei socialis,* 42.

94. *Centesimus annus,* 11.

95. Scriptural passages that suggest God's special love of the poor include Luke 1: 46–55; 1 Cor.: 26–29; Luke 6: 20–26.

96. For example, when the U.S. bishops cite this principle in the 1986 pastoral letter, *Economic Justice for All,* they take great pains to propose a reformist agenda that supports neither the status quo nor radical extremism. They assert that "the poor have the single most urgent economic claim on the conscience of the nation" (no. 86). The bishops recognize a dual obligation to address the immediate needs of the poor as well as to reform structures to improve their opportunities to participate more broadly in the benefits of social life (nos. 88–91).

97. For an insightful treatment of desperate exchanges and "trades of last resort," see Michael Walzer, *Spheres of Justice: A Defense of Pluralism and Equality* (New York: Basic Books, 1993), 97–103, 120–21.

98. Ryan, *Distributive Justice,* 357.

2

THE HISTORICAL CONTEXT OF U.S. WELFARE POLICY

To set the stage upon which the drama of the most recent episodes of welfare reform have unfolded, this chapter analyzes just enough of the history and development of U.S. welfare policy to shed light upon the central features of recent policy debates. Chapter 3 explains the details of the welfare reform law of 1996. This present chapter concludes with a brief consideration of one of the most frequently debated topics with profound implications for how America regards its poorest members: the role of private charitable organizations and other faith-based voluntary efforts to alleviate poverty and provide social services.

Because this part of our study is concerned with political and socio-historical realities rather than theological argumentation, its methodology is quite different from that of the previous chapter on Catholic social teaching. Chapter 1 appeals to theological principles to consider how certain policy directions might be justified on moral grounds. By contrast, chapters 2 and 3 make only the most minimal ethical assumptions in evaluating the feasibility and desirability of policy proposals. Moreover, as we analyze various policy rationales in these chapters, we will have occasion to appeal to what is often loosely referred to as American political culture. This term from political science refers to a set of generally shared convictions and commonly revered norms for determining which social practices are fair and desirable. It would, of course, be simplistic to claim that unanimous agreement reigns among all Americans on any topic, particularly on the contested terrain of social policy. Nevertheless, it is possible to identify a relatively stable core of public opinion regarding the kinds of institutions and practices that are fair and desirable.[1] As would be expected in any democracy, the convictions prevalent among the American populace play an influential (if not determining) role in public policy formation. Indeed, our public laws and social policies may be viewed as a text from which a perceptive observer might glean the underlying social values we share as a nation.

Few Americans would dissent from a certain small set of convictions that will here be assumed to shape social policy. Among the most central of these controlling ideas are these three propositions: (1) people should earn their living through paid employment if such work is a realistic and available option for them; (2) government should act to shield children from the worst effects of poverty; and (3) public policy should foster the formation and stability of two-parent families. Since conflict among even such general guidelines for sound policy is inevitable, one of the perennial tasks facing policymakers is to strike a balance among competing values. For example, a decision to increase the size and availability of welfare benefits bolsters the achievement of the second of these objectives at the possible expense of the first and third. Conversely, decisions to scale back welfare benefits and restrict eligibility compromise the second objective in the interest of pursuing the other two.

Another factor complicating policy analysis is that the relative strength and popularity of these shared objectives seem to shift over time. New eras witness varying climates of opinion among both political leaders and the general populace. How, then, does this contribute to explaining the sweeping welfare reform of 1996 and the shape of the reauthorization debate after 2002? Although these changes would not have occurred without widespread support among both political leaders and the general public, it is nevertheless important to avoid a false interpretation of the attitudinal shift reflected in the most recent rounds of welfare legislation. It is not necessarily the case that Americans have simply become less compassionate in their attitudes toward the needs of poor families. Alternative explanations are available. It is also possible that the transformation of the welfare debate in recent years primarily reflects a general increase in the level of public dissatisfaction with government programs, including greater distrust of the efficacy of federal efforts in fighting poverty. In other words, frequently expressed arguments about general government inefficiency and the more specific charge that nothing works in fighting poverty may have persuaded many Americans to withhold support from antipoverty programs, and this may account for the force and direction of certain policy shifts of the recent past.

As we survey below the winding history of American social policy, it is wise to heed the findings of most experts in the field of public opinion. The majority of studies find that there is a basic continuity in the fundamental desires of the American people in social policy.[2] Even when the nation endorses a new departure in policy (as it did when the 1996 law abandoned the income entitlement of the former AFDC program), we should examine the evidence with an eye towards the interplay of continuity and change and not focus exclusively on novel dimensions of policy, as dramatic as they might seem. While in the 1990s we witnessed the endorsement of a new policy strategy for addressing poverty, this need not be interpreted as an utter abandonment of underlying goals, such as a commitment to alleviate childhood poverty where possible. The basic objective of six decades of previous policy remained, despite the political decision to strike a new balance between the social policy goals of enforcing work requirements and providing a floor of income for the "deserving poor." Indeed, the consensus that some low-income families continue to merit substantial public assistance demonstrated something of a revival in subsequent state policies and in congressional proposals during the reauthorization debates starting in 2002.

THE ROOTS OF AMERICAN SOCIAL POLICY

Many civilizations have contributed to contemporary American understandings of what is possible and what is desirable regarding collective action to alleviate the effects of poverty. Our current ideas and practices reflect an eclectic heritage that shapes our awareness of private forms of almsgiving and public arrangements for poor relief around the world. However, no legacy has influenced our policy more directly than the English Poor Laws. The legacy of these laws not only set the context for the earliest public welfare measures adopted by the colonies that would become the United States, but also has continued to play a role as the primary point of reference for American policy makers seeking lessons from other societies.

Several episodes in the long history of English social welfare legislation are particularly worth examining. They reveal a consistent tendency for relief arrangements to be conceptually and practically linked with the tasks of establishing discipline within the labor force and developing and sustaining a competitive market for free labor. The Statute of Laborers, enacted in 1349 during the reign of King Edward III, sought to control the widespread practice of begging by restricting the movement and fixing the wages of potential laborers. This landmark measure was a response to the social upheavals associated with the end of serfdom and the shortage of labor caused by the Black Death and other plagues.[3] Subsequent Tudor and Elizabethan Poor Laws "established the principle of a legal, compulsory, secular, national (although locally administered) provision for relief."[4] Those to whom assistance was extended during this era, although presumably unable to work, were nonetheless subject to considerable shame and stigma because of their inability to support themselves. Localities provided a mix of indoor relief (in which the unemployed received money and in-kind assistance to help them survive) and outdoor relief (which required such paupers to take up residence in a poorhouse or workhouse). The need for each, as well as the expense of each, expanded whenever economic conditions worsened.

In 1795 a new set of poor relief arrangements was tried, first in Berkshire, then more generally throughout England. Called the Speenhamland system, it provided wage subsidies for farmworkers whose earnings left them below the subsistence level. This system of income supplementation had the advantage of shielding agricultural laborers somewhat from the worst effects of the economic upheavals of the dawning industrial age. However, its disadvantages included high expenditures of public funds, direct work disincentives that threatened long-term dependency for recipients, and complex unintended effects on productivity and mobility that forestalled the establishment of a national industrial labor market. Thomas Malthus famously added a new rationale for the repeal of the Speenhamland subsidies. He argued that, according to the supposedly inexorable law of population, overgenerosity in poor relief would only lead to social disaster by encouraging an unsustainable increase in the number of those living at a level of bare subsistence.[5]

Gertrude Himmelfarb argues that the reforms contained in the subsequent New Poor Law of 1834 accepted only a fraction of the recommendations that Malthusians proposed. Rather than repealing all forms of assistance, the new law emphasized a key distinction between those applicants worthy of aid (the "deserving poor," such as the sick, aged, and widows with young children) and the able-bodied poor who did not merit assistance because they were potentially part of the workforce. In order to discourage overgenerosity to those not in genuine need and to deter new applicants from seeking relief, the workhouse came to be used as a locus for administering a harsh work test. Conditions there were to be so severe (indeed, prisonlike, as the novels of Charles Dickens attest) that no one with any other options at all would voluntarily choose the terms of poor relief. This rationale for such arrangements is often referred to as the principle of less eligibility, whereby the instrument of relief also serves as the test of relief. The New Poor Law became infamous because of the way it degraded and in a sense criminalized the poor, diminishing the freedom and social status of those unfortunate enough to require assistance.[6]

Regarding the other side of the Atlantic, colonial and nineteenth-century American relief arrangements reflected the intellectual legacy of the English Poor Laws. The triumph of a distinctively American version of individualism and the nearly unchallenged ascendency of free-market liberalism on these shores reinforced three central features of the English poor relief system: (1) its tendency to denigrate and even criminalize the poor; (2) its drawing of moral boundaries between worthy and unworthy; and (3) the enforcement of a rigorous work ethic. The Puritan ethos that constitutes one strand of American intellectual culture gave rise to a gospel of self-help that so emphasizes personal responsibility that it eclipses other social values, such as solidarity and compassion, that would support more ambitious public assistance efforts.[7] The desire of these early generations of Americans to relieve the misery of their less fortunate neighbors was no doubt genuine, but was checked by widespread reluctance to induce the socially destructive consequences that they supposed would accompany overgenerosity. These fears placed a premium on the rigid control of the distribution of welfare assistance, whether by means of indoor or outdoor relief.[8]

As members of a frontier society, where opportunity seemed limitless, Americans perhaps found it even easier than their English counterparts to blame the poor for their own poverty. Further, ready at hand were widely accepted theological justifications that supported the value of self-reliance and viewed the maintenance of inequality as somehow divinely ordained. When prosperity is interpreted as a sign of divine favor, it becomes morally hazardous to lift the losers in economic competition above the level they attain through their own work effort. Against this intellectual backdrop, it was easy for eighteenth- and nineteenth-century American policy makers not only to impose strict limits upon the generosity of relief and eligibility for it, but also to ignore the structural economic issues that made reliance on social provision necessary for some segment of the population. If poverty stubbornly persists in an increasingly prosperous society, the most genuine need seemed to be for moral reform on the individual level, not for systemic change to address the deeper causes of poverty.[9]

American relief arrangements in this era followed the English tradition inasmuch as they reflected serious concern not only for people threatened by destitution, but also for the social goal of maintaining labor force discipline. In the interest of deterring potential workers from dependence upon assistance, the institutions and administrators of relief came to regulate the lives of the poor in numerous ways, some of them objectionable on a number of grounds, both ethical and practical in nature.[10] In her study of how American social welfare policy has affected the cause of gender justice, Mimi Abramovitz recounts the many ways policy has served to regulate the lives and roles of women in particular. The maintenance of a patriarchal family ethic has been an implicit goal of relief arrangements and welfare policy in every era, from colonial times (when the family was considered "a cell of righteousness") to nineteenth-century industrialism (with its moral reform charity efforts to support conventional family life) through the Progressive Era's scientific and environmental reform movements and finally to the rise of the casework approach of the social work profession of the current era.[11]

For a variety of reasons, relief arrangements, as determined by legislators and administered by public authorities, are not neutral in their social effects. One key factor in this is the social stigma that attaches to all recipients who, for whatever reasons, engage in those types of behavior (such as low attachment to labor markets and independence from male breadwinners) that welfare policy seeks to discourage. Welfare program rules may be likened to a text that, for better or worse, encodes the values of particular forms of a family ethic and a work ethic.[12] In every era, public policy has served not only as a means of material assistance, but also as a potent instrument of social control. Those who flout accepted social standards are subject to punitive treatment.

All these features of welfare policy can be detected in the AFDC program. It originally came into existence as ADC (Aid to Dependent Children) under Title IV of the Social Security Act. This measure, part of the Second New Deal, was signed into law by President Franklin Delano Roosevelt on August 14, 1935. Although historians universally consider the act a major social policy landmark, it would be a serious mistake to view this first comprehensive federal welfare program for families as completely discontinuous from previous policy developments on the state and local levels. Theda Skocpol alerts us of the need to revise the conventional wisdom regarding the narrative of social policy. The standard version suggests that the New Deal represents a "big bang" of social reform consisting of many unprecedented "extensions of federal power into the country's economic and social life."[13] A less familiar but very influential story is that of the antecedent phases of U.S. social provision, something that proceeded on two fronts that Skocpol links by noting their common conceptual rationale. They were based upon solidarities of gender as opposed to those solidarities of class position that accounted for the development of advanced welfare states in many European nations.[14] The first was a system of generous military pensions for veterans of the Civil War, adopted in stages during the Reconstruction Era and beyond. It was designed to reward soldiers of the Grand Army of the Republic for their service to the nation and to protect them from the indignities of poverty in their old age. The second consisted of a series of measures that brought the United States to the brink of establishing a truly maternalist style of welfare state nearly a generation before the New Deal. It included forty-six state-run Mother's Pension programs for "deserving" (mostly widowed) single mothers and a federal program (administered from 1921 to 1929 by the Children's Bureau under the Sheppard–Towner Act) to advance the provision of health care for mothers and infants.

These two "precocious social spending regimes" left a legacy of predispositions and attitudes within the collective memory of Americans. As it turned out, much of this legacy was negative. Startling levels of patronage and corruption plagued the administration of veterans' benefits. The maternalist programs were discredited by objections to the cost of thus "honoring motherhood" and by second thoughts regarding the programs' basic rationale, best summarized by the claim that "motherhood creates entitlements."[15] At the very least, these programs demonstrated that political support could be mobilized to enact national social provision for goals identified with the common good of all Americans. The United States might still be considered a welfare state laggard compared to many European nations with highly developed social assistance programs. Yet the achievements of the Progressive Era had demonstrated that there were possibilities within the American political culture for mobilization beyond what many expected from a nation dominated by an ethos of rugged individualism and a laissez-faire style of economic life.

THE NEW DEAL AND ITS LEGACY

The centerpiece of the New Deal's social legislation, the Social Security Act of 1935, merits careful attention in any study of subsequent welfare policy. This breakthrough measure reflects both continuity and noteworthy discontinuity with previous American social policy. Of course, if there had been no Great Depression, there would have been no Social Security Act. Sudden economic constriction and unprecedented massive unemployment promoted a profound rethinking of social policy during the 1930s. The seemingly random distribution of economic misfortune made a mockery of the work ethic upon which earlier policy approaches to poverty had been based. Harry Hopkins's realization, amidst the severe social dislocations of the Depression, that "the poor are not a class apart who are to be pitied, but are . . . just like the rest of us, with the same hopes, aspirations and appetites,"[16] was emblematic of a dawning appreciation of the structural causes of poverty. New assumptions about the nature of poverty allowed at least some of the poor to be viewed more as victims than as culprits. Individuals or families might suffer dramatic declines in income or wealth for reasons completely beyond their control, as when stock values plummeted, factories closed, jobs were lost, labor markets crashed, crops withered, and illness struck. The national emergency sparked a renewed sense of social solidarity similar to the wartime solidarity that prompted the citizens of many European nations to make remarkable sacrifices during armed conflicts and to forge comprehensive social assistance regimes once the struggles had ended.[17]

The solidarity of emergency led many to the conclusion that something must be done to improve income security in the United States. Still, diverse factors would influence the precise form these measures would take. Roosevelt's Committee on Economic Security found itself buffeted by ideological and popular pressures on all sides as it attempted to draft what eventually became the Social Security Act.[18] The major concern of the deliberations was to provide replacement income to the unemployed and elderly poor. These goals were accomplished by the establishment of such programs as Old Age Insurance (popularly called Social Security), Unemployment Insurance, Disability Insurance, and Worker Compensation. The federal commitment of resources to these programs, based as they are on a contributory principle (one in which attachment to the labor market serves as the key basis for entitlement to transfer payments), was impressive. As such, it dwarfed in size and scope the grant-in-aid public assistance programs (Old Age Assistance, Aid to the Blind, Aid to Dependent Children, and their successor programs) that are noncontributory in nature.

There are three especially noteworthy features of this structure set up in the 1930s and still largely in place today. First, it places the American welfare state on a categorical basis, with distinct programs targeted to address separate categories of need. This characteristic distinguishes the American approach to social policy from those European welfare states featuring universal programs for guaranteed income maintenance and the provision of basic goods (housing, nutrition, health care) as rights of social citizenship.[19] In this respect, the Social Security Act displays continuity with the heritage of state-run programs that it largely replaced, for it established a patchwork of programs (now national in scope and funding) with varying eligibility requirements rather than a seamless social safety net.[20]

Second, as already noted, the Act's primary concern was the establishment of a social insurance system in which the predominant rationale for the distribution of benefits was to support workers through earnings fluctuations over their life cycle, including benefits to cover spells of unemployment, disability, and eventual retirement. This minimized the potential redistributive effects of the legislation and reaffirmed the traditional work ethic. Without a history of attachment to the labor market and contribution to program funds, individuals could lay claim to benefits only by establishing themselves as belonging to categories of citizens who were not expected to engage in paid employment (the elderly poor, the permanently disabled or blind, and—at least at the time—single mothers with young children).

Third, the system was set up so that these latter categories constituted a lower tier or track of a stratified welfare state. The distinction between the entitlements of the upper and lower tiers may be measured in at least three ways. One is in terms of benefit levels. Programs in the upper stratum of social insurance are consistently more generous than the others, providing recipients with a more adequate standard of living than the normally sub-poverty level of welfare benefits.[21] This type of discrimination introduces a peculiar mode of irrationality into the structure of U.S. programs, for it means that children may be divided arbitrarily into categories that receive starkly different treatment. For example, those children "fortunate" enough to be the offspring of a formerly working but now deceased parent receive far more generous assistance (from the Social Security program) than those unlucky enough to be growing up in one-parent families receiving welfare alone.

A second measure is the use of means testing to limit eligibility for the lower tier of benefits. This criterion introduces earnings disincentives, notch effects, and other, similar complications for welfare recipients, who find themselves in the unenviable position of having to negotiate their way through an irrational system. Third, the American welfare state introduces significant levels of stigma into some transfer programs by subjecting recipients to more rigorous, frequent, and potentially degrading scrutiny in order to determine initial and continuing eligibility. For example, in the ostensible interest of reducing fraud and establishing more reliable verification of demonstrated need, welfare caseworkers have on occasion conducted such intrusive procedures as midnight home visits to enforce the no-man-in-the-house rule upon single mothers receiving welfare. The overall effect has been not only to stigmatize recipients of this lower tier of programs, but also to make their very livelihood more precarious by rendering their continued eligibility more conditional and subject to revocation than has ever been the case for the upper stratum of programs. In addition, in all three of these instances, the differential effect of these program rules on men and women is quite marked. The highly gendered basis of U.S. social assistance is demonstrated by the fact that women disproportionately find themselves in the lower tier of social program participation.[22]

The Social Security Act certainly deserves high praise for institutionalizing an active and constructive role for the federal government in establishing a decent floor of income for many categories of Americans in a time of dire economic distress. Its implicit acknowledgment of structural causes of poverty was a great step forward, for it challenged the dominant assumption that low incomes result exclusively from the moral failings of the individuals suffering their consequences. Nevertheless, we should not allow the positive accomplishments of the Social Security Act to obscure its failure to address a number of unresolved issues (such as the pressing needs of groups systematically excluded from adequate coverage) and its tendency to introduce inequities and even irrationalities into the national system of social provision, as the subsequent history of American social policy attests.

THE "PERMANENT CRISIS" OF AFDC

When the AFDC program was terminated by lawmakers in 1996, the magnitude of the change startled many. A sixty-year federal commitment to provide guaranteed cash income to poor families was wiped away with the stroke of a pen. However, those policy observers with the most acute sense of historical perspective marveled that the program had lasted as long as it did. Scholars studying American social policy have long noted the conflicts of goals and values that have perennially plagued our poor relief efforts in general and AFDC in particular. R. Kent Weaver describes welfare policy as a constant struggle to avoid a series of four traps that in the end proved to be an insurmountable challenge: the dual clientele trap, the perverse incentive trap, the federalism trap, and the money trap.[23] Anne Marie Cammisa describes endemic confusion within AFDC program rules and implementation regarding the four possible ways government can address poverty: prevention, rehabilitation, income assistance, and deterrence.[24] Michael B. Katz recounts the numerous shortcomings and irrational aspects of the program, many of them stemming from a failure to adapt program goals to a rapidly changing cultural context. Katz reaches a surprising conclusion about the longevity of the program:

> Contrary to conservative myths AFDC was not expensive. . . . The cost of AFDC benefits, annually about $22 billion, constituted only about 1 percent of the federal budget and 2 percent of federal entitlement spending. . . . The

real secret of AFDC's persistence lay in its cheapness. It is hard to imagine a less expensive way to keep millions of nonworking people alive.[25]

Any social program with such modest selling points will find itself challenged, since social policy is always about more than the minimal goal of low-cost subsistence. It was on the playing field of cultural values and moral content that AFDC was in the end perceived as having two strikes against it.

However one may choose to portray the proximate causes of the demise of AFDC, it is wise to consider the permanent crisis in this program within the larger context of the American welfare state, replete as it has always been with lacunae and unresolved tensions. Many of the objectionable aspects of welfare policy may be attributed to a combination of factors relating to the original design of the programs, a failure to adapt program rules to changed social realities (such as the massive entry of women into paid labor markets in recent decades), and flawed methods of implementing and amending the Social Security Act. Inevitably, however, criticism of AFDC centers upon the issue of program goals.

The legacy of the English Poor Laws and previous American social policy handed AFDC a muddle of objectives and conflicting aims from its inception. The most obvious function of the program, namely providing material assistance to low-income families, was complicated (some would say compromised) by a concomitant desire to enlist welfare policy to serve other social goals, such as the enforcement of the work ethic or a bourgeois family ethic. Using social policy to enforce such moral boundaries runs the risk of cutting at cross-purposes to the well-being of the economically marginalized.[26]

But nothing regarding welfare policy comes easily, not even the seemingly straightforward task of identifying program goals. Pinpointing policy objectives is complicated by the recognition that policy rationales, social conditions, and political cultures change over time. Judith M. Gueron (at the time president of the Manpower Demonstration Research Corporation, a highly regarded independent agency), in 1994 testimony before a congressional subcommittee, offered this summary of changes in welfare policy goals over the previous sixty years:

> When the federal government got into the welfare business in 1935, the aim was to help poor children. AFDC was intended to give poor mothers the same opportunity to stay at home with their children and out of the labor force that other mothers had. It represented . . . a national commitment to the idea that a mother's place is in the home. Since then, a series of changes—women pouring into the labor market, the increasing costs of welfare, the growing numbers of single-parent families, and concern about long-term dependency— undermined the 1930s view that welfare should provide an alternative to work and raised questions about the equity of paying one group of women to

stay home on AFDC while others were working, often not by choice. The focus shifted toward trying to make welfare a route to work. Welfare reform proposals since the 1970s have sought to balance the original anti-poverty goal against a new anti-dependency goal, always under pressure to minimize costs.[27]

Accompanying this shift in program goals was a corresponding replacement of the original principle of entitlement with a new principle of reciprocal obligation. Because of this change, program rules gradually subjected recipients to the new expectation that they would engage in either work or activities (such as education and job training) that would lead to steady employment.

As this new rationale took root, program rules began to feature encouragements for work activity. The 1962 Amendments to the Social Security Act introduced the first work incentives for welfare mothers. It was followed by the institution in 1967 of the Work Incentive (WIN) program that altered benefit formulas to encourage work and mandated that states adopt work incentives for at least a certain percentage of their AFDC caseloads. Lax enforcement and generous provisions for exemptions prevented these innovations from truly changing the nature of AFDC, despite a series of new regulations and opportunities in the 1970s (under President Jimmy Carter's Community Employment Training Assistance program and the Plan for Better Jobs and Income) and the 1980s (under provisions of the Omnibus Budget Reconciliation Act signed by President Ronald Reagan in 1981).[28]

The Family Support Act of 1988 (FSA) was hailed as a promising bipartisan effort to enact a new consensus to transform AFDC from an entitlement into a work-preparation program. However, like previous initiatives, it was ineffective because of a failure to commit adequate resources to the task of rendering private sector employment feasible and attractive to welfare mothers. In the case of FSA, most of the failure may be attributed to the states, very few of which committed enough of their own funds to draw down their full federal allotment of matching funds under the Job Opportunity and Basic Services (JOBS) program in the years FSA was in effect.[29]

Even this brief narrative of those events in the history of AFDC that bring us to the threshold of the most recent welfare reform debates indicates the tremendous force of shifting priorities upon program administration. When ADC was adopted, its goal of keeping families intact despite the absence of a male breadwinner was widely accepted, for it reflected family forms and value orientations prevalent in America at the time. Linda Gordon confirms this: "ADC, along with the Children's Bureau's program for maternal and children's health services, were the least controversial parts of the Social Security Act. To support ADC was, literally, to support motherhood. . . . Almost no one opposed ADC. Its symbolic resonance evoked the most generous emotions among voters."[30] The alternatives to committing federal resources to social provision for such poor families were considered unpalatable. Without some financial assistance, children without resident fathers would be sent to orphanages and single mothers would be forced to enter labor markets on terms considered unacceptable at the time. The status of these recipients as the "deserving poor" was bolstered by the fact that 81 percent of the recipients of ADC in its start-up year of 1935 were widows and their young children; families started by the birth of an illegitimate child numbered less than 5 percent of recipients.[31]

However, as the makeup of the welfare population changed over the next several decades, AFDC became harder to defend in terms of the maintenance of those moral boundaries drawn by a traditional family ethic. Welfare was increasingly utilized by families sundered by divorce, separation, or desertion. More recently, a sharp increase in illegitimacy has raised further suspicion not only about the moral quality of the recipients, but about the program itself. Critics accused AFDC of complicity in these disturbing trends because the program acted as a disincentive for work and marriage. By cushioning the effects of nonwork and promiscuity, AFDC appeared to many observers to be encouraging antisocial behaviors.[32]

The very nature of these perspectives, shifting as they do over time, underlines a constant in social attitudes among Americans: single motherhood has always been defined as a problem. The tendency to resort to moralistic posturing and blaming the victim when this subject is raised may be attributable to a truth articulated in Linda Gordon's observation that "everything about single motherhood is charged with the emotional and moral intensities that saturate social phenomena concerned with sex, reproduction and the family."[33] As long as shared social mores lead Americans to draw sharp moral distinctions between deserving and undeserving poor, our collective social disapproval of single motherhood will find eventual expression in political and administrative forms. Even those to whom established programs make a formal offer of social assistance will experience the effects of this invidious distinction. This may take the form of social stigma attached to participation in a program or the threat that benefits (in any program within the politically vulnerable bottom tier of social provision) will be cut off or saddled with even more conditions, as happens anew in every round of welfare reform.

Herbert Gans identifies this type of social disapproval as the underlying but often submerged cause of a periodically renewed "war against the poor."[34] The only authentic alternative is to institutionalize a true universalism in income guarantees. This is a move that many other advanced industrialized nations have completed (although some have backed away in recent years from particular welfare commitments), but that admittedly seems increasingly less likely in the contemporary political atmosphere of the United States. Indeed, the failure of the original Social Security Act to enact universal entitlements to health care, income support, and even job opportunities is sometimes poignantly referred to as the original sin of the American welfare state.

These reflections on the problematic status of welfare recipients allow us to interpret the recent pressure favoring welfare-to-work initiatives in the proper context. Such work-based approaches as workfare emerge not just as another strategy to assist a needy population, but rather as an attempt to add an entirely new goal and rationale to welfare programs. Alongside the established objectives of preventing severe material deprivation and reinforcing social judgments associated with the traditional family ethic, the goal of rehabilitating this population of single mothers is now added. If welfare recipients can be cajoled or even coerced into fulfilling the terms of the work ethic, then programs that encourage and enforce work may possibly drag this segment of society back across a key moral boundary, from a vilified status as violators of social mores to one of moral worthiness.

From the perspective of political culture, the overriding goal seems to be eliminating social deviancy within a family. If this cannot be fully accomplished by adding a male breadwinner, then it can at least be approximated by forcing single mothers to become self-sufficient breadwinners. Policy affecting single mothers is now oriented not just to establishing "floors" (minimum income entitlements) but also to providing "doors" (means of escaping poverty through earnings). This mirrors the strategy of empowerment stressed for other demographic groups in the War on Poverty during the 1960s. Increasingly, this latter goal is crowding out the former, as politically popular welfare-to-work strategies replace income maintenance approaches to alleviating the poverty associated with single parenthood.

No treatment of the interaction of American welfare policy and social mores could be complete without mention of the neuralgic issue of racial discrimination in policy formation and implementation. U.S. social policy has contained racial as well as gender subtexts in every era, both before and after the Social Security Act. State programs prior to 1935 allowed wide discretion to local officials who enjoyed the prerogative of discriminating between worthy and unworthy recipients in the distribution of benefits such as mothers' pensions. This situation resulted in great disparities in the assistance that white and black families could expect to receive in most states.[35] For a variety of reasons (spanning overt racism, the geography of jurisdictions, the accidents of social location, and employment patterns), African American women were disproportionately excluded from the category of respectable widows who received most of the available assistance in that era.

The Social Security Act, because of political concerns that shaped its provisions and mode of implementation, failed to correct this racial asymmetry. Because President Roosevelt needed the support of influential white southern Democrats in Congress, he allowed what Jill Quadagno, a scholar of the history of social programs, calls the "weaving [of] racial inequality into his new welfare state."[36] In the upper tier of income maintenance programs, this took the form of excluding domestic and agricultural workers from many contributory programs, even those with the smallest probability of exerting redistributive effects. Such measures achieved the racially motivated goal of preventing public funds from reaching many southern black workers. In the lower tier of public assistance programs, the desire to prevent black families from receiving welfare benefits led members of Congress from the South to champion a new form of the states' rights argument. They succeeded in eliminating key clauses in the proposed legislation that set national standards for the ADC-AFDC program. "Southerners simply would not allow the federal government to dictate standards or set benefit levels," Quadagno writes. "They sought control over any social program that might threaten white domination, so precariously balanced on cotton production."[37] The consolidation of programs in subsequent decades left many racial asymmetries unaddressed, since AFDC administration patterns consistently allowed state and local authorities to exercise wide discretion in program implementation. Racial disparities and even blatant discrimination in welfare program design and implementation persist to this day. Literature treating the most recent evolution of welfare policy provides statistical and anecdotal evidence of racial bias in current policy administration, whether intentional or not.[38]

It was only with the civil rights movement and welfare rights explosion of the 1960s that African Americans in large numbers began to overcome the systematic discouragement that prevented them from applying for AFDC and receiving the share of benefits to which they are legally entitled. Recent decades have witnessed a closer match between the numbers of black mothers eligible for benefits and the number actually receiving them. However morally ambiguous they may appear to be, such data constitute an encouraging sign that we are moving closer to "an equal opportunity welfare state."[39] While this trend surely counts as progress toward greater fairness, these developments also contain the unfortunate but real peril of sparking a racially motivated backlash against new (although unfounded) stereotypes of welfare mothers. In painting the face of welfare black and invoking race to serve as a powerful wedge issue, the program's detractors have contributed to the political delegitimation of welfare. By tapping into deeply ingrained attitudes of a racially divided America, they have further eroded support for public assistance programs.[40] Unfortunately, it continues to be the case that when we view the welfare system through the lens of race, many aspects of the system come into sharper focus.

Our consideration of the history of U.S. social policy in this chapter has revealed a number of features of our welfare system that rightly cause concern. These include the gendered nature of the policy inheritance; a history of racism within program administration; and conflicts among such program goals as providing material sustenance to the truly needy, discouraging behavior judged deviant by prevalent social mores, and attempting to rehabilitate recipients of welfare. As America approached the 1990s, only a modest subset of these concerns from our ambiguous policy heritage rose to prominence in the public eye. Concerns about racial and gender justice were eclipsed by a renewed desire to enforce the work ethic and traditional family norms. These goals were converted into new public laws by politicians who openly cited the public's preference for welfare changes that could be accomplished by a partial withdrawal of government from economic life rather than for policies that would necessitate costly new interventions. The momentum of welfare reform during the 104th Congress (1995–97) was greatly enhanced by such aspects of the contemporary national mood as a renewed desire for budgetary restraint and a rising skepticism about the effectiveness of government in pursuing its policy goals. Our next chapter examines the outcomes of the policy process.

THE ROLE OF CHARITABLE AND FAITH-BASED ORGANIZATIONS IN THE SOCIAL WELFARE SYSTEM

If frustration with government ineffectiveness was one of the key cultural factors shaping the welfare reform law of 1996, then an important corollary was a sturdy confidence on the part of the public that charitable and voluntary efforts would play a vital role in filling the new gaps in social service delivery. Particular attention fell upon faith-based organizations. Viewed with suspicion by some and with unbounded hope by others, the charitable efforts of religious congregations and their affiliated nonprofit organizations came under unprecedented scrutiny at the turn of the millennium.

In the early 1990s, conservative critics of the moribund AFDC program faced a dual task. The easy half of their agenda consisted of launching an attack on the increasingly unpopular welfare system. The harder part was coming up with attractive alternatives to government programs, so that their proposals would include at least some provisions for continuing assistance to American families in need. Conservative voices over these years converged on a work strategy combined with a charity strategy. One clear expression of this combination appeared in a 1994 publication of the Cato Institute, a libertarian think tank in Washington, D.C.:

> We should eliminate the entire social welfare system for individuals able to work. That includes eliminating AFDC, food stamps, subsidized housing and all the rest. Individuals unable to support themselves through the job market should be forced to fall back on the resources of family, church, community, or private charity. . . . When it comes to charitable giving, Americans are the most generous people on earth. Every year we contribute more than $120 billion to charity. Surely, we can find private means to assist individuals who need temporary help.[41]

While this prescription for the total elimination of all welfare programs for the able-bodied is extreme, the emphasis on the role of private charity is very much in line with more mainstream conservative recommendations for how the poor may replace the income lost as a result of the welfare reform process. The Republican authors of the 1994 "Contract with America" devote an entire chapter of their 1995 follow-up document to outlining an agenda for how private initiative and voluntarism in this "nation of good neighbors" may replace the efforts of a shrunken federal government.[42] The benefits of thus liberating people to engage in civic responsibility may be measured not only in terms of how material needs are met, but also in terms of the spiritual renewal that accompanies broad popular empowerment through the enhanced exercise of individual responsibility. The authors of the "Contract with America" conclude their argument with this look backward and forward in time:

> When we say that we need to rely more on the genius and goodness of all our citizens to foster genuine solutions to our social, economic and moral problems, we are calling for a return to what once was called a "civil society." This is the Jeffersonian notion—long accepted in this nation until the birth of the modern welfare state—that America needed effective but limited government in order to liberate people to engage in civil responsibility. Civil responsibility meant being a good citizen. With amazing clarity of vision, Jefferson predicted that the larger government grew, the more it would crowd out individual responsibility in a civil society.[43]

This spirited passage makes two related claims that bear investigation. The first invokes the notion of a golden age of times past when the flourishing of private charitable works provided for the needs of the less fortunate in society without resort to the impersonal, centralized action of governmental agencies. The second is the claim that government efforts to relieve poverty wind up crowding out and displacing private initiatives and neighborly assistance. Each has continued to command attention since the passage of the 1996 welfare overhaul, especially in light of its "charitable choice" provisions.

It would be impossible in a brief treatment of this aspect of public welfare to evaluate these two claims in a definitive way. Indeed, both defy the kind of quantitative measurement that would be necessary either to refute or to prove these claims to the satisfaction of neutral observers. Perhaps the best place to start even a tentative evaluation is with the following observation, one that should be acceptable to both proponents and opponents of the impetus toward the privatization of social services. To wit, there is a great difference between the warm feel of assistance that is offered and delivered on a face-to-face basis and the cold feel associated with officer-client relations within an impersonal bureaucracy. The former has the advantages of superior responsiveness to particular needs, a greater likelihood of establishing a personal rapport, and the potential of challenging recipients to make sincere efforts toward self-improvement and eventual self-sufficiency. This is particularly true of programs run under the auspices of religious bodies. The latter (the cold officer-client relationship) suffers from the limits of the organizational cultures of rigid bureaucracies that tend to be rule-based rather than outcome-oriented.[44] All too often, such systems wind up sacrificing flexibility and human values and settling for the goal of standardized expectations and performance. Emblematic of such disheartening consequences within welfare systems are caseworkers who limit their efforts on behalf of their clients to the narrow parameters of official job descriptions. This is likely to include the determination and verification of program eligibility but only rarely the motivation of human spirits to overcome barriers to employment and richer achievement. All too frequently, the behaviors that perpetuate the dependency of recipients are simply assumed rather than aggressively challenged.

An often-quoted 1996 *Wall Street Journal* op-ed column, in the course of pressing an argument for the privatization of welfare, further explicates this contrast:

> Under government entitlement programs, beneficiaries do not have to explain how they plan to change their behavior or even to show a willingness to change. By contrast, the best private charities often make assistance conditional on behavioral changes. Overall, the private sector has shown that only through hands-on management—direct, personal contact between aid giver and recipient—can we help the poor without encouraging dependency.[45]

In a volume frequently cited in the welfare reform debates, Marvin Olasky portrays as a great "tragedy" the progressive substitution of depersonalized dependence for genuine compassion within American relief arrangements. He laments the tendency for bureaucracies to treat the people they serve as clients rather than as neighbors. The potential for personal challenge and moral uplift is sacrificed to the felt need to eschew moral judgmentalism, to guarantee professional standards, and to insure uniform operating procedures.[46]

Olasky's work serves as an instructive reminder of the virtues of an ethic of private initiative and of the dangers of indiscriminate giving (sometimes called the "helping conundrums" or "Good Samaritan dilemmas"). Indeed, it inspired other impressive scholarly efforts to revive the virtues associated particularly with nineteenth-century charitable organizations and movements.[47] The ongoing debate on the potential of private charities as it unfolded during the 1990s turned out to be productive in a number of ways. The concluding sections of this chapter treat two sets of outcomes from this debate: first, an emerging consensus of opinion regarding charities; and second, legislative developments seeking to enact it.

The New Consensus on the Contribution of Charities

To speak of a new consensus regarding charitable efforts runs the risk of overstating the case. There is still ample friction between supporters and opponents of further privatization of social services. Yet it is possible to

identify a number of areas of broad agreement. Once the dust of controversy had settled, most parties to the debate recognized that the work of
Olasky and his disciples was neither stubbornly wrongheaded nor a flaw-
less blueprint for America's future social services. Reviving contemporary
awareness of the virtues associated with charitable efforts of generations
past turns out to be a constructive contribution. It need not be interpreted
as a flight of nostalgic fantasy; nobody seriously expected or really desired
to turn back the clock one hundred years or more, to a time characterized
in fact by far greater insecurity on the part of the poor.[48] With a modicum
of patience and good will, Olasky's insights may be translated into an
agenda for incremental improvement in the actual system of social provision we have inherited as a nation.[49]

For example, some observers found it helpful to juxtapose Olasky's appeal to principles inspired by past practices with social philosopher Michael
Walzer's analysis of contemporary relief arrangements. First, Walzer acknowledges the obvious constraint that "bureaucracy is unavoidable given
the size of contemporary political communities and the range of necessary services."[50] Second, he insists that "some modern substitute is sorely
needed" for the essential "mobilization of altruistic capacities" that characterized social provision in earlier times, before the "professionalization of
social work" displaced efforts that had proceeded on a voluntary basis.[51]
Although many features of our welfare efforts are dictated by necessity (e.g.,
its reliance on public finance by means of involuntary taxation), we can at
least hope to approximate some of the virtues associated with systems that
tapped into voluntarism and neighbor-to-neighbor assistance.

Walzer's suggestions for how state action might be able to recapture the
vital and beneficial aspects of mutual aid are described in his 1988 essay,
"Socializing the Welfare State."[52] The nationwide organization of social
provision need not cancel out such goods as local empowerment and voluntary involvement in distributive arrangements, as long as the political
system remains committed to the principle of broad participation in the
processes of decision making and in the delivery of social services. Such desirable elements as hope, care, accountability, discernment, and involvement can be preserved, Walzer maintains, within the context of "a lively and
supportive welfare society framed, but not controlled, by a strong welfare
state."[53]

Walzer is not alone in articulating a "both-and" rather than an "either-
or" approach to the role of government and private agencies in social services. The 1990s witnessed many prominent politicians and public figures
staging publicity, legislative, and even electoral campaigns that invoked similar principles.[54] As we entered the first decade of the new millennium, the
rough edges of Olasky's arguments were rounded off somewhat, including
the dubious claim, mentioned above, that government efforts somehow
crowd out private voluntary activities. Research conducted by such expert
groups as Twentieth Century Fund and Independent Sector (a coalition of

nonprofit foundations and charities) sorted out the tangle of statistics and claims about patterns of spending and giving across American society.[55] By the end of the 1990s, a convincing case had been made that huge cuts in public spending to reduce poverty could not conceivably be replaced by the charitable efforts of private nonprofits. Indeed, what emerged was a clearer picture of just how dependent the major private charities are upon government funding sources, so that private-public partnerships are ultimately among the most vital aspects of the social services delivery system.[56] As time passes, the many voices favoring American civic renewal demonstrate increasing adherence to the consensus opinion that charitable voluntarism, while highly desirable and perhaps particularly in need of encouragement today, is not a viable substitute for government's antipoverty efforts. Our laudable efforts to support a revival of philanthropy and compassion should always retain an awareness that government's role remains indispensable. The most promising path to improving public relief arrangements, then, is one of augmentation, not wholesale replacement.

This emerging consensus, of course, pertains to more than just social services. All collective social action ideally follows the contours of the mediating structures of civil society and respects the workings of local and voluntary associations.[57] This insight reflects the theme of subsidiarity that we encountered in surveying the heritage of Catholic social thought in the previous chapter. The efforts of neighborhood groups, religious organizations, professional bodies, and charitable societies are properly considered the first resort for addressing problems such as poverty. It is when the texture of civil society is unable to cope with large-scale problems that government action is justified. In the complex, diverse, increasingly mobile society of the present age, informal and voluntary arrangements would be simply unable to supply the accountability necessary to provide adequately for the needy. Unless the mechanism of universal taxation continues to enforce individual contributions to antipoverty efforts, members of society would surely yield to the temptation to become free riders on the sacrifices of others. Without the accountability that only government can insure, citizens would face no effective sanctions against the natural proclivity to shirk their share of responsibility for the least fortunate. In the absence of government involvement in social welfare provision, it would become a certainty that many of the neediest families would fall through the cracks of piecemeal, unsystematic charitable relief.

"Charitable Choice" and Faith-Based Initiatives

The new consensus soon inspired legislative efforts to fine-tune the way government and private charities forged partnerships for social service delivery. The realization that massive privatization of social services would prove impossible without structural changes prompted conservative legislators to propose new and constructive arrangements. Republican John Ashcroft, later President George W. Bush's attorney general but at the time a senator from Missouri, took the lead. He attached a little-noticed amendment to the 1996 welfare reform bill. The measure received approval and became section 104 of the law. It consists of eleven brief paragraphs that came to be known universally by the alliterative phrase "charitable choice."

Charitable choice has come to mean many things to many parties, some of whom project upon the law their deepest fears (of government corrupting the mission of churches or of religious influence upon government threatening to turn our polity into a theocracy).[58] The actual wording of the statute suggests an intention that is quite modest in scope. The law encourages states (since states now run their own welfare systems with sharply reduced federal oversight) to involve local religious groups to participate in social services and welfare-to-work programs in more active ways than previously possible. So charitable choice is not a new funding stream or programming initiative, but merely a revised set of options and conditions regarding how states may use the federal welfare block grants they receive. Religious groups may now compete for contracts and voucher arrangements for social service delivery on an equal basis with other providers. The law includes a number of key protections, such as the stipulation that secular alternatives to faith-based programs must be available, as well as the enumeration of a variety of rights of beneficiaries eligible for services.[59]

Previously, legal restrictions against direct governmental assistance to religion complicated social service contracting. In order to avoid violations of the prevailing interpretation of the "no establishment" clause of the First Amendment to the U.S. Constitution, religious bodies set up their own 501(c)(3) nonprofit organizations to run their charitable outreach. Because these agencies (such as Catholic Charities, Lutheran Social Ministries, Jewish Federations, and Salvation Army agencies) are considered religiously affiliated but not pervasively sectarian, they could administer state-funded programs as long as they observed certain codes of conduct. No religious discrimination was allowed as the basis for hiring staff or accepting applicants. Proselytizing and overt displays of religious behavior were also prohibited. Under the new charitable choice guidelines, while government money still may not be used for worship or evangelization, religious congregations may now administer social service programs directly, without the buffer of creating a more neutral legal entity. Religious providers may run programs in their customary meeting spaces with no need, for example, to remove crosses or other religious symbols from the walls. By allowing program staff to use spiritual language and to appeal to moral principles and religiously inspired values, charitable choice seeks to free faith-based groups to provide their distinctive social service contribution: motivating people to improve their lives and to overcome barriers to their personal and social advancement.

While certain policy observers seized upon charitable choice, praising it or demonizing it depending upon their agenda, for several years the vast majority of Americans remained unaware even of its existence. One journalist who regularly covers religious news later admitted that "Section 104 flew in under the media's radar. . . . The coverage of charitable choice has not been sufficient to register even a blip on the radar screen of public awareness."[60] Then, in July 1999, an NBC-*Wall Street Journal* poll "found 76 percent of Americans in favor of giving federal funds to private groups, including religious organizations, to deal with social problems."[61] This discovery of support for the basic principle behind charitable choice practically insured that awareness of this issue would surface in the contentious 2000 election. Actually, to their credit, the eventual major party nominees had already gone on record, in each case expressing solid support for charitable choice. Al Gore had addressed the topic in a May 24, 1999, appearance at an Atlanta drug rehabilitation center run by the Salvation Army.[62] George W. Bush was already known as the first governor aggressively to implement charitable choice, and his first major campaign speech (on July 22, 1999, at a Methodist church in Indianapolis) spelled out his plan to "rally the armies of compassion." One of the primary ways Bush proposed to enact "compassionate conservatism" was by honoring the pledge he announced that day: "In every instance where my Administration sees a responsibility to help people, we will look first to faith-based organizations, charities and community groups that have shown their ability to save and change lives. We will make a determined attack on need by promoting the compassionate acts of others."[63]

The marked resemblance of the campaign rhetoric of Bush and Gore on this topic prevented charitable choice from becoming a wedge issue in the close and divisive election of 2000. Indeed, both candidates, along with their running mates, Dick Cheney and Joseph Lieberman, went out of their way to highlight plans to extend the charitable choice principle to government programs beyond welfare. The closing years of the Clinton administration had already witnessed modest progress along these lines. The 106th Congress considered a number of bills in 1999 and 2000 that contained charitable choice measures. By June 2000, *Congressional Quarterly* counted seven such major pieces of pending legislation covering housing subsidies, education and literacy programs, parenting skills promotion, substance abuse treatment, health counseling, and public health services. In each case, legislative sponsors on both sides of the aisle endorsed the principle that faith-based providers should not only be allowed, but positively encouraged to apply to administer federal grants for a wide variety of social services. Qualms about potential constitutional issues and civil rights concerns in the implementation of such grants delayed action on these proposals until after the 2000 election.[64]

It was, of course, George W. Bush who acquired the opportunity to advance this agenda during subsequent sessions of Congress. Throughout 2001 and 2002, Bush's ambitious plans for a religious charities or faith-based bill that would remove numerous barriers to more direct religious involvement in social service delivery were thwarted time and time again. One recurring sticking point was the proposal to give religious groups an

exemption from the state and local laws that forbade organizations contracting with government to discriminate in certain ways in hiring program
staff. When the House of Representatives finally passed a bill Bush deemed
acceptable, the Senate stalled its progress for many months until a version
featuring responses to practically all potential objections could be hammered out.[65] Compromise became necessary to placate skeptical senators,
many of them concerned about eroding the constitutional separation of
church and state. The result was a bill so sharply scaled back that little remained except meager packages of tax credits and incentives to encourage
charitable giving.[66] The more substantial proposals for enhanced partnerships between charities and government and for more direct financing of
church-sponsored social services had been eviscerated in the legislative
process.[67]

The Senate did finally approve its version of the faith-based legislation
(titled the Charity, Aid, Recovery and Empowerment Act, or CARE) on
April 9, 2003. The 95 to 5 margin of its passage was matched by the 408
to 13 vote for a companion measure in the House on September 17, 2003.
But by this time, the long-delayed and frequently amended legislation was
so watered down that it no longer contained any language at all acknowledging a special role for religious organizations (as opposed to secular
nonprofit agencies) and their competition for government social service
funding.[68] Further, it did not bode well that less than a month later, when
Congress was again taking up proposals for enhanced faith-based provisions (in this case as part of the reauthorization of the Workforce Investment Act of 1998), sharp divisions in both chambers immediately surfaced
once again.[69] The future of this neuralgic category of legislation and the
very principle of charitable choice that lies behind it remain very much in
doubt at present, languishing as it has for years in Congress. In retrospect,
although enhanced social service provision by religious groups did not at
first emerge as a wedge issue, faith-based initiatives have increasingly come
to be perceived as yet another partisan battleground, with each party eager
to deny significant victories to the other. Further, the prospect of numerous
appropriations measures and other bills regarding social programs being
held hostage to legislators' agendas regarding funding for faith-based initiatives is horrifying to all those who fear an increase in the political and budgetary gridlock that has so plagued Washington in recent years.[70]

Despite these setbacks in winning congressional approval for a full-
fledged faith-based initiative, President Bush accomplished certain of his
objectives by means of executive orders and similar actions that do not require legislative action. A mere week after taking office, he established a
White House Office of Faith-Based and Community Initiatives. Its mandate
was "to establish policies, priorities, and objectives for the Federal Government's comprehensive effort to enlist, equip, enable, empower and expand the work of faith-based and other community organizations to the
extent permitted by law."[71] The new office was at first staffed by John J.

DiIulio Jr. and Stephen Goldsmith and, after February 2002, by James Towey (who resigned in early 2006). All were considered pragmatic moderates who brought excellent credentials to this new initiative. Further bypassing Capitol Hill, Bush also set up parallel offices to encourage and coordinate faith-based programs, initially in five federal departments (Justice, Education, Labor, Housing and Urban Development, and Health and Human Services), and by spring 2006 in eleven federal agencies.[72] Each was to serve as a clearinghouse for collaborative efforts and was charged with circumventing bureaucratic barriers to religious involvement in the delivery of government-funded social services. Even without congressional action, numerous contracts and many large grants (in the vicinity of $2 billion by 2004) to faith-based groups were made available through these departments.[73] Among their other accomplishments so far, these offices have already sponsored a nationwide series of seminars to train up to five thousand religious groups on ways to use current law to win federally funded contracts.[74] Even in his second term, with Congress still stalled on this divisive topic, Bush continued to hold conferences and sponsor publicity events to announce progress in channeling greater social service funding through faith-based organizations and to encourage additional religious groups to apply for newly available federal grants.[75]

It might seem tempting to characterize these faith-based initiatives as merely a passing political fad or even as a public relations ploy. Charitable choice still lacks sufficient legislative consolidation to determine whether it will survive as a permanent feature of American social policy. However, regardless of the outcome of current disputes over the shape of relevant laws, the question of the involvement of faith communities in social service provision is here to stay. The nation cannot afford to forfeit the opportunity to enlist the energy and good will inspired by religion in addressing pressing social problems like drug addiction, homelessness, the need for foster care, affordable housing, job training, and family counseling. A recent survey found that 92 percent of religious congregations engage in activities related to human services or welfare, but that only 2 percent to 3 percent participate in a joint venture with government or receive any public funding.[76] It is in the interest of all Americans—religious congregants, government officials, taxpayers, and program participants alike—to insure that the potential contribution of religious communities is not squandered by a widespread failure to form public-private partnerships.

Extending the principle of charitable choice may not be the solution to all the problems in this area of policy, but it is certainly an initiative worthy of further attention, study, and effort. Many relevant goals need to be balanced, and principles like government neutrality toward religion and nondiscrimination in the hiring of staff for public-funded projects must be respected. Government agencies should be assured that public funds are expended on appropriate projects in ways that respect program rules, all while preserving the religious character that renders these charities distinctive from secular programs. Religious providers should be neither inordinately favored nor discriminated against, but should experience a level playing field in the competition for grants and contracts. Further, such initiatives will surely require constant fine-tuning in order to "chart a course that avoids both naive triumphalism about the opportunities and exaggerated fears about the dangers" of religious involvement in public programs. [77] Yet the potential gains for more effective social policy when religious groups forge partnerships with government continue to outweigh the persistent difficulties of implementation. The promise of tapping into the positive energies (recall the themes of volunteerism, participation, grassroots and neighborhood-based support) of enhanced religious social service provision renders these faith-based initiatives well worth the challenges they present to our system of welfare and related social services. In the end, the Bush administration's inability to "put meat on the bones of compassionate conservatism" through successful faith-based initiatives must be counted as a lost opportunity for our nation as it seeks to meet serious social needs and to improve the lives of its disadvantaged citizens. [78]

NOTES

1. Benjamin I. Page and Robert Y. Shapiro, *The Rational Public: Fifty Years of Trends in Americans' Policy Preferences* (Chicago: University of Chicago Press, 1992), chaps. 3, 4, and 8.

2. Ibid. See also R. Kent Weaver, Robert Y. Shapiro, and Lawrence R. Jacobs, "Public Opinion on Welfare Reform: A Mandate for What?" in *Looking Before We Leap: Social Science and Welfare Reform,* ed. R. Kent Weaver and William T. Dickens (Washington, DC: Brookings Institution, 1995), 109–28.

3. Joel F. Handler, *The Poverty of Welfare Reform* (New Haven, CT: Yale University Press, 1995), 10.

4. Gertrude Himmelfarb, *The De-Moralization of Society: From Victorian Virtues to Modern Values* (New York: Alfred A. Knopf, 1995), 127.

5. These effects are treated in considerable detail in Karl Polanyi, *The Great Transformation: The Political and Economic Origins of Our Time* (Boston: Beacon Press, 1944), esp. 77–85, 280–88.

6. Himmelfarb, *The De-Moralization of Society,* 131–33.

7. John E. Tropman offers an intriguing argument about alternatives to the Protestant ethic and its influence on American approaches to social policy. With appropriate caveats, he proposes a contrasting model he calls the Catholic ethic. Although a full examination of his claims would take us too far afield from the focus of this present study, his two major works on this topic shed much light on considerations relevant to welfare policy: *The Catholic Ethic in American Society: An Exploration of Values* (San Francisco: Jossey-Bass Publishers, 1995); *The Catholic Ethic and the Spirit of Community* (Washington, DC: Georgetown University Press, 2002).

8. Michael B. Katz, perhaps the foremost scholar of American poor relief arrangements, offers insightful historical perspectives on such policies in *The Undeserving Poor: From the War on Poverty to the War on Welfare* (New York: Pantheon

Books, 1989). Pages 9–15 contain a particularly informative commentary on the cultural aspects of these trends in early American policy.

9. Katz calls this the supply-side interpretation of poverty. He comments that "often despite powerful evidence, [it] has coursed through American social thought for centuries." Ibid., 7.

10. For a compelling account of the interaction among relief-giving, political processes, and the threat of civil disorder, see Frances Fox Piven and Richard A. Cloward, *Regulating the Poor: The Functions of Public Welfare*, updated ed. (New York: Random House, 1993).

11. Mimi Abramovitz, *Regulating the Lives of Women: Social Welfare Policy from Colonial Times to the Present* (Boston: South End Press, 1988).

12. In her essay "Women, Welfare and the Politics of Need Interpretation," Nancy Fraser argues that many welfare state program rules, despite a veneer of seeming neutrality, encode an "unmistakable gender subtext" with "a common core of assumptions concerning the sexual division of labor." It is when these assumptions become increasingly counterfactual that programs undergo a legitimation crisis. This essay appears in Nancy Fraser, *Unruly Practices: Power, Discourse and Gender in Contemporary Social Theory* (Minneapolis, MN: University of Minnesota Press, 1989), 144–60, with the phrases cited above at 149.

13. Theda Skocpol, *Protecting Soldiers and Mothers: The Political Origins of Social Policy in the United States* (Cambridge, MA: Harvard University Press, 1992), 4.

14. Ibid., 528.

15. Linda Gordon, *Pitied but Not Entitled: Single Mothers and the History of Welfare, 1890–1935* (New York: The Free Press, 1994), chap. 3.

16. From a speech by Harry Hopkins, May 10, 1935. Quoted in James T. Patterson, *America's Struggle Against Poverty 1900–1980* (Cambridge, MA: Harvard University Press, 1981), 46.

17. One contemporary economist, looking back upon the drafting during the 1940s of the Beveridge Report that became the cornerstone of the British welfare state, characterizes this development by observing: "Just as there could be no atheists in foxholes, there were no aristocrats in bomb shelters. The common sacrifices of war brought home to the British middle class the unpleasant realities of gross social inequality." Robert Kuttner, *The Economic Illusion: False Choices Between Prosperity and Social Justice* (Boston: Houghton Mifflin Co., 1984), 32.

18. For a revealing account of these deliberations, especially the racial and gender-based agendas that placed pressures on the parties involved, see Gordon, *Pitied but Not Entitled*, chaps. 6–10.

19. For a historical and cross-national comparative perspective on modern systems of social provision, see T. H. Marshall, *Social Policy in the Twentieth Century*, 3rd rev. ed. (London: Hutchinson and Co., 1970). An excellent comparison of the features of the welfare-state regimes of most industrialized nations appears in Gosta Esping-Andersen, *The Three Worlds of Welfare Capitalism* (Princeton, NJ: Princeton University Press, 1990).

20. Handler, *The Poverty of Welfare Reform*, 20–21.

21. Comparisons of benefit levels across programs are notoriously difficult because of such factors as complex formulae in the determination of benefit packages, the overlap of multiple benefits, and variation in state contribution in matching-fund programs. However, as one benchmark for comparison, statistics gathered in the

early 1990s revealed that no state offered AFDC recipients a basic cash payment
that raised their family income above 80 percent of the poverty line. In the lowest-benefit states, the figure is in the range of 40 percent. The average AFDC family of three in 1995 received cash and food stamp benefits that brought its income
up to two-thirds of the poverty line. These figures appear in Sharon Parrott,
"How Much Do We Spend on Welfare?" (Washington, DC: Center on Budget
and Policy Priorities, August 4, 1995). Developments in the era of the TANF program have complicated the calculations but have not changed this basic situation.
The subpoverty levels of AFDC and TANF benefits are not experienced by most
Social Security beneficiaries, such as recipients of survivors' benefits.

22. See Gordon, *Pitied but Not Entitled*, chap. 10, for an elaboration of the features
    of this stratification of programs. The author attributes these features to domi-
    nant social attitudes at the time of the institutionalization of the Social Security
    Act and laments how their perpetuation has relegated women receiving welfare
    to a type of second-class citizenship.

23. R. Kent Weaver, *Ending Welfare as We Know It* (Washington, DC: Brookings
    Institution Press, 2000), 43–52.

24. Anne Marie Cammisa, *From Rhetoric to Reform: Welfare Policy in American
    Politics* (Boulder, CO: HarperCollins, 1998), 25–26.

25. Michael B. Katz, *The Price of Citizenship: Redefining the American Welfare
    State* (New York: Henry Holt and Co., 2001), 318.

26. A variety of such critiques of the development of welfare policy appear in the
    dozen insightful essays contained in Elizabeth Bounds, Pamela K. Brubaker, and
    Mary E. Hobgood, eds., *Welfare Policy: Feminist Critiques* (Cleveland, OH: The
    Pilgrim Press, 1999).

27. United States Congress, House of Representatives, Committee on Ways and
    Means, Subcommittee on Human Resources, *Family Support Act of 1988: Hear-
    ings before the Subcommittee on Human Resources*, 103rd Congress, second
    session, March 15, 1994 (Washington, DC: GPO, 1994), 38.

28. Historical accounts of these events are widely available. Martin Gilens analyzes
    these gradual changes in welfare policy with a particular emphasis on public per-
    ceptions; see his intriguing volume, *Why Americans Hate Welfare: Race, Media
    and the Politics of Antipoverty Policy* (Chicago: University of Chicago Press,
    1999), esp. 178–84. For an account that makes explicit connections to the even-
    tual shape of the 1996 welfare law, see Ladonna A. Pavetti, "Welfare Policy in
    Transition: Redefining the Social Contract for Poor Citizen Families with Chil-
    dren and for Immigrants," in *Understanding Poverty*, ed. Sheldon H. Danziger
    and Robert H. Haveman (Cambridge, MA: Harvard University Press, 2001),
    229–77.

29. An analysis of the failure of these efforts to encourage employment is offered in
    Gary Burtless, "The Effect of Reform on Employment, Earnings and Income,"
    in *Welfare Policy for the 1990s*, ed. Cottingham and Ellwood, 103–45.

30. Gordon, *Pitied but Not Entitled*, 254–55.

31. Statistics appear in Ben J. Wattenberg, *Values Matter Most* (New York: The Free
    Press, 1995), 164.

32. The major proponents of these charges were Robert Rector, Charles A. Mur-
    ray, and Lawrence M. Mead. Their arguments are described in some detail in
    chapter 3.

33. Gordon, *Pitied but Not Entitled*, 17.

34. Herbert J. Gans, *The War Against the Poor: The Underclass and Antipoverty Policy* (New York: HarperCollins Publishers, 1995).
35. Gordon, *Pitied but Not Entitled,* chap. 5; Skocpol, *Protecting Soldiers and Mothers,* 471–79.
36. Jill Quadagno, *The Color of Welfare: How Racism Undermined the War on Poverty* (New York: Oxford University Press, 1994), 20.
37. Ibid., 21–22.
38. See Kenneth Feingold and Sarah Staveteig, "Race, Ethnicity and Welfare Reform," in *Welfare Reform: The Next Act,* ed. Alan Weil and Kenneth Feingold (Washington, D.C.: Urban Institute Press, 2002), 203–19; Kenneth J. Neubeck and Noel A. Cazenave, *Welfare Racism: Playing the Race Card Against America's Poor* (New York: Routledge, 2001).
39. Quadagno, *The Color of Welfare,* 9.
40. See Gilens, *Why Americans Hate Welfare,* esp. chap. 7 ("Racial Stereotypes and Public Responses to Poverty").
41. Michael Tanner, "Ending Welfare as We Know It," *Policy Analysis,* no. 212 (July 7, 1994), 23.
42. "Empowering Citizens, Communities, and States," chap. 9 in *Restoring the Dream: The Bold New Plan by House Republicans,* ed. Stephen Moore (New York: Times Books of Random House, Inc., 1995), 203–25.
43. Ibid., 224–25.
44. On this point, see two works by Lisbeth B. Schorr: "What Works: Applying What We Already Know about Successful Social Policy," *American Prospect,* no. 13 (1993): 43–54; *Common Purpose: Strengthening Families and Neighborhoods to Rebuild America* (New York: Anchor Books of Doubleday, 1997), esp. part 1.
45. John C. Goodman, "Welfare Privatization," *Wall Street Journal,* May 28, 1996, A18. The same author's fuller treatment of this contrast appears in "Why Not Abolish the Welfare State?" *Common Sense* 2 (winter 1995): 63–72.
46. Marvin Olasky, *The Tragedy of American Compassion* (Washington, DC: Regnery Gateway, 1992) esp. 192–97. See also Olasky's sequel, *Renewing American Compassion: How Compassion for the Needy Can Turn Ordinary Citizens into Heroes* (New York: The Free Press, 1996).
47. Himmelfarb's *The De-Moralization of Society* appeared in 1995. See also Joel Schwartz, *Fighting Poverty with Virtue: Moral Reform and America's Urban Poor 1825–2000* (Bloomington: Indiana University Press, 2000).
48. An overview of responses to Olasky's work in the midst of this debate, both supporting and criticizing his agenda, appears in Joseph P. Shapiro, "Marvin Olasky's Appeal: A Golden Age of Charity," *U.S. News and World Report,* September 9, 1996, 52–53.
49. A particularly insightful collection of essays from academics and social activists who engage the themes of this new consensus in creative ways is *Who Will Provide? The Changing Role of Religion in American Social Welfare,* ed. Mary Jo Bane, Brent Coffin, and Ronald Thiemann (Boulder, CO.: Westview Press, 2000).
50. Walzer, *Spheres of Justice,* 94.
51. Ibid.
52. Walzer's essay "Socializing the Welfare State" appears in Amy Gutman, ed., *Democracy and the Welfare State* (Princeton, NJ: Princeton University Press, 1988), 13–26.

53. Ibid., 26.

54. This list includes Lamar Alexander, William J. Bennett, Dan Coates, Joseph Lieberman, Al Gore, and, of course, George W. Bush.

55. Summaries of these reports and findings that appeared in the popular media in the mid-1990s include: Peter Steinfels, "As Government Aid Evaporates, How Will Religious and Charity Organizations Hold Up as a Safety Net for the Poor, the Sick and the Elderly?" *New York Times*, October 28, 1995, 11; Joseph P. Shapiro, "Can Churches Save America?" *U.S. News and World Report*, September 9, 1996, 46–51; Milt Freudenheim, "Charities Say Government Cuts Would Jeopardize Their Ability to Help the Needy," *New York Times*, February 5, 1996, B8.

56. Statistics suggest that private charities are not as private as is frequently assumed. Large portions of their operating budgets come directly or indirectly from government sources. Of the estimated $87 billion that private charities spent on social services in 1996, for example, just over half (50.1%) came from government funding, and indicators in subsequent years suggest that this percentage is growing. Each of the nation's three largest religiously affiliated social service agencies (Lutheran Social Ministries, Catholic Charities USA, and Jewish Federations) in that year received between 54% and 62% of its operating budget from government sources. Statistics come from Freudenheim, "Charities Say," B8.

57. A prominent figure in advocating the renewal of American civic life in recent years is Brookings Institution scholar and journalist E.J. Dionne, Jr. See for example the volume of essays he edited, compiled, and introduced, titled *Community Works: The Revival of Civil Society in America* (Washington, D.C.: Brookings Institution Press, 1998).

58. Regarding the allegedly corrupting influence of government, see, for example, Melissa Rogers, "Charitable Choice: A Threat to Religion," *Sojourners*, July–August 1998, 28–30. The author, associate general counsel of the Baptist Joint Committee on Public Affairs in Washington, D.C., argues that charitable choice is "unconstitutional, unwise and unnecessary" and "leads to dangerous government-church entanglement." Her statement echoes the arguments of many other religious professionals, especially in Evangelical Christian communities, that accepting government funds in this new way might undermine the integrity and independence of church ministries, compromising their missions. The most prominent voice of those concerned about incipient theocracy is Barry Lynn of the organization Americans United for Separation of Church and State. After the law's passage, Lynn warned: "Even though the statute says it can't happen, it will be impossible for this not to essentially pay for evangelism." Quoted in Laurie Goldstein, "Religious Groups See Larger Role in Welfare," *New York Times*, December 14, 1997, 39.

59. The full text of section 104 and an excellent commentary upon its provisions appears in the pamphlet "A Guide to Charitable Choice: The Rules of Section 104 of the 1996 Federal Welfare Law Governing State Cooperation with Faith-based Social-Service Providers" (Washington, DC: Center for Public Justice, January 1997).

60. David Weiner, "Missing the Boat on Charitable Choice," *Religion in the News* (June 1998): 8.

61. Dennis R. Hoover, "Charitable Choice and the New Religious Center," *Religion in the News* (spring 2000): 4.

62. Ibid.
63. Quoted in Adam Clymer, "Filter Aid to Poor Through Churches, Bush Urges," *New York Times,* July 23, 1999, A1, A10.
64. David Nather, "Funding of Faith-Based Groups Spurs New Civil Rights Debate," *Congressional Quarterly Weekly,* June 10, 2000, 1385–87. As this article explains, the one area where charitable choice was legally applied beyond welfare-to-work programs under the TANF law was the Community Services Block Grant. It was reauthorized in 1998 under PL 105-285, a measure that explicitly allowed these antipoverty funds to be administered by faith-based organizations.
65. The bill was numbered HR 7. Passed by the House in July 2001, it languished while the Senate refused to consider companion measures.
66. Helen Dewar, "Senate Bill to Aid Charities Retooled," *Washington Post,* March 28, 2003, A15. The Senate bill during 2002 was labeled S 1924, cosponsored by Republican senator Rick Santorum of Pennsylvania and Democratic senator Joseph Lieberman of Connecticut.
67. A comprehensive account of the prehistory and subsequent legislative fate of these Bush proposals through late 2003 is contained in Amy E. Black, Douglas L. Koopman, and David K. Ryden, *Of Little Faith: The Politics of George W. Bush's Faith-Based Initiatives* (Washington, DC: Georgetown University Press, 2004).
68. Sheryl Gay Stolberg, "Senate Passes Version of Religion Initiative," *New York Times,* April 10, 2003, A18.
69. Adam Copperman and Juliet Elperin, "House to Vote on Church Programs: Bill Will Allow Hiring Based on Beliefs," *Washington Post,* May 8, 2003, A29. The bill won approval in the House of Representatives on May 9, 2003 by a vote of 220 to 200, but was thrown into a contentious Senate chamber where action was repeatedly blocked by legislators poised to hold up the entire Workforce Investment Act legislation because of objections to the charitable choice provisions in the proposed bill.
70. A thoughtful and remarkably balanced consideration of the merits and flaws in the Bush proposals before Congress is found in *Faith-Based Initiatives and the Bush Administration: The Good, The Bad and the Ugly,* ed. Jo Renee Formicola, Mary C. Segers, and Paul Weber (New York: Rowman and Littlefield Publishers, 2003). Developments from 2003 to early 2005 are covered in Dennis R. Hoover, "The Faith-Based Initiative Re-ups," *Religion in the News* (Spring 2005): 18–20.
71. The White House Office of the Press Secretary, *Executive Order: Establishment of White House Office of Faith-Based and Community Initiatives* (Washington, DC, January 29, 2001), 1.
72. Elisabeth Bumiller, "Bush Urges More Money for Religious Charities," *New York Times,* March 10, 2006, A16.
73. Bill Swindell, "Faith-Based Offices an End Run Around Languishing Legislation," *Congressional Quarterly Weekly,* November 2, 2002, 2861–62.; Richard W. Stevenson, "Rules Eased on Financing Social Work," *New York Times,* September 23, 2003, A20.
74. "Faith-Based Initiative to Get Push: Bush to Implement Parts of Proposal," *Washington Post,* August 31, 2002, A22.
75. Elisabeth Bumiller, "Bush Says $2 Billion Went to Religious Charities in '04," *New York Times,* March 2, 2005, A17.

76. Anna Greenberg, "Doing Whose Work? Faith-Based Organizations and Government Partnerships," in *Who Will Provide?* ed. Bane, Coffin, and Thiemann, 187–88.
77. Mark Chaves, "Religious Congregations and Welfare Reform: Assessing the Potential," in *Can Charitable Choice Work? Covering Religion's Impact on Urban Affairs and Social Services,* ed. Andrew Walsh (Hartford, CT: The Leonard E. Greenberg Center for the Study of Religion in Public Life at Trinity College, 2001), 136.
78. Black, Koopman, and Ryden, *Of Little Faith,* 272.

3

AT THE CROSSROADS: THE WELFARE REFORM LAW OF 1996

The welfare system limped into the 1990s, staggering under the weight of nearly universal disfavor. Critics cited a litany of statistics and disturbing trends—including rising AFDC rolls, mounting program costs, and escalating rates of illegitimacy—in efforts to prove that the system was broken. The incremental reforms of the previous decades, including the most recent federal welfare legislation, the Family Support Act of 1988, appeared ineffective in the face of such a crisis of legitimacy. The status quo was nearly without defenders. Even many liberal Democrats cheered candidate Bill Clinton's 1992 promise to "end welfare as we know it." The question facing policy makers was no longer whether to undertake an ambitious reform of the welfare system, but rather precisely how to go about a dramatic restructuring of U.S. welfare policy.

The writings of new critics of AFDC had supplied the intellectual underpinnings for drastic versions of welfare overhaul. During the Reagan years figures such as Charles Murray, Lawrence Mead, and George Gilder had risen to prominence in the world of think tanks and academia by proposing bold new courses for social policy. However, the actual agents of welfare reform turned out to be the new Republican congressional majority elected in November 1994 on the strength of its "Contract with America." This campaign document included a plank (number three on its list of ten agenda items) titled "The Personal Responsibility Act." To keep their promises on welfare, the new majority (under its leader, Speaker of the House Newt Gingrich) speedily introduced a welfare reform proposal into the opening session of the 104th Congress as bill HR 4 in January 1995. This plan of the Republican House leadership quickly eclipsed a number of rival bills, including Clinton's own long-delayed proposal, one that had languished in Congress since June 1994, even while he enjoyed a Democratic majority in both houses. The original version of HR 4 passed the House within Gingrich's first hundred days as Speaker, but it took sixteen more months, two vetoes, and a number of revisions and amendments before it was signed into law by President Clinton on August 22, 1996. Despite the compromises and challenges the bill underwent during a series of legislative battles (at the committee level, in the full Senate, and in joint conference committee), the original welfare bill's central provisions remained basically intact. They were outlined by this list that appeared in a March 1995 document of the Republican Party:

1. Require work for benefits.
2. Turn back most of welfare to the states to encourage experimentation and cost-effectiveness.
3. Stop subsidizing illegitimacy.
4. Make welfare a temporary safety net, not a lifetime support system.
5. End the open-ended entitlement feature of welfare by block-granting programs to the states and establishing enforceable spending caps.
6. Renew the vital role of private institutions, such as charities, Boys and Girls Clubs, and neighborhood groups to serve as support networks.[1]

The organizing principle of this chapter follows that list, with a few adjustments. The six sections below analyze the major provisions of the 1996 welfare reform law, reflecting as they do the Republicans' objectives listed above. Recall that the sixth objective on the list, regarding the role of private institutions and charities in serving the poor, was treated at the end of chapter 2. What follows, then, is an analysis of these six features of the 1996 welfare overhaul: (1) the block-granting of the program; (2) time limitation of benefits; (3) work requirements; (4) anti-illegitimacy measures; (5) other new conditions on benefits; and (6) nonwelfare provisions of the 1996 law.

In each section below, the task is to describe the provisions of the 1996 law and to characterize the social, behavioral, and philosophical assumptions behind them. Despite their seeming diversity, these measures constitute a unified welfare policy strategy. To lay the foundation for the moral analysis of subsequent chapters, we will contrast this recently adopted strategy to the policy it replaced, especially the categorical income guarantees of the former AFDC program. An analysis of the actual effects of each facet of post–1996 welfare policy is postponed until chapter 5 below, so the focus in this present chapter is upon what was known when, in 1996, policymakers indeed stood "at the crossroads." By investigating the rationale behind the new law, we will, in addition, gain some insight into the content and framing of the welfare reform debate to which religious voices, particularly the U.S. Catholic bishops, sought to make a constructive contribution.

THE BLOCK-GRANTING OF WELFARE

This aspect of the 1996 welfare law is not just one item among the others on the list of reforms, but rather constitutes the framework of all the other policy innovations. Block grants have for decades served as a mechanism for project management and revenue sharing between the federal government and state and local jurisdictions. Alongside the more targeted categorical grants and the less restrictive general-purpose grants, block grants are a well-established arrangement for program financing and standard setting. Proponents of block-granting federal programs were often advocates of the related agenda of the new federalism that had appeared sporadically in national policy debates for decades before the "Contract with America." Presidents Nixon and Reagan had crafted initiatives under this rubric in hopes of altering the ways roles and funds were shared among various levels of government.[2]

Supporters of the proliferation of block grants argue that a devolution of funding and decision-making authority toward lower levels of government improves efficiency and enhances responsiveness to local needs. Only by reversing the trend toward centralization, the argument runs, will government be able to serve citizens more effectively. However, as research conducted by the political scientist Michael Rich demonstrates, "the balance between accountability and flexibility" is a highly complex phenomenon, particularly in redistributive programs with funding and authority shared by multiple levels of government.[3] Careful consideration of the history of those arrangements that constitute alternatives to block grants suggests that it is by no means a foregone conclusion that Washington is a poor partner for states in their efforts to assist low-income Americans.[4]

By 1995, newly elected majorities of Republicans in Congress and in the statehouses (speaking through the National Governors' Association) were expressing their support for a bold transformation in the funding and administrative structure of AFDC. The program had for decades been a cooperative venture between states and the federal government in the form of an open-ended matching grant. According to this arrangement, the states were required to match federal expenditures approximately dollar for dollar, with the matching rate varying somewhat according to a given state's fiscal capacity and poverty rate.[5] In the interest of increasing state flexibility and discretion in its programs for poor families, welfare reformers were calling for replacing the matching grants (the mechanism that gave AFDC its entitlement nature) with block grants, a system that distributes a fixed sum to each state in a given year according to a predetermined formula. Under a block grant system, there is generally no requirement that states match federal funds in any way, although the 1996 welfare law did require states to demonstrate a substantial "maintenance of effort" by spending 75 percent to 80 percent of what they previously spent on welfare.

To complete the details of this new state-federal funding arrangement, members of both houses of Congress participated in a legendary horse-trading session as the welfare bill moved towards its final form. They agreed to a series of compromise measures that established an annual TANF pool of $16.5 billion and the fixed proportionate shares each state would receive annually from 1996 to 2002, the expected life of the legislation they were hammering out. Under the new TANF system that replaced AFDC, states enjoy increased freedom from federal oversight so they can design and administer their own programs. They are required only to submit annual reports to the federal Department of Health and Human Services to document how they are using their federal monies to support poor families by providing benefits, education, job training programs, and ancillary services. With this action, Congress also consolidated two additional sets of block grants, for child care and social services, so that they would be shared among the states on a similar basis.

The 1996 law also set up two additional funds, termed "high performance grants," for which states would compete over the following five years. States achieving the highest success rates in meeting program goals for reducing illegitimacy and moving welfare recipients into work would share these bonuses. Overall, compared to the previous welfare-funding mechanism, the new block grant system is far less categorical in nature, in the sense that unlike AFDC, it is not targeted for specified purposes and does not contain uniform federal standards for program administration. Nevertheless, the 1996 law also introduced some new restrictions. For example, states are discouraged (by financial penalties) or even legally prohibited from using funds to assist certain categories of newly ineligible recipients, as is described in the sections below on time limits, work requirements, and sanctions.[6]

Any ethical analysis of recent changes in the American welfare system must address the merits of this transition from the entitlement-based system of AFDC to a block grant system that shares fixed federal TANF grants with states. A 1995 study conducted by the Brookings Institution uses the following four policy goals as a framework to evaluate the advantages and disadvantages of shifting to a block grant approach for federal welfare policy.[7]

First is the goal of promoting innovation and evaluation of possible improvements in welfare policy. Supporters claim that employing the block grant mechanism frees states to experiment with new approaches for encouraging the social goods of work effort and family stability. The successes of pioneering states might then be repeated nationwide. Opposing arguments at the time emphasized the risk of removing federal oversight from welfare programs in such a broad way. In the mid-1990s, the Clinton administration attempted to accomplish the same goal through alternative means, namely, by applying a series of waivers (granted through the Department of Health and Human Services) allowing states to experiment with novel welfare program features according to formal state requests. Forty states had received at least one such waiver by the time the welfare bill became law in 1996. By expediting the waiver process, Clinton sought to encourage state experimentation in an incremental way even before the block grant approach was adopted as law. Opponents of block-granting welfare cited the waiver process as evidence that the goals of experimentation and innovation are not incompatible with retaining the entitlement nature of the AFDC system, and they argued that these goals do not require new funding mechanisms with attendant risks and unknown effects.

A second policy goal is preventing a race to the bottom, a common way of referring to the alarming prospect of interstate competition to adopt increasingly stringent welfare rules and stingier benefit packages. Among the risks associated with block-granting welfare is that new funding arrangements may create incentives for states to reduce welfare spending in order to make its welfare programs less attractive to present and potential recipients. High-benefit states fear becoming welfare magnets, especially if the block grant system exacerbates previous disparities in benefit levels and triggers interstate migration of recipients. Concern about this troubling prospect prompted Congress to include a "state maintenance of effort" provision in the 1996 law. At the time, critics argued that only a "maintenance of effort per capita" (a measure never seriously considered in the final bill) would truly protect poor citizens of budget-strapped states from severe hardship once low-income families had been stripped of the federal welfare entitlement. As we shall see in chapter 5, the worst fears about a race to the bottom did not come to pass. However, available studies on the topic do not definitively allay the full range of concerns about the negative effects of devolution on the availability of adequate welfare benefits.[8]

A third policy goal is the equitable distribution of welfare funds to states and individuals eligible for assistance. Efforts to pursue this objective involve the desire to establish some broad limits upon the state-to-state variation of welfare benefit levels. As we have already seen, there have always been high-benefit and low-benefit states, even under the open-ended matching grant system of the previous entitlement-based AFDC program. Any funding system that ties federal contributions to the level of spending commitments made by individual states, with their wide variety of histories and political cultures, will yield some glaring disparities. The outcome of the congressional bargaining over TANF grant distribution to the states perpetuates most of the inequities in per capita federal funding reaching poor residents of each state. As a result, there is still far more federal money available for the average poor child in Connecticut (to cite one example of a traditionally high-benefit state) than there is for a similar child in Mississippi (a perennially low-benefit state). Factors such as variability in the rates of population growth and change in poverty rates across the states exacerbate these concerns about inequity. Only a sharply revised block grant sharing system, one that considers the actual level of need of the poor families in each state as the central criterion for its distributional formula, would truly address this dimension of justice in the distribution of welfare resources.

A fourth goal of welfare-funding mechanisms is to pool the risk of economic difficulties, such as the hardships that accompany cyclical or regional recessions. Whenever recessions reduce the number of jobs available, they increase the need for public funds for poor relief. Unfortunately, this usually occurs at precisely the point in the business cycle when state revenues drop off because, in reducing earnings and production, recessions also reduce a state's tax base. Because of its entitlement nature, the former AFDC program served beneficially as a countercyclical measure in the tradition of neo-Keynesian macroeconomic policy, for it expanded government spending to match whatever level of need might be generated by a recession. Since annual TANF block grants are capped, they cannot exhibit this flexibility to adapt to changing economic conditions. No additional federal TANF funds flow into a state during a recession, and the opportunity to use the program to alleviate regional or cyclical hardship is squandered.[9]

Proponents of the new federalism cite several cogent arguments in making their case that block grants constitute an improved pattern of program funding and control. The states may indeed be better loci for certain programs, serving as laboratories of democracy more accessible to common people as devolutionists claim. The argument that creative solutions to social problems are more likely to take hold on the local level commands intuitive appeal, at least on the surface. However, to make this argument convincingly requires a consistent commitment to a wider agenda of change. Why did the 104th Congress choose to block grant only those programs in the lower tier of the American welfare state, preserving the security of the upper tier programs for the middle class (including Social Security, Disability Insurance, and Unemployment Insurance) according to an entitlement principle? In the interest of equity, there ought to be a principled rationale supporting such sweeping changes in how the broad array of government programs and functions will be reassigned to the federal, state, or local levels. Without such a plan for comprehensive rethinking of the management of all social programs, the decision to subject welfare alone to devolution is subject to the charges of opportunism, bad faith, or arbitrary application of the principles of federalism.

The opponents of block-granting welfare cite a number of objections to this innovation. On the practical level, there arose an often-expressed concern that the welfare efforts of many states continue to suffer because they do not possess adequate administrative or information-management capabilities crucial to implementing the full range of welfare programs. Indeed, these concerns were born out by more than anecdotal evidence suggesting that, at least in the first months and years after the 1996 law went into effect, the transition to state control of previously federal functions was anything but smooth. Accounts abounded of debilitating confusion in state welfare offices as efforts to serve and monitor program recipients lagged under the weight of new responsibilities.[10]

Opponents also cited more fundamental reasons, on the level of program design and philosophy, to support the argument that block grants are inappropriate funding mechanisms for income maintenance programs. In numerous welfare debates spanning several decades, the late Senator Daniel Patrick Moynihan of New York pointed out the shortcomings of any distribution formula that would lock into place existing disparities in state commitments to poor families. Moynihan renewed his previous calls to move welfare policy in the opposite direction, toward greater equity, if not uniformity, across the states. Several years earlier, he had argued in print that "AFDC should be a national program, with national benefits that keep pace with inflation, in exactly the same way that Survivors' Insurance is a national program with national benefits."[11]

The poverty researcher Katherine McFate raises yet another objection to the block-granting of AFDC: the likely differential effects of such policy innovations upon distinct geographical and racial groups. McFate fears that further disproportionate harm will accrue to certain segments of the population that have traditionally suffered from the lack of national uniformity in program standards:

> The purpose of our federal welfare system is to insure some kind of support is available to needy families with children regardless of their residence. The poor are not evenly distributed across the United States. States in the Deep South have higher rates of poverty, especially black poverty, than states in other regions of the country, for obvious historical reasons. The majority of AFDC recipients in all the states of the Deep South are black; the majority of southern state legislators are white conservatives. It was largely because southern states lacked the resources and political will to provide assistance to their needy citizens that the federal government originally began applying more federal standards to assistance programs. Although the proponents of block grants argue that state governments have improved their operations dramatically over the past 30 years, benefit levels in the South remain much lower than in other areas of the country.[12]

Other commentators have explicitly linked the impetus for block-granting welfare to larger historical trends in U.S. social policy. Carl Rowan notes how this new movement for states' autonomy harkens back to the earlier pre–civil rights era when the phrase "states' rights" served as a codeword for racism and justified states' decisions "to cut people off" (from civil rights as well as social assistance) by covering over a hidden racist agenda with seemingly pragmatic arguments.[13] Also writing during the mid-1990s, Margaret Weir views the retreat of the federal government from many of its previous social policy commitments as part of a distressing and larger trend of "fragmentation of the public sphere." She fears that welfare reform will be just one of the hallmarks of a coming era of exacerbated racial exclusion and "the politics of defensive localism." The more policy prerogatives fall upon local jurisdictions, the easier it will become for social policy to come under the sway of "thinly veiled exploitations of racial fears and antipathies."[14] Bureaucracies based in Washington may have their drawbacks and inefficiencies, but robust federal partnership in social programs serves a vital function as a guarantor of social safety nets and as a counterweight to the tendency of local forces to segregate and neglect low-income people, especially the minority poor.

TIME LIMITATION OF BENEFITS

The 1996 welfare law gives states wide new flexibility, including the discretion to deny aid to any low-income family or category of such families. Somewhat paradoxically, the law also contains a number of restrictions on how states may spend their federal TANF funds. As both a goal and effect of the law, these provisions tie the hands of state and local governments in the administration of welfare programs. The legislation explicitly disqualifies certain categories of people from receiving this assistance. Quite a few such restrictions, often referred to as conservative mandates, were proposed early in the congressional welfare debates of the mid-1990s. Only a few of them were eventually incorporated into the final version of the 1996 legislation. This section examines the rationale behind the most important of these new restrictions: the exclusion from further assistance of people receiving benefits beyond a specified time period.

The 1996 welfare reform law set a basic time limit of five years. Beyond that federal lifetime limit of sixty months, recipients are ineligible for cash assistance that comes from federal sources (although they may retain eligibility for in-kind assistance such as food stamps and Medicaid coverage). States may offer assistance from their own in-state funding sources to recipients whose federal clock has expired, and some states have indeed opted to do so. Since states may exclude any category of recipients they choose, they are also free to adopt a time limit as short as they wish. Seventeen states (accounting for about one-quarter of the national welfare caseload) initially imposed a time limit of less than sixty months, some as short as two years. Other states opted for a lifetime limit of sixty months but imposed fixed period time limits, such as a limit of twenty-four months of benefit receipt in any sixty-month period.[15]

Two clarifications regarding time limits are in order. First, the time limit applies, strictly speaking, only to adults. Therefore, states retain the option of continuing to distribute even the federally funded portion of benefits to children beyond the five-year limit. Eight states have chosen merely to reduce, not completely to terminate, a family's benefits to reflect the loss of the portion allotted for the adult member or members. It is also worth noting that time spent as a child in a household receiving AFDC or TANF does not count against the record of an adult applicant or recipient. Second, by virtue of what is called a hardship exemption, states may exempt up to 20 percent of their caseloads from the time limits. As we shall see below, this exemption, combined with the caseload reduction credit, was a significant factor in mitigating the most stringent demands of the new welfare system in its first years of operation.

It is difficult to evaluate the arguments for and against time limitation of welfare benefits in isolation, since this principle is only one element of a much larger package of interrelated policy measures. One of its major effects and goals is to increase the incentive for welfare recipients to search for work and to retain jobs. These activities are, of course, profoundly affected by work incentive and work requirement measures adopted by individual states (the topic of a later section of this chapter). Even before considering how time limitation interacts with the work requirements of our current welfare system, it is necessary to describe two aspects of time limitation: (1) the forms it may take and (2) the rationale behind these measures.

Two versions of time limitation were considered in the public debates leading up to the 1996 overhaul. They came to be known as soft and hard time limits. Each won a number of supporters, particularly once it became evident that the efforts of the Family Support Act of 1988 to facilitate the employment of adults receiving AFDC had fallen short of their goals. Throughout the early 1990s, welfare rolls were growing and costs were rising. A proliferation of exemptions from the work incentives and requirements enacted by the welfare amendments of the previous three decades had undermined the purposes of updated welfare policy. The politicians' desire to "get tough" with welfare recipients was frustrated by program constraints that reduced pro-work measures to mere paper formalities. Hard time limits were proposed as the most direct way to enforce the end of long-term recipiency. No exceptions would be made for welfare-collecting families headed by able-bodied adults once they had exhausted the fixed time limits. Proponents of soft time limits preferred to apply this same basic principle in a more flexible way, by making exceptions for those participants in work preparation programs whose sincere efforts to find employment nevertheless left them jobless after the normal time limit had expired.

The Republicans' "Contract with America" urged the adoption of hard time limits, arguing that any half-measure would only serve to muddy the waters by sending the same mixed signals that had frustrated earlier efforts at welfare reform. Several amendments considered in the Senate deliberations on successive versions of the welfare bill sought to modify this provision, but they never seriously challenged the basic framework of the Republican-sponsored House bill (HR 4). On the state level, Governor

Tommy Thompson of Wisconsin emerged as a pioneer in adopting the principle of hard time limits through his Wisconsin Works (or W-2) program.

President Clinton's 1994 welfare reform proposal was something of a hybrid between soft and hard versions of time limitation. The Clinton plan included the sanction of reducing benefits to recipients who do not cooperate with welfare-to-work programs, but it counted various work preparation activities (including education and job training) as roughly equivalent to actual work effort. It also included provisions for creating many thousands of public-sector jobs of last resort and subsidizing private-sector jobs for recipients who had reached the time limit, although not nearly enough funding would be made available for work slots for all who would likely apply for them. Consequently, Clinton's plan was criticized by time limit hawks for invoking the rhetorical force of the phrase "two years and out" without imposing the strict measures that would make this outcome a reality. It was also criticized by time limit doves for not following through on Clinton's 1992 campaign promise (the often-forgotten second half of his pledge to "end welfare as we know it") to guarantee work opportunities to all able-bodied adults who had exhausted their eligibility under the time limit rule.[16]

A purer example of soft time limits is Project Zero, sponsored by Michigan governor John Engler and presented to the federal Department of Health and Human Services early in 1996 as part of a waiver request.[17] It allows for the continuation of assistance to families whose adult members, because of unfavorable labor market conditions, learning disabilities, and other extenuating circumstances, are unable to find private-sector jobs despite sincere efforts toward work preparation during the period of ordinary welfare eligibility. Engler's program emphasizes the notion of reciprocal responsibilities between government and recipients. It places Michigan "among the few states that acknowledge the basic need to take care of welfare parents who do everything the state asks but still cannot find a decent-paying job."[18] Because adult recipients who exceed the five-year time limit are no longer eligible for federal TANF funds, any benefits they receive (unless they are counted among the state's 20 percent hardship exemption from time limits) in soft time limit states such as Michigan and Vermont must come exclusively from state and local funding sources.

Despite their differences, what hard and soft time limits share is a common rationale that justifies drastic measures in order to break a supposed cycle of dependency in which America's poor families find themselves. The account of dependency that most deeply influenced the welfare reform debates of the 1990s was that of Charles Murray in *Losing Ground: American Social Policy 1950–1980*.[19] Here, Murray argues that the paradox of the persistence of poverty in the affluent, opportunity-filled United States can in large part be explained by the perverse incentives created by public policies, especially by means-tested social programs. Overgenerous welfare policy has built a "poverty trap" that creates an environment in which less advantaged members of society experience disincentives to engage in responsible behavior regarding work, sex, and family life. Murray contends that, by cushioning the effects of failure for this segment of our population, we unwittingly reward and reinforce dysfunctional values that perpetuate a supposed cycle of dependency. Despite their original good intentions, expensive social programs send all the wrong signals to the vulnerable. They destigmatize irresponsibility and actually punish achievement. Only a dramatic restructuring of social policy (Murray was a pioneer in recommending, even in the early 1980s, the total abolition of AFDC) will adequately change this incentive structure and liberate those trapped in the cycle. If we really wish to help low-income Americans, we will enforce the tough-minded discipline that will serve them better in the long run than the myopic compassion that has hindered their ability to become self-sufficient. Murray concludes his book with the assertion, "When reforms finally do occur, they will happen not because stingy people have won, but because generous people have stopped kidding themselves."[20]

Murray's analysis of social policy and its effects is based on several key assumptions about human nature and psychology. In his view, people are rational calculators, seeking to maximize their short-term gains and choosing courses of action solely on the basis of cost-benefit analysis. The decisions of people with sharply limited economic prospects to avoid work, to stay on welfare, to refuse to marry, and to bear illegitimate children are based on the fact that such behaviors pay off more often than their alternatives. Murray borrows several principles from the rational choice school of economic theory in presenting a series of "thought experiments" that demonstrate the salience of the perverse incentives he claims exist within the American legal and educational systems as well as in our social policy. In all these cases, the lines of causality supposedly run from economic incentives, through the coldly calculating minds of individuals, and finally to socially destructive behavior.

Murray's portrayal of the root causes of poverty stands in stark contrast to two alternative theories of the poverty paradox. Each of these approaches relies on significantly different anthropological assumptions. The first is the culture of poverty, a loosely connected school of thought that dates from the work of ethnographer Oscar Lewis. The most important feature of the poor, it contends, is not the measurable economic variable of low income, but qualitative cultural differences that render part of the population socially distant from the mainstream. The subculture of the poor displays certain shared values and patterns of behavior (low work motivation, sexual promiscuity, a proclivity toward escapism, a disproportionately present-time orientation favoring immediate gratification). These patterns possess the adaptive advantage of helping the less privileged cope with the daily pressures and deprivations of their environment, but these same features also stigmatize those who display them, reinforcing their social isolation.[21]

As an explanation of the cause of poverty, the culture of poverty has been used in a number of ways. It can serve as a neutral set of descriptive categories, as a basis for blaming the poor for what are perceived to be their dysfunctional values, or even as an opportunity to romanticize the alternative cultural practices and values of the poor.[22]

A second alternative to Murray's theory of poverty is an approach shared by the members of another loose-knit school of thought regarding the determinants of socioeconomic status. These theorists employ the tools of what is called structuralism. Its most notable contemporary proponent is William Julius Wilson, an urban sociologist who has taught at the University of Chicago and at Harvard University. Wilson's influential works seek to explain the persistence of serious poverty among residents of minority groups and inner-city neighborhoods in terms of the limited economic opportunities available to them due to forces beyond their control. Such forces include the lingering effects of historical racial discrimination; geographical barriers to employment; deteriorating job prospects in rapidly changing labor markets; and declining opportunities for education, stable marriage, and social mobility.[23]

Structuralism shares one set of common assumptions with Murray's theory of poverty: it too explains the persistence of low incomes primarily in terms of economic, not cultural forces. This accords structuralists like Wilson much more room for hope for change, since improvement depends primarily on changing certain key economic conditions, not on somehow altering the cultural inheritance or deeply ingrained personal characteristics of the poor. However, in other ways, the perspectives of Murray and the structuralists are precise opposites. Whereas Murray's agenda for improving the lives of the poor is to urge government to scale back its supposedly counterproductive economic interventions, Wilson calls for more ambitious governmental efforts to shape the economic environment so as to reduce the unfair barriers to economic opportunity for the least advantaged members of society.

Because of their contrasting assumptions about the causes of long-term poverty, Murray and the structuralists judge the principle of time limitation of welfare benefits in directly opposite ways. Since Murray views welfare benefits as part of a system of governmental overgenerosity that traps people in an intergenerational cycle of poverty, a drastic measure such as cutting off eligibility for benefits is a necessary step to establish new rules of the game. Structuralists like Wilson judge this to be the wrong medicine for the ailment of intergenerational dependency. Since their diagnosis is that massive economic forces have blocked the upward mobility of certain sectors of the population, structuralists contend that the proper prescription is not to withdraw continued income support from disadvantaged people. Rather, the most appropriate and effective strategy for poverty reduction is to commit greater resources to the task of extending real opportunity for economic advancement and eventual self-sufficiency.

The divergence in these theories of poverty began as a scholarly disagreement over the interpretation of economic data. However, when policy makers turned their attention to the adoption of time limits during the welfare reform debates of the 1990s, the theories of Murray and the structuralists assumed prominent public profiles, with high stakes riding on their rival claims. Charles Murray's work was often cited explicitly by Speaker of the House Newt Gingrich and other supporters of time limitation.[24] Their arguments for abolishing open-ended eligibility for AFDC as one way of replacing the culture of dependency with an opportunity society frequently invoked concepts (such as "the welfare trap" and "perverse moral signals") introduced by Murray.[25] Conversely, the arguments of Wilson and other structuralists were frequently cited by opponents of time limits. They generally contend that it is the existence of systematic barriers to employment, not some perverse desire to pursue a lucrative welfare career path, that accounts for most welfare recipiency. The alternatives to time limits most frequently proposed include structuralist measures to assist marginalized people in their efforts to join the economic mainstream.[26]

Without doubt, the idea of time-limiting welfare benefits has gained considerable support among the American populace in recent decades.[27] Both the enactment of time limits in the 1996 welfare law and the noteworthy absence of challenges to retaining this feature of welfare policy in the reauthorization debates so far suggest that, at least in these rounds of the debate over social policy, Murray's analysis proved more persuasive than that of the structuralists. Care must be taken, however, in interpreting the significance of this seeming victory. Welfare reform is a complex process involving numerous clusters of values and competing modes of social analysis, so the resulting legislation must not be characterized as a referendum on the tenability of a single theory of poverty. Charles Murray offers a simple (indeed monocausal) explanation for persistent poverty: the rules of social programs create an alluring trap. The broad embracing of time limits suggests that American audiences, at least in the past decade, have for the most part been satisfied with this seemingly straightforward explanation of the causes of long-term dependency. Evidently, Americans have not yet felt the need to dig for the more complex and potentially more satisfactory answers to the questions often asked by structuralist analysts, such as: Why does our affluent society still feature long-term poverty? None of this, however, precludes the possibility of changed public perceptions in subsequent rounds of welfare reform.

WORK REQUIREMENTS

Because the 1996 law devolves most authority for welfare program design and administration to the state level, its provisions for work requirements contain few details regarding specific arrangements. Instead, this federal law issues mandates to the states, spelling out a series of conditions that must be fulfilled in order for states to receive their full share of the allotted TANF grants. The sections of the law that address work requirements specify certain penalties that states will incur for noncompliance, such as forfeiting a percentage of their block grants if work participation quotas are not met. In contrast to previous eras in the history of federal welfare policy, states are free to develop work programs and to subject recipients to any work-related requirements they choose, as long as their use of TANF funds follows three sets of rules.

First, to avoid penalties, each state must enforce minimum work participation rates for its welfare caseload. This annual participation rate started with an initial 25 percent in 1997 and rose by five-percentage-point increments each year to reach 50 percent in 2002. This level of half the caseload is still in effect as of this writing in 2006, although the Republican plan for reauthorization supported by the Bush administration has repeatedly proposed raising the level to 70 percent. Second, the law lists twelve categories of activities in which recipients may engage in order to be counted toward the state's work participation rate. Included are an upper track of seven categories of direct engagement in work (in private and public sectors, including community service and subsidized on-the-job training) and a lower track of work preparation activities (attending secondary school, vocational education programs, and job skills training). No more than 20 percent of a state's recipients may count toward its work participation rate through this second category of work activities. Third, the law sets a minimum number of hours per week for participation in these activities in order for recipients to count toward the state's work percentage goals. This requirement started at twenty hours for single parents and rose in stages to thirty hours after 2000.

The remainder of this section examines the debate over the underlying rationale for these innovative welfare measures. In the four decades since AFDC rules first included work incentives and recommendations, never had such strict regulations enforced work as a condition for receiving welfare benefits. The growing appeal of work requirements over these decades represents the triumph of a set of attitudinal assumptions that favor an employment strategy over a guaranteed-income strategy as the best way of assisting poor families. A consensus has developed that views work as the primary answer to the problem of welfare dependency.

The policy analyst Richard Nathan traces the evolution of the workfare principle from these new assumptions. He describes an initial period of opposition to this new synthesis of policy thought and administrative practice before its ascendency in the 1980s:

> In the seventies, the word workfare was used in a narrow way to refer to the idea that . . . welfare recipients should be required to work, even in make-work jobs, in exchange for receiving benefits. Liberals on social policy is-

sues—and this included most welfare administrators—heaped abuse on this idea, calling it "slavefare" and rejecting it out of hand.[28]

In few states did workfare really get off the ground until its terms of reference changed—away from the punitive enforcement of a quid pro quo and toward a commitment of public resources that offered low-income families opportunities for real advancement.[29] The occasion for the birth of this new-style workfare was the establishment in 1981 of the Community Work Experience Program that provided participants with "an array of employment and training services and activities, job search, job training, education programs and also community work experience."[30] Numerous studies of the effectiveness of such workfare programs, both before and after the Family Support Act of 1988 restructured the federal commitment to them, indicate generally modest but occasionally encouraging results.[31] It remains debatable whether the high cost per participant of these workfare programs and their ancillary services is justified by the level of increased earnings and reduced welfare dependency they produce.

For a variety of reasons that we shall investigate in chapter 5, to date very few states or localities have actually set up sizable workfare programs, despite early predictions that this would be necessary under the terms of the work requirements in the 1996 law. Although it is impossible to predict future shifts, one thing is clear: any ambitious new workfare initiatives to be set up in the near future will draw upon a set of key assumptions that have already contributed to earlier episodes in the development of workfare. These elements of an emerging workfare consensus were captured in a 1987 comment by Senator Moynihan before the Senate Finance Committee: "Conservatives have persuaded liberals that there is nothing wrong with obliging able-bodied adults to work. Liberals have persuaded conservatives that most adults want to work and need some help to do so."[32] Any future development of the workfare principle will surely reflect two pieces of, by now, conventional wisdom. The first is that single mothers should be expected to work because of the psychological satisfaction and emotional benefits associated with holding a job. The second is that an employment strategy is in the best interest of poor families because it enhances their long-term prospects for self-sufficiency and membership in the mainstream of society.[33]

However, if there is a new phase of workfare ahead, it may also be shaped by another, much harsher set of assumptions about human behavior and the role of public policy in enforcing such social virtues as the traditional work ethic. These ideas constitute the "new paternalism" advocated by political scientist Lawrence Mead. Operating with an uncompromisingly punitive version of the culture of poverty hypothesis, Mead proposes the theory that the simple refusal of the poor to work is the major cause of welfare dependency. He posits that the members of a "behavioral underclass" have been so pathologically damaged by the prevalence of an "entitlement mentality" that they no longer have the psychic ability to respond to economic incentives in-tended to encourage greater work effort.[34] This is what separates the opin-ions of Lawrence Mead from those of Charles Murray. Whereas Murray recommends the defunding of welfare programs as a means to restoring the normal incentive structures to which poor families will presumably respond by leading lives of self-sufficiency, Mead's view of the corruption of human nature itself by welfare leads him to despair that simply cutting welfare will suffice. Murray's stated goal of making the virtue of work once again a ne-cessity for all the welfare poor is disputed by Mead, who claims that "it is less and less apparent that self-interest alone would lead recipients to work."[35] For Mead, the only true and sustainable solution to the entrenched habits of dependency is the active enforcement of work discipline by govern-ment. Social policy must surrender its previous (and, Mead claims, counter-productive) goals of extending greater freedom and opportunity to less fortunate citizens. It must now pursue the very different goal of transform-ing the basic life direction of a deviant class within society.

Mead advocates radical reassessments of the role of social policy and the nature of workfare as one of its key instruments. A new "authoritative social policy" would function as one arm of a tutelary regime seeking to instill in citizens those desirable qualities that will produce acceptable behavior.[36] This proposal goes much further than ordinary civic conceptions of the role of government, a long tradition of thought that links statecraft with soulcraft and recognizes a legitimate role for government in fostering certain kinds of virtues.[37] Since, according to Mead's perspective, government can no longer assume basic social competencies, it must take a maximal approach to the task of communicating social expectations, using social policy as a tool to compel its citizens to comply with basic rules for what Mead calls "social functioning."[38]

Mead's understanding of workfare stands in sharp contrast to the new-style workfare that seeks to commit new resources to enhance opportunity and social mobility. In the "custodial democracy" advocated by Mead, workfare becomes a primary way for government to exercise the "social ob-ligations of citizenship."[39] In order for acceptable levels of social discipline to be restored, low-wage work must come to be seen as a duty of the de-pendent poor, no longer as an option to which they might be enticed by eco-nomic incentives.

The "new paternalism" Mead advocates contains a paradox.[40] The struggle against dependency requires not a reduction of government inter-vention, as might be supposed, but actually justifies greater intrusion by public authorities into the lives of those accused of shirking responsibilities. In attributing long-term poverty to deeply ingrained behavioral dysfunc-tions of the poor, Mead cannot be content with a social policy that merely decreases the availability of welfare benefits (as Murray's brand of laissez-faire recommends). Rather, Mead seeks to couple public assistance with rig-orously enforced work obligations.

It is not difficult to imagine numerous objections to Mead's claims. William Julius Wilson articulates one pivotal criticism from a structuralist perspective:

> Despite Mead's eloquent arguments the empirical support for his thesis is incredibly weak. It is therefore difficult for me to embrace a theory that sidesteps the complex issues and consequences of changes in American economic organization with the argument that one can address the problems of the ghetto underclass by simply emphasizing the social obligations of citizenship.[41]

Besides those objections concerning the causes of the social problem of nonwork are serious questions about the practice of "work enforcement" that Mead recommends. What checks will be employed to insure that such work is performed on favorable and nonexploitative terms that respect the basic human rights of workfare participants? Will any barriers to employment (disabilities, family obligations, lack of skills, or work preparation) be considered legitimate excuses for not engaging in workfare activities? By what rationale is the largely unpaid work of child care systematically excluded from Mead's accounting of the social obligations of citizenship? Perhaps most importantly, where will the new work positions come from? If new workers are not needed in the private sector, why should a polity create an artificial situation of full employment (via make-work, public-sector jobs) if the labor of some segment of the population is truly not required for purposes of useful economic production? Such questions raised in response to Mead's proposals have the potential to touch off an important debate that transcends merely technical matters (such as data on job availability and work behavior of the poor) to prompt a reevaluation of the traditional work ethic in advanced societies experiencing a diminished need for paid labor.

It is difficult to judge precisely how much influence the thought of Lawrence Mead has exercised on the welfare reform debates of the past two decades. The notoriety of his writings (and even congressional testimony) suggests that at least his appeals to certain cultural values (accountability, reciprocity, the work ethic), if not his actual recommendations for enforcing work discipline among the members of what he calls a dependent underclass, have found a deep resonance among the American public and national policy makers. The fact that the original welfare bill in 1995 was titled the Personal Responsibility Act indicates something about the rationale and agenda that produced the 1996 law. However, since the most recent federal welfare law remains a skeletal framework for the state programs that actually enforce work requirements, it proves impossible to measure the precise level of Mead's direct influence upon recent policy. Nevertheless, one undeniable effect of the 1996 law and subsequent developments has been to enforce an unprecedented increase in work obligations among welfare recipients.

ANTI-ILLEGITIMACY MEASURES

The very first words of Title I of the 1996 welfare law are: "Marriage is the foundation of a successful society." The act emphasizes that marriage is "an essential institution" that depends on "responsible fatherhood and motherhood."[42] When the lawmakers enumerated the four goals of the revised welfare system, two of these goals related to family structure: "to prevent and reduce the incidence of out-of-wedlock pregnancies . . . and to encourage the formation and maintenance of two-parent families."[43] No article of the welfare reform consensus received more support in Congress at that time than the conviction that a reduction in out-of-wedlock births would surely reduce the magnitude of welfare dependency. Indeed, the major factor preventing sterner measures to discourage and even to punish illegitimate births was the devolutionary nature of the 1996 law. Because so much control over welfare program administration was simultaneously being shifted away from the federal level, it would be up to individual states to fashion the precise steps to take in support of marriage.

Early in the welfare debates of the 104th Congress, conservative legislators introduced several proposals featuring a wide array of very strict measures to punish illegitimacy. Among these conservative mandates were family caps (the policy of denying additional benefits to a family upon the birth of a new child) and teenage mother exclusions. Such measures, if enacted as mandatory restrictions upon the states, would make entire categories of people ineligible for any welfare assistance. The final version of the bill gave states the option of adopting such restrictions but did not require them to do so. The firmest message on illegitimacy contained in the law was the restriction that no state could offer welfare assistance to a mother under the age of eighteen unless she lived with a parent or guardian and continued to be enrolled in high school.

Congress sent a more diffuse message when, as part of the same law, it allocated over one-half billion dollars over six years to the fight against out-of-wedlock births. Fifty million dollars per year was added to the existing Maternal and Child Health Block Grants to promote sexual abstinence through education. Even more significantly, Congress set up a sizable illegitimacy bonus program. This consisted of a system of financial incentives to reward those states that demonstrate the largest decline in the proportion of illegitimate births (without increasing abortions). In each of the four years from 1999 to 2002, the five states compiling the best results in this regard were awarded twenty million dollars each. The yearly announcement of the awards was generally an occasion to reaffirm the laudable goal of encouraging marriage, but it also prompted criticism of the program for a lack of focus and a dearth of provisions to foster the sharing of information among states regarding what works in family formation programs.[44]

The dissatisfaction with existing anti-illegitimacy measures (as well as the subsequent drawn-out controversy over attempts to expand marriage promotion programs during the reauthorization debates) reflects a perennial set of problems concerning this topic within American social policy. Part of the problem may be attributed to a confusion of goals. It is simply unclear how to go about identifying the best strategy to reduce illegitimacy, or even precisely which of the many related outcomes (more marriages, less cohabitation, greater presence of biological fathers in the lives of their out-of-wedlock children) is most desirable, given the numerous social constraints. Another problem involves a confusion of data. One recent survey of many relevant studies on the topic concluded that, although social scientists know much about "how poverty rates vary dramatically by family structure . . . , the declining proportion of married-couple families reflects [such] a variety of interrelated trends"[45] that firm conclusions about causes and effects elude even those who have spent decades studying these data. Social policy that seeks to steer a course around such gigantic uncertainties seldom pleases many observers.

Opponents of these measures often characterize the effort to discourage out-of-wedlock births as a dangerous foray into social engineering, and even as a potential violation of the reproductive rights of low-income single women.[46] These objections are not to be taken lightly. Nevertheless, support for proposals to use social welfare policy as a tool to fight illegitimacy has undeniably deepened in American politics in recent years, now extending to practically all parts of the political spectrum. On the right, both Charles Murray and Lawrence Mead have shifted their focus noticeably in recent years.[47] Whereas the topic of work enforcement formerly occupied most of the attention of these two influential policy analysts, the topic of family formation occupies center stage in their most recent writings on welfare. Further to the center and even the left of the political spectrum, both Jean Bethke Elshtain and Marian Wright Edelman argue for more ambitious and effective anti-illegitimacy efforts.[48] Each echoes the findings reported in the text of section 101 of the 1996 welfare law, citing the ample data demonstrating a correlation between better outcomes for children and the presence of two parents in a household. Few doubts remain about the high social costs associated with pregnancy among unmarried teens. A 1996 independent study estimates that government spends at least seven billion dollars each year dealing with the consequences of teen pregnancy.[49]

However, the existence of a consensus that something should be done to prevent extramarital births should not be allowed to paper over an ongoing disagreement among policy analysts regarding the causes of illegitimacy. A key question remains: To what extent does welfare contribute to the problem of illegitimacy in the United States? It is easy enough to observe the data regarding the sharp rise in illegitimacy rates in the past forty years and its leveling off during the past decade at the rate of approximately one-third of all births. The challenge is to find an interpretation of those data, generally agreeable to well-informed observers, that makes sense of all these trends in terms of key causal factors.

Conservatives frequently favor an economic interpretation. Charles Murray, in an argument reflecting the concern he has manifested in recent years about illegitimacy, ventures the blunt claim that "welfare causes illegitimacy," or in other words, "the generosity of welfare benefits has a relationship to extramarital fertility."[50] Two years before the enactment of the 1996 welfare law, he predicted that illegitimacy would decline by 50 percent if all welfare were eliminated. William F. Lauber and Robert Rector of the Heritage Foundation posit an even tighter linkage between welfare recipiency and the conscious reproductive behavior that precedes illegitimate births. Writing in 1995, they claimed:

> Most unwed mothers conceive and deliver their babies deliberately rather than accidentally. . . . They are very much aware of the role welfare will play in supporting them once a child is born. Thus, the availability of welfare plays an important role in influencing a woman's decision to have a child out of wedlock.[51]

George Gilder, also writing a matter of months before the welfare law's passage, labeled welfare a "promiscuity entitlement" that discourages marriage by displacing the economic role of the father of the illegitimate children it encourages.[52] These are the types of arguments that inspired the attempt to enact mandatory teenage mother exclusions, family caps, and other categorical welfare restrictions—items proposed as drastic but necessary efforts at behavior modification. The actual provisions of the 1996 law, consisting of rules that generally leave it up to states to determine eligibility, are only a remnant of a much broader agenda regarding out-of-wedlock births.

Although generalizations are difficult to make, most liberals and structuralists favor an interpretation of these same data that is more cultural than economic in nature.[53] They attribute illegitimacy to complex social factors rather than crass calculations of gains on the part of potential welfare recipients. In this view, the linkage between family structure and poverty is not as simple as may appear at first glance. The lines of causality run primarily from a starting point of economic disadvantage through collective social mores to an end point of welfare dependency, not, as many conservatives contend, from overgenerous welfare benefits directly to undesirable behaviors such as promiscuity and illegitimacy.[54] In support of these claims, numerous studies may be cited that demonstrate no correlation between the levels of welfare benefits and rates of illegitimacy over a span of time or across geographical jurisdictions.[55] Rather, illegitimacy emerges primarily as one effect of enormous cultural shifts that influence the attitudes and behaviors of all social groups, not just those with low incomes. The effects of the sexual revolution, trends toward delayed marriage, increased economic independence of women, new patterns of schooling, work, and parenting—all these factors contribute to the surge in extramarital births.[56] The salience of noneconomic explanations for this phenomenon suggests that welfare reform measures aimed at reducing illegitimacy will not be effective and will serve only to punish single mothers and their children. The picture emerging from the most careful studies of the problem of nonmarital births suggests that this is a population in need of far more discerning treatment than conservatives recommend. The remedy for the high rate of illegitimacy in the current generation of childbearing Americans is far more complex than what is imagined in the diagnoses of some of the most vocal commentators on welfare reform.[57]

Given the persistence of such deep disagreements over the relationship between welfare and illegitimacy, it is not surprising that the 1996 law drew back from staking out a definitive strategy to counter illegitimacy. While the text of the law does highlight family formation and structure as one of the social concerns relevant to welfare policy, it nevertheless leaves to individual states the delicate task of addressing reproductive behavior as part of the personal responsibility agenda. Chapter 5 offers a summary of how states have enacted the seventeen provisions in the 1996 federal law that relate to these family formation objectives.[58]

OTHER NEW CONDITIONS ON BENEFITS

This section considers three sets of welfare measures enacted by the 1996 welfare law: (1) changes in child-support enforcement; (2) withdrawal of benefits to legal immigrants; and (3) the imposition of Learnfare. While these three measures might seem quite disparate, targeted as they are at different populations, they nevertheless share a common approach. Each attempts to accomplish a policy goal through a strategy of offering incentives and disincentives (often referred to as carrots and sticks, a metaphor that derives from techniques for training beasts of burden) to modify problematic human behavior.

The least controversial of the three is a series of measures that empower states to facilitate enhanced collection of child-support payments. Under the elaborate provisions of Title III of the 1996 law, states are required to implement new, tougher policies to punish nonresident parents whose child-support payments are in arrears. Applicable sanctions even include the suspension of driver's and professional licenses in cases of noncompliance. Federal assistance is offered to states in setting up registries of child-support orders and enhancing enforcement and collection of these payments. The law establishes an improved Federal Parent Locator Service and a system of income withholding for violators in interstate child-support cases. The 1996 law also institutes new formulas for determining eligibility for welfare benefits in families where child-support payments from absent parents are received. These measures to expedite enforcement and to establish uniform procedures are not actually policy innovations, but merely an extension of successful provisions of previous legislation, such as the Family Support Act of 1988.[59]

There are few serious objections to these attempts to hold accountable deadbeat dads (as parents who do not comply with child-support awards are dubbed in common parlance). At the time of the passage of the 1996 law, an annual total of $34 billion in such court-ordered awards were going uncollected. Efforts to beef up enforcement held the inviting prospect of eliminating the need for a significant portion of federal and state welfare expenditures.[60] Controversy arises, however, whenever policies intended to implement these popular goals turn to specific strategies, such as the mandatory establishment of paternity as the basis for any future child-support payments. The 1996 law strongly encourages the states to document the paternity of each newborn. States may designate this as an option for the parents, who on a voluntary basis may consent to having their social security numbers recorded on birth certificates. Or, in the absence of parental cooperation, states may now even go so far as to order genetic matching of babies and suspected fathers if circumstances warrant. For those who apply for welfare, the federal law specifies certain mandatory practices: states must invoke a penalty equal to at least 25 percent of welfare benefits upon families that do not cooperate with state authorities in establishing paternity and child-support orders.

The rationale behind these measures is to use the threat of financial sanctions to secure compliance from welfare mothers hesitant to identify the absentee fathers of their children. As one welfare administrator admitted, "The whole goal is to make it her problem in addition to the government's problem."[61]

This is where strenuous ethical objections to the new child-support measures potentially arise. Such requirements may place custodial parents in impossible situations, especially when single mothers come under the pressure of threats from the men who fathered their children. The well-documented risk of physical or emotional harm in such cases suggests that there is often more at stake than meets the eye in invoking the threat of such sanctions in order to "improve the memory" of a welfare mother. Because paternity identification may create unreasonable burdens on the women and children involved, there is a need to make prudential exceptions to regulations requiring the establishment of paternity. Sometimes neither the carrot nor the stick seems capable of addressing all the relevant needs and concerns in appropriate ways. Policy measures based on principles of behavior modification run the risk of treating human motivation too simplistically. Program values must remain flexible enough to accommodate the complexities of real-life human families and the often very difficult circumstances they face. While encouraging paternal responsibility may be an indispensable part of effective welfare reform, ethicists may judge this provision of the 1996 law too blunt an instrument to suit its purposes.

A second carrot and stick measure is Learnfare. Although it receives no explicit attention in the 1996 law, this form of welfare sanction became a policy option available to the states with the revocation of the entitlement to welfare. Of all the behavioral conditions likely to be imposed upon families receiving welfare benefits from the states, Learnfare emerged as one of the most initially appealing measures. It takes a desirable social goal, namely the compiling of a satisfactory school attendance record by minors in low-income families, and makes a given family's eligibility for welfare contingent upon meeting this goal. Under the Learnfare principle, any family not meeting these attendance requirements is subject to penalties, including reductions in the cash assistance it receives or even complete termination of benefits (the full-family sanction) as punishment for egregious truancy.

Even before the passage of the 1996 law, thirty-four states had already received federal waivers granting them permission to experiment with various programs linking welfare benefits to school attendance.[62] The earliest program started in 1988 in Wisconsin, where Governor Tommy Thompson made it one of the five pillars of his statewide welfare overhaul. The results of that Learnfare experiment have been intensely scrutinized. A 1992 study by researchers at the University of Wisconsin's Employment Training Institute found that "it has not changed attendance patterns of low-income families."[63] One commentator described the results in more dramatic fashion:

> Learnfare was a disaster. In the first year of the program, the drop-out rates actually increased in Milwaukee, where most of the Learnfare sanctions occurred. Errors in record-keeping and lack of follow-up meant that many families lost their benefits for no reason at all. A federal judge issued an injunction against the program in 1989. In the injunction order he wrote: "This is a situation where the survival and dignity of individuals and families are involved. These people should not be made homeless and hungry in the name of social experimentation."[64]

Other states, most notably Connecticut, have instituted similar measures only to reap such disappointing results that Learnfare was largely abandoned as a policy option.[65] Nevertheless, various states have periodically revived experiments with Learnfare after 1996, if only because the temptation is so strong to attempt quick fixes that seek to accomplish several goals at once.[66] In this case, the laudable goals of encouraging sound parenting practices, punishing truancy, and lowering welfare costs proved attractive enough to lure dozens of states into Learnfare experiments. However, even aside from its failure to demonstrate statistical improvements in school attendance, Learnfare may be criticized on ethical grounds. It has the effect of stigmatizing welfare recipients by imputing unproven motives and behaviors to low-income citizens. It holds families' essential lifelines of assistance hostage to conditions often beyond the control of at least some members of the family. Like a parallel initiative called

Immunofare, Learnfare is objectionable because it arbitrarily singles out welfare-dependent families with the implicit suggestion that poorer parents will neglect their children unless coerced to do otherwise by the threat of government sanctions.[67]

A third set of welfare restrictions introduced by the 1996 law involves legal immigrants. These new provisions are contained in Title IV of the law, labeled Restricting Welfare and Public Benefits for Aliens. Previously, only illegal (or undocumented) immigrants had been ineligible for most means-tested entitlement benefits. The welfare reform law further specifies the narrow conditions under which the undocumented are eligible for emergency medical care and other special assistance from federal agencies. A sweeping effect of the 1996 law is that legal immigrants for the first time are denied assistance from federal programs, including food stamps, Medicaid, and Supplemental Security Income (or SSI, the means-tested program for the elderly and disabled). The only exceptions written into the 1996 law were for U.S. military personnel, veterans, political refugees, those granted legal asylum, and those who have worked for ten years in this country. All other immigrants would have to be granted full legal citizenship in order to gain eligibility for these safety net programs. Nearly half a million beneficiaries, mostly elderly or disabled poor, lost their eligibility when the law took effect. Another half million faced the loss of their health insurance within five years because of Medicaid restrictions contained in the 1996 law.[68] States retained the prerogative of using some of their TANF block grant funds to offer services to immigrants who qualify because they arrived before 1996, but no state assistance to subsequent immigrants may draw upon federal funding sources. States and localities faced the prospect of having to bear the full cost of any other aid, even most emergency assistance, that they would choose to offer to noncitizens.

Numerous overlapping goals and strategies prompted these measures. One major motive was surely the massive cost savings of these measures. Congress in the mid-1990s was under intense pressure to comply with the terms of the Balanced Budget Amendment (it would soon become the Balanced Budget Act of 1997) and was on the lookout for savings to offset any new program expenditures. The Congressional Budget Office (CBO) estimated that these cuts in program eligibility for noncitizen legal immigrants would save $23.8 billion over the five fiscal years 1997 to 2002, representing 44 percent of the overall budgetary savings from the entire 1996 welfare bill.[69] Although immigrants comprised only 5 percent of all recipients of the affected programs, awareness of these calculations rendered them especially vulnerable as targets of major cuts.

Another strong motivation for these immigrant provisions was the desire to advance the personal responsibility agenda. As we have already seen, lawmakers sought to use the 1996 legislation to encourage only those behaviors deemed socially constructive. This rationale is surely evident in additional provisions of the law that "increase the circumstances under which an immigrant's sponsor would be considered financially responsible for that individual."[70] All these aspects of the legislation may be viewed as attempts to use sanctions to modify behavior so that all groups become less dependent upon government assistance. However, certain demographic groups appear to have been targeted disproportionately, and it is no accident that immigrants suffered the largest cuts, for these newcomers represent a special case. For them, the rules of social policy may be used as an instrument of behavior modification not only to motivate financial independence, but also to deter them from arriving in the United States in the first place.

It is not strictly necessary to impute racism, nativism, or xenophobia to the proponents of these policies in order to recognize the intent of the 1996 welfare law in this regard: to function as a deterrent against dependency by the immigrants deemed most likely to take advantage of government benefits. Ample public evidence reveals this clear purpose. During Senate deliberations in July 1996 on the final version of the bill, Senator Rick Santorum (R-PA) cited the argument that elderly legal immigrants take advantage of their eligibility for social benefits and use the United States as a "retirement haven."[71] Governor Pete Wilson of California praised the 1996 law as "the kind of step that needs to be taken to prevent federal taxpayers from being inundated with persons who come, especially late in life, and become public charges."[72] In sum, supporters see these measures as a needed response to a distressing pattern by which legal immigrants, drawn by the lure of generous benefits, have taken unfair advantage of the U.S. system of social provision. By restricting such assistance, American social policy implements a principle captured in a comment Senator Phil Gramm of Texas liked to repeat during his public career: "Immigrants should come . . . with their sleeves rolled up, ready to go to work, and not with their hands out, ready to go on welfare."[73]

Opponents of these measures cite numerous practical concerns, such as the fear that severe burdens may be imposed upon local hospitals and that private social service agencies will have to fill the gap in the safety net left by the federal withdrawal. Opponents also question the prevailing assumptions about the motivation of legal immigrants in coming to the United States. As one legal advocacy group protesting these measures contended:

> There is no evidence to support either the thesis that large numbers of immigrants come to the U.S. seeking welfare, or that immigrant benefits constitute a large portion of total welfare expense. Immigration and Naturalization Service data establish that the vast majority of both legal and illegal immigrants come to the U.S. to work, join family members or to flee persecution, not to seek welfare benefits. Overall, 95 percent of immigrants support themselves or are supported by family members and/or sponsors. Only 2.3 percent of immigrants who entered the U.S. during the 1980s from nonrefugee countries received public benefits, a welfare receipt rate approximately 30 percent lower than that of U.S. citizens.[74]

The immigrants most likely to apply for means-tested benefits are the elderly and political refugees, two subgroups hardly likely to be jolted into self-sufficiency by the threat of withdrawing benefits. If a greater deterrent is indeed desired to prevent future immigration of those most likely to become dependent on means-tested benefits, then the blunt tool of eliminating categorical eligibility for programs should be replaced by more precise instruments of policy. Perhaps what is called for is more careful case-by-case determination of immigrant admission or improved screening of immigrants' sponsors by immigration officials already charged with this task. It is debatable whether subsequent policy measures regarding immigration have adequately appropriated and reflected these insights. The rancorous debate over comprehensive reform of U.S. immigration policy that broke out in 2006 certainly was not marked by careful attention to such matters.

OTHER PROVISIONS OF THE 1996 WELFARE LAW

The 1996 welfare overhaul legislation (Public Law 104-193) included a number of provisions besides those relating to welfare per se (in the narrow sense of means-tested cash assistance to qualifying families). This section describes changes in six categories of assistance related to welfare insofar as they tend to serve the same low-income families. The six programs affected are: (1) food stamps; (2) federal assistance in child care services; (3) child nutrition programs; (4) Supplemental Security Income for Disabled Children; (5) Medicaid; and (6) Social Services Block Grants. Most underwent funding reductions and program rule changes, as outlined below.

The federal food stamp program has been the target of periodic calls for repeal, cutbacks, and, most recently, transformation into a system of capped block grants to states. Unlike AFDC, it survived the 1996 welfare overhaul, retaining its status as an open-ended entitlement to all who qualify. However, it was scaled back in significant ways in this round of reform. Spending reductions have been imposed on the food stamp program due to a number of changes: across-the-board cuts in benefit levels (allotments per recipient meal fell from eighty cents to sixty-six cents); tighter eligibility standards (fewer deductions were allowed in means-test calculations); less generous indexing of benefits to inflation; the imposition of new work requirements for able-bodied recipients; and new efforts to reduce fraud, state error rates, and other funding miscalculations in the program. Indeed, the majority of the fifty-six sections in Title VIII, the part of the law that deals with food stamps, enumerate a long series of disqualifications, rendering ineligible many categories of former recipients. Initial estimates placed the cost reductions associated with these changes at $28 billion over six years, amounting to a 20 percent annual reduction in program spending once all the provisions were fully implemented.

The two innovations that most change the nature of the food stamp program are a pair of related measures that parallel the major changes in the cash welfare program: time limitation and work requirements. Both apply to able-bodied food stamp recipients between eighteen and fifty years of age who do not receive an exemption (as do pregnant women, those residing in areas with over 10 percent unemployment, and, in some states, parents of children under age six). Nonexempted recipients are limited to three months of eligibility over any three-year period. After three months, applicants may continue to receive food stamps only if they are working at least twenty hours per week or are enrolled in a workfare or approved job-training program. Although states enjoy some increased discretionary power in administering food stamps under the 1996 law, they have no authority to issue hardship exemptions for food stamp recipients unable to comply with these rules. Because no new funds were set aside for the creation of work or job-training slots for affected people, this provision has the effect of denying food stamp assistance to people who are willing to work if given the opportunity.[75] This is an especially harsh provision, since food stamps represent the sole safety net program for which many low-income individuals are eligible.

Regarding the second of these six items, the 1996 welfare law changed substantially the funding structure of federal assistance to child care services. It created a unified child care block grant to the states, replacing previous programs that had provided federal funds for child care for children in three categories: (1) those considered at risk; (2) those in AFDC families that required child care in order to allow parents to participate in work or training programs; and (3) those in families in the first year of transition from AFDC to employment. The latter two programs had provided child care assistance on an open-ended entitlement basis, so that the federal government had matched state spending on child care with no upper limit. By contrast, Title VI of the 1996 law creates a capped Child Care and Development Block Grant, a consolidated fund over which states, in keeping with the necessity of not exceeding their federal allotments, exercise a high level of discretionary control. Only a few federal guidelines apply to state use of these funds, such as the stipulation that at least 70 percent of each state's allocation be used for low-income, single-parent families. Abolition of the entitlement status means that, at least in some states, a parent who cannot afford the day care required to participate in a work or training program may be cut off from TANF assistance when the time limit is reached. The ethical issue raised here concerns whether these arrangements place parents in the impossible situation of choosing between the immediate well-being of their children (as substandard day care or a total lack of supervision constitute risk factors) and the long-term economic security of their families.

To its credit, the 1996 law had the net effect of increasing the actual level of federal funding for child care. Over six years, the consolidated block grants included a base allocation of $7.2 billion (to be divided among states according to a formula based on past spending patterns) and additional grants to qualifying states of up to $6.7 billion, for a total of $13.9 billion. However, various CBO studies available to legislators at the time raised serious doubts about whether these new funds would be adequate to meet the increased demand for child care as the expanded work requirements and time limits would be taking effect. One CBO report calculated that, assuming that states meet their work requirement percentage targets and that then current patterns of need for such assistance persisted, federal child care funding would run $1.8 billion short in fiscal year 2002.[76] The new child care needs of the flood of single parents being channeled into the workforce threatened to overwhelm even the enhanced system of federal assistance for these services. Opponents argued that only a funding mechanism providing open-ended entitlements to day care would be flexible enough to meet such increased needs for child care assistance, but this is precisely what the law was revoking.

In a third category of federal spending, child nutrition programs, far fewer changes were made. Despite long deliberations during which a capped block grant approach was seriously considered, the school lunch program and the Women, Infants, and Children (WIC) nutrition program remained practically untouched by the 1996 law. However, an estimated $2.9 billion in cost savings were earmarked through modest reductions in two programs: (1) the Child and Adult Food Care Program that subsidizes meals provided to children in day care centers; and (2) the Summer Food Service Program for Children that supplies meals in low-income areas when school lunches are not available.[77]

The cuts in a fourth category, Supplemental Security Income for Disabled Children, are both more significant and more concentrated in their effects. In order to achieve cost savings of $7 billion over six years, the law trimmed this program by restricting the types of disabilities that qualify children for assistance. At the time, the CBO predicted that, based on the language of Title II of the 1996 welfare law, approximately 22 percent of previously eligible low-income children would no longer qualify. By 2002, some 315,000 children who would have been eligible for assistance under the previous rules would be denied benefits. The changes are largely a response to the perception that this particular program had been abused through fraudulent claims and inappropriate allowances by doctors who exaggerated existing minor disabilities in their assessments of children in low-income families. At the time of the bill's passage, several alternatives to such sharp reductions in the SSI rolls, such as a proposal for more modest changes in the approved List of Impairments, were rejected.[78]

In a fifth category of federal assistance, Medicaid coverage for the health needs of low-income families, sweeping changes were narrowly averted in the final weeks of the 1996 welfare reform deliberations. Medicaid benefits had long been automatically tied to the receipt of AFDC. With the revoking of the categorical entitlement to welfare assistance under the TANF system, Medicaid coverage for millions of poor women and children could have been jeopardized. The danger was averted when congressional leaders accepted an amendment to the nearly completed welfare bill that linked eligibility for Medicaid to the AFDC rules in effect in each state as of July 1996. Thus, regardless of how a state used its TANF funds or how it implemented time limitation and work requirements, low-income families continued to receive Medicaid coverage on the same basis as they did under AFDC. We will review more recent developments regarding Medicaid coverage in chapter 5.

The sixth change involves the Social Services Block Grants, a long-standing method of federal revenue sharing with the states. The 1996 law trims the size of these allotments by 15 percent, so that in each year from 1997 to 2002, only $2.35 billion would be available to the states. Of all the features of the welfare law, this provision attracted perhaps the least attention at the time, although one *New York Times* news story, published exactly one month after President Clinton signed the bill into law, sounded an alarm with a prediction that these vital funds would be sorely missed. The loss of the federal dollars would have a powerful and adverse impact upon the actual delivery of social services in subsequent years. This same article noted that these appropriations had been used "for hundreds of purposes, typically to help the elderly poor stay out of nursing homes, to pay for shelters and day care, to rehabilitate juvenile criminals, and to rescue children from parental abuse or neglect."[79] The funding cuts amounted to $420 million annually, an amount that states would be unable easily to replace. This placed local governments in the difficult position of having to choose which subgroups of the poor they would continue to serve and which vital social service programs would be eliminated for lack of resources.

THE WAY FORWARD

As this chapter demonstrates, the 1996 law dramatically restructured America's welfare arrangements. The termination of the entitlement principle changed welfare from an income-support system into a work-based system in which a limited amount of transition assistance is available. The resources that remain are explicitly intended to encourage struggling families to take advantage of employment opportunities. A key ethical question then emerges: Does the new welfare system make this type of opportunity effective in practice? In other words, does it provide the conditions that will make work available and make work pay for America's poorest families?

We have already examined the arguments of the proponents of the personal responsibility agenda. The predictions of Charles Murray, Lawrence Mead, Robert Rector, and other conservative analysts rest on the assumption that the psychological effects of a sharp break from previous welfare policy will accomplish most of the desired goals. With the culture of dependency and welfare entitlement in the rearview mirror, they sanguinely predict, the new version of American social policy will benefit everyone. The private sector will provide sufficient opportunities for earnings to all those formerly dependent on public assistance.

Opponents, for their part, call attention to the unfulfilled second half of the title of the 1996 law. Conspicuous by its absence in the Personal Responsibility and Work Opportunity Reconciliation Act is any provision or funding for actual job opportunities. In order to address the disadvantages that lock millions of former welfare recipients into poor employment prospects, massive additional resources are required—in education, skills enhancement, job training, and placement services. The provisions of the 1996 federal welfare law did not reflect this concern, nor would the states be able to supply the resources for the needed investments in human capital. In their honest moments, commentators from across the entire political spectrum admitted that converting the welfare system into a work-based system would require substantial new expenditures.[80] The compromises hammered out by our lawmakers in 1996, however, entirely omitted any new funding to turn the law's work-based solution into an effective and realistic jobs-based solution.

Further reflections on this topic of "what is missing in welfare reform" appear in chapters 5 and 6, where issues regarding the implementation and attempted reauthorization of the 1996 law are examined. Before moving to those most recent developments in the ongoing saga of welfare reform, it will be instructive to address the topic of chapter 4: the contribution of the U.S. Catholic bishops to the welfare reform debates. Examining the message of these prominent religious commentators on public policy will allow us to compare the claims of the personal responsibility agenda with an alternative discourse that also considers a healthy dose of the social responsibility we have already seen (in chapter 1) within the tradition of Catholic social teaching.

NOTES

1. Stephen Moore, ed., *Restoring the Dream: The Bold New Plan by House Republicans* (New York: Times Books of Random House, 1995), 170.
2. See Timothy Conlan, *New Federalism: Intergovernmental Reform from Nixon to Reagan* (Washington, DC: Brookings Institution, 1988); Paul E. Peterson, *The Price of Federalism* (Washington, DC: Brookings Institution, 1995).
3. Michael J. Rich, *Federal Policymaking and the Poor: National Goals, Local Choices and Distributional Outcomes* (Princeton, NJ: Princeton University Press, 1993), 341.
4. A spirited statement of the arguments supporting governmental decentralization is found in Newt Gingrich, *To Renew America* (New York: HarperCollins Publishers, 1995), chap. 2. In this bestseller, the former Speaker of the House lists several fiscal and even "spiritual" advantages of dramatically curtailing the size and role of the federal government. Interestingly, Gingrich frequently cites the

states' rights language of the Tenth Amendment of the U.S. Constitution in mounting his case for devolution.

5. Poorer states with traditionally low AFDC benefits thus received a greater federal matching share than high-benefit states. Despite this sliding matching formula, low-income children in Mississippi (perennially the lowest-benefit state) received only 20 percent of the federal matching funds reaching similar children in the most generous state (in the early 1990s, Connecticut). The disparity in the actual federal dollars per capita that a state draws down under such open-ended matching grants as AFDC is due to widely varying spending commitments made by the states themselves. Statistics above appear in Robert D. Reischauer and R. Kent Weaver, "Financing Welfare: Are Block Grants the Answer?" in *Looking Before We Leap,* ed. Weaver and Dickens, 23.

6. For more detailed information regarding specific features of the law, consult the text of the law itself: "The Personal Responsibility and Work Opportunity Reconciliation Act of 1996," HR 3734, 104th Congress, 2nd Session, Public Law 104-193. The full text appears in *United States Statutes at Large,* vol. 110 (Washington, DC: Government Printing Office, 1997), part 3: 2105–2355. Two excellent sources providing helpful summaries of this 250-page law are: Jeffrey L. Katz, "Welfare Overhaul Law," *Congressional Quarterly Weekly Report,* September 21, 1996, 2696–2705; David A. Super et al., *The New Welfare Law* (Washington, DC: Center on Budget and Policy Priorities, August 14, 1996).

7. Reischauer and Weaver, "Financing Welfare," 13–26. The authors conclude that the shortcomings of a block grant approach greatly outweigh any advantages it might offer.

8. See the preliminary data and early analysis available in *Welfare Reform: A Race to the Bottom?* ed. Sanford F. Schram and Samuel H. Beer (Baltimore, MD: Johns Hopkins University Press, 1998). Chapter 5 revisits this concern.

9. The only exception to this general picture are two provisions in the 1996 law. First, over the law's first five years, a total of $2 billion was set aside as a contingency fund into which states affected especially severely by unemployment could tap to fund extraordinary welfare demand. Second, lawmakers set up a Rainy Day loan fund of $1.7 billion to finance emergency social service needs over that same five-year period. As it turned out, states hardly ever even eyed these recession-triggered federal funding pools because the national economy was so strong from 1996 to 2001. An Urban Institute volume that went to press just as recession was hitting early in 2002 called upon the reauthorization process to beef up such measures "to ensure that program rules and funding respond to the many different challenges TANF will face in worse economic times . . . includ[ing] a more effective mechanism for increasing funding when needs increase . . . [due to] labor market conditions." See the co-editors' "Introduction" in *Welfare Reform: The Next Act,* ed. Weil and Feingold, xxvii.

10. Accounts of state administrative difficulties, particularly in the early months after the 1996 overhaul, are numerous. A November 1996 computer error in New York City resulted in the wrongful termination of welfare benefits to six thousand recipients. Vivian Toy, "Welfare Offices Issue 6000 Emergency Checks," *New York Times,* November 28, 1996, B14. "Bureaucratic and administrative difficulties and contradictions in the delivery of public assistance" were cited as a major topic of concern in the state of Massachusetts in 2001. Donna Haig Friedman et al., *After Welfare Reform: Trends in Poverty and Emergency Service Use*

in Massachusetts (Boston: Center for Social Policy, John W. McCormack Institute of Public Affairs at the University of Massachusetts at Boston, June 2001), 3. Many first-hand stories of dangerous, even life-threatening cutoffs due to welfare agency clerical errors are available, none more poignant than those found in the case studies presented in LynNell Hancock, *Hands to Work: The Stories of Three Families Racing the Welfare Clock* (New York: HarperCollins Publishers, 2002).

11. Daniel Patrick Moynihan, "Welfare Reform: Serving America's Children," *Teacher's College Record* 90 (Spring 1989): 340.

12. Katherine McFate, *Making Welfare Work: The Principles of Constructive Welfare Reform* (Washington, DC: Joint Center for Political and Economic Studies, 1995), 33.

13. Carl T. Rowan, "Back to State's Rights," *Washington Post*, November 5, 1995, C7. See also n. 4 of this chapter supra.

14. Margaret Weir, "Urban Poverty and Defensive Localism," *Dissent* (summer 1994): 338.

15. Complete statistics on state options in setting time limits appear in Ladonna A. Pavetti and Dan Bloom, "State Sanctions and Time Limits," in *The New World of Welfare,* ed. Rebecca Blank and Ron Haskins (Washington, DC: Brookings Institution Press, 2001), 245–69. Pavetti and Bloom divide state time limit policy into the three categories of "stringent, lenient and moderate." They point out that two states, Michigan and Vermont, have chosen to circumvent federal time limits altogether by increasing the state contribution to families making good faith efforts at financial independence beyond the five-year mark. Note that the task of tabulating state policies during the late 1990s is complicated by several factors, including policy reversals and the effects of earlier waivers, some of which expired during this period and were replaced by a variety of new time limit options.

16. The 1994 Clinton plan required $9.3 billion in additional government spending over five years, much of it for the creation of public-sector job slots and for services (such as child care and job training) that would make welfare-to-work plans feasible. Despite the high cost, the administration's own estimates were that the AFDC caseload would drop by no more than 20 percent by the year 2000. Clinton administration officials had earlier floated proposals for a far more expensive program to create 1.3 million public-sector jobs for former recipients, but scaled that number back to 400,000 jobs over a six-year period. The high costs and low expected payoffs soured many observers on the Clinton plan, but served as a sobering reminder of the difficulty of translating welfare reform slogans into effective work-based programs. In this task, neither hard nor soft time limits constitute silver bullets of any sort. For a comprehensive account of the development of the Clinton welfare initiative, see Weaver, *Ending Welfare as We Know It,* chap. 9.

17. Its name derives from the goal of completely eliminating unemployment among welfare recipients. For details on program features, see Jason DeParle, "Aid from an Enemy of the Welfare State," *New York Times,* January 28 1996, sec. 4, p. 4.

18. "John Engler, Welfare Maverick," *New York Times,* March 21, 1996, A24.

19. Charles Murray, *Losing Ground: American Social Policy 1950–1980* (New York: Basic Books, 1984).

20. Ibid., 236.

21. Michael B. Katz offers a succinct and particularly insightful analysis of these concepts in *The Undeserving Poor: From the War on Poverty to the War on Welfare* (New York: Pantheon Books, 1989), 6–35.

22. Oscar Lewis himself, in his many works describing the lives of the poor in Western society, alternately assumes the first and third of these three options. See, for example, *The Children of Sanchez* (New York: Random House, 1961). A major figure in urban sociology whose works often drew criticism for blaming the poor is Edward Banfield. He offers his version of the culture of poverty most clearly in his controversial work, *The Unheavenly City Revisited* (Boston: Little, Brown and Co., 1974).

23. These works of William Julius Wilson include: *The Declining Significance of Race: Blacks and Changing American Institutions* (Chicago: University of Chicago Press, 1978); *The Truly Disadvantaged: The Inner City, the Underclass, and Public Policy* (Chicago: University of Chicago Press, 1987); and *When Work Disappears: The World of the New Urban Poor* (New York: Albert A. Knopf, 1996).

24. See Gingrich's *To Renew America*, 78.

25. Moore, ed., *Restoring the Dream*, 59–61, 193.

26. One emblematic example of such structuralist argumentation against time limits appears in Association of the Bar of the City of New York, "Report and Recommendations on HR 4, 'The Personal Responsibility Act of 1995,'" *Record of the Association of the Bar of the City of New York* 50 (June 1995): 493–521.

27. See R. Kent Weaver, Robert Y. Shapiro, and Lawrence R. Jacobs, "Public Opinion on Welfare Reform," in *Looking Before We Leap*, ed. Weaver and. Dickens, 109–28. This study collects data from ten public opinion surveys conducted in the mid-1990s. Each indicates support for the time limitation principle by a substantial majority (generally between 74 percent and 92 percent) of the public.

28. Richard P. Nathan, "Will the Underclass Always Be with Us?" *Society* 24, no. 3 (March–April 1987): 61.

29. A notable exception was California under Governor Ronald Reagan. There, program development and implementation proceeded quite rapidly in the 1970s.

30. Nathan, "Will the Underclass Always Be with Us?" 61.

31. A detailed and well-balanced analysis of the findings of dozens of such studies conducted by the Manpower Demonstration Research Corporation appears in Judith M. Gueron and Edward Pauly, *From Welfare to Work* (New York: Russell Sage Foundation, 1991), with Cameran M. Lougy. A rich source of data and analysis of workfare programs in the United States, Canada, and the United Kingdom in recent decades is Jamie Peck, *Workfare States* (New York: Guilford Press, 2001).

32. Quoted in Lawrence M. Mead, *The New Politics of Poverty: The Nonworking Poor in America* (New York: Basic Books, 1992), 201.

33. Robert D. Reischauer lists additional elements of this consensus (at least as it existed as he wrote in 1987) in "Welfare Reform: Will Consensus Be Enough?" *Brookings Review* 5 (Summer 1987): 3–8.

34. Lawrence M. Mead, *Beyond Entitlement: The Social Obligations of Citizenship* (New York: The Free Press, 1986), 22.

35. Ibid., 90.

36. Ibid., 11; Mead, *New Politics of Poverty*, 181.

37. One current representative of this tradition is social commentator George F. Will. See his *Statecraft as Soulcraft: What Government Does* (New York: Simon and Schuster, 1983).
38. Mead, *Beyond Entitlement*, chap. 3.
39. Mead, *New Politics of Poverty*, 183; chapter 11 ("The Common Obligations") of Mead's *Beyond Entitlement* lists four further obligations alongside work. They are: supporting one's family; fluency in English; learning enough in school to become employable; and abiding by the law.
40. Mead, *New Politics of Poverty*, 183. This phrase also appears in the title of a volume on the same topic that Mead later edited: *The New Paternalism: Supervisory Approaches to Poverty* (Washington, DC: Brookings Institution Press, 1997).
41. Wilson, *The Truly Disadvantaged*, 161.
42. *United States Statutes at Large*, vol. 110, part 3, 2110. See n. 6 supra for full citation.
43. Ibid., 2113. This part of section 401 of the law is cited prominently and analyzed in Gwendolyn Mink, *Welfare's End* (Ithaca, NY: Cornell University Press, 1998), 66.
44. Upon the September 2002 announcement of the second round of these awards, Cory Richards, vice president for policy of the Alan Guttmacher Institute (a nonprofit research organization focusing on reproductive health issues), remarked: "About the best you can say for the bonus is that it advertises the issue. There's no requirement that the states tell the government what they're doing to bring down the rates, or even that they do anything at all, so there's no way states can learn from each other's successful programs. The federal government gives no guidance to the states as to what they should or shouldn't do to bring down the rates." Quoted in Tamar Lewin, "Cut Down on Out-of-Wedlock Births, Win Cash," *New York Times*, September 24, 2000, sec. 4, p. 5.
45. Maria Cancian and Deborah Reed, "Changes in Family Structure: Implications for Poverty and Related Policy," in *Understanding Poverty*, ed. Danziger and Haveman, 69–96.
46. Christopher Jenks and Kathryn Edin, "Do Poor Women Have a Right to Bear Children?" *American Prospect*, no. 20 (1995): 43–52; Iris Marion Young, "Making Single Motherhood Normal," *Dissent* (Winter 1994): 88–93; Dorothy Roberts, "Welfare's Ban on Poor Motherhood," in *Whose Welfare?* ed. Gwendolyn Mink (Ithaca, NY: Cornell University Press, 1999), 152–67.
47. Already by 1994, Charles Murray had come around to this opinion: "These observations have led me to conclude that illegitimacy is the central social problem of our time." Murray, "What To Do About Welfare," *Commentary* 98 (December 1994): 27. By 2001, his assessment was so unequivocal on this point that he was invited to author a long chapter on the topic of family formation for a Brookings Institution volume of essays on welfare reform. There, he wrote that "high-density nonmarital parenthood is the driving force behind the creation and persistence of an underclass." Murray, "Family Formation," in *The New World of Welfare*, ed. Blank and Haskins, 137–68; Mead's essay in a 1996 volume on welfare reform demonstrates a concern for family structure not apparent in his earlier writings. See "The Poverty Debate and Human Nature," in *Welfare in America: Christian Perspectives on a Policy in Crisis*, ed. Stanley W. Carlson-

Theis and James W. Skillen (Grand Rapids, MI: William B. Eerdmans Publishing Co., 1996); 209–42. Mead's contribution to a 2001 volume on welfare includes a declaration of his fervent hope that future reforms will help "to deter unwanted pregnancy" and "to help children and strengthen marriage," important elements of genuine reform he believes have been neglected. Mead, "The Politics of Conservative Welfare Reform," in *The New World of Welfare*, ed. Blank and Haskins, 201–20. Further evidence of the evolution of Mead's thought appears throughout the volume he co-authored with Mary Jo Bane, *Lifting Up the Poor: A Dialogue on Religion, Poverty and Welfare Reform* (Washington, DC: Brookings Institution Press, 2003), esp. 53–106, which contains Mead's essay "A Biblical Response to Poverty."

48. "We also know, from . . . dozens of other reliable sources, that children growing up in single-parent households are at greater risk on every index of well-being: crime, violence, substance abuse, mental illness, dropping out of school, and so on." Jean Bethke Elshtain, "Single Motherhood: Response to Iris Marion Young," *Dissent* (Spring 1994): 268; "Adolescent parenthood is no longer a viable option for thriving and progressing in society. . . . Teenage pregnancy is a problem because it very often precludes the completion of education, the securing of employment, and the creation of a stable relationship." Marian Wright Edelman, *Families in Peril: An Agenda for Social Change* (Cambridge, MA: Harvard University Press, 1987), 56–57.

49. The study was sponsored by the Robin Hood Foundation, a charitable organization based in New York. It measured increased costs to government associated with the approximately 175,000 annual births to mothers of ages fifteen to nineteen, of whom 72 percent are unmarried. The figure of $7 billion is dominated by medical care, AFDC, foster care expenses, and opportunity costs from lost productivity and tax revenues. See Stephen A. Holmes, "Public Cost of Teen-Age Pregnancy Is Put at $7 Billion This Year," *New York Times*, June 13, 1996, A19.

50. Murray, "What To Do About Welfare," 29.

51. Robert Rector and William F. Lauber, *America's Failed $5.4 Trillion War on Poverty* (Washington, DC: The Heritage Foundation, 1995), 27–28.

52. George Gilder, "End Welfare Reform as We Know It," *American Spectator* (June 1995): 26.

53. An excellent example of a liberal and structuralist interpretation of family formation issues is Kristin Luker, *Dubious Conceptions: The Politics of Teenage Pregnancy* (Cambridge, MA: Harvard University Press, 1996). Throughout the book, Luker argues that the timing of the first birth, especially among poor American women, is an outcome of many factors, so that pregnancy among unmarried teens is properly considered neither a simple cause of poverty nor a clear result of the availability of welfare.

54. A long-neglected body of evidence contradicts such claims of conservatives. It documents the high number of teenage mothers who are, as one study phrased it, "the abused prey of older men" and who "deserve legal protection rather than demonization." Mireya Novarro, "Teen-age Mothers Viewed as Abused Prey of Older Men," *New York Times*, May 19, 1996, 1, 18.

55. Much evidence could be cited to support this claim, including numerous studies conducted specifically in direct response to the analysis of Charles Murray. The data from dozens of governmental and independent sources, the great majority

of which find virtually no demonstrable causal link between welfare and single-parent families, are summarized in Tufts University Center on Hunger, Poverty, and Nutrition Policy, *Statement on Key Welfare Reform Issues: The Empirical Evidence* (Medford, MA: Tufts University Center on Hunger, Poverty, and Nutrition Policy, 1995).

56. For an analysis of how these social trends interact with rates of marriage and illegitimacy, see Robert D. Mare and Christopher Winship, "Socioeconomic Change and the Decline of Marriage for Blacks and Whites," in *The Urban Underclass*, ed. Christopher Jencks and Paul E. Peterson (Washington, DC: Brookings Institution, 1991). Other essays in the same volume offer corroborating observations about the causes of the behavioral patterns of one social group of particular concern, namely urban underclass teens.

57. Kristin Luker takes on Murray's arguments directly. She compiles an impressive array of arguments and statistical comparisons to document the complexities of the causes of teen and nonmarital pregnancy, making a strong case that welfare benefits in isolation possess little causal power in explaining this phenomenon. See Luker's *Dubious Conceptions*, chap. 5.

58. For a review of how states have opted to implement the anti-illegitimacy provisions of the 1996 welfare law, see three studies on recent state programs to reduce nonmarital births, which appear as chaps. 16–18 in *Welfare Reform and Beyond: The Future of the Safety Net*, ed. Isabel V. Sawhill et al. (Washington, DC: Brookings Institution, 2002).

59. An excellent overview of how these 1996 provisions built upon existing child support enforcement legislation and changed "the fiscal relationship between recipients and noncustodial parents" appears in James L. Wolk and Sandra Schmahl, "Child Support Enforcement: The Ignored Component of Welfare Reform," *Families in Society: The Journal of Contemporary Human Services* 80, no. 5 (September–October 1999): 526–30.

60. See David T. Ellwood, *Poor Support: Poverty in the American Family* (New York: Basic Books, 1988), 163–74; Robert I. Lerman, "Child-Support Policies," in *Welfare Policies for the 1990s*, ed. Cottingham and Ellwood, 219–46.

61. The statement is from Michael Henry, director of the Virginia Division of Child Support Enforcement, quoted in Peter Baker, "Virginia Targets Welfare Moms in Effort to Track Down Absentee Dads," *Washington Post*, July 31, 1995, A1, A12.

62. Michael B. Katz, *The Price of Citizenship: Redefining the American Welfare State* (New York: Henry Holt and Co., 2001), 95–96.

63. Ellen Nakashima, "Learnfare Starts Off Slowly in Virginia," *Washington Post*, February 12, 1996, D1, D5. For a summary of other studies of similar programs, see Dirk Johnson, "Wisconsin Welfare Effort on School Is a Failure, Study Says," *New York Times*, May 19, 1996, 20.

64. Ruth Cuniff, "Big Bad Welfare," *The Progressive* 58 (August 1994): 20.

65. See Jonathan Rabinovitz, "Welfare Cuts for Truancy Are Stalled: Task Force in Hartford Finds Problems in Plan," *New York Times*, May 7, 1996, B1, B4.

66. Anemona Hartiocollis, "Experiment on Truancy Advances: Attendance Is Tied to Welfare Benefits," *New York Times*, September 12, 1997, A35. This account of a pilot program in three New York City schools illustrates the lingering appeal of Learnfare for state officials even after the publication of the disappoint-

ing Wisconsin results. Governor George Pataki urged the New York City Board of Education to institute this local trial.

67. Immunofare programs enacted in certain states sanction welfare families for failure to maintain adequate child immunization histories. Jill Duerr Berrick points out the faulty premises of this policy: "The effect is based on the assumption that low-income women are not aware of the importance of vaccinations and that they are not concerned about the health of their children." Berrick, *Faces of Poverty: Portraits of Women and Children on Welfare* (New York: Oxford University Press, 1995), 156. Berrick further argues that there is no evidence to suggest that low incomes or welfare recipiency are correlated with willful neglect of the needs of children for schooling or vaccines. An ongoing experiment in various counties in Georgia, including control group experimentation dating from 1993, suggests only very modest, although not negligible, increases in inoculation rates when sanctions are threatened. See Associated Press, "Georgia Threat to Cut Welfare Seen to Boost Vaccinations," *Boston Globe*, July 15. 2000, A4.

68. These figures are Congressional Budget Office estimates reported in Super et al., *The New Welfare Law*. Calculations are complicated by two factors: (1) slight differences between the way the 1996 law treats new arrivals after 1996 and those who arrived earlier; and (2) new spending by some states to offset severe hardships.

69. Statistics cited in Ladonna A. Pavetti, "Welfare Policy in Transition" in *Understanding Poverty*, ed. Danziger and Haveman, 266. These estimates proved to be overstated because some SSI and food stamp benefits would eventually be restored for especially needy immigrants who had arrived before 1996. Subsequent changes regarding the eligibility of immigrants will be treated in chapter 5. For a review of the debate on further changes during the 107th Congress, see Kelly Field, "Immigrants' Benefits Revisited," *CQ Weekly*, February 15, 2003, 399.

70. "Provisions of the Welfare Bill," *Congressional Quarterly Weekly Report*, August 3, 1996, 2193.

71. Quoted in Robert Pear, "Senate Votes to Deny Most Federal Benefits to Legal Immigrants Who Are Not Citizens," *New York Times*, July 20, 1996, 9.

72. Quoted in Tim Golden, "If Immigrants Lose U.S. Aid, Local Budgets May Feel Pain," *New York Times*, July 29, 1996, A1, A12.

73. Quoted in ibid.

74. Association of the Bar of the City of New York, "Report and Recommendations on HR 4, 'The Personal Responsibility Act of 1995,'" *Record of the Association of the Bar of the City of New York* 50 (June 1995): 510.

75. At the time, the CBO offered initial estimates that in an average month, one million individuals will be in this situation (i.e., denied food stamps because of an inability to find work). See Super et al., *The New Welfare Law*, 17–23.

76. For details of these CBO studies, see Super et al., *The New Welfare Law*, 12–14.

77. For details, see ibid., 22–23, or the text of the law, Title VII, subtitle A (National School Lunch Act) and subtitle B (Child Nutrition Act of 1966).

78. Jeffrey L. Katz, "Welfare Overhaul Law," 2699; Super et al., *The New Welfare Law*, 29–30.

79. Peter Kilborn, "Little-Noticed Cut Imperils Safety Net for the Poor," *New York Times*, September 22, 1996, 1, 16.

80. William Julius Wilson (see *The Truly Disadvantaged*, 150–51) had advocated a multibillion dollar public-sector work program to provide "jobs of last resort." Clinton's 1994 welfare proposal included $9.3 billion to make welfare-to-work programs feasible. The CBO projected that by 2002, $5.6 billion would be required annually to meet the work requirements of the 1996 law. Even the Republicans' "Contract with America" called for a jobs program of $10 billion over five years. Each of these proposals is discussed in Super et al., *The New Welfare Law*, 10–11.

4

The Bishops' Contribution to the Welfare Reform Debate

Given the history of American social policy and recent developments in the ongoing debate over welfare, what does the tradition of Catholic social teaching say about contemporary welfare policy? Is there a distinctive Catholic position amidst this contested terrain? What ethical concerns about recent rounds of welfare reform arise from the social thought of the Catholic Church?

Two methods of addressing these questions present themselves. The first would be to conduct an independent scholarly investigation of how the themes of universal Catholic social teaching apply in the specific context of American social policy. Such a study would build on the contents of chapter 1 above and would attempt to link foundational Catholic concerns about proper social order and concern for the poor to detailed conclusions about welfare program rules and policy choices in the specific national context of the United States. A major pitfall of this methodology is the likelihood that any such application of principles to concrete realities will reveal too much about the ideological commitments and political biases of the observer, and far too little about the actual policy implications of Catholic social principles.

A second method is simpler and probably more reliable. Instead of launching a deductive inquiry that would attempt to determine appropriate applications of Catholic social teaching, this approach relies primarily upon observation. What positions and proposals regarding welfare reform were in fact staked out by leaders of the Catholic community in the United States during these recent rounds of welfare reform? Did authentic spokespersons of the Catholic social tradition advocate any noteworthy principles and priorities regarding the well-being of the welfare poor at pivotal junctures of the welfare debates? This second approach is the method that will guide this chapter.

It should come as no surprise that the principal voice of the Catholic community in the United States on public policy issues such as welfare reform is that of the Catholic bishops. Indeed, one of the advantages of the Catholic model of ecclesial polity is its clarity regarding who rightfully exercises teaching authority. Although there are other important sources of wisdom within the Church (the legitimate role of theological scholarship, the due recognition of lay expertise, the reception of teachings according to the *sensus fidelium,* or sense of the faithful), it is proper to identify the hierarchy of the Church as holders of solemn teaching authority. By virtue of his office, each bishop exercises this magisterial authority within a given diocese. Increasingly important in recent decades, particularly on matters of ethical teachings on issues of social justice, is the collective exercise of teaching authority in national episcopal conferences. In the United States, all the bishops work together in a collegial way through the United States Conference of Catholic Bishops, or USCCB, which was introduced in chapter 1. Through its semiannual plenary meetings, through the work of ongoing committees, and through the maintenance of a professional staff in Washington, D.C., the Bishops' Conference is an indispensable vehicle for the teaching and advocacy efforts of the over two hundred American bishops who take part in it.[1]

One of the important tasks of the U.S. Bishops' Conference is the preparation and promulgation of statements and pastoral letters about issues of social justice and public policy. Chapter 1 identifies the application of social teachings of the universal Church to local circumstances as a critical mandate of each local Christian community. The leadership of bishops, both individually and collectively, is vital in bringing the message of social justice to contemporary political and economic issues. The U.S. bishops have taken their role as "carriers" of the tradition of Catholic social teaching very seriously ever since their first major statement on economic justice, the groundbreaking Bishops' Program for Social Reconstruction in 1920. Chapter 1 cites *Economic Justice for All,* a 1986 pastoral letter that stands as the U.S. bishops' most comprehensive statement to date on economic aspects of social justice. The bishops publish certain documents regarding public policies on a regular basis in the form, for example, of annual Labor Day messages and quadrennial pre-election statements that address current issues of moral concern and call for the exercise of prudent political responsibility. Other similar documents are ad hoc in nature, as the bishops seek to respond to issues of contemporary import regarding the entire range of social, economic, and political concerns.

Bishops' statements relating specifically to welfare and poverty in recent years take their place in a long pedigree of efforts on many fronts to serve as a public church. The idea that public advocacy for justice is a core dimension of contemporary ministry is well established in Catholic circles. The commitment to witness publicly for social values is specifically incarnated in local diocesan peace and justice offices as well as in state-level Catholic Conferences that lobby for social justice in state capitals. On the national level, the public church mandate inspires all the work of one particular department of the Bishops' Conference, namely the Office of Social Development and World Peace.[2] This office is a clearinghouse for official Catholic efforts to track legislation on justice issues, to lobby Congress and government agencies for constructive social change, and to engage in public dialogue on domestic and foreign policy. Its staff of lay researchers, project directors, and policy specialists serves as the bishops' major resource in public church advocacy.

THE NEW WELFARE CONSENSUS OF THE 1980S AND THE BISHOPS' DEMURRAL

Among the many policy issues they addressed in the 1986 pastoral letter *Economic Justice for All,* the U.S. bishops singled out public welfare programs as a key element of fighting poverty. Paragraphs 186–214 of this document consist of a set of seven guidelines for action to address the problem of poverty in an affluent America. The final item on that list calls for a "thorough reform of the nation's welfare and income-support programs."[3] In the subsequent five paragraphs, the bishops advocate a series of measures to accomplish two tasks: (1) to improve the welfare system as it existed in the mid-1980s; and (2) to go beyond that system through new initiatives to make welfare arrangements better fit the values (as they are developed throughout the entire pastoral letter) of family, work, and community.

In the first of these two categories fall the bishops' suggestions for national eligibility standards and uniform minimum benefit levels for AFDC recipients. These measures are proposed in order to eliminate distressing state-to-state disparities in safety net provision, including the great variations in the levels of and eligibility requirements for welfare benefits. As noted in chapter 2, it is no secret that these glaring differences are at least partially the legacy of racial discrimination and bias against ethnic minorities. The bishops also call for welfare benefit levels that will allow families that find themselves temporarily dependent upon public assistance to live in dignity rather than in desperate need and constant insecurity.

In the second category are the bishops' suggestions to redesign welfare programs so that they will henceforth "assist recipients, wherever possible, to become self-sufficient through gainful employment."[4] Several concrete measures to fulfill this goal are listed, including job creation programs for welfare recipients, coordinated with such services as job training, work placement, counseling, and child care. The bishops also mention the need to address "notch effects" that discourage people from leaving the welfare rolls. This occurs when, for example, "under current rules, people who give up welfare benefits to work in low-paying jobs soon lose their Medicaid benefits."[5] By implementing such changes in program rules, the U.S. welfare system would make progress toward observing a prudential rule of thumb identified by the bishops: "Individuals should not be worse off economically when they get jobs than when they rely only on public assistance."[6]

Although the bishops' treatment of welfare in 1986 was relatively brief and was folded into a long and wide-ranging document, it was not over-looked in policy circles. The welfare reform bill that passed during the very next Congress, the Family Support Act (FSA) of 1988, included numerous measures that reflect many of the same concerns and even some of the same strategies embraced by the bishops. This bipartisan legislation amended AFDC program rules in several ways. It eliminated some of the most egre-gious notch effects (by means of provisions for transitional Medicaid cov-erage and more generous earnings disregards in determining eligibility for cash benefits). It also made new federal resources available to states for ser-vices (such as child care and job training) designed to ease the transition from welfare to work. Although the 1988 law espoused an enhanced work strategy that increased work incentives and introduced new work expecta-tions for nonexempt AFDC recipients, it resolutely reaffirmed the principle that the federal government should commit significant resources to unem-ployed single parents. The FSA thus represents a firm response to the assault on welfare spending during the "mean season" of the 1980s, an era when pressures for sharp cuts in AFDC had surfaced from the more extreme voices echoing through Washington during the Reagan years. The welfare consensus of the late 1980s thus constituted a positive welfare consensus (one committed to continuing the desirable elements in the existing pro-grams and making improvements, even at substantial cost), not a solely neg-ative one (focused on cutting social services budgets and introducing punitive measures into the welfare system).

The bishops' welfare recommendations in *Economic Justice for All,* then, found resonance within the wider community of public policy discourse. The years at the very end of the Reagan era witnessed a noteworthy convergence of opinion across the political spectrum on how most sensibly to approach the topics (family stability, dependency, work obligation, teen pregnancy) that most directly frame welfare as a policy issue. The findings of several blue-ribbon and scholarly studies sponsored by private groups and govern-ment agencies indicated the existence of the new consensus that was imple-mented through the FSA of 1998.[7] The consensus centered around the growing conviction that paid employment rather than cash transfer pay-ments should be the primary strategy to raise the incomes of needy families. The convergence of opinion along these lines justifies a greater commitment on the part of federal and state governments to tailor programs (such as job training and subsidized child care) to the needs of single-parent families. The overriding goal is to empower single mothers to make the transition from welfare to work—precisely the policy goals the FSA sought to achieve.

Social ethicist Philip Land, SJ, devotes an entire volume, *Shaping Welfare Consensus* (1988), to identifying the precise contribution the bishops made to this new convergence of opinion. Land sees enough similarities between the bishops' recommendations and the FSA to validate the claim that the bishops did indeed play a significant role in changing the eventual policy outcome. He also notes that the basic tenets of Catholic social teaching lead the bishops to espouse certain distinctive positions about the proper role of government in pursuing the common good in modern societies—positions seldom reflected in partisan policy debates. Although much overlap exists between the position of the bishops and those of liberals and conservatives who joined together in a temporary consensus on welfare in the late 1980s, the bishops harbor significant reservations about many popular policy directions. Land concludes:

> The Bishops hold a middle ground between conservatives and liberals on the welfare function of the state. But it is a proper ground of its own, and not simply a picking of ideas from one side and the other. . . .
>
> Quite apart from the Bishops' position within the consensus on welfare reform, the Pastoral holds foundational views about welfare. While being the object of severe attacks from within and outside the Catholic community, these views are both defensible and a powerful contribution to welfare policy in general.[8]

Among those distinctive "foundational views about welfare," Land lists several themes and principles of Catholic social teaching we have already seen: the preferential option for the poor, subsidiarity, the recognition of the phenomena of socialization and interdependence, and the challenge of fostering more robust elements of economic democracy.[9] However, there is one area of Catholic social teaching not treated in the analysis of chapter 1 above that provides the basis for the U.S. bishops' most prominent point of disagreement with the new welfare consensus of the late 1980s. This is the issue of family life and, more specifically, how best to shape welfare policy so that it preserves the dignity of these families and relieves some of the burdens placed upon single-parent families.

The prevailing bipartisan wisdom that shaped the Family Support Act of 1988 and, in more dramatic fashion, the welfare reform law of 1996, includes a key conviction that the Catholic bishops refuse to accept in its simplest form. This is the belief that the well-being of female-headed families will unambiguously be advanced by moving single mothers into work outside the home, through whatever arrangements prove successful in expediting this transition. Both the 1988 and 1996 laws contain provisions that permit, encourage, and even require the states to develop programs (such as workfare and mandatory participation in job training or work activities, combined with increasingly stringent hardship exemptions) that force mothers to leave their young children in day care while they work outside the home. The former AFDC program rules that generally exempted mothers with children under the age of three from work requirements were abrogated by the 1996 law. Since that law took effect, states are free to impose work requirements upon new mothers as soon after delivery as they wish, and many states have adapted timetables measured in weeks or months, rather than years. The significance of this issue regarding work requirements in the early months of motherhood is not to be slighted; demographers estimate that one in eight welfare mothers is caring for a child under age one, and fully one in five has a child under age two.[10] Supporters of these rule changes point, of course, to cultural trends that witness increasing numbers of mothers, both affluent professionals as well as low-income service workers, whether single or married, opting for paid employment. Reliance upon purchased day care continues to grow, as the former cultural norm of mothers devoting themselves to full-time care of their own children is increasingly eclipsed.

In *Economic Justice for All,* the U.S. bishops' most substantial demurral from the new welfare consensus is their rejection of welfare rules that, according to their implicit interpretation of what is good for families, weaken family life because they force single mothers with preschool children to work outside the home. While the bishops offer no objection to programs and policies that encourage (through incentives and transitional assistance) single mothers to choose to work, particularly on schedules of their own choosing, they view it as a violation of the dignity of these families positively to force mothers of young children into paid employment. The bishops' words demonstrate that this stance is based not on some quaint longing for a golden age of blissful domesticity, but upon a coherent and highly principled set of priorities:

> Society's institutions and policies should be structured so that mothers of young children are not forced by economic necessity to work outside the home. The nation's social welfare and tax policies should support parents' decisions to care for their own children and should recognize the work of parents in the home because of its value for the family and for society.[11]

This particular statement of the bishops' own distinctive version of a "family values" argument echoes the concerns of a key passage in the very first chapter of the same pastoral letter: "The economic and cultural strength of the nation is directly linked to the stability and health of its families. . . . When families are weak or break down entirely, the dignity of parents and children is threatened."[12]

When the bishops thus explicitly link public policy with "the ability of families to fulfill their roles in nurturing children," they are drawing from a long tradition of concern for family life in papal encyclicals and other Vatican documents.[13] Frequently, the ability of mothers to remain at home to nurture their children in the early years of childhood is a focal point of this concern. For example, Pope Pius XI's 1931 encyclical *Quadragesimo anno* identified this concern as part of its rationale (within the dominant patriarchal model of the time) for supporting the notion that the "wage paid to the workingman should be sufficient for the support of himself and his family." Only under this condition can we hope to counteract "the abuse whereby mothers of families, because of the insufficiency of the father's salary, are forced to engage in gainful occupations outside the domestic walls to the neglect of their own proper cares and duties, particularly the education of their children."[14]

Vatican documents in recent decades have added some measure of gender sensitivity and an awareness of the changed economic role of women, even while retaining this basic commitment to the idea that there is intrinsic value to full-time parenting. In the face of the massive entry of women (many of them mothers) into the paid labor force of most industrial societies, the argument increasingly takes the form of recognizing that some mothers of young children surely will choose to work outside the home, but that none should be forced by economic necessity to do so. The Second Vatican Council document *Gaudium et spes* and John Paul II's *Familiaris consortio* (Of Family Partnership) made this argument in summary form, but were later surpassed by two Vatican documents that treated this topic at greater length and in even more noteworthy ways.[15]

The first of these two was *Laborem exercens,* the 1981 encyclical of John Paul II. Section 19 treats the topic of women and work in a way that may surprise observers who expect a mere repetition of earlier church pronouncements on traditional gender roles within family life. Toward what he calls "a social re-evaluation of the mother's role," John Paul acknowledges the complexity of modern life, highlights the conflicting goals confronting families and especially mothers with young children, and lauds the potential of government policies to reduce the costs associated with some of these trade-offs. John Paul II repeats the traditional Catholic call for the "family wage," but adds a second category of government action to insure the income of families, namely "through other social measures such as family allowances or grants to mothers devoting themselves exclusively to their families."[16] In the context of U.S. social policy, this is accurately interpreted as a call for a welfare policy that insures a single mother the ability to delay her entry into paid employment until her children are of school age.

While this passage from *Laborem exercens* does not signal a sharp break from traditional Catholic positions on gender roles, it does make an often overlooked advance. Here the innate mission of motherhood emerges as a source of women's legitimate claims against social institutions that might threaten their aspirations and advancement. Note how the emphasis in the following lines of John Paul's encyclical falls upon the task of expanding the range of free choices available to mothers, not upon any rationale of subordinating women or restricting their options for their work or home lives:

> It will redound to the credit of society to make it possible for a mother—without inhibiting her freedom, without psychological or practical discrimination, and without penalizing her as compared with other women—to devote herself to taking care of her children and educating them in accordance with their needs, which vary with age. Having to abandon these tasks in order to take up paid work outside the home is wrong from the point of view of the good of society and of the family when it contradicts or hinders these primary goals of the mission of a mother. . . .
>
> But it is fitting that [women] should be able to fulfill their task in accordance with their own nature, without being discriminated against and without being excluded from jobs for which they are capable, but also without lack of respect for their family aspirations and for their specific role in contributing, together with men, to the good of society. The true advancement of women requires that labor should be structured in such a way that women do not have to pay for their advancement by abandoning what is specific to them and at the expense of the family, in which women as mothers have an irreplaceable role.[17]

If public policies based on this moral analysis were implemented, many women would find themselves in an improved economic position. Their desires to pursue the goods of motherhood and professional careers would be better supported by laws (including antidiscrimination measures and provisions for flextime and parental leave, besides welfare laws) that recognize the social contributions of both paths and that protect the ability of women, whether married or single, to succeed in either or both, according to their wishes. Although they begin from very different perspectives, John Paul's updated version of the Catholic Church's analysis of family life converges in this key respect with the position of mainstream feminist thought. These unlikely allies both argue that public policies, including welfare laws, advance the cause of gender justice when they support women's aspirations to exercise more choice in the question of whether to stay home with their young children. This interpretation of the meaning of justice for low-income single mothers is clearly at odds with the American welfare law of 1996— a law that enforced work participation quotas, ended the entitlement status of AFDC, and gave to the states new freedoms to force single mothers into workfare. In thus supporting greater freedom of choice for women in this regard, the Catholic version of family values distinguishes itself from various positions of the Religious Right that, if implemented fully into civil law, would sharply curtail these same rights and liberties of women.

The second document that makes the argument that mothers should not be forced by economic necessity to work outside the home is the Vatican

"Charter of the Rights of the Family." It was published in 1983 and is addressed "to all states, international organizations, and all interested institutions and persons" in an attempt to promote respect for family rights.[18] While most of the norms and principles listed herein are mentioned in previous church documents, the Charter is valuable in that it serves as an orderly "model and a point of reference for the drawing up of legislation and family policy, and guidelines for action programs" to insure that families are strengthened by public policies.[19] Article 10 of the Charter deals with the matters most relevant to social welfare policy. The full text of this article reads as follows:

> Families have a right to a social and economic order in which the organization of work permits the members to live together and does not hinder the unity, well-being, health and the stability of the family, while offering also the possibility of wholesome recreation. a) Remuneration for work must be sufficient for establishing and maintaining a family with dignity, either through a suitable salary, called a "family wage," or through other social measures such as family allowances or the remuneration of the work in the home of one of the parents; it should be such that mothers will not be obliged to work outside the home to the detriment of family life and especially the education of the children. b) The work of the mother in the home must be recognized and respected because of its value for the family and for society.[20]

The Charter is even more explicit than previous documents regarding the importance of the work of mothers within the home. It emphasizes protecting mothers from the necessity of working outside the home, both when an alternative breadwinner is available (through policies that promote a "family wage") and when, as in the situation of single welfare mothers, no source of income besides public assistance is available. The Charter surpasses previous church documents in explicitly stating that the social contribution of homemakers should be "recognized," "respected," and even "remunerated." The universal Catholic Church thus proposes an argument (one that the U.S. bishops would later borrow) for the continuation of a social policy that recognizes a welfare entitlement for mothers of young children—an entitlement free from such onerous conditions as mandatory workfare requirements. Amidst the welfare debates of the 1990s, the American bishops would adapt this argument to the U.S. social context as part of their distinctive message. Theirs was one of the very few voices to advocate the position that welfare benefits should continue to be understood as part of a societal obligation to provide single mothers with favorable material conditions to support their work inside or beyond the home.

In writing *Economic Justice for All* and in drawing from these Vatican teachings on family life, the U.S. bishops thus demurred from one significant element of the welfare consensus that enjoyed support from both liberals and conservatives, Democrats and Republicans, in recent rounds of recurring welfare reform debates. A brief look at one additional document will serve as a helpful transition to our investigation of the U.S. bishops' specific contribution to the welfare debates during the Clinton and Bush administrations.

In 1991, three committees of the Bishops' Conference (Domestic Social Policy, International Policy, and Marriage and Family Life) coauthored *Putting Children and Families First: A Challenge for Our Church, Nation and World*. This seventeen-page pastoral letter was approved by the assembled bishops near the end of the year and published in 1992. Both chronologically and conceptually, it serves as a bridge between two rounds of welfare policy debate: the one that produced the Family Support Act of 1988 and the one that produced the welfare overhaul of 1996. In this document the bishops focus more intensely on the project they had identified five years earlier in *Economic Justice for All*: subjecting all public policy to a particular form of moral scrutiny. They call upon their audience to judge policies by their effects on family life, especially that of the poorest and most vulnerable in our nation and abroad.

The 1992 letter includes a section that offers policy suggestions for assisting children in low-income families. Two paragraphs in particular reflect the bishops' awareness of the gap between the ethical goals of Catholic social teaching and the actual achievements of the United States (in its social policy as well as in our common cultural practices) on a key matter that affects the ability of poor families to live in dignity:

> At a time when most mothers of young children are employed at least part time, our society sometimes loses sight of the value of parental care of young children. As preschoolers in day care becomes [sic] the norm, we fear the work of mothers in the home is becoming devalued, since it does not offer the economic rewards or recognition of other work. Our conference strongly supports effective voluntary programs to equip parents with education and job skills. We oppose compulsory and poorly designed efforts to require them to hand over to others the daily care of their preschool children. The fact that children are poor and in need of government aid does not take away their basic human right to be cared for by their parents if that is their family's choice.[21]

The pastoral letter's policy recommendations include two trajectories. First, the bishops identify specific ways the policy process had produced unsatisfactory outcomes in the years immediately preceding the publication of this document. The Family Support Act of 1988, while generally reflecting a majority of the bishops' earlier welfare recommendations, nevertheless had ignored their call to reject measures that pressure mothers with young children to take paid employment outside the home. The bishops thus express concern that poor mothers will not enjoy the same level of choice in child-rearing arrangements as financially self-sufficient families.

Second, the document serves as a vehicle for the bishops to register their broader discontent with the general drift of welfare policy and public sentiment toward a more punitive stance vis-à-vis poor families headed by single mothers. The years of the George H. W. Bush administration (1989–1993) had witnessed an economic recession that caused welfare rolls to rise sharply and left many states in fiscal crisis, making it more difficult for them to devote to federally mandated welfare-to-work programs the resources necessary to empower single mothers to prepare for employment on reasonable terms. Public frustration with the costly Job Opportunity and Basic Services (JOBS) program grew, as its provision of job training and other services (spelled out in the FSA of 1988) came to be perceived as a luxury that states could not afford. In the years 1990–1992, most public discussion of how to improve the program focused on promoting more drastic measures to implement an employment strategy (giving welfare mothers fewer choices) rather than on developing an income- and service-based strategy (one that would offer these women more choices about the terms and timelines for their efforts toward self-sufficiency).[22] The bishops' expression of concern about how such trends would threaten the dignity of family life (forced reliance on fee-for-service day care is emblematic of such sharply constrained options) may indicate their prescience regarding how far the policy debate would drift in subsequent years in the direction of options they considered objectionable. By the mid-1990s, policy makers were considering replacing work incentive and preparation with a system of strict and mandatory work enforcement.

DOCUMENTS OF THE U.S. CATHOLIC CHURCH ON
WELFARE REFORM: 1994–96

As the nation braced for the contentious welfare debate of the middle 1990s, concern about the policy outcome rippled through the Catholic community. Alongside the Bishops' Conference, the national offices of Catholic Charities decided to speak out. Early in 1994, Catholic Charities USA released an eighteen-page position paper titled *Transforming the Welfare System*.[23] It was commissioned by the Social Policy Committee of Catholic Charities USA and drafted by the dozen members of an ad hoc AFDC work group.

A word about Catholic Charities USA and its relationship to the Bishops' Conference is necessary. Although Catholic Charities USA is a nonprofit organization that is formally and juridically independent of the Bishops' Conference, it nevertheless maintains a close working relationship with the bishops, since it represents the Catholic Church as its national network of social service agencies.[24] Because of these organizational ties and the similarity of the policy recommendations of these two groups, it is advisable to treat their welfare reform statements together.

The most substantial document on welfare reform published by the Bishops' Conference is a statement titled "Moral Principles and Policy Priorities on Welfare Reform."[25] Because it was approved by the bishops at a meeting of the administrative board of the USCC in March 1995, fourteen months after the publication of the Catholic Charities USA document, it has the advantage of being able to respond to the events of the intervening months. These include the announcement of the Clinton welfare reform proposal, the unveiling of the Republicans' "Contract with America," the November 1994 electoral victory and new congressional majorities of the Gingrich-led Republicans, and the early success of the Personal Responsibility Act, the initial version of which had already passed in the House of Representatives.

A number of subsequent documents, briefings, and letters from individual bishops, groups of bishops, or USCC offices advance the arguments contained in the March 1995 statement, but none substantially deviates from its basic message. These later documents generally repeat, apply, and update the arguments of the major statement upon which they obviously draw. A careful perusal of both public and internal documents emanating from the Bishops' Conference during the tumultuous months of welfare reform debate in 1995–96 confirms the consistency of the message articulated by these Catholic leaders during this turning point for U.S. social policy.[26] The bishops made strenuous efforts to stay on message during these pivotal months.

The core of the bishops' message is evident from the very outline of "Moral Principles and Policy Priorities on Welfare Reform." The document begins with a brief contextualization of the welfare reform debate and a reminder of the urgency and potential consequences of policy deliberations on welfare. It then establishes the bishops' reason for writing: "Our purpose is not to make any partisan point, but to share our principles and experience in hopes they will help lift up the moral dimensions and human consequences of this debate."[27] Quickly, the document introduces a series of six concerns that provide both a checklist for future political action on the issue and an outline for the remainder of the document:

> We will advocate for welfare reform which:
>
> A. Protects Human Life and Dignity;
>
> B. Strengthens Family Life;
>
> C. Encourages and Rewards Work;
>
> D. Preserves a Safety Net for the Vulnerable;
>
> E. Builds Public/Private Partnerships to Overcome Poverty; [and]
>
> F. Invests in Human Dignity.[28]

Rather than simply rehearsing point by point the claims and appeals of this document (or the other Bishops' Conference literature that repeats and echoes its concerns), the final section of this chapter distills the bishops' recommendations into five propositions. Each of the five represents not only an interpretation of part of the bishops' specific message on welfare reform, but more broadly applies a piece of the general social wisdom contained in universal Catholic social teaching. We already encountered a cluster of such general principles for social policy when chapter 1 above introduced this list: (1) social membership must be universal; (2) make a preferential option for the poor; and (3) do not place people in impossible situations. The list of five propositions that follows constitutes a specification of those earlier, more general principles. Although in a sense they may be applied to challenges facing societies in any part of the world in any era, these guidelines appear here because they address issues that surfaced prominently in the course of recent debates over American social policy.

FIVE GUIDELINES FOR SOCIAL POLICY

By way of preliminary clarification, two potential misunderstandings regarding these five propositions must be avoided. Each involves the question of ownership. First, strictly speaking, these propositions belong solely to this author, not to the bishops or to any official instrument of Catholic social teaching. As a Catholic ethicist, I seek not to put words into the mouths of the bishops, but to tease out the premises and ethical commitments implicit in the bishops' message about welfare policy. While most of the citations in the remainder of this chapter (which lists and explains these five principles) refer to documents of the bishops or Catholic Charities USA, the interpretation remains solely mine. Second, the insights contained in these propositions are available to any policy observer, regardless of theological, ideological, or political commitment. The compatibility of these principles with the framework of Catholic social teaching by no means precludes their adoption by any other party to the discussion regarding welfare reform. Indeed, advocates for any number of causes who locate their base of support anywhere across the political spectrum may well discover resonance and felicitous overlap between these propositions and their own recommendations. The distinctiveness of the Catholic position in this instance involves perhaps more the style of and motivation for social concern than the practical conclusions that Catholic voices, official or not, might reach.

Focus on the Struggle against Poverty Itself, Not Merely against Welfare Dependency

The documents on welfare reform from Catholic sources repeatedly contend that the proper focus of social policy should be on fighting poverty, not solely on reducing welfare rolls and program costs. This claim is sharply at variance with the agenda of government budget cutting that has prevailed in recent decades. Especially as elections approach, both major parties consistently scramble to portray themselves as supporters of smaller government and practitioners of fiscal responsibility. As noted above, since the 1970s both liberals and conservatives have subscribed to a welfare-to-work agenda that appeals to the electorate's desire to encourage (and eventually even to enforce) self-sufficiency among welfare recipients. What separates this dominant perspective from that of the U.S. bishops is not differing estimations of the value of work, but rather a fundamental disagreement regarding how to balance the seemingly conflicting social goods of self-sufficiency and income security.[29] The bishops' statements repeatedly display a much greater concern that low-income families be shielded against the worst effects of poverty and material deprivation, regardless of whether these families contain a working adult whose earnings are sufficient to lift the family above the poverty line.

This difference of opinion between the bishops and the dominant discourse on welfare highlights a deeper question at stake regarding social priorities. We usually think of poverty and welfare dependency as closely related phenomena. Prevailing attitudes by and large lump them together as barely distinguishable. If welfare rolls and expenses were sharply curtailed, the temptation would be to declare victory over this problem, whatever the actual conditions experienced by low-income families. But the perspective of Catholic social teaching insists on a more careful practice in problem definition. This more inclusive lens employed by the U.S. bishops not only inquires into the actual outcomes for the poorest families, but consistently prioritizes their well-being. Declining levels of welfare dependency may be a desirable trend, but if it is not accompanied by progress for the former recipients, it is ultimately an illusory gain.

Awareness of the problem of poverty itself has waxed and waned on the nation's policy agenda over recent decades. The demand for remedial action against poverty resurfaces periodically but somehow proves hard to sustain for very long. For decades at a time, poverty seems to loom as nothing more than a background condition of life—something perceived as vaguely unpleasant but, in the absence of clear strategies for improvement, ultimately tolerable.[30] In the mid-1960s, at the height of the War on Poverty sponsored by President Lyndon Johnson, a firmer-than-usual commitment to insuring broad economic security for all surfaced. Suddenly, for the first time in over a generation, antipoverty efforts commanded national attention and action. Perhaps the temporary popularity of Johnson's agenda may be attributed to the skillful way in which the appealing ideal of extending equal opportunity to all was invoked as both the goal and mechanism of social progress. Since the late 1970s, however, the more narrow goal of curtailing welfare dependency has emerged in the minds of most public policy observers as more salient and appropriate, or at least as more attainable. The shift in emphasis was caused in part by a backlash against the perceived failure of expensive antipoverty programs.

Fighting poverty and reducing dependency on government benefits, then, appear as goals that are in tension with each other. Of course, there is no simple inverse relationship between these two policy objectives nor between policy measures designed to address each. In fact, Charles Murray and like-minded critics of government policies that supposedly foster intergenerational cycles of dependency argue that, in the long run, poverty will increase when dependency on welfare benefits rises. The influence of Murray's analysis on both the welfare plank of the Republicans' 1994 "Contract with America" and on the 1996 welfare law is readily apparent. Each subscribes to the social theory Murray adopted and explicated in his book, *Losing Ground: American Social Policy 1950–1980.* When government offers overly generous welfare benefits, it reduces the incentive for people to engage in efforts for self-improvement. By cushioning the effects of irresponsible behavior, welfare encourages nonwork, dropping out of school, promiscuity, and out-of-wedlock births—the very factors that cause increases in poverty. Only by radically altering the social landscape, Murray argues, particularly the prevailing expectations regarding work and self-sufficiency, can welfare reform break the back of this "poverty trap."[31]

Backers of the 1996 law defended the abrupt change in welfare policy as necessary to signal a sharp break with the failed policies of the past. They contended that only by sending an unambiguous message could government propel potential welfare recipients into the responsible work and family behaviors that constitute the only true long-term solution to the plight of America's poorest families. The authors of the legislation were convinced that they had discovered the elusive silver bullet capable of reducing both poverty and dependency simultaneously. Even as they voiced their confidence that the nation would find in these measures a long-term solution to a frustrating logjam, legislators also acknowledged the likely short-term costs of these expected gains. For example, in a statement made shortly after the passage of the 1996 law, Representative E. Clay Shaw Jr., a Florida Republican who wrote much of the welfare bill, readily indicated his awareness of how the overhaul would affect millions of families. He justified the funding cuts and the abrogation of the entitlement status of welfare with these words: "There will be a certain amount of turmoil in making these changes, and there will be some stories of hardship that tug at all our hearts. But I'm confident that many people will be helped and will take control of their lives, which otherwise would have been destroyed by a corrupt welfare system."[32]

The Catholic bishops rejected the idea that short-term pain (particularly when it is likely to be endured by children in families losing welfare benefits) could justify long-term aggregate gain, however it might be measured. Their opposition to those welfare overhaul proposals was not based on technical arguments about the size and likelihood of these projected eventual improvements in poverty indices. Rather, their objections to this type of welfare policy were more ethical than macroeconomic in nature. Any strategy that not only tolerates, but actually relies for its success upon severe deprivations for a portion of the population is morally unacceptable. The bishops' documents express strong disapproval of the drift of policy away from its former income-maintenance goals. As the earlier emphasis on antipoverty efforts was eclipsed by a new strategy featuring antidependency measures almost exclusively, low-income families were forced to endure intolerable burdens. Even if the harsh employment strategy proves in the long run to be the coveted silver bullet that brings down poverty and dependency simultaneously, the bishops still deem it unacceptable to rely on policies that are sure to cause such severe hardships, even if only temporarily. Especially in the absence of new public commitments of resources for work preparation and job placement for those who run up against the time limits and work requirements, the bishops find it impossible to justify the way the 1996 welfare law forced poor families into desperate situations.[33]

Acknowledge Insuperable Barriers to Employment Where They Exist
The bishops are eager to communicate a pro-work message, but unlike supporters of the 1996 welfare law, they also take pains to recognize that work is not always a feasible or desirable solution to every family's income needs. Sound policy is sensitive to whether a given family contains an adult who may reasonably be expected to hold a full-time paid work position. The following lines from "Moral Principles and Policy Priorities on Welfare Reform" illustrate particularly well the dual track the bishops suggest for how social policy should interact with these families:

> Those who can work ought to work. Employment is the expected means to support a family and make a contribution to the common good. . . . Real reform will offer education, training and transitional help to those who exchange a welfare check for a paycheck. The challenge is to ensure that reform leads to productive work with wages and benefits that permit a family to live in dignity. Rigid rules and arbitrary time lines are no substitute for real jobs at decent wages and the tax policies which can help keep families off welfare.
>
> For those who cannot work, or whose "work" is raising our youngest children, the nation has built a system of income, nutrition and other supports. Society has a responsibility to help meet the needs of those who cannot care for themselves, especially young children.[34]

In drawing a distinction between these two groups, the bishops' analysis begs the question: What are the relevant factors in determining whether (and how much) work should be expected of a given single mother? While the bishops raise the question, only in the longer Catholic Charities USA document, *Transforming the Welfare System*, is a detailed treatment of this issue offered. Here we find an acknowledgment of a crucial but often overlooked aspect of the welfare issue: the need to disaggregate the welfare caseload into distinct varieties of people and demonstrable patterns of welfare use. Reflecting on the then-current profile of program use, the authors of that 1994 document note that "AFDC recipients can be divided into recognizable groups," one of which consists of the approximately "30% who are chronic or persistent users. Many of these long-term users have severe learning disabilities or serious health problems. Policies or programs of intervention must take into account the differences."[35]

A major advantage of the approach of these Catholic voices is a willingness to consider some welfare recipients as unlikely candidates (at least in the short term) to become independent workers. Catholic Charities USA and the bishops reach this conclusion via two routes. One is through their retrieval of the traditional family life themes found in Catholic social teaching, the documents of which reserve a special place for the role of the mother in the early childhood of her offspring. From this intellectual inheritance the bishops find support for the idea that mothers in this position ought to enjoy the option of choosing to make their social contribution exclusively in the home (rather than through paid employment) during this period of their lives.[36] Welfare reform, they conclude, should be informed by an awareness that there are other parenting responsibilities besides breadwinning. Legislation that disregards the necessity and value of homemaking and child-rearing tasks trivializes this type of work and dishonors those who contribute to social well-being by performing it.

The second route to the conclusion that not all welfare mothers are easily converted into independent jobholders involves paying attention to the data regarding the phenomenon of welfare cycling. Careful studies of welfare recidivism and "spell dynamics" conducted during the early 1990s by researchers Mary Jo Bane and David T. Ellwood revealed that a substantial percentage of welfare recipients at that time were neither simply long-termers nor short-termers.[37] Rather, many single mothers were attempting to make "work exits" from welfare, but despite their best efforts at boosting their earnings, they were periodically forced by circumstances back onto the public assistance rolls.[38] These data documenting how hard it was to "make work exits stick" suggested to many critics of the 1996 reforms that the work-based system was doomed to fail, leaving many vulnerable families in dire straits. These studies demonstrated to their satisfaction that it was unrealistic to expect labor markets entirely to replace benefit programs as a reliable source of income for all families that previously depended upon welfare on a steady, or at least periodic, basis. The prospects of these single mothers in labor markets were simply too precarious to expect a work-based system to function adequately.

Besides the logistical and financial difficulties associated with their child care responsibilities, this population of single mothers disproportionately experiences a host of personal problems, low attainment levels of work skills and life skills, and other difficulties that limit their marketability to employers. In order to succeed in the job market, many welfare recipients need to overcome a range of disabilities—whether physical, emotional, or educational in nature—any one of which may constitute a significant impediment to holding a job on a sustainable basis. New data about these barriers to successful employment continue to appear.[39] Such barriers to employment render these single parents less likely to be hired initially, to maintain steady employment, and to be promoted into jobs that can support their families without the need for further assistance. The effects of these constraints and disadvantages show up in statistical data that indicate the high likelihood that welfare recipients will cycle back into dependency when their efforts to move from welfare to work run up against these barriers. The imposition of time limits and sanctions in the 1996 welfare reform law sharply curtails these options for support when employment is not meeting the needs of such hard-pressed families.

In replacing the previous income maintenance strategy with a nearly exceptionless work strategy as the answer to the problem of welfare dependency, the 1996 law operates on the questionable assumption that success in labor markets is entirely a function of moral will. It dismisses researchers' hard-won demonstration of the complexities of deep-seated barriers to employment in favor of a simple model in which labor effort translates readily and immediately into workplace success. Since they commit no new resources to training and education, the terms of the 1996 law indicate a further assumption that the nonwork behavior of most members of this group is easily remediable, requiring no more human capital than is already possessed by these single mothers. The bishops criticize these aspects of the legislation, pointing out its failure to recognize the many complex factors that account for the great variability of earning potential among welfare mothers. In place of the law's rigid requirements, the bishops call for "incentives [that] should be tailored to a particular family's needs and circumstances, not 'one size fits all' requirements."[40] Similarly, Catholic Charities USA affirms the "recognition that AFDC recipients are a heterogeneous population," so it is inevitable that the best approach is one that addresses members "of this population according to their differing needs and focus[es] on investing in families."[41]

Recall that these documents from Catholic sources were published over a year before the eventual version of the 1996 welfare bill was finalized. For that reason, they are obviously unable to comment extensively on program details and specifics of the legislation. Rather, their enduring value lies in how they analyze basic policy directions and critique them from the ethical perspective of the tradition of Catholic social thought. In this brief section, we have noted how the thrust of the law's reliance on a work solution to welfare is at variance with the Catholic approach. While work is unambiguously an important social good, the documents criticize the approach of the welfare reformers for relying so single-mindedly on paid labor as a solution to the problems of low-income families.

Supporting work is only one of several legitimate goals of social policy. Any welfare system that ignores other social objectives, such as promoting healthy family life and providing income security for those in distress, ignores the distinctive needs and features of the welfare population. An adequate consideration of these factors reveals three truths: (1) for some welfare mothers, work is impossible; (2) for others, the costs of work (measured in both personal and social terms) outweigh the benefits; and (3) where work is feasible, it must be supported by investments in human capital, such as government-sponsored job preparation programs. To overlook these important aspects of the welfare question is to run the risk of punishing poor families for failing to deliver what they simply cannot achieve. The bishops forthrightly express their fear that pursuing such a policy strategy turns the war against poverty into a war against the poor.

Respect Certain Absolute Moral Prohibitions for Policy

One of the strengths of Catholic social teaching, as we saw in chapter 1, is its explicit awareness of the various levels at which moral reasoning proceeds. Documents in this tradition are quick to distinguish between core principles that are always central and relevant to the ethical task, on one hand, and the prudential judgments that pertain to specific applications of moral directives in actual circumstances, on the other hand. Our highest moral aspirations sometimes require compromise and accommodation amidst the messiness of policy deliberations, especially when they play themselves out in a situation of moral and social pluralism and unsure outcomes. As a result, the church recognizes that a variety of opinions may often be held and a diversity of strategies may be pursued by people of good will faced with difficult policy decisions. An appealing feature of Catholic social thought is the way it combines a seriousness about preserving absolute moral values with a prudential flexibility regarding decisions in the rough-and-tumble world of public policy.

Aspects of the welfare reform debate, however, prompted Catholic voices to resort on occasion to rather solemn pronouncements concerning firm limits in what is morally acceptable in this area of policy. Certain phrases the bishops use in "Moral Principles and Policy Priorities on Welfare Reform" suggest the invocation of absolute moral imperatives (especially concerning the policy goal of guaranteeing the well-being of children) as a justification for their policy recommendations. We need not read too creatively between the lines to detect this style of moral appeal. The bishops call for the preservation of "the federal government's role and responsibilities in fighting poverty." This task includes "provid[ing] an essential safety net for vulnerable children" and continuing "entitlement programs which provide essential supports for poor children."[42] The document introduces these positions collectively as "a matter of moral consistency."[43]

Similarly, the Catholic Charities USA document alludes to a set of solemn moral imperatives that rightly constrain public policy. It does not hesitate to use the language of "should," "must," and "basic obligations," especially when it treats the topic of children's welfare. Two statements from *Transforming the Welfare System* are emblematic of this approach: (1) "Investing in our children and their families is fundamental to the well-being of society and constitutes a basic obligation of each citizen and the state"; and (2) "The purpose of public policy is to enable all people to live with dignity."[44]

Although neither document (nor the other welfare reform statements from official Catholic sources described above) employs the technical ethical terminology of "deontological constraints" or "absolute moral prohibitions," it is clear nevertheless that the authors of these documents consider certain options for social policy strictly off-limits. For example, regarding the issue of family caps and teenage mother exclusions (two of the conservative mandates that the 1996 law eventually permitted states to adopt, although did not require), the bishops could not have been firmer in their opposition.[45] They cite the potential harm these measures might cause to innocent children, both those who might be aborted because of new financial incentives to limit family size and those whose families will be deprived of welfare benefits because of such policy innovations. The bishops judge these measures intolerable. No attempt to justify them in terms of eventual social benefits could ever conceivably override these stern moral objections to the deleterious short-term impact of such policies. Social policy strategies that directly or indirectly cause harm to an already disadvantaged segment of the population are not reconcilable with Catholic social principles such as the preferential option for the poor. Putting children at greater risk of victimhood to abortion or severe deprivation runs counter to our solemn duties to protect innocent life, no matter what eventual benefits might accrue to taxpayers or members of future generations.

The bishops see wise social policy as being constrained by a prohibition against harming poor children, or even against serving as an accomplice in situations where innocent children are placed at risk by the irresponsible behavior of their parents. Catholic Charities USA laments the unfortunate fact that, when children "are victims of their parents' choices . . . , all society can do is to protect and nurture the children."[46] In the absence of a culturally acceptable and financially feasible way to separate children from their irresponsible parents, the Catholic documents call for the continuation of the principle of categorical entitlement to welfare benefits. While they have sometimes been misused by parents who rely upon them as something other than as a last resort, reliable income maintenance measures are the only way to guarantee protection against dire poverty for all America's children, regardless of the conditions of their birth.

Recent U.S. policy debates have emphasized what is wrong with entitlements, particularly the risk of introducing perverse incentives and signaling permissiveness on the part of a government that has been faulted for asking too little of poor families. These Catholic documents, conversely, issue a reminder of what is right about recognizing entitlements. To abandon the child-protecting role that entitlements have played during six decades of

American social policy is to violate a moral prohibition against damaging the life prospects of children in low-income families.

So far, this section has focused on regard for children, born and unborn, as a key source of moral concern about the 1996 welfare law. These documents also defend the principle that single mothers themselves should be considered among the deserving poor. Although less obviously than is the case with children, this is a population whose special situation commends its members as worthy recipients of special assistance. There are more reasons to favor income support for low-income mothers than the truth contained in the maxim that "it is impossible to assist children without helping their entire family." The bishops recognize a host of factors that might prevent a given single mother from finding and retaining a job that might lift her family into financial independence. Even though more and more women are succeeding in labor markets once closed or hostile to them, sound policy recognizes the formidable barriers to adequate employment, already mentioned in the previous section, facing this particular demographic group. To lay the blame for persistent poverty upon the supposed irresponsibility or low work motivation of single mothers of young children is to ignore the genuine reasons for the struggles these women daily face.

For public policy to restrict sharply single mothers' eligibility for benefits through sanctions and time limits is objectionable from the standpoint of Catholic social teaching. As these documents argue, such policies threaten to place single mothers and their children in impossible situations, at the mercy of economic forces beyond their control. Particularly in the absence of new job opportunities or adequate resources to support the increased work effort it requires of single mothers, the 1996 welfare law violates standards of social justice by exposing millions of vulnerable women and children to new financial burdens, income insecurity, and serious personal risk.

Recognize "Carrots and Sticks" without Subscribing to a Reductionist View of the Human Person

Catholic social teaching in general, and recent church statements on welfare reform in particular, display a "both-and" style of thinking that balances two sets of concerns. On the one hand, public policy should be realistic, taking into account the effects of human selfishness and calculating prudent responses to the possibility of abuse. Within the context of social policy, such concessions to the inevitable human condition of sinfulness must be carefully crafted so that the interaction of programs and people is suitably calibrated. It is necessary for legislators to build into public laws acceptable incentive structures that encourage responsible behavior through the operation of rewards and sanctions.

On the other hand, good policy respects the complexities of human subjecthood and the transcendent character of human persons. As free and spiritual beings, humans are never to be treated merely as objects to be manipulated. When chapter 1 above investigated this aspect of Catholic moral anthropology, it revealed Catholic social teaching's consistent opposition to various versions of reductionism (materialism, scientific behaviorism, economism), especially in the encyclicals of Pope John Paul II. Each version of reductionism violates human dignity by treating persons in ways that ignore their spiritual dimension and disregard their aspirations for goods that transcend the material.

The tension between these two poles of policy analysis is readily apparent in the U.S. Catholic Church's statements on federal welfare reform. Particularly in the two major documents on this topic, there is a careful interplay of what is predictable and what is indeterminate about human behavior. At one pole, the documents recommend practical measures to restructure welfare program incentives in order to encourage better outcomes. Each document repeatedly appeals to the principles, namely responsibility and accountability, that should be more consistently encoded into program rules and structures. These two words become shorthand expressions of the Catholic officials' support for a strategy of implementing "carrots and sticks" in a more effective and rational way. The bishops in particular accord the principle of reciprocity a prominent place in their welfare recommendations. In fact, they explicitly state that their welfare project is one of "proposing alternatives that provide assistance in ways that safeguard children but do not reinforce inappropriate or morally destructive behavior."[47]

The bishops also volunteer an opinion on the sensitive matter of the proper balance of carrots and sticks: "Genuine welfare reform should rely on incentives more than harsh penalties."[48] Catholic Charities USA presents a more detailed description of desirable incentive structures in welfare programs. Its document, *Transforming the Welfare System*, includes several recommendations for changing programs in order to "make work pay." These include revising the formulas for "earnings disregards" and "asset standards" that help determine eligibility for welfare benefits and better coordinating welfare with an expanded Earned Income Tax Credit (EITC).[49] The penultimate paragraph of the document appeals for an improved incentive structure: "We must be willing to build into our welfare system responsibility and accountability on the part of both the recipient and the giver of public assistance."[50]

However, at the other pole of this policy analysis, it is wise to recall that the analogy of carrots and sticks is based on the handling of beasts of burden and does not provide entirely appropriate guidance for considering the complexities of human behavior. In the interest of promoting human dignity, we must not portray people as if they are the equivalent of mules nor fashion policies that treat them as little more than brutes. Accordingly, these Catholic documents nowhere claim that measures to revise program incentives exhaust all the goals of welfare reform or respond to all the diverse needs of America's poor families. Because the participants in the program are human persons, whose lives are marked by freedom and complexity, no regime of monetary incentives can account for all the values at stake in social assistance. Nor should any attempt at behavior modification be expected to succeed in exerting some crass form of control over the personal decisions of low-income people. Families make their decisions regarding work, marriage, child-bearing, and relocating on the basis of many factors, not all of them quantifiable and predictable in terms of monetary or material incentives. Sound policy recognizes that people act for a variety of reasons that transcend financial payoffs, including intangible motives bound up with personal aspirations and preferences, the desire to strike the most fulfilling balance between paid employment and home life, and even fundamental priorities such as the yearning to spend quality time with one's young children.

To subscribe uncritically to the cynical maxim that "society witnesses more of whatever behavior government subsidizes" is to adopt an unduly mechanistic view of human nature. Focusing all of our welfare reform energies on revising incentive structures to discourage dependency and encourage work effort risks employing a simplistic version of rational-choice theory as a mask for condescending to welfare recipients. This demeans the aspirations of program recipients for a better life than welfare could ever offer.[51] Single mothers who rely on public assistance are thus treated as if they operate according to a different (and far simpler) mode of rationality than other members of society, for whom monetary rewards presumably do not completely determine day-to-day behavior, much less life-shaping decisions.

The bishops register their protest against this brand of reductionism in such repeated calls for flexibility in program standards as this: "Increased accountability and incentives should be tailored to a particular family's needs and circumstances, not 'one size fits all' requirements. Top-down reform with rigid national rules cannot meet the needs of a population as diverse as poor families."[52]

Catholic Charities USA incorporates similar insights into its welfare document, in a section labeled "Tailor Investments to Families":

> A significant shift in the philosophy underlying AFDC is critical. We must move from maintaining families at a subsistence level to tailored investing in families. This means moving from scrutinizing eligibility and qualification requirements to becoming partners with beneficiaries. . . .
>
> Assistance providers must be retrained to become partners who respond to recipients in culturally appropriate ways. . . . A contract must be forged to specify the responsibilities of both the recipient and the agency providing assistance and make them both accountable for results.[53]

This proposal, in emphasizing direct personal contact and individualized sets of expectations, implicitly passes judgment upon bureaucracies that, without supplementation, are incapable of treating people in ways that respect and enhance their dignity. This does not constitute a reason to abandon all hope, as do certain observers such as Marvin Olasky, that public assistance programs can play a constructive role in the lives of poor families. Rather, it offers a chastening reminder (one very much in line with the Catholic principle of subsidiarity) of the limits of rule-bound government bureaucracies.

Like any regulations, incentive clauses in welfare program rules may be good servants but are invariably "bad masters." In other words, while it may be wise to employ such incentives, policymakers should not allow a reductionist perspective to control the entire agenda of how laws and people interact. Certainly, welfare reform, present and future, should improve the implementation of carrots and sticks so that program rules better reflect our shared values regarding family and work. However, in accord with the Catholic Church's insistence upon respecting human transcendence, an overemphasis on tinkering with financial incentives in social policy must be avoided, for it runs the risk of encoding in law a crass reductionism. To expect an overly tight correlation between material incentives and behavioral outcomes not only invites policy failure, but also risks riding roughshod over such normative values as human dignity and individual freedom.

Avoid Fostering the Demonization or Marginalization of Recipients of Public Assistance

These documents from American Catholic leaders challenge lawmakers to adopt policies that invite welfare recipients further into the mainstream of society, rather than allowing them to be excluded. In so doing, they echo key principles of the social teaching of the universal church: the preferential option for the poor; the full recognition of human dignity; equal social participation of all; a consistent concern for social cohesion; solidarity; and universal social membership. In fact, the bishops' major 1995 document on welfare reform makes explicit mention of "an option for the poor," "solidarity with the poor and vulnerable," and the "call to participation."[54] In seeking to dispel the notion that the welfare poor are in any way to be regarded as a deviant subpopulation separated from the rest of society by virtue of supposedly distinctive pathologies, the bishops offer a caveat that highlights the disturbing prevalence of deep social problems throughout U.S. society, not just among our poorest families:

> Children thrown from windows, found in dumpsters, and abused in their homes are tragic symptoms of culture in disarray and a welfare system in urgent need of real reforms. It is worth noting that it is not just low-income families that sometimes engage in destructive behavior. Personal irresponsibility, family disintegration, and loss of moral values touches not just the "down and out," but also the "rich and famous" and the rest of us.[55]

This reminder is very much in line with the recent scholarship of ethicist Julia Fleming, who finds in Catholic social teaching the seeds for a renewed commitment to protecting the good name of all people, especially the disadvantaged.[56] As individuals and as identifiable demographic groups, low-income people struggle to defend their right to a good reputation, free from unfair charges that denigrate and malign them. All members of society, as part of the preferential option for the poor to which we are called, have an obligation to elevate the social status of poor families. By extension, the public policies we support must also advance this imperative. Of course, the issues pertaining to marginalization and demonization are often quite subtle. A given policy proposal or the social theory behind it seldom explicitly advocates the further stigmatization of recipients.[57] However, in the absence of deliberate efforts to foster greater inclusion of low-income families in the mainstream of society, social programs tend (even if inadvertently) to isolate recipients. They may come to serve as a wedge dividing a "deserving us" from an "undeserving them." Every child who cringes in fear of peer ridicule when queuing up for a free breakfast before school or when furtively flashing a pass to receive a subsidized school lunch well knows the meaning of stigmatization. In assessing the ways means-tested programs contribute to stigma, the "how" of program administration and public perception is often as important as "what" assistance is actually being offered. As the bishops urge: "We must resist the temptation to see poor women, minority families, or immigrants as either passive victims or easy scapegoats for our society's social and economic difficulties."[58]

The Catholic Charities USA statement addresses head-on the question of how much progress can realistically be expected toward the goal of empowering low-income single parents and their children to achieve a place in the mainstream of society. The document lists the numerous barriers to economic success faced by this diverse group and then enumerates ten social conditions that must be addressed before eventual success could be completed.[59] Against this backdrop of daunting challenges, it then identifies this goal for welfare policy in the short term: "to help these people obtain an adequate level of financial and social stability in an interdependent society."[60] This modest goal corresponds to the document's earlier description of what constitutes an adequate condition for social life: "Human dignity is reflected in one's ability to live life manifesting a healthy balance between autonomy and interdependence."[61]

Like the bishops, Catholic Charities USA does not imagine that the welfare population will quickly and easily achieve complete financial independence. Rather, it reflects a sober recognition of the need for a continuation of substantial assistance to poor families. Mirroring the bishops' position, Catholic Charities USA advocates re-envisioning this assistance as "tailored investments in families," not just as means of subsistence that society grudgingly doles out in highly stigmatized poor relief efforts. If the approach we take amounts to nothing more than warehousing people, public policy has failed all of us. Both documents propose reframing welfare as part of a social contract in which government as well as the private sector become partners with recipients.[62]

If complete and immediate financial independence is not to be expected for our poorest families even according to the rosiest scenario of wise policy choices combined with favorable social and economic conditions, then these struggling families may at least hope for a diminution of stigma and social marginalization. The bishops venture the hope that by emphasizing the triad of "hope, opportunity and investment [that] are essential to the transition" from welfare to work, the "othering" of the welfare poor by those who distrust them and their motives may be curtailed.[63] Catholic Charities USA looks forward to a day when a revised message will accompany a welfare check. Instead of being an occasion for the communication of stigma-laden suspicion, the granting of assistance will be perceived in this more constructive way:

> The community makes a fitting investment in a family. This says to a family: "We believe in you. We believe you can succeed and we are here to help you do so." In turn, the recipient says to the community, "Thank you for investing in me and my children. I will do all I can to make sure this investment pays off for us and for the community."[64]

In thus emphasizing mutual gains and enhanced accountability, this approach to welfare reduces stigma by treating recipients in ways more in accord with the standards of the mainstream of society, although still within the parameters of realistic expectations about the earning potential of single mothers. If welfare is to serve as a bridge into the social mainstream, a first step must consist of altering programs and their perception so that they reduce the social distance between recipients and the rest of the population.

We will return to the topic of public church contributions to social policy debates in chapter 6, updating this coverage to account for the events of the past decade. The Catholic bishops and other Church-based groups made their voices heard when the welfare law of 1996 was due to be reauthorized. In reprising their role as advocates for a more compassionate welfare policy, these religious voices addressed their task with a mixture of hope and resignation. Obviously, the recommendations of the bishops and like-minded spokespersons of religious social concern for the poor did not carry the day in the mid-1990s. The welfare overhaul was carried out over their strenuous objections and despite their vocal support for alternative courses of action. Over the subsequent decade, none of them expected a sharp reversal of any of the major elements of the 1996 overhaul: the block-granting of welfare; the imposition of time limits; work requirements; and the whole array of sanctions and cutbacks in social services. But they did maintain a high profile, daring to hope that they would receive a fair hearing for their suggestions for improving the welfare system. While the debate over welfare reform in 1995–96 yielded few tangible results as far as actual influence on the outcomes of policy debates, the religious community continued subsequently to serve as a voice of conscience informing our nation's social policy.

In the case of the Catholic Bishops' Conference, the contribution to public discourse continues to be guided by an agenda that defies easy categorization as either politically conservative or liberal in conventional ways. Rather, the welfare policy message presented by these Catholic voices reflects distinctive religious concerns about healthy family life, parenting priorities, and social justice. These themes, like the five more specific propositions examined in this chapter, are drawn from the rich tradition of Catholic social teaching and will surely continue to shape the policy advocacy of Catholic leaders in future social policy deliberations.

NOTES

1. The current name, USCCB, is the successor to several other titles (noted in chapter 1) used for this body over the past century. The latest name change came in 2001 when the bishops ceased using separate titles for the actual assembly of bishops (since the 1960s it had been called the National Conference of Catholic Bishops, or NCCB) and the nonprofit professional agency serving the U.S. bishops (it had been called the United States Catholic Conference, or USCC). Since this recent reorganization, the USCCB (or its commonly used shorthand name, the Bishops' Conference) refers to both the assembly of bishops itself and the various offices and departments that constitute the permanent staff serving the bishops. To avoid anachronism, this chapter uses titles in effect at the time of events and publications treated herein.
2. Abundant information about this department, its staffing, and its projects is readily available at http://usccb.org/sdwp.
3. U.S. Bishops, *Economic Justice for All* (Washington, DC: USCC Office of Publishing and Promotion Services, 1986), 210.
4. Ibid., 211.
5. Ibid.
6. Ibid.
7. The recommendations of several such studies are summarized in a report of the Working Seminar on Family and American Welfare Policy, sponsored by the Institute for Family Studies at Marquette University. The institute's volume, *The New Consensus on Family and Welfare,* was published simultaneously by Marquette University in Milwaukee and the American Enterprise Institute for Public Policy Research in Washington, D.C., in 1987. The study's ten policy recommendations, drawn from the findings of several earlier commissions on welfare, are much more moderate than the welfare recommendations contained, for example, in the Republicans' "Contract with America," written eight years later.
8. Philip S. Land, SJ, *Shaping Welfare Consensus: U.S. Catholic Bishops' Contribution* (Washington, DC: Center of Concern, 1988), 157.
9. Ibid., 145–51, 171–84.
10. Statistics appear in Jack P. Shonkoff, "Connecting the Dots for Poor Children," *Boston Globe,* July 24, 2003, A11. In this op-ed column published amidst the debate over the reauthorization of TANF, the author, the dean of the Heller

School for Social Policy and Management at Brandeis University, cites the findings of medical and behavioral studies of child development to argue against the
adoption of stricter work requirements for new mothers.

11. U.S. Bishops, *Economic Justice for All,* 297.
12. Ibid., 18.
13. Ibid., 206.
14. *Quadragesimo anno,* 71.
15. *Gaudium et spes,* 67; Pope John Paul II, *Familiaris Consortio: Papal Exhorta-
    tion on the Family* (Washington, DC: USCC Office of Publishing and Promotion
    Services, 1981), nos. 23, 81.
16. Here in *Laborem exercens,* 19, the family wage is described as "a single salary,
    given to the head of the family for his work, sufficient for the needs of the fam-
    ily without the other spouse having to take up gainful employment outside the
    home." Interestingly, the original Latin text leaves the gender of the parents
    playing each of the roles of breadwinner and homemaker indeterminate.
17. Ibid., 19.
18. "Introduction" to Holy See of the Roman Catholic Church, "Charter of the
    Rights of the Family." See *Origins* 13, no. 27 (December 15, 1983): 461.
19. Ibid., 461.
20. Ibid., 463.
21. United States Catholic Conference, *Putting Children and Families First: The
    Challenge for Our Church, Nation and World* (Washington, DC: USCC Office
    of Publishing and Promotion Services, 1992), 10.
22. On these alternative strategies and the history (up to 1994) of the welfare pro-
    grams that implemented them, see Rebecca M. Blank, "The Employment Strat-
    egy: Public Policies to Increase Work and Earnings," in *Confronting Poverty:
    Prescriptions for Change,* ed. Sheldon Danziger, Gary D. Sandefur and Daniel
    H. Weinberg (Cambridge, MA: Harvard University Press, 1994), 168–204.
23. Catholic Charities USA, *Transforming the Welfare System: A Position Paper of
    Catholic Charities USA* (Alexandria, VA: Catholic Charities USA, January 24,
    1994).
24. The website www.catholiccharitiesusa.org contains abundant information about
    this organization, which constitutes the nation's largest private network of vol-
    untary social service agencies. Its national office in Alexandria, Virginia, coor-
    dinates the network of over 1,600 affiliates or branch agencies and engages in
    lobbying and advocacy in Washington, D.C.
25. United States Catholic Conference, "Moral Principles and Policy Priorities on
    Welfare Reform: A Statement of the Administrative Board of the United States
    Catholic Conference," *Origins* 24, no. 41 (March 30, 1995): 673–77. It was
    originally published by the USCC on March 19, 1995 as a stand-alone work,
    but the page numbers of the more readily available *Origins* version will be ref-
    erenced below.
26. Individually and collectively, the bishops sent dozens of letters to policy makers
    during these months, urging them to implement principled approaches to wel-
    fare reform and to adopt policies that would protect the poor and vulnerable,
    including the unborn. At the time, the USCC Department of Communications
    publicized many of these through a series of press releases. The texts of several
    of these letters were subsequently published in *Origins,* the documentary news
    service of the Bishops' Conference. For example, a February 16, 1995 letter from

the Catholic bishops of Florida to elected officials in that state appeared as "Promoting Meaningful Welfare Reform" in *Origins* 24, no. 37 (March 2, 1995): 609–12. A long January 13, 1995 letter from Bishop John Ricard of Baltimore, in his capacity as chairman of the USSC Domestic Policy Committee, to members of the House and Senate and officials of the federal Department of Health and Human Services, appears as "Factors of Genuine Welfare Reform" in *Origins* 24, no. 34 (February 9, 1995): 564–66. Similar messages about the dangers of a punitive version of welfare reform were folded into several documents routinely published by the Bishops' Conference. One such regular statement was the annual Labor Day Message; see "A Shifting, Churning Economy" in *Origins* 25, no. 12 (September 7, 1995): 199–200. Another was the bishops' quadrennial "Statement on Political Responsibility"; see the paragraphs treating welfare reform and family life that appear in the text of the 1995 statement appearing in *Origins* 25, no. 22 (November 16, 1995): 369, 371–83. The same points are repeatedly covered in internal memoranda of the USCC shared (by means of bimonthly mass mailings, subsequently replaced by electronic bulletins and website postings at www.usccb.org/sdwp) with affiliates such as diocesan offices of peace and justice. A large number of backgrounders, policy updates, and action alerts on welfare reform appeared during 1995–96. For further information on these categories of documents from the Bishops' Conference, see Thomas Massaro, SJ, *Catholic Social Teaching and United States Welfare Reform* (Collegeville, MN: Liturgical Press, 1998), 146–49.

27. United States Catholic Conference, "Moral Principles and Policy Priorities on Welfare Reform," 675.

28. Ibid., 675–77.

29. All the documents from the Bishops' Conference surveyed in the above section are unambiguously pro-work. The bishops' statements never deny that the welfare system as it existed before 1996 needed to be reformed so that it would better support and encourage employment. One of the six featured recommendations of the United States Catholic Conference's "Moral Principles and Policy Priorities on Welfare Reform" is "to encourage and reward work" since "those who can work ought to work" (676). The distinctive concerns of the bishops come to the fore when they interpret that call for work as necessarily including a variety of supports to make the work activity of single parents beneficial and sustainable (through the provision of day care, fair terms of employment, and income supplementation when necessary to lift a family above the poverty line).

30. The political scientist John W. Kingdon introduces an illuminating distinction between the terms "problem" and "condition" in just this way in his influential volume, *Agendas, Alternatives and Public Policies* (New York: HarperCollins Publishers, 1984), chap. 5.

31. Murray, *Losing Ground*, esp. part 4.

32. Quoted in Robert Pear, "Actions by States Hold Keys to Welfare Law's Future," *New York Times*, October 1, 1996, A22. At the time, Shaw served as chair of the Human Resources Subcommittee of the House Ways and Means Committee.

33. United States Catholic Conference, "Moral Principles and Policy Priorities on Welfare Reform," 676. The section titled "Preserves a Safety Net for the Vulnerable" includes the complaint: "We cannot support reform that destroys the structures, ends entitlements and eliminates resources that have provided an essential

safety net for vulnerable children or permits states to reduce their commitment in this area."

34. Ibid.

35. Catholic Charities USA, "Transforming the Welfare System," 7.

36. Not explicitly mentioned in these documents is the possibility that it could be the father who chooses to forego paid employment to exercise the function of primary nurturer of the family's children. Although it is admirable to advert to this contingency in the interest of addressing gender asymmetries, this is unfortunately not often a viable option, since the vast majority of welfare families feature nonresident fathers. Households headed by a single mother generally must rely on day care for preschoolers if the mother takes on paid employment.

37. See Bane and Ellwood's coauthored volume, *Welfare Realities: From Rhetoric to Reform* (Cambridge, MA: Harvard University Press, 1994), esp. chaps. 2 ("Understanding Welfare Dynamics") and 3 ("Understanding Dependency"). No study of comparable substance has been published since the 1996 overhaul, but census data suggest the persistence of many of the same dynamics regarding the need for income assistance by this same population. However, under new program rules featuring time limits and many categories of sanctions, benefits are obviously not available to many who would previously have applied for and collected them.

38. Ellwood estimates that only 40 percent of women leaving welfare at that time actually earned their way off the rolls. Since barriers to work are so prevalent, he reflects, it is "no wonder the most common way to leave welfare permanently is via marriage, not work" (ibid., 152).

39. Besides ordinary physical and medical disabilities, welfare mothers are disproportionately affected by medical conditions that are particularly rampant in the poor neighborhoods they tend to inhabit. One such condition is chronic asthma, an ailment that often adversely affects employees' reliability and prospects for advancement. Another hindrance to steady employment is substance abuse and addiction. Joseph A. Califano Jr., a former secretary of the (then) federal Department of Health, Education and Welfare, has in recent years studied the problem extensively. In 1996 he estimated that "at least 20% of women on welfare—as many as one million mothers—have drug or alcohol problems severe enough to require treatment." Califano, "Welfare's Drug Connection," *New York Times*, August 24, 1996, 23. As his claims were confirmed by independent studies of the matter (see Joe Sexton, "Dependency's Double Edge," *New York Times*, November 9, 1997, 37), Califano continued to speak out about the grim dangers to this population of addicted welfare recipients of implementing the 1996 welfare law.

In 2002 he wrote again to express his fears that the welfare reauthorization process would exacerbate the plight of these welfare mothers affected by substance abuse and addictions, which he now claimed constituted "the bulk of the remaining caseload." Califano, "To Reform Welfare, Treat Drug Abuse," *Washington Post*, September 18, 2002, A29. Somewhat surprisingly, his plea for more generous provisions allowing this vulnerable population to participate in alcohol and drug rehabilitation programs as part of welfare reauthorization was met with a stinging rebuke two weeks later, when the *Washington Post* published a rebuttal of sorts. In this later op-ed, two academics (one a professor of public health, the other of criminology) dispute Califano's characterization of the problem and claim that his sloppy style of argumentation undermines the work of researchers at Columbia University's National Center on Addiction and Substance Abuse, the very center Califano directs. These coauthors claim that, contrary to Califano's version, "these problems appear to affect a small minority of welfare recipients" and that "this wildly overstated account reinforces false stereotypes about who is on welfare." The authors fear that "Califano's inflammatory rhetoric . . . reinforces widespread suspicions that welfare clients are beyond help and not worthy of our assistance." Harold Pollack and Peter Reuter, "Myths About Drugs and Welfare," *Washington Post*, October 1, 2002, A21. Although it remains difficult to adjudicate this sensitive debate, all parties can perhaps agree that this exchange illuminates many of the issues at stake in making generalizations regarding the behaviors and characteristics of welfare recipients.

A 1996 medical study finds that welfare mothers suffer from debilitating emotional problems (such as posttraumatic stress disorder and major depressive disorders) at much higher rates than the general female population. Regarding major depression, welfare mothers registered a lifetime incidence rate of 40 percent, compared with 21 percent for all women. See Ellen L. Bassuk et al., "The Characteristics and Needs of Sheltered Homeless and Low-Income Housed Mothers," *Journal of the American Medical Association* 276, no. 8 (August 29, 1996): 640–46. The correlation of welfare recipiency, especially long spells on public assistance rolls, with low educational attainment is well established. Urban Institute research found that 63 percent of mothers who were on the welfare rolls for five years or longer in the 1980s had not completed high school. Few women with higher education experience were on welfare. For further data, see the statistical charts accompanying "Spelling the End of Welfare as We Know It," *New York Times*, August 4, 1996, sec. 4, p. 3. The related issue of how to treat learning-disabled welfare mothers under the TANF system surfaced in 1998 when a class action suit filed in Boston petitioned the Commonwealth of Massachusetts for more lenient exemption policies for this population. Although the judicial ruling in the case refused to stop the time-limit clock for the plaintiffs who claimed the state was discriminating against them unfairly, the case publicized the plight of women in such straits. It even led a major newspaper to editorialize on the need for heightened awareness of and more sensitive policies toward welfare recipients with dyslexia; attention-deficit disorders; and other, often undiagnosed, learning disabilities (as well as more severe problems such as mental illness) as they face job markets. See Doris Sue Wong, "Suit Says Welfare Slights the Disabled," *Boston Globe*, August 12, 1998, B1, B6; Doris Sue Wong, "Learning-Disabled Welfare Recipients Lose Ruling," *Boston Globe*, August 27, 1998, E8; "Mental Illness and Welfare Reform," *Boston Globe*, September 9, 1998, A18.

The findings of some of the most recent studies on barriers to employment are summarized in Ladonna A. Pavetti, "Helping the Hard-to-Employ," in *Welfare Reform and Beyond*, ed. Isabel V. Sawhill et al., 135–42. Researchers generally divide these barriers into categories such as "human capital deficits," "logistical obstacles," and "personal and family challenges." One refreshingly original study asked five hundred welfare recipients in the San Joaquin Valley in California for their own answer to the question, "What things do you think prevent you from finding work?" The respondents' accounts appear in Michael Carley and Donna Hardina, "Going to the Source: AFDC Recipients' Perspectives on Their

Unemployment," *Journal of Poverty* 3, no. 3 (1999): 53–70. An excellent survey of possible policy responses to the multiple types of barriers to employment is Sheila R. Zedlewski and Pamela Loprest, "Will TANF Work for the Most Disadvantaged Families?" in *The New World of Welfare*, ed. Blank and Haskins, 311–34.

40. United States Catholic Conference, "Moral Principles and Policy Priorities on Welfare Reform," 675.
41. Catholic Charities USA, *Transforming the Welfare System*, 7.42. United States Catholic Conference, "Moral Principles and Policy Priorities on Welfare Reform," 676.
43. Ibid.
44. Catholic Charities USA, *Transforming the Welfare System*, 3, 4.
45. "Denying needed benefits for children born to mothers can hurt the children and pressure their mothers toward abortion and sterilization. . . . Proposals that deny benefits to children because of their mother's age or dependence on welfare. . . , whatever their intentions, are likely to encourage abortions. . . . In seeking to change the behavior of parents, these provisions hurt children, and some unborn children will pay with their lives." United States Catholic Conference, "Moral Principles and Policy Priorities on Welfare Reform," 675–76.
46. Catholic Charities USA, *Transforming the Welfare System*, 11.
47. United States Catholic Conference, "Moral Principles and Policy Priorities on Welfare Reform," 676.
48. Ibid., 675.
49. Catholic Charities USA, *Transforming the Welfare System*, 9.
50. Ibid., 12.
51. One particularly egregious example of this unfortunate proclivity is found in the welfare reform proposals in chap. 4 of Robert Rector and William F. Lauber, *America's Failed $5.4 Trillion War on Poverty* (Washington, DC: Heritage Foundation, 1995). All twelve of the "steps to genuine welfare reform" advocated therein consist of thinly veiled attempts at social engineering that proceed on the assumption that a one-to-one correlation exists between desirable human behavior and financial incentives encoded into public laws. The proposal places heavy reliance on family caps, teenage mother exclusions, strict workfare enforcement, and tax breaks for married couples as means to reduce illegitimacy, as if these "additional incentives to encourage constructive behavior" hold the potential to serve as a panacea for solving this complex social problem. (41)
52. United States Catholic Conference, "Moral Principles and Policy Priorities on Welfare Reform," 675.
53. Catholic Charities USA, *Transforming the Welfare* System, 7.
54. United States Catholic Conference, "Moral Principles and Policy Priorities on Welfare Reform," 675.
55. Ibid., 676.
56. Julia Fleming, "The Right to Reputation and the Preferential Option for the Poor," *Journal of the Society of Christian Ethics* 24, no. 1 (Spring–Summer 2004): 73–87.
57. By way of exception, Lawrence M. Mead's *The New Paternalism: Supervisory Approaches to Poverty* (Washington, DC: Brookings Institution Press, 1997) openly considers the poor to be deviant from the rest of American society. Charles Murray and like-minded supporters of further drastic reductions in so-

cial programs do not necessarily advocate this position as an anthropological claim, but it may be argued that the effects of their proposals (upon both the material conditions and public perceptions of low-income Americans) would contribute to further stigmatization and marginalization of the poor. The 1990s also witnessed frequent calls for a related notion: the revival of shame. These appeals occurred more prominently in journalistic venues such as editorial pages than in academic circles, although scholars William J. Bennett and Gertrude Himmelfarb were noteworthy promoters of such notions. Moreover, it is arguable whether making a distinction between actions worthy of shame (out-of-wedlock childbearing, drug use) and particular populations associated with shameful behavior changes the nature and intent of such discourse.

58. United States Catholic Conference, "Moral Principles and Policy Priorities on Welfare Reform," 677.

59. The ten conditions are: (1) "a vibrant economy must provide career opportunities"; (2) "all workers need a level playing field"; (3) "the educational system needs major changes"; (4) "adequate health care must be available"; (5) "the supply of affordable housing must be increased"; (6) "our society must provide greater support for family life"; (7) "quality, affordable child care should be universally available"; (8) "our society must place renewed emphasis on the value of marriage"; (9) "teen-agers and young adults must have attractive life-options"; and (10) "America must address both the societal roots and the individual episodes of domestic violence." Cited phrases are interspersed among several paragraphs of Catholic Charities USA, *Transforming the Welfare System*, 4–5.

60. Ibid., 12.

61. Ibid., 4.

62. Catholic Charities USA, *Transforming the Welfare System*, 7–9; United States Catholic Conference, "Moral Principles and Policy Priorities on Welfare Reform," 677.

63. United States Catholic Conference, "Moral Principles and Policy Priorities on Welfare Reform," 677.

64. Catholic Charities USA, *Transforming the Welfare System*, 8.

5

Implementing Welfare Reform, 1996–2006

This chapter describes the major developments in the process of implementing the welfare reform law of 1996. Its purpose is straightforward: to supply an overview of the most important events, trends, and issues that affected and characterized our nation's implementation of that welfare overhaul. A brief treatment like the one in this chapter can present only a summary account of these complex developments. A comprehensive investigation of all the relevant aspects of our national experience of welfare policy in the decade or so after the passage of the 1996 law would no doubt fill many volumes. This is particularly true now that we have entered the era of what is sometimes called the newest New Federalism. Because the 1996 law devolved so much authority away from the federal government, the new center of gravity for welfare policy became the states, each of which represents a unique landscape of policy choices, demographics, and economic realities. These factors and others interact in complex ways that resist easy summary in a synoptic account.

Another serious constraint regarding what can be stated with certainty about the welfare system during these years is the simple unavailability of much important data. Poverty researchers have long been familiar with the frustrations associated with attempting to produce timely analysis of policy outcomes when the crucial measurements they need for their work take years to be collected, collated, interpreted, and published. Festering questions plague researchers: How reliable are the numbers in government reports? What are the shortcomings of their sampling methods and what do they leave out? How can we separate out the effects of multiple simultaneous changes in our quest to assess the influence and success of a given policy? In the absence of definitive data, how may we adjudicate conflicting claims about policy effects?

Further problems and challenges complicate the task of reaching even tentative conclusions about the causation of social changes using aggregate statistics that often conceal more than they reveal, particularly in the case of multifaceted policy changes like welfare reform. In one of the earliest comprehensive reports on the effects of the 1996 law, the veteran researcher Richard Nathan highlights the inadequacy of current social services information infrastructure. He laments its inability to tell policy makers precisely what they most want to know about the outcomes of welfare reform, particularly regarding the task of "tracking individuals on the perimeter of the welfare system."[1] In this October 1997 report of the independent Rockefeller Institute of Government, Nathan offers a series of recommendations for improvement, including this one: "The most crucial start-up challenge now is the creation of information systems to manage state and local welfare and social programs and track recipients both during the time and after they receive cash benefits and social services."[2] Because the task of monitoring welfare reform has normative significance as our nation searches for social policies that address poverty more adequately, the failure to commit adequate resources to track these social effects must be judged a serious breach of the ethical obligations of government.

Despite these frustrations regarding the findings we have yet to discover and confirm, there are nevertheless certain elements of the landscape of welfare reform implementation that are beyond dispute. This chapter presents the major ones. The first part of this chapter surveys further developments in federal policy during the span of years from 1996 to 2006, including so-called technical adjustments and policy corrections as well as some new federal initiatives in welfare-related programs. The second part describes initial reactions to and concerns about the 1996 law and offers a tentative report on the actual outcomes of welfare reform so far as we can know them as of this writing. The indices of caseload reduction and changes in poverty rates emerge as important (although far from sufficient) measures of the success of the 1996 law. The third part of this chapter offers a glimpse at developments and trends on the state and local levels, the arenas where welfare reform measures like time limits, sanctions, and work requirements are actually implemented.

FURTHER DEVELOPMENTS IN FEDERAL WELFARE POLICY, 1996–2002

The months immediately following President Bill Clinton's signing of the welfare law on August 22, 1996 witnessed a scramble by the affected demographic groups and jurisdictions to adjust to the changed policy environment. State legislatures rushed to adopt plans to mesh their existing welfare arrangements with the new federal framework, hastening to meet filing deadlines to register their plans and program standards with federal agencies. In many cases, this process was complicated by the need to integrate preexisting waivers and exemptions from the former federal AFDC rules into new state policies aimed at compliance with the new TANF program. State and local welfare administrators then took up the next phase of implementation: translating the federally approved state plans into concrete strategies and operating procedures to be followed by caseworkers and frontline welfare officials.

The potentially jarring abruptness of the policy changes was mitigated somewhat by staggered deadlines for a number of the law's provisions, so that the phase-in of the program restructuring and policy changes proceeded over a period of several months, not all at once when the law took effect on October 1, 1996. Perhaps the most disruptive aspects of welfare reform implementation were not felt at welfare offices specifically, but rather were weathered by the Immigration and Naturalization Service. Great tumult was associated with the desperate efforts of hundreds of thousands of recent immigrants to complete the process of procuring American citizenship. Their eagerness to beat the mid-1997 deadlines that threatened to leave all non-naturalized immigrants without a safety net garnered considerable media coverage during those critical months.[3]

Two choruses competed for attention in the months just after the signing of the welfare bill. First, conservative supporters of the legislation, aware of the pressure to soften its provisions, called for patience and forbearance. For example, Representative E. Clay Shaw Jr., the Florida Republican responsible for the writing of the bill and the actual codification of many of the law's features, frequently urged listeners to give the new legislation time to work before tinkering mischievously with it. Shaw was adamant that he and his Republican allies in Congress were willing to support only those technical corrections that would prove necessary to hasten the success of the law.[4] Second, President Clinton, eager to mollify the liberal allies whose advice he spurned in approving the law, signaled his support for a broader set of policy corrections. Clinton looked for opportunities to provide a "softer welfare landing" than the original text of the law allowed. His long-term strategy was to propose restoration of certain categories of funding that had been cut by the welfare legislation. In the short run, he signed numerous executive orders and worked closely with Donna Shalala, the secretary of Health and Human Services, to enact the most generous interpretations of the law's provisions. Although Clinton did not want to appear to be reopening the issue entirely, even after his reelection in November 1996 took some of the peril out of this prospect, he nonetheless secured a few noteworthy victories in easing the harshest effects of the welfare law.[5] On many of these items, Clinton was able to cite the support of the National Governors' Association. Even though a majority of the fifty governors were Republicans, they were keenly aware of the many ways this legislation threatened hardships for the people, the economies, and the public finances of their states.[6]

The high point of Clinton's push for restoring substantial welfare funding came with the submission of his annual budget plan in February 1997.

The administration's opening bid in the budget process proposed to ratchet up spending on an array of programs for the poor by $21 billion, much of it to cushion the impact of the welfare law even as it was still being phased in.[7] The largest piece of Clinton's proposal that survived the particularly intense congressional budget battle that year was an allocation for $3 billion over the two fiscal years 1998 and 1999. The grant program in question was intended to assist states in creating job programs for people making the transition from welfare to paid employment and would be administered through the Department of Labor. The funding of this Welfare-to-Work Program (WtW) was incorporated into the provisions of the Balanced Budget Act of 1997 (Public Law 105-333, passed in final form August 5, 1997). It targeted long-term welfare recipients who met strict qualifications that placed them in the category of hard-to-employ. The program of job training and support services, relying as it did upon local Private Industry Councils for administration and coordination, eventually disappointed most observers, producing only modest results. Michael B. Katz describes the outcome in this way:

> Its eligibility requirements undermined WtW's potential success. States had difficulty finding clients who met the strict criteria. As a result, in the first eighteen months, WtW spent only about 8 percent of its first year's money. After one year, Philadelphia's WtW program, Greater Philadelphia Works, enrolled only 7,995 of the 15,000 welfare recipients it had targeted. Just over half [sic], 3,800, were placed in jobs, and half of those quit or were fired. Compared to other projects across the nation, however, the Philadelphia program succeeded: its 3,800 job placements were one-fifth of the national total.[8]

Throughout his second term, Clinton used the bully pulpit of the office of president to push a parallel program, the Welfare-to-Work Partnership, that shared many of the goals of the WtW program. The Partnership was a private nonprofit effort to enlist companies to hire from the welfare rolls. It was assisted greatly by a series of very generous tax incentives championed by the Clinton administration.[9] Although it started slowly and the rhetoric surrounding the Partnership consistently exceeded any actual sustained progress toward its goal of hiring fully one million out of the pool of four million welfare mothers, "by March 1999, 10,000 companies in the Welfare-to-Work Partnership had hired 410,000 welfare recipients."[10] Even discounting the inevitable backsliding of newly hired workers who return to the welfare rolls for an assortment of reasons, these raw numbers remain quite impressive. The strong economy and tight labor markets that prevailed in the late 1990s made these successes possible.

Another policy correction addressed by Congress in 1997 concerns the Family Violence Amendment. It "allows states to identify domestic violence victims among the caseload and exempt those clients from program requirements," including time limits and work participation rules.[11] When the 1996 law was passed, legislators came under pressure (generated by studies showing unusually high correlations of welfare recipiency and violent abuse) to include some compassionate exceptions for victims of domestic violence.[12] Democratic senators Paul Wellstone and Patty Murray secured inclusion of an amendment, in section 402 (a)(7) of the law, allowing (although not obliging) states to waive time limits for benefits received by women in this precarious situation. States that approved this Family Violence Option (the vast majority of states did eventually adopt some version of it) were soon faced with uncertainty about how to interpret these exemptions. Were such women to be counted as part of each state's allowed exemption of 20 percent of its welfare caseload? Or were such hardship exemptions to be counted above and beyond that baseline ratio? If the former interpretation prevailed, then "abused women would be forced into competition with other groups for protection and help, and many would not receive the waivers they need because states risk losing their funding if they do not follow the guidelines of the welfare law."[13] During 1997, both houses of Congress voted affirmatively on clarifications that allowed battered women to be granted exemptions above each state's general level of 20 percent.[14]

Women coping with the effects of domestic abuse comprise one disadvantaged group whose newly exacerbated needs were addressed by legislation subsequent to the 1996 welfare law. Legal immigrants are another such group. They too won a measure of public sympathy for the hardships they initially endured under that legislation and likewise found some remedy in later congressional action. The welfare law of 1996, in conjunction with the Immigration Reform Act of the same year, sharply limited the public benefits for which noncitizens are eligible. Legal complexities regarding these provisions abound, including key distinctions among categories of immigrants (such as refugees, asylees, those with substantial work histories, those who arrived before 1996, and newcomers after that date). The upshot was that 90 percent of immigrants lost their eligibility for cash assistance, food stamps, and Medicaid. The effects of the law included "striking declines in benefit use" even among those immigrants who still retain eligibility for certain means-tested benefits.[15] These trends suggest that the impact of the 1996 legislation on participation rates can be attributed as much to the communication of a general atmosphere of hostility on the part of the government toward resident aliens as to the technical details of revised eligibility criteria for specific programs. As increasing awareness of the hardships associated with these social services cuts arose during 1997, thoughtful expressions of protest surfaced on editorial pages of major media as well as in more specialized scholarly journals.[16] It seemed that the American populace needed just a bit of prompting to remember that the vast majority of immigrants are more aptly characterized by the adjective "hardworking" than "freeloading."

Congress responded to this uptick in pro-immigrant sentiment by approving certain of President Clinton's requests to restore a significant fraction of the lost benefits. In the budget deal struck in mid-1997, disabled legal immigrants who arrived before 1996 saw their SSI and Medicaid benefits restored.[17] The next year, food stamp benefits were restored to certain categories of immigrant children, the elderly, and the disabled—even those who had not yet become citizens.[18] Other incremental modifications in subsequent years, many of them the result of pressure from the congressional delegations of high-immigration states such as California and New York, consolidated further gains. For example, the Farm Bill of 2002 (Public Law 107-171) reinstated food stamp benefits for adult legal immigrants who have lived in the United States for at least five years. Nevertheless, as the reauthorization of the welfare law loomed, this vulnerable group remained largely outside the protective sphere of coverage from means-tested benefits. A survey of immigrant eligibility published in 2001 summarized their plight this way:

> Immigrants who entered the country since August 22, 1996 . . . are restricted from receiving most public benefits for five years; they are barred from receiving food stamps and SSI benefits unless they accumulate ten quarters of work. States decide whether legal immigrants will be eligible for Medicaid, TANF and Social Services Block Grants after the five-year bar.[19]

Even though the cause of restoring benefits to legal immigrants gained popularity after 1996, progress toward this goal was retarded by the sheer expense of extending social service coverage to this population on a national basis.[20] Individual states displayed extraordinary generosity in providing emergency assistance out of their own budgets and compensating for the withdrawal of federal assistance from some of the neediest people within their borders. Budgetary constraints continued to be cited as a major factor limiting the rollback of the harshest provisions of the 1996 welfare law. Even in the extremely prosperous years of the late 1990s, when government coffers were flush with tax revenues due to a booming economy, the perception that fiscal responsibility demanded very slow or no growth in outlays for social services prevented dramatic reversals of any provisions of the welfare overhaul. The sole exception to this general rule was the inauguration of a new category of health care programs: federal assistance for State Children's Health Insurance Programs (SCHIPs).

In response to alarming statistics regarding the ten million children who lacked health insurance at the time, the budget agreement negotiated in the summer of 1997 allocated $24 billion over five years for state-run programs to assist in extending medical coverage for this population. This assistance was particularly targeted to youngsters in families among the working poor, especially those reporting too much income to qualify for Medicaid but too little to afford private health insurance.[21] As it was initially set up under

Title XXI of the Social Security Act, SCHIP is neither a simple block grant program nor an entitlement. In most states, it operates as an enhancement of the Medicaid program, expanding eligibility according to set formulas that measure family income and need. The program shares federal money with the states on a matching grant basis but includes many conditions for local implementation.

From the start, SCHIP was plagued by numerous administrative problems. Particularly as the program got off the ground, most states had difficulty complying with all the requirements and receiving federal approval for their expenditures. By the fall of 2000, as much as 45 percent of the intended total allocation up to that point remained unspent.[22] Over two dozen states eventually missed the final deadline for drawing down their shares of the federal pool, and so in October 2002 were stripped of their untapped allotments.[23] Furthermore, a fierce debate erupted when the Bush administration was discovered to be offering waivers to states that proposed to spend their shares of the federal funds on health programs for childless adults, seemingly frustrating the original purpose of the program.[24] All the while, approximately 8.5 million children remained uninsured, despite the fact that SCHIPs had enrolled nearly 2.3 million children.[25] The expansion of health care coverage for low-income children evidently requires more than just this one particular new program, however fervently advocates for the poor have welcomed its addition.

THE FALLOUT OF THE 1996 OVERHAUL: FEARS, REACTIONS, AND RESULTS

Among all the operations of government, social policy exhibits effects that are perhaps the least predictable and the hardest to penetrate with numerical analyses alone. The significance and effects of measures like welfare reform involve the interaction between objective items such as program rules and the behavior of millions of real-life people in all their subjectivity. For that reason, this section on the effects of the 1996 welfare law pays as much attention to matters involving fears and perceptions as it does to quantitative data in assessing the complex outcomes of the major policy overhaul.

Predictions of Hardship
In the summer of 1996, as a congressional conference committee finalized details of the welfare bill and as President Clinton braced to sign it, much speculation centered on the likely effects of the measure. The most widely cited estimates came from a report released July 26 by the Urban Institute, a highly respected independent Washington-based research center that specializes in social and economic policy. Relying on sophisticated econometric projections, the study estimated that the combined effects of the policy changes surveyed in chapter 3 above would push 2.6 million people below

the poverty line, including 1.1 million children. These figures would have represented a 12 percent increase in childhood poverty. The study estimated that when all the law's measures were implemented, the annual poverty gap (the total amount of income that would be required to lift all poor families with children exactly to the government-defined poverty line) would rise by $4 billion dollars (a 20 percent increase). Some households would suffer dramatic decreases in income. The 8.2 million families most affected by the law were projected to lose an average of $1,300 annually.[26] At the time, the credibility of the Urban Institute report was bolstered by how closely its predictions matched the figures earlier released by the Congressional Budget Office and the Clinton administration's Office of Management and Budget.[27]

A word about the perils of such projections is in order, particularly because the harshest of these predictions did not come to pass. The key source of uncertainty in estimating the effects of any social legislation concerns how people will respond to incentives written into public laws. In the case of these welfare rule changes, the increase in poverty rates involves complex interactions regarding three factors: (1) lost benefits; (2) replacement of those benefits by increased work effort and earnings; and (3) the formation of fewer single-parent families requiring public assistance. In this unusual case of a law that introduces new applications of the principle of federalism, the projections were further complicated by additional uncertainty regarding how states would react in selecting their own local policy options (e.g., regarding time limits and sanctions).

Although its estimates were necessarily based on unconfirmed assumptions about the reactions of families and states to the new federal law, the Urban Institute's behavioral and policy assumptions actually turned out to be quite accurate. The Urban Institute, like the authors of earlier government reports, chose to follow parameters that were fairly conservative (in other words, those that would yield predictions of smaller rather than more dramatic increases in poverty rates). As it turned out, the largest factor that introduced error into these projections was the extraordinary prosperity the nation experienced in the five years after the law passed. In 1996, nobody could have predicted such a mighty economic boom, one characterized by tight labor markets, higher wages for workers, historically low unemployment rates, and a stock market surge that shifted most American industries into overdrive for several years. This hospitable economic climate surely accounts for much of the gap between the expectation that child poverty would increase substantially and the actual outcome. Census Bureau statistics reveal that child poverty decreased approximately one percent each year during the late 1990s—years that witnessed two simultaneous developments (the phase-in of the new welfare system and an unprecedented economic surge) whose effects are impossible to separate. Accounting for the role economic prosperity played in seeming to make welfare reform work greatly complicates ethical evaluations of these policy changes, as well as the central challenges regarding reauthorization of the welfare law.

The Urban Institute report and various similar government studies were not the only indications of deep concern expressed at that time about the plight of low-income families as they were being stripped of a major portion of their safety net. In the months after the passage of the welfare overhaul, Senator Daniel Patrick Moynihan continued to dispute numerous claims of supporters of the law. In a particularly spirited op-ed article titled "The Big Lie of 1996," which appeared in the *New York Times* in January 1997, Moynihan derided the facile claims of right-wing politicians and pundits who proposed an optimistic reading of social changes promoted by the new law. Rather than heralding an end to the urban underclass and the possibility that economic growth will at last filter down to inner cities, Moynihan warns, the welfare overhaul threatens to bring only greater "chaos" and heightened "disaster" to adults and children at risk.[28]

Two months earlier, a similar note of concern was struck by Mary Jo Bane, one of several prominent Clinton administration officials who resigned in protest over the law (others included Peter Edelman and Wendell Primus). Shortly after stepping down from her post as assistant secretary for children and families at the Department of Health and Human Services, Bane penned a *New York Times* op-ed piece that bore the title "Stand By for Casualties." Bane identified the new block grant funding mechanism and inadequate federal monitoring of state efforts as among the features of the welfare law that exposed poor children to sharply increased risk. She predicted that dire consequences would result from the loss of the welfare entitlement, and called for the restoration of at least some uniform federal protections for the most vulnerable families.[29]

A further set of concerns wrapped up with welfare reform involves the geography of poverty and the impact of policy changes on the street level. To some observers, the time limits and work requirements contained in the 1996 law raised the specter of a horrifying scenario for American cities. They feared that large numbers of current residents of inner cities would come under immense pressure to abandon their neighborhoods as the welfare time limit clock ticks down toward eventual cutoffs. Facing an inadequate supply of jobs and greatly eroded income support programs, urban families with declining prospects might well face heightened incentive to relocate to areas with more robust employment opportunities.[30] The resulting mass exodus from especially depressed urban districts, expedited by looming time limits that hit affected populations all at once, potentially threatened to strip certain cities of large shares of their population and to disrupt local economies. Shortly before the welfare law's enactment, one commentator, noting that cities like New York, Philadelphia, and Milwaukee contain over half of their respective states' welfare caseload, expressed the fear that "we will have created a 'welfare dust bowl' in our inner cities."[31] In an analogous way, other predictions about the hardship associated with welfare reform focused on disproportionate burdens falling upon hard-pressed sectors of the population, particularly minority ethnic groups. This particular ethical concern receives a closer look in chapter 6.

Campaigns of Resistance

The prospect of government policy exposing poor families to such increased levels of hardship galvanized certain groups of welfare reform resisters across the country. Although they never received large amounts of media attention, protests against the direction of welfare reform must be counted among the significant developments associated with the adoption of the 1996 law. Even before the bill's passage, the Children's Defense Fund, a Washington-based advocacy group, staged a massive demonstration at the Lincoln Monument on the National Mall. Reminiscent of the protests against the Vietnam War a generation earlier, the June 1, 1996 Stand for Children rally sought unsuccessfully to persuade lawmakers to reject the legislation at the last possible moment. Subsequent protest actions broke out at various stages of the law's implementation in several states, including at the Massachusetts State House on the occasion of the first benefit cutoff date and at a New York City welfare office that pioneered enforcement of a harsh regime of drug screening and sanctions against substance abusers.[32]

Early in 2002, as the task of reauthorizing the 1996 law loomed before Congress, a newly formed coalition called National Campaign for Jobs and Income Support emerged to take the lead in advocating for the interests of low-income people. Claiming the support of organized labor and as many as one thousand member affiliates, this group was led by a young activist named Deepak Bhargava and burst onto the Washington scene with great rapidity and boldness. The group adopted the unconventional tactic of targeting for protest not President Bush or congressional conservatives, as might be expected, but rather some of the most liberal legislators, including New York representative Charles Rangel and Senator Hillary Rodham Clinton. Bhargava explained his intention to embarrass these usual allies of the poor by attacking them from the left, scolding them for signaling their willingness to compromise with conservatives in the welfare reauthorization debates.[33]

A more subtle form of protest was undertaken by certain religious congregations and church-based social service providers. Already by the end of 1996, a group of Maryland pastors was publicizing its refusal to cooperate with the state's new welfare rules, signaling its resistance to the idea that churches should fill gaps in social services previously provided by government.[34] In New York City, the backlash by religious groups was even larger and came to be sharply focused on opposition to Mayor Rudolph Giuliani's version of workfare, the Work Experience Program (WEP). By mid-1997, seventy religious and nonprofit agencies in the city's five boroughs had banded together in organized efforts to discourage Giuliani's plans by refusing to enter contracts that involved workfare participants.[35] The sentiments expressed by the pastor of Manhattan's Judson Memorial Baptist Church, in a 1998 *Sojourners* magazine article titled "Insult to the Poor," are revealing:

> Judging WEP to be a moral disaster, my church has joined with the Urban Justice Center to co-sponsor the WEP Campaign of Resistance. Since we launched the campaign in summer 1997, more than 200 congregations and not-for-profit agencies have pledged that they will not participate as WEP placement sites. . . . We believe that rejecting the path of complicity and demanding a new program based on what people really need is a positive move for faith-based communities.[36]

These comments reflect a widespread reluctance on the part of many congregations and religious leaders to cooperate with the measures contained in the 1996 welfare reform law. The new challenge of negotiating the subtleties of the law's charitable choice provisions (treated in chapter 2 above) has understandably received the most media attention.[37] However, when they consider the welfare law and its impact in local communities, most religious bodies find themselves grappling with more mundane decisions and familiar dilemmas, such as whether to continue to cooperate with specific programs such as the ones mentioned above. The option of boycotting objectionable government initiatives associated with welfare reform occasionally places congregations in the unenviable position of choosing strict adherence to principles of fairness over long-standing commitments to programs ostensibly geared to help poor families.[38]

Fears Regarding the New Federalism: A Race to the Bottom?

Among the most common fears about the effects of the 1996 law was a set of concerns that came to be expressed in terms of two colorful metaphors: a race to the bottom and welfare magnets. At issue here is the specter of interstate welfare migration, in which needy families presumably would be drawn to cross jurisdictional lines in order to obtain higher benefits or to qualify for more generous terms of treatment, such as extended time limits in certain states. While the landscape of AFDC had always featured higher- and lower-benefit states, it was feared that the TANF system in effect after 1996, because it removed so much of the previous federal oversight, would exacerbate interstate differentials in benefit levels and program rules. With the advent of this regime of capped block grants, states experienced new incentives to discourage in-migration of the poor and to compete with neighboring states for the dubious distinction of featuring stingier welfare provisions.

The salience of arguments about a race to the bottom in this new era of welfare hinges on two sets of behaviors: (1) how low-income families respond when faced with an incentive to relocate; and (2) how the policymaking process within the states reacts to these fears and new realities. Regarding the first item, it turns out that poor families display no particular propensity to uproot themselves and to move across state borders in search of higher benefits. After conducting a careful review of available research on the relationship between residential mobility and welfare receipt, one policy analyst concludes that "there is little empirical evidence to support welfare-magnet arguments."[39] The true determinants of mobility patterns among low-income families turn out to involve not welfare benefits at all, but rather such factors as the availability of employment opportunities and proximity to family and established social networks. As a result, the vast majority (one educated estimate is 90 percent) of relocations of welfare recipients consists of intrastate migration.[40]

Regarding the second item, the most important finding of researchers is that "there is little direct evidence that welfare-benefit levels are influenced by competitive pressure from neighbors."[41] Although states naturally keep an eye on the welfare policies of their neighbors (in a dynamic termed "policy diffusion"), historic patterns of interstate benefit variation reveal only the weakest of causal linkages to be at play. One careful empirical study of state welfare policy between the years 1976 and 1994 concluded that the welfare policies of most states during this era displayed only very modest sensitivity to the policy choices of neighboring states.[42] A close examination of policies adopted by the six New England states in the years immediately after the 1996 welfare law also reveals ample evidence to lead researchers "to reject race-to-the-bottom arguments."[43]

Rather than participating in a dramatic race to the bottom that, some predicted, would entail sweeping across-the-board cuts in benefit levels, states responded to the 1996 law in a more subtle and unexpected way. Between 1996 and 1998, as many as fifteen states passed welfare residency requirements, evidently seeking to deter in-migration of poor families by treating newcomers differently when they applied for benefits. In a majority of these cases, this entailed states choosing to offer newly arrived families only a certain percentage of the TANF benefits received by long-term state residents, at least during a given family's first year of residency.[44] Because the form of this discrimination closely matched the object of previous U.S. Supreme Court rulings on welfare rights, the matter soon became grist for the legal process. Advocates for the poor cited the Supreme Court's *Shapiro v. Thompson* decision in 1969 that struck down similar residency requirements in an earlier era. In so acting, the court issued a ruling that is widely cited as establishing the right to travel as a constitutional guarantee. Initial rounds of legal appeal in 1997 played out in courts in California and Pennsylvania in cases that hinged on the right to equal protection guaranteed under the Fourteenth Amendment.[45] Finally, in its 1999 decision in *Saenz v. Roe* (119 S. Ct. 1526, 1999), the Court struck down the provision of the 1996 welfare reform law that these fifteen states had cited in defense of their revised eligibility standards.[46] With the outlawing of such "two-tier-benefit schedules," the nation witnessed what appears to be the final act in an acrimonious debate over whether a race to the bottom is an allowable, or beyond that, perhaps even an inevitable result of the putative phenomenon of welfare magnets.[47]

On the several other occasions when welfare reform found its way into the courts, litigators discovered a changed landscape. Court decisions involving access to welfare benefits during the previous decades of the AFDC program tended to hinge upon the existence of a welfare entitlement. Since Congress had revoked this entitlement in writing the 1996 legislation, attorneys defending welfare clients could no longer rely on statutory law in the accustomed way to advance their arguments. Nevertheless, occasional legal victories for low-income plaintiffs were secured during the first years of TANF. In December 1998 and January 1999, Federal District Court Justice William Pauley III issued a pair of decisions regarding the treatment of welfare applicants by New York City's Human Resources Administration. Over the objection of the city's lawyers, Pauley ordered welfare caseworkers to discontinue certain practices introduced by the city's Human Resources Commissioner, Jason Turner. "Work first" and similar policies that consistently diverted applicants from access to emergency benefits were ruled objectionable because, as Justice Pauley determined, they "were literally putting people's lives in danger" and depriving them of "the very means by which to live."[48]

A 5–4 decision of the U.S. Supreme Court on February 28, 2001 represented another victory for advocates of the poor. In *Legal Services Corporation v. Velasquez* (case no. 99-603), the Court overturned an attempt by Congress to restrict the scope of publicly funded legal services for welfare recipients. In an effort to bolster and defend the recently passed 1996 welfare law, Congress had sought to bar legal services lawyers from attempts to amend or challenge existing law, specifically regarding benefit reductions. The sharply contested Supreme Court decision ruled that muzzling these attorneys in such a way would constitute a violation of the First Amendment right to free speech. The text of the court's decision expresses the fear that, left in place, this restriction would "distort the legal system" and would serve as an illegal means "to insulate the government's laws from judicial inquiry."[49] The editorial staff of a major newspaper called the removal of "Congress's gag rule" upon Legal Services Corporation attorneys representing indigent clients an important victory for "free speech for the poor."[50]

Measurable Effects of Welfare Reform

Against the background of these legal and policy developments, we now turn to an examination of the results of welfare reform to date. We have already alluded to what are undoubtedly the two most important outcomes in the years 1996 to 2006: a massive decline in the welfare caseload across the nation and modest (though temporary) progress in reducing poverty rates. The sheer numbers are staggering. From a historic peak in the national welfare caseload at 5.1 million families in 1994, the welfare rolls plummeted to 2.1 million families in March 2001, before reaching a plateau and even rising slightly in the months after that due to the onset of an economic slowdown. The excruciatingly slow and shallow recovery that spanned 2002 to 2006 had little effect on the raw numbers of those receiving TANF benefits. The overall national drop of approximately 58 percent over this span of time was of course not uniformly distributed. However, every single state recorded unprecedented declines in families receiving welfare, from dips of just over 30 percent for Rhode Island and Hawaii to precipitous free falls of approximately 90 percent for Idaho and Wyoming.[51] Whatever else might be said about the experience of social policy during these years, it must not be denied that the changes represented by these numbers are truly remarkable. Welfare recipiency had for decades been a particularly stubborn social indicator, never falling below three million families from the early 1970s until after the welfare overhaul of 1996. One group of senior policy analysts marveled: "The rapidity and breadth of change have been stunning."[52]

According to most public assessments, welfare reform was a success simply because it achieved the single objective of shrinking substantially the public assistance rolls. But judging these large declines in caseload to constitute true social gains, of course, depends upon changes in other indices and variables during these same years. We cannot rely on one indicator, however dramatic, in isolation to tell the whole story of what happened to America's poorest families during the years in question. Often consulted to round out the picture in this regard are various measures of poverty in the United States, including the overall poverty rate, the child poverty rate, and the rate of extreme poverty.

By any calculation, the welfare reform of 1996 did not produce the severe social catastrophe prophesied by many of its critics. Using the standard government measures of income and family needs, poverty rates for the period in question, 1996 to 2006, remained well within the range of recent national experience. Since the mid-1960s, overall poverty rates have rarely strayed from the relatively narrow range of between 11 and 15 percent.[53] The latter half of the 1990s produced a very modest downturn in poverty, from approximately 14 percent down to 12 percent. The Census Bureau's fall 2001 statistics on poverty and income recorded a poverty rate of 11.3 percent, the lowest in a generation. Most of that gain is rightly attributed to the unrelenting economic expansion of these years, a fact that is reinforced by subsequent data. The poverty rate rose to 11.7 percent in 2002 and 12.5 percent in 2003, reflecting the economic downturn that began in 2001. The uptick in poverty to 12.7 percent by the end of 2004 surprised many observers, as it prompted the disturbing realization that the effects of a mild economic rebound were not filtering down to the least affluent households. The sluggish recovery brought some good news regarding aggregate economic growth (the economy grew a very encouraging 3.8 percent during 2004), but it still left thirty-seven million Americans below the poverty line.[54]

Of course, it is crucial to the endeavor of evaluating welfare reform to narrow down the analysis so as to measure poverty trends among the target population only. Ideally, researchers seek to single out exclusively those families directly affected by welfare reform, generally single-parent families with children. The child poverty rate is one measure often used as a reasonably accurate stand-in for this specific population. When we track the child poverty rate in recent years, we find that it followed the same basic pattern as the general poverty rate, declining gradually but consistently through the years just after 1996. While it is certainly good news that welfare reform did not spark the predicted increase in childhood deprivation, nevertheless the persistence of poverty in the households of over twelve million American children continues to occasion a good deal of soul-searching with the release of each government report on the topic.[55] From a 1995 level of 20.8 percent, child poverty fell to 16.9 percent in 1999 and 16.2 percent at the time of the 2000 census, before rising again in rough proportion with the overall poverty rate increases after 2001. However, the poverty rate for African American children remained much higher, a stubborn 30.9 percent even in 2000, a year of peak prosperity for the nation as a whole.[56]

The numbers regarding the well-being of black children look even more bleak when we consider a subgroup of the poor, namely those families living in extreme poverty—defined as those with disposable incomes of one-half the poverty line or less. For example, the poverty line for a family of three is about $14,000; below $7,060 a three-person family is considered to be extremely poor. In 2000 there were 686,000 black children living in extreme poverty, but by the end of 2001 the number had risen sharply to 932,000, representing the highest level since the category was introduced in government statistics in 1980. These numbers suggest that the recession (the first since the 1996 overhaul) had disproportionately hurt these particularly vulnerable families, who for a variety of reasons fared much worse than the larger population. While the poverty rate for all black children had fallen from 41.5 percent in 1995 to 30 percent in 2001, the economic circumstances of these particularly hard-pressed families with the fewest resources, especially now with welfare reform's trimming of the safety net, had deteriorated precipitously.[57] The loss of public benefits, especially in conjunction with declining work prospects, was leaving hundreds of thousands of families in dire straits, and the impact appears to be increasingly concentrated among members of minority groups.

Interpreting the Data: The Search for Explanations

Having examined these major trends regarding poverty rates and the welfare caseload since the 1996 overhaul, we now search for some tentative explanations for what has transpired thus far. Many interpretations of these data are possible, although some are clearly more plausible than others. For example, those seeking to attribute the decline in the welfare rolls primarily to changes in family structure occasioned by the 1996 law have difficulty building a solid case. Notwithstanding that this is undoubtedly an important social indicator, data regarding nonmarital births and family formation in recent years do not offer any significant encouragement. No measurable increase in marriage rates occurred. The only detectable progress is a leveling off of previous rates of increase in births to unmarried couples, and even the slowing of this rate of increase was not sustained after 1997. The slight improvements that have occurred may be attributed in part to social and legal changes not directly related to welfare policy, such as new state and local child-support enforcement procedures and larger social and cultural shifts.[58]

There is much more solid evidence supporting the claim that a major factor in the decline of welfare recipiency is simply that fewer new applicants are entering the welfare system to replace those who inevitably leave. The new culture of welfare offices is one that places unprecedented demands upon applicants to conduct a rigorous job search (the work first strategy) and to use public assistance only as a last resort. Even given the relative rarity of ambitious state and local workfare programs, the mere threat of enforcing work participation requirements has had the effect of smoking out recipients or potential applicants who possess alternatives to welfare. This approach has, in effect, closed (or at least restricted) the intake valve of the welfare caseload. Like a reservoir being drained gradually but not replenishing itself, the sheer volume of the caseload has receded considerably. By adding "new diversion policies that deflect claimants toward job searches or private assistance rather than adding them to the rolls," many states have created "cultural and administrative climates that have . . . functioned to deter eligible families from claiming benefits."[59] In certain cases, such diversion is no doubt an ethically defensible or even laudable strategy, for it provides incentive to those able to succeed in labor markets with a bit more effort. In other cases, where recourse to work is problematic for a given family, and where substantial barriers to employment preclude adequate earnings, deterring families from applying for benefits they desperately need is not only counterproductive but potentially dangerous and ethically objectionable.

It has proven very difficult for policy analysts to sort out the interplay of factors that account for a variety of changes in welfare outcomes since the 1996 overhaul. Ron Haskins and Wendell Primus argue that a majority of the gains so far, as well as potential further gains, are intricately wrapped up with the distinctive problems and struggles of female-headed families, particularly those consisting of never-married women with their children.[60] Only by fully comprehending the work and family challenges they face, and by finding ways to assist them as they navigate uncharted waters in this new era of diminished eligibility for benefits, can we expect further gains. Besides the simultaneous decline in caseloads and poverty rates, we must also take account of the marked increase during these same years in the share of single mothers working outside the home. Between 1993 and 2000, this figure (one that matches the basic profile of the typical adult welfare recipient) rose remarkably, from 59 percent to 74 percent, as did the earnings of single mothers.[61] Lively debate continues to focus on both the consequences and the causes of this large increase in work effort on the part of this key demographic group.

One experienced social policy observer, Douglas Besharov of the American Enterprise Institute, summarizes available recent studies on this topic and ventures an estimate of the relative effects of three causal factors at play in welfare outcomes. First of all, in his estimation, the 1996 law itself, by virtue of the way "it changed the expectations and the 'atmospherics' of the program," accounts for 25 percent to 35 percent of the decline in caseloads.[62] Recipients nationwide clearly responded to the new pro-work message it sent. But the welfare overhaul did not single-handedly account for the halving (and then some) of the welfare rolls. A second factor in caseload reduction was the strong economy. Favorable economic conditions during the late 1990s created a particularly strong demand for the low-skilled labor that welfare recipients typically offer. Entry-level positions were scooped up in record numbers by single mothers, including never-married women as well as divorcees, who might otherwise have turned to welfare benefits for income. Besharov estimates that 35 percent to 45 percent of the caseload decline can be attributed to economic prosperity, which emerges as having played an indispensable role in the success of welfare reform. Richard B. Freeman, a distinguished Harvard economist, stated the case more starkly: "Absent the late 1990s boom, the new welfare policies might have been a disaster. But in the strong labor market, they succeeded beyond anyone's expectation."[63]

A third factor is "sharply increased aid to low-income, working families," primarily in the form of the Earned Income Tax Credit (EITC).[64] This category also includes noncash work-support programs usually considered ancillary to welfare, such as enhanced child care subsidies, extended Medicaid coverage, housing subsidies, and other transitional assistance. As an unabashed conservative, Besharov hastens to add that he does not approve of this third factor, even though he attributes 20 percent to 30 percent of the welcome welfare caseload decline to it. He claims that it would be a dangerous thing if the United States adopted an ambitious "European-style social welfare state" that might threaten to "saddle the economy with immense transfer systems that create troubling distributional inequities, stifle business investment, create huge work and marriage disincentives." While he objects to the "startling expansion of the welfare state," Besharov nevertheless concedes that welfare reform could not have produced such impressive changes in the social landscape without the work-support benefits the federal and state governments have already implemented.[65] His liberal opponents on welfare reform underline the fact that EITC and similar benefits available to the working poor are precisely the things that made possible both exits from the welfare rolls and the very survival of many families once their welfare cases are terminated.[66]

Assigning percentages to these three particular causal factors may to a certain extent be instructive, but this procedure should not be allowed to mask the inextricable nature of multiple complex social realities associated with welfare reform in recent years. Because it is impossible to disaggregate the many factors that played a role in producing the effects we have seen, it is advisable to avoid the temptation of oversimplification. For example, those who wish to attribute almost all the positive effects and progress noted above to the 1996 legislation in isolation would do well to recall that the trend toward caseload reduction was already well under way during the years 1994 to 1996, before the law had passed (although some small share of the changes may be attributed to federal waivers to states in effect by mid-1996).[67] Even more of the caseload reduction had occurred before the full implementation and phase-in of the law (and certainly before its more delayed aspects, such as time limits, started to exert their impact) months and even years after the October 1, 1996 date when the welfare reform law went into effect.

How Have Welfare Leavers Really Fared?
Above all, what welfare policy analysts are eager to know more about is the well-being of "leavers." This term refers to welfare recipient families, usually consisting of single mothers and their children, who depart from the welfare rolls and turn to alternative sources of income or support. Any comprehensive evaluation of the 1996 welfare reform depends to a great extent upon the answers to such questions as: What survival strategies have welfare leavers turned to? Have they by and large succeeded in keeping their families together and even improving family stability? Have their incomes risen or dropped since 1996?

Naturally, there is great variety in the experience of former welfare recipients. Indeed, one of the major lessons that emerges from what we do know for certain about welfare leavers is that the outcomes that they face largely depend upon the characteristics that a given family displays. In other words, families whose members display similar sets of skills and work histories, on one hand, or similar problems and barriers to employment, on the other hand, tend to share similar prospects for success. One careful observer of welfare families, Michael Massing, divides the welfare caseload into three groups, each with a distinctive set of challenges and expectations as they move from welfare to work. The most well positioned are the heads of households whom Massing refers to as "ready-for-prime-time workers." For the most part, these welfare leavers are job ready, requiring at most modest preparation for jobs that will allow them to advance in the labor market and to provide adequate income for their families. The middle group consists of the "eager beavers." These are welfare recipients who, despite enthusiasm for the transition to work and willingness to cooperate with program rules, still require significant levels of job training, coaching, and similar preliminary activities to equip them for job success. Massing calls the third category the "willing but unable." Because of a host of medical, emotional, and family problems, these welfare recipients face a steep uphill battle in the struggle for financial independence. Since they will probably never fully overcome the disadvantages that preclude full self-sufficiency, Massing concludes, a small but adequate public assistance system that offers a long-term safety net must be maintained to insure the survival of families sharing this type of profile.[68]

Precisely how many welfare recipients fall into each of these categories? Before the 1996 reform practically forced progress toward answering this question by ending the entitlement status of welfare, we could only speculate. For example, one educated guess came from Gary Burtless, a senior fellow at the Brookings Institution. Even before the legislation was finalized and passed into law, he estimated that

> about a quarter or more of the welfare mothers who would be pushed into the work force when their benefits ran out would succeed in maintaining a job, earning at least as much as they now receive on welfare. But about half the mothers pushed off welfare would be worse off than they are now, earning less than they now get on welfare. And another one-quarter of recipients are going to be in such severe difficulty that they will have to give up their children or, in trying to keep their families together, they will spend time as homeless people.[69]

By virtue of the measures contained in the 1996 law, recipients have in effect been prompted to sort themselves out according to the three categories cited by Massing and Burtless. By displaying their relative abilities to cooperate with the work requirements, time limits, and other provisions of the law in the years since it passed, welfare recipients revealed what they were capable of achieving and where they stood vis-à-vis potential self-sufficiency. All that remains to be done, it might seem, is to measure the outcomes and assess the numbers of those able to make successful welfare exits. Well-designed leaver studies would hold the promise of accomplishing just that task.

Unfortunately, there is no single and most obviously reliable source of information regarding the transition off welfare. A number of frustratingly incomplete leaver studies gradually surfaced, offering fragmentary evidence of what happened to the earnings of the millions of low-income families no longer on the welfare rolls. By the middle of 1999, mainstream media outlets were covering the release of some of the preliminary reports, mostly based on data compiled and interpreted by official federal and state government sources and independent poverty research institutes.[70] A few early reports on the earning achievements of leavers appeared in scholarly journals during these same months.[71] While considerably significant even in isolation, data on earnings alone are, of course, only one part of the overall picture of leaver well-being that researchers were seeking to detail. As time passed, frustration with narrow and one-dimensional measures of these outcomes grew.

Perhaps the most reliable summary of the findings of early leaver studies was compiled by Ron Haskins, a major player (as a Republican congressional staffer) in the actual writing of the 1996 welfare law and an astute observer of its effects. In an essay published by the Brookings Institution in 2001, Haskins surveys all the available findings regarding the effects of the 1996 reform on family income and poverty, including leaver studies (of admittedly uneven quality) from forty-three states. He offers a three-statement summary of his own conclusions in light of these data:

> First, most mothers with children who have left welfare have more money than they had when they were on welfare. . . . Second, child poverty has declined substantially since the enactment of welfare reform. Third, there is a small to moderate-sized group of mother-headed families that are worse off than they were before welfare reform. Again, these generalizations capture what has happened in a strong economy; what will happen when the economy goes sour remains to be learned.[72]

To avoid accusations that he is providing an overly optimistic interpretation of the data, Haskins concedes that there are blemishes in the portrait he paints regarding the success of welfare reform. He acknowledges: "The evidence also shows a group of mothers and children in the bottom fifth who have less income when they leave welfare. For these mothers, the system of low-wage work and the EITC is not working well."[73] In addition, Haskins considers "especially compelling" the data reviewed above regarding an alarming increase in families in extreme poverty, with disposable incomes under half the federal poverty line.[74]

Reviewing the same fifty or so leaver studies available as of 2001, Ladonna Pavetti (a senior fellow at the highly respected Mathematica Policy Research group in Washington, D.C.) largely agrees with Haskins on the basic thrust of the initial findings. However she takes pains to emphasize two particular aspects of the picture that the preliminary data reveal. First, Pavetti calls attention to the meager gains typically achieved even by families considered to be success stories. Even among those who have "gained a foothold in the labor market" and raised their standard of living in the wake of welfare reform, "the earnings of welfare leavers are generally not sufficient to bring them up to the poverty line."[75] Pavetti issues a reminder of a problem endemic to low-wage work, namely, the paucity of key fringe benefits, when she observes: "In addition to low wages, most working recipients do not receive paid vacations, sick leave or employer-sponsored health insurance."[76]

Second, Pavetti adverts to the disturbingly large number of families who seem to have fallen through the cracks of the reformed welfare system alto-

gether and who report earnings from neither welfare benefits nor employment. The proportion of former recipients who find themselves in such dire
straits is perhaps as high as 30 percent, a figure that includes a disproportionate number of families who lost benefits due to sanctions. Pavetti notes
that "so far there is limited information on how these families make ends
meet and whether their disconnection from the labor market and TANF is
temporary or permanent."[77] These cases of hardship go a long way toward
explaining another finding of leaver studies: that as many as "27 percent
of welfare leavers report having problems providing enough food for their
families, and that 15.9 to 21.7 percent report difficulty paying utility
bills."[78]

Researchers have attached the shorthand phrases "missing mothers" and
"foundering families" to the category of former welfare recipients who seem
not to have replaced their benefits through reported earnings. Based strictly
upon what we know about their reported financial situation alone, we
would be justified in the expectation that hundreds of thousands of them
should have starved to death by now. It is possible to imagine possible sce-
narios for how these families support themselves: unreported earnings from
off-the-books or black-market employment; and reliance on the generosity
of private charities, relatives, friends, or domestic or intimate partners. In
most cases, a combination of these and perhaps further alternative sources
of support most likely plays a role in the daily lives and budgets of these
families.

Continuity and Change in the Welfare System: Eligibility and Program Participation Rates

One might conclude that, at least in the narrow sense of the observations
contained in the preceding paragraph, not much seems to have changed
with the 1996 welfare reform. Even in the era of the AFDC entitlement,
practically all low-income single mothers were forced to piece together a
patchwork of support from multiple sources of income, for the simple reason that welfare benefits were generally so meager. In research conducted in
the final years of the AFDC system, Kathryn Edin and Laura Lein found
that welfare mothers exercised great resourcefulness and even stunning cre-
ativity in filling the substantial gap between what welfare offered and what
they truly needed to support dignified family life.[79] Only one out of 214
women interviewed by Edin and Lein in four cities in the mid-1990s reported being able to make ends meet on welfare and associated benefits
alone.[80] Mothers helped their families get by through a variety of coping
strategies, a high number of which were technically against the rules and
regulations of the welfare system. From this research, we might find encouragement in the realization that poor families turn out to have somewhat
greater resources than are officially acknowledged. Yet we might simultaneously be discouraged that most estimates of the poverty line (and thus most
calculations of appropriate benefit levels) undercount the actual needs of

these unfortunate families who have historically been practically forced to lie about their sources of income.

However, the wider picture of welfare reform suggests that a great deal has indeed changed since the 1996 law took effect. Chapter 3 surveys the restrictions on eligibility for benefits under the federal cash welfare programs, and the final section of this present chapter examines the ways state implementation has affected eligibility for TANF benefits. But beyond the question of technical eligibility for welfare, an additional concern involves the sharply declining actual participation rates for the two largest federal programs offering in-kind benefits: food stamps and Medicaid. The statistics in question are often referred to as take-up rates and are calculated by dividing the number of people actually receiving benefits by the raw number of those eligible for the benefit in a given period. In the case of both the food stamp and Medicaid programs, even though the 1996 welfare law mandated only marginal changes in eligibility criteria, the take-up rates for the programs fell precipitously, to an extent far beyond anyone's expectations given the modest changes in program rules.

Regarding food stamps, these trends represent a major departure from previous experience in the use of this form of food assistance. Although our ability to perform precise calculations is limited by endemically incomplete data on monthly family income and assets, one observer of the decline offers this estimate:

> food stamp take-up fell by 24 percent between 1993 and 1999, and the decline accelerated following welfare reform. Consequently, by 1999 as many as 4 million children were living in households eligible for, but not receiving, food stamp assistance. The decline appears particularly pronounced among both single-parent and married-couple families with earnings. Given that a major objective of welfare reform is to encourage work and to promote marriage, these changes are of special concern.[81]

Early in 2001, the Department of Agriculture reported that 12 million people were eligible for food stamps but were not receiving them. The 24.9 million recipients in 1996 had shrunk to 17 million by the beginning of 2001. Diminished need for food stamps due to economic prosperity accounted for only a fraction of this decline of over 30 percent.[82]

The declining participation rates for food stamps are bound up with a number of technical issues regarding the administration of the food stamp program. By giving states new authority to set welfare eligibility rules, the 1996 law provided incentives for states to divert poor families from applying for any social benefits at all, even the few remaining federal entitlements such as food stamps. At the very least, it is fair to surmise that states no longer promoted such applications as aggressively as they once did. Other factors contributing to sharply lower take-up rates include widespread confusion among families leaving welfare who are unaware that they may still be eligible for food stamps (many leavers indeed retain eligibility) and the hassle factor associated with visiting social service offices to retain eligibility for (often reduced) benefits, especially on the part of families whose adult members are now working, at least part-time, in accordance with work requirements.[83] A number of possible reforms have been suggested (including simplifying application forms, enrollment procedures, and program rules) for reducing the barriers that the working poor must surmount in order to acquire and retain food stamps for which they are fully eligible.[84]

The decline in Medicaid participation rates hinges on some of the same causes, but also reflects certain issues particular to this program. As our nation's major public health insurance program for the indigent, Medicaid provides essential coverage for approximately forty million Americans, at an annual cost exceeding $150 billion. Since its 1965 inauguration under Title XIX of the Social Security Act, Medicaid has worked according to a vendor payment system along with a joint federal-state financing system that allows states to set payment rates and methods within general federal guidelines. As reported in chapter 3, the architects of the 1996 welfare overhaul struck a compromise that preserved eligibility for Medicaid on the part of all families who would qualify for TANF benefits, but nevertheless in principle de-coupled Medicaid coverage from welfare eligibility.

Since the mid-1990s, the nation has witnessed a significant erosion in Medicaid take-up rates among those eligible. Many of those who found themselves without coverage were members of families that had recently left welfare. One study estimated that 675,000 people (420,000 of them children) lost Medicaid coverage and were without health insurance during 1997 "as an unintended consequence of welfare reform."[85] A sizable number of them were actually eligible for Transitional Medical Assistance, a new program that provides Medicaid coverage for one year for low-income families leaving welfare. However, large numbers of people did not take advantage of this benefit and found themselves among the ranks of the approximately forty-five million uninsured Americans.

Compounding this unfortunate and wrongful erosion in coverage was widespread confusion about eligibility among potential applicants, local officials, and providers. Many families containing certain members (usually adults) who do qualify for Medicaid failed to realize that other family members (usually children) were also eligible. The computer systems of government offices sometimes did not appreciate this complication, either.[86] One study of these disturbing trends attributed the problem to state policies that erected "more significant hurdles to obtain benefits, . . . either formal diversion programs or added steps . . . that diverted or discouraged families from applying for Medicaid, even if they were eligible."[87] Although the causal factors were complex and seemed to shift somewhat after 1998, the consensus remains that it was increasingly restrictive state administrative practices, rather than tighter federal eligibility rules, that accounted for most of the decline in Medicaid enrollment in the wake of the welfare reform law of

1996.[88] Concern for this population is heightened by the all-or-nothing nature of Medicaid's categorical eligibility, a program feature that has drawn recurring criticism for its seeming unfairness and that has perpetuated the problem of notch effects causing families to lose their entire benefit when their income or assets rise even quite modestly.

Even accounting for the effects of these technical explanations for the decline in Medicaid and food stamp take-up rates, policy analysts admit to a certain degree of bafflement about the downward trend in participation rates. An emerging consensus emphasizes this insight: the effects of the 1996 welfare overhaul somehow run deeper than the letter of the law and its actual provisions. Beyond the details of eligibility criteria and benefit standards contained in the legislation is a strong psychological effect associated with its get-tough message. One effect is evident in the behavior of recipients, who seem increasingly hesitant to apply for benefits, perhaps to avoid the bureaucracy, scrutiny, and hassle associated with participation in such programs, or perhaps for fear of rejection, stigma, or ridicule. These families settle for making do with their own limited resources despite their continuing eligibility for certain benefits. Second, the clarion call to steer welfare recipients onto the road to independence as quickly as possible surely affects local welfare officials. In their zeal to close public assistance cases, they seem often to overlook the fact that these families often still need (and indeed maintain full eligibility for) certain benefits, such as food stamps and Medicaid, even if they no longer qualify for cash assistance. Problems relating to the interaction between programs (such as the de-linking of welfare from Medicaid) compound the wrongful rejections, miscalculations, and mistakes that occur in social service offices.

One final significant change in welfare arrangements since the 1996 overhaul regards the topic of child-only cases. A 2002 publication of the Urban Institute reports that these cases have come to account for a larger share than ever (approaching 35 percent, up from 10 percent in 1990) of the welfare caseload. In certain states, particularly in the rural South and those with high levels of immigration and urban problems, approximately half of all TANF cases now fit this category.[89] It is composed of poor children who do not live with their parents at all or whose parents do not qualify for public assistance (often because of their immigration status or because they have been sanctioned under state rules). The single largest group consists of children being raised by grandparents or other relatives, often because their parents are jailed, are struggling with addictions, or have lost custody as a result of abuse or neglect. Other cases involve foster care or similar arrangements to cope with homelessness that results in family breakup, whether temporary or permanent in nature. Monthly checks are sent to the adults in the household to care for the children, even though the adults in these families are not themselves eligible (although some may collect SSI or other types of benefits).

Growing awareness of this disturbing trend failed to yield immediate clarity about its significance, as researchers found themselves frustrated that they could not "pinpoint the forces driving parents and children apart."[90] By 2002, the publication of new research on the topic by the Rand Corporation, Mathematica, and the Urban Institute confirmed previous analyses of census data on child-only cases and contributed to renewed consternation about the effects of welfare reform on family life. Even some supporters of the 1996 law began to wonder whether it was time to reassess their previously optimistic analysis of the changing welfare landscape, as numerous anecdotes (if not actual hard data) suggested that many new instances of family separation, dissolution, and hardship turned out to be unintentional consequences of the welfare legislation.

Although some aspects of the problem are unrelated to poverty or welfare, the total number of children living apart from both parents had reached a startling new high of 2.3 million nationwide by 1999.[91] Of these, slightly over one million children (in 782,000 families) were TANF recipients.[92] Many thousands more are eligible for TANF benefits but do not collect because they fear the stigma of welfare, are unaware of their eligibility, or have been wrongly denied assistance. One calculation estimated that between 1996 and 2002, the number of black urban children living without a parent rose by two hundred thousand. Although in some cases these children are potentially better off under the care of adults besides their parents, on the average children living with neither parent experience higher rates of school failure, mental health problems, psychological trauma, and delinquency than other children, even those living with a single mother.[93]

The increasing prevalence of child-only cases is a sobering reminder of several important truths about welfare in the new millennium. First, it serves as a counterbalance to overly optimistic portrayals of outcomes so far. Along with the discouraging data about the rising number of families surviving with income below half the poverty line, child-only cases provide eloquent testimony that a significant portion of low-income American families are indeed doing worse under welfare reform. While it is easy to cheer statistics such as declining welfare caseloads, it is important to pay attention to this indication that many thousands of children in our nation are still deprived of stable and secure living arrangements—whether despite or because of the shape of our welfare laws. Second, it reminds policy observers not to rely on overly narrow definitions of success in measuring outcomes. While social scientists prefer to work with easily quantifiable metrics like median gains in income or employment rates, it is important to remember that averages may conceal as much as they reveal. The ability to cite aggregate statistics demonstrating overall social gains offers little comfort to the families who find themselves utterly unable to cope with new program rules and requirements.

The measure of success for welfare legislation must somehow consider whether our laws are making it harder or easier to keep intact the most troubled families. Heroic efforts to hold together and to stabilize the most fragile families all too often meet with frustration that could be alleviated by more responsive and compassionate policy and administration. Even though family members themselves bear ultimate responsibility for their own success or failure, the most enlightened public policy takes account of the interaction between law and actual human behavior and responds appropriately to alleviate hardship and even to anticipate ways of preventing it. Sound welfare policy will always have an eye toward the long-term outcomes most important to families. These certainly include building job skills and enhancing educational attainments that position low-income people for good jobs down the road. Beyond work-related items, they should also include more holistic concerns such as building up parenting skills and prioritizing mundane goals such as guaranteeing ample time to spend with one's children in the course of an average day or week.

In short, a complete picture of family well-being will consider environmental and behavioral factors that bear directly or indirectly on policy outcomes. It is important not to lose sight of the broadest objectives of our nation's social service system, namely to assist families in their efforts to thrive. Cost cutting and financial independence, while legitimate foci as far as they go, must not displace or crowd out key elements of the larger picture. Reviewing these lessons illustrates the wisdom of a quote that reportedly hung on the wall of Albert Einstein's office at Princeton: "Not everything that counts can be counted, and not everything that can be counted counts." While the 1996 welfare overhaul posted solid numbers on some of the broadest aggregate measures traditionally associated with welfare reform (declining caseloads, rising average income of leavers), a careful examination of the details of its outcomes reveals a rather mixed picture of accomplishment. It is only when we restrict our purview so sharply that it includes merely caseload reduction and diminished short-term dependence of families upon government benefits that welfare reform appears to be an unqualified success story.

PATTERNS OF STATE IMPLEMENTATION

Because the 1996 welfare law ushered in a new era of federalism, block-granting the welfare program for the first time in our nation's history, the center of gravity for welfare policy is now the fifty states. It is impossible to evaluate the new TANF system without paying thorough attention to the way states have chosen to implement it. The major problem complicating this task is that there is no single way that can be described in a simple fashion. With the accomplishment of the welfare overhaul of 1996, state governments acquired numerous options regarding their welfare programs and have followed a wide variety of paths in implementing their newfound freedom. The numerous policy directions the states have chosen resist easy summary. This concluding section of the present chapter attempts merely to survey the major trends and to outline the most significant developments regarding state implementation in the years following the 1996 welfare reform law.

Perhaps the single best source of information regarding how states exercised their policy options in appropriating the 1996 federal overhaul to their particular contexts is the Urban Institute in Washington, D.C. In 1997, this independent, nonprofit, and nonpartisan research center launched an impressive project titled Assessing the New Federalism. It is described in Urban Institute literature as

> a multi-year project designed to analyze the devolution of responsibility from the federal government to the states for health care, income security, employment and training programs, and social services. Researchers monitor program changes and fiscal developments. . . . The project studies changes in family well-being. The project aims to provide timely nonpartisan information to inform public debate and to help state and local decisionmakers carry out their new responsibilities more effectively. Key components of the project include a household survey, studies of policies in 13 states, and a database with information on all states and the District of Columbia, available at the Urban Institute's Web site.[94]

The project is especially helpful for present purposes, since it uses 1996 as the base year and measures changes in policy and family well-being after that. Indeed, the stated goal of the project's featured publication series (titled State Policy on Income Support and Social Services) is to "describe how states reshape programs and policies in response to increased freedom to design social welfare and health programs to fit the needs of their low-income populations."[95] This is precisely what the following paragraphs hope to do in the briefest of summary form.

For decades, governors and state officials, including many welfare administrators, had sought expanded control over their local programs and had repeatedly requested greater independence from federal oversight. With the passage of the welfare overhaul in the summer of 1996, they suddenly received all they hoped for. At first the magnitude of the change, coupled with the complexities and even ambiguities of the legislation, had the effect of overwhelming state officials. Upon emerging from a meeting in early September 1996 with several hundred state welfare administrators seeking clarifications about their newfound authority, one federal official remarked: "States are like the dog that ran after the car and finally caught it. Now they are not sure what to do with it. It's amazing what happens when you wish for something and actually get it."[96] Eventually, state officials, acting under the additional constraint of what their own state legislatures mandated, fumbled their way toward full implementation of the new TANF system.

What policies did the states devise? The consensus among policy observers is that every single state enacted policies that complied with federal directives by reducing the availability of public assistance to single mothers (the traditional welfare recipient population) and by greatly increasing their incentive to work. The states accomplished these objectives by means of varying packages of regulations. A 2001 Brookings Institution overview of the content of these state programs offers a typology that highlights five key state options. First, "overall work incentive," a metric that includes the strength of a given state's welfare-to-work programs and the frequency with which it enacts a strategy of diverting applicants from benefits toward rapid employment, is measured on a scale of "strong" to "mixed" to "weak," with a majority of states in the middle category. Second, "benefit generosity" is tallied as "low," "high," or "medium." The nearly even distribution of states among these three groupings confirms the finding that most states made only minor modifications in the level of actual cash benefits for those who still qualify and receive welfare. Third, the category of "earnings disregards" records the levels (low, medium, or high) at which states allow recipients to earn income without forfeiting all their welfare benefits. Phase-in rates and break-even points are taken into account in the rankings, which break down nearly evenly among the three classifications. Fourth, state policy on a wide array of sanctions is scored as "strict," "moderate," or "lenient," with fully one-half of states falling into the strict category. Fifth, a given state's time limit policy is measured on this same scale, with seventeen states registering as "strict," twenty-five as "moderate," and only nine in the "lenient" category.[97]

Other typologies of state policies are readily available. Thomas Gais and R. Kent Weaver offer the simplest categories of any such accounting. Their treatment of selected policy changes that states have chosen to adopt identifies just two categories: "policies enhancing access to supports" and "policies restricting access to supports." While acknowledging the existence of "substantial heterogeneity in packages of state choices," these authors consider the list of positive and negative incentives generally enacted by states to be less than daring. The authors' 2002 essay describing the list of carrots and sticks barely disguises its disappointment over the nearly total absence of creative innovations on the part of "policy outliers," that is to say, states that experiment with novel policy features that differ from a mainstream of "policies reflecting a conservative approach to the goals of work, independence and marriage."[98] It is easy to agree with the implied criticism of the results of welfare reform. After all, much of the initial attraction of the welfare reform movement of the 1990s involved the promise of progress associated with states serving as laboratories of democracy and learning from each other's best practices. In the absence of substantial experimentation, much of the shine comes off this system of enhanced federalism.

The tendency for states, within the obvious remaining constraints of their newfound liberty regarding welfare, to spurn more radical changes has its positive aspects, of course. Ladonna Pavetti notes that "nearly all states have maintained a cash benefit structure and benefit level for non-working families that are comparable to those that were in place prior to 1996."[99] The good news contained in this development is that, contrary to the predictions of some welfare experts, the feared race to the bottom did not occur. The only two states that greatly modified the basic shape of their former AFDC programs are Idaho and Wisconsin, each of which shifted to a flat grant that now ignores the variable of household size in determining welfare benefits offered to a given family. By and large, between 1996 and 2006 states did not conduct wholesale changes in policy beyond what the federal welfare law mandated. The major exceptions to this generalization are the adoption of family caps (by twenty-three states), the lowering of work exemptions for mothers with very young infants (reduced by twenty-two states, where mothers of children under twelve months now are subject to work requirements), and the adoption of intermittent time limits (by fourteen states) as well as lifetime time limits lower than the federally mandated sixty months (by six states).[100]

Why do states adopt the welfare policies that they do? Gais and Weaver briefly address the question of the causal factors that influenced state policy making after 1996. They note an intriguing correlation between states with a prevalence of political conservatism and a high percentage of African Americans, on one hand, with the adoption of more restrictive policy options newly available to states (family caps, shorter time limits, immediate work activity requirements, particularly strong sanction regimes, etc.), on the other hand.[101] A more detailed model of predictors of state policy choices is presented by Pamela Winston in her book *Welfare Policymaking in the States* (2002). The author conducts three extensively researched case studies of states (Texas, Maryland, and North Dakota) that vary substantially in size, types of constituencies, and dominant political cultures. One particularly noteworthy finding of Winston's research is the important role played by public interest and advocacy groups representing the interests of low-income families in the corridors of power in state capitals. Where they are present (as in the case in Maryland) to speak up strongly for the otherwise underrepresented poor citizens in state legislatures, welfare arrangements are far more likely to reflect the actual needs of low-income families than when no such advocacy community is on the scene to voice its concerns (as was the case, by and large, in Texas during the years studied). Winston's actor-centered analysis of the play of interests inside the institutions that set state welfare policy adds much to our understanding of the process and outcomes of post-1996 welfare reform.[102]

If one wished to pursue a wider research agenda regarding the variability of state policies during the early years of the TANF system, the path would surely include further case studies of the policy deliberations and outcomes in individual states. Among the most interesting states to study would be Wisconsin and New York. By virtue of their ambitious workfare programs, these two states stand out as outliers in policy innovation. New York, a state featuring one of the highest welfare caseloads in the nation, is one of seven states (along with California, Maryland, Ohio, Florida, Colorado, and North Carolina) that opted to devolve most welfare program decision-making responsibilities to its constituent counties.[103] Richard P. Nathan of the Albany-based Rockefeller Institute of Government describes the pattern of "state-supervised/county administered systems" as "an arrangement in which states set policy goals, prescribe administrative arrangements, and provide funds, but [where] the basic legal responsibility is lodged at the county level."[104] The resulting second-level devolution challenged counties to expand their administrative capacities, especially in the struggle to implement innovative programs to meet the new work requirements for welfare recipients.

Extensive media coverage of these efforts on the part of county governments, most notably of New York City's ongoing struggles to enhance the effectiveness of its Work Experience Program, occasionally proved embarrassing to the local social service departments, politicians, and state officials who received blame for their failures. One particularly revealing series of *New York Times* articles in April 1998 amounted to an exposé of problematic aspects of the New York City workfare program, including its punitive treatment of welfare recipients, the dead-end nature of the work experiences, and the tendency of the program to displace higher-paid civil servants with less expensive, nonunionized workers.[105] Despite some impressive rhetoric surrounding the goals and philosophy of the Work Experience Program, championed by the popular mayor Rudolph Giuliani and his controversial and hard-charging welfare commissioner, Jason Turner, New York's workfare program was repeatedly accused of exploiting the very people it set out to serve.

In the last decade of welfare reform, no state has attempted a more ambitious transformation of previous arrangements than Wisconsin. Led during the 1990s by Governor Tommy Thompson (who was subsequently appointed as President George W. Bush's secretary of health and human services), Wisconsin has hovered near the top of the list of states in achieving caseload reduction, cutting its welfare rolls by approximately 90 percent in the course of the 1990s. By rebuilding the safety net unambiguously around work rather than welfare benefits, Thompson's Wisconsin Works (or W-2) program refashioned poor relief in radical ways, first under a series of federal waivers, then within the contours of the welfare law of 1996. A national spotlight was focused on the vicissitudes of the program by the journalism of Jason DeParle, a *New York Times* reporter who provided a series of snapshots of program functioning and outcomes during the late 1990s.[106]

Wisconsin's strategy consists of eliminating traditional cash welfare benefits and replacing them with a complex system of guaranteed employment. Recipients are placed on one of four work tracks. First, those deemed work-

ready (approximately 35 percent of TANF recipients in the state find themselves in this category) are expected to find work in ordinary job markets
but are eligible for earnings supplements and an array of benefits such as
subsidized child care, health insurance for one year, and federal and state
income tax credits. Second, a handful of recipients whose job searches are
unsuccessful are eligible for up to six months of subsidized employment, an
arrangement in which the state underwrites employers at levels up to three
hundred dollars per month to support the job slot. A third option (utilized
by about 43 percent of TANF recipients at a given time) consists of community service jobs that the state pays public or nonprofit agencies to create. These positions are limited to nine months and pay much less than the
minimum wage, so that even with income supplements and benefits from
other programs like food stamps, holders of these jobs are mired substantially below the poverty line. Finally, 22 percent of Wisconsin's caseload is
deemed not ready to work but is still responsible for logging forty hours per
week in such activities as drug rehabilitation or physical therapy, supplemented by job training or education. They are eligible for similar income
supplements and in-kind assistance, but their basic stipend provides even
less cash income than the other three tracks.[107]

Several conclusions emerge from the Wisconsin welfare experiment. Its
experience confirms the insight that running a jobs-based program is usually much more expensive than using cash welfare to maintain families at
an income level close to the poverty line. Job search and preparation activities are costly and time-consuming, particularly once the most promising
recipients have been placed and the remaining caseload features the highest
barriers to employment. It is easier to mandate work for all than actually to
find adequate positions in the private job market suitable for the entire caseload, so subsidized and public sector employment becomes the provider of
jobs of last resort for the least job-ready. Indeed, Wisconsin was the pioneer
of a stunning trend in national welfare spending. Because most other states
emulated its emphasis on work over benefits, the overall national percentage of welfare spending that went toward job preparation and work supports increased from 23 percent in 1997 to 56 percent in 2002. In other
words, the percentage of total welfare spending that consisted of cash benefits fell from 77 percent to 44 percent over five years. In this reapportionment of funds, Wisconsin led the way.[108]

From an ethical perspective, the actual outcomes of these efforts for the
well-being of families surpass in importance such measures as the cost and
employment effectiveness of uncompromising versions of work-based programs like Wisconsin's. Of course, it is important to pay attention both to
aggregate statistics and to the hardships and successes that are experienced
by particular families. In this regard, good policy analysis always exhibits a
binocular quality. It makes room for insights and concerns that derive from
individual cases where people and programs interact but is not driven solely
by anecdote. It pays heed to quantifiable measures of success but is not a

slave to the raw numbers. In the case of Wisconsin's recent welfare history, each of these indices offers room for encouragement, but also room for grave concern.

For all the innovative efforts in place in Wisconsin, families have experienced an overall decrease in their level of income security. Only the most successful welfare leavers enjoy significant gains in family income above the admittedly modest level that welfare benefits formerly offered. The success stories consist of families well positioned to take advantage of work-support services and incentives, but clearly not all are able to do so. Because of low prevailing wages even for those who find jobs, many families suffer earnings declines and the associated hardships of inability to pay their monthly bills. A 2004 three-state survey (which included New Jersey and Washington along with Wisconsin) reported that "between half and three-quarters of [welfare participant] families had incomes below the poverty line . . . and a quarter of families in various studies reported that they sometimes or often did not have enough food, or had housing problems (utility disconnection, eviction, or homelessness)."[109]

In the absence of an income safety net, many thousands of families cannot afford even the bare necessities of life. Shortages of child care, lack of health insurance, the unavailability of transportation to many jobs—all these exacerbate the struggles of low-income families in the era of ambitious welfare reform in Wisconsin. Due to time limits and sanctions, many families simply fell through the cracks of the system, with 38 percent reporting no income at all for months at a time and still other families unraveling in a variety of ways. Official Wisconsin sources report a sharp increase during the years 1990–2000 in infant mortality rates, particularly among minorities, and of placements of children in foster care (up 32 percent), particularly in Milwaukee (up 51 percent), the city that features the densest concentration of low-income families.[110] Further social indicators could be cited to detail Jason DeParle's conclusion that, despite bold policy changes intended to improve their situation, many aspects of life for poor families in Wisconsin remain unchanged at best, and in many cases are significantly worse.[111]

How successfully have we appropriated the lessons of these several years of welfare reform? What moral concerns remain unaddressed? By surveying ethical issues at stake in the long-delayed reauthorization of the 1996 welfare law, the final chapter explores the question of what American society has learned from recent experience of social policy overhaul.

NOTES

1. Richard P. Nathan, "The Newest New Federalism for Welfare: Where Are We Now and Where Are We Headed?" in *Rockefeller Reports* (Albany, NY: Nelson A. Rockefeller Institute of Government, October 30, 1997), 6.
2. Ibid., 1.

3. Much news coverage at the time focused on the fears and hardships endured by these immigrants, as well as the backlog of citizenship applications that clogged the naturalization pipeline for many months. See, for example, Celia Dugger, "Backlog Threatens Immigrants Seeking Citizenship," *New York Times,* March 7, 1997, A1, A26. In a few highly publicized cases, despair over lost benefits and associated hardships contributed to the tragic suicides of recent immigrants. For coverage of one such case in New York City, see Clifford Levy, "In Mayor's Race, Clash on Workfare and Immigrant's Suicide," *New York Times,* February 23, 1997, 34. The author of one wide-ranging essay on the effects of this legislation, particularly upon communities of immigrants in California, claims knowledge of "the suicides of scores of elderly and disabled immigrants [due to] the welfare reform bill." Lynn H. Fujiwara, "Asian Immigrant Communities and the Racial Politics of Welfare Reform," in *Whose Welfare?* ed. Mink, 100–31.

4. Quotations to this effect attributed to Representative Shaw at the time of the bill's passage appear in Jeffrey L. Katz, "Welfare: After 60 Years, Most Control Is Passing to States," *Congressional Quarterly Weekly Report,* August 3, 1996, 2190–96. When the Clinton administration was assembling its laundry list of eighty desired changes to the welfare bill just two weeks after the 1996 election, Shaw's House colleague, Republican Bill Archer of Texas, echoed Shaw's resistance to any wholesale changes. See Judith Havemann, "Republicans Steadfast on Welfare Overhaul," *Washington Post,* November 23, 1996, A4.

5. Robert Pear, "Clinton Considers Moves to Soften Cuts in Welfare," *New York Times,* November 27, 1996, A1, A19.

6. Barbara Vobjeda and Judith Havemann, "Governors Seek Changes in Welfare Reform Law," *Washington Post,* February 1, 1997, A1, A12.

7. The $21 billion figure was much higher than most observers expected from Clinton at the time. See Judith Havemann and Barbara Vobjeda, "A $21 B Plan to Cushion the Poor," *Washington Post,* February 5, 1997, A6.

8. Katz, *The Price of Citizenship,* 330.

9. See Robert Pear, "Clinton Will Seek Tax Breaks to Ease Paths off Welfare," *New York Times,* January 28, 1997, A1, A12.

10. Katz, *The Price of Citizenship,* 329–30.

11. Sheila R. Zedlewski and Pamela Loprest, "Will TANF Work for the Most Disadvantaged Families?" in *The New World of Welfare,* ed. Blank and Haskins, 313.

12. Among the primary advocates spearheading the cause of greater recognition for victims of abuse was the National Organization for Women Legal Defense and Education Fund. The major research on the prevalence and dynamics of domestic abuse as it affects welfare recipients is particularly well summarized in Nichola L. Marshall, "The Welfare Reform Act of 1996: Political Compromise or Panacea for Welfare Dependency?" *Georgetown Journal on Fighting Poverty* 4, no. 2 (Spring 1997): 333–45.

13. Demie Kurz, "Women, Welfare and Domestic Violence," in *Whose Welfare?* ed. Mink, 145–46.

14. Actually, this progress remains somewhat fragile because, although both houses of Congress approved the more generous interpretation, a House-Senate conference committee in the fall of 1997 failed in the end to enact this clarification. For details, see "Appropriations: GOP Leaders Pull out of Deal," *Congressional Quarterly Weekly Report,* November 1, 1997, 2688. In the absence of definitive congressional approval, the additional exemptions are being granted by the

Department of Health and Human Services on a discretionary basis. For details, see Kurz, "Women, Welfare and Domestic Violence," 145; Sanford F. Schram, *After Welfare: The Culture of Postindustrial Social Policy* (New York: New York University Press, 2000), 82; Mink, *Welfare's End*, 114.

15. Michael Fix and Ron Haskins, "Welfare Benefits for Non-citizens," in *Welfare Reform and Beyond*, ed. Sawhill et al., 208.

16. Mickey Kaus, "How the GOP Discredits Welfare Reform," *Washington Post*, April 25, 1997, A27. The author chides congressional conservatives for intransigence in blocking proposals for loosening provisions of the law, such as "grandfathering in" additional categories of recent immigrants; Sharon M. Keigher, "America's Most Cruel Xenophobia," *Health and Social Work* 22, no. 3 (August 1997): 232–37.

17. Sue Kirchoff, "Some Benefits for Immigrants Won't Lapse," *Washington Post*, May 3, 1997, A11.

18. Lizette Alvarez, "In New Retreat, Senate Restores Food Stamps for Legal Immigrants," *New York Times*, May 13, 1998, A1, A18. That eventual 1998 legislation, PL 105-185, restored food stamp benefits to about one-third of the nine hundred thousand people who had been cut off in 1996.

19. Pavetti, "Welfare Policy in Transition," 266. The most comprehensive recent account of how immigrants are faring with respect to this loss of benefits appears in section 3 ("Immigration: Transforming the Demographics of Low-Income Families") of *Assessing the New Federalism: Eight Years Later*, ed. Olivia A. Golden et al. (Washington, DC: Urban Institute, 2005).

20. Dana Carney, "GOP Casts a Kinder Eye on 'Huddled Masses': Lawmakers, Candidates Are Backing Away from Immigration Crackdown of the Mid-90s," *Congressional Quarterly Weekly Report*, May 15, 1999, 1127–29; Field, "Immigrant Benefits Revisited," 399.

21. For a survey of statistics and conditions that caught the eyes of policy makers at the time, see Peter Kilborn, "Unlearned, Unhealthy, and Mostly Uninsured," *New York Times*, August 5, 1997, A10.

22. Robert Pear, "40 States Forfeit Health Care Funds for Poor Children," *New York Times*, September 24, 2000, 1, 26.

23. Robert Pear, "States Forfeit Unspent U.S. Money for Child Health Insurance," *New York Times*, October 14, 2002, A15.

24. Robert Pear, "Study Finds Children's Aid Goes to Adults," *New York Times*, August 8, 2002, A1, A19.

25. John Mullahy and Barbara L. Wolfe, "Health Policies for the Non-elderly Poor," in *Understanding Poverty*, ed. Danziger and Haveman, 293.

26. Sheila R. Zedlewski et al., *Potential Effects of Congressional Welfare Reform on Family Incomes* (Washington, DC: Urban Institute, 1996). Figures cited here are contained in a timely summary of the report, titled *Urban Institute Study Confirms That Welfare Bill Would Increase Child Poverty*, published by the Center on Budget and Policy Priorities (Washington, DC: July 26, 1996), that was widely circulated and more readily available to legislators and media in those critical days than the original Urban Institute study itself.

27. One example of media coverage of these earlier reports from official government sources is Allison Mitchell, "Greater Poverty Toll Is Seen in Welfare Bill," *New York Times*, November 10, 1995, A27. In some cases, routine government re-

ports on the predicted effects of subsequent versions of the legislation were either canceled or kept confidential, possibly to avoid public relations embarrassment.

28. Daniel Patrick Moynihan, "The Big Lie of 1996," *New York Times,* January 28, 1997, A13.

29. Mary Jo Bane, "Stand By for Casualties," *New York Times,* November 10, 1996, sec. 4, p. 13.

30. One news story reporting early expressions of concern about this phenomenon is Joe Sexton, "The Trickle-Up Economy: Poor Neighborhoods Fear a Disaster if Welfare Is Cut," *New York Times,* February 8, 1996, B1, B9. Depressed rural areas with limited employment opportunities feared outflows of population due to similar welfare-related factors. See the description of various state programs to address this problem in Jon Jeter and Judith Havemann, "Rural Poor May Seek Greener Pastures: Welfare Recipients Face Relocation as a Result of Work Rules," *Washington Post,* October 14, 1996, A1, A18.

31. Mark Alan Hughes, "Welfare Dust Bowl," *Washington Post,* September 25, 1995, A23.

32. Hilary Sargent, "Sit-in at State House Urges Reprieve of Benefit Cutoff," *Boston Globe,* December 1, 1998, B4. Thirty people were arrested in this culmination in Boston of ongoing statewide demonstrations in support of recipients' rights. An impressive coalition of many Massachusetts advocacy groups participated; Donna De La Cruz, "20 Held After Protest on NYC Welfare Policy," *Boston Globe,* December 8, 1999, A9.

33. Robin Toner, "Rallies in Capital Protest Bush Welfare Proposals," *New York Times,* March 6, 2002, A17; Raymond Hernandez, "Clinton's Stance on Work-fare Alienates Her Liberal Allies," *New York Times,* May 22, 2002, A24.

34. Jon Jeter, "Welfare Plan Rebuffed by Maryland Clerics," *Washington Post,* December 12 1996, A1, A24.

35. Steven Greenhouse, "Nonprofit and Religious Groups to Fight Workfare in N.Y.," *New York Times,* July 24, 1997, A1, A24.

36. Peter Laarman, "An Insult to the Poor," *Sojourners,* May–June 1998, 37.

37. See, for example, Laurie Goodstein, "Churches Are Wary of Government Aid to Assist the Needy," *New York Times,* October 17, 2000, A1, A25.

38. This dilemma is treated in Diego Ribadeneira, "With Eye on Funds, Focus Turns from Pantry to Workplace," *Boston Globe,* December 1, 1998, B1, B4.

39. Scott W. Allard, "Revisiting *Shapiro:* Welfare Magnets and State Residency Requirements in the 1990s," in *Welfare Reform: A Race to the Bottom?,* ed. Sanford F. Schram and Samuel H. Beer (Washington, DC: Woodrow Wilson Center Press, 1999), 62.

40. Schram, *After Welfare,* 103.

41. Allard, "Revisiting *Shapiro,*" 67.

42. Mark Carl Rom, Paul E. Peterson, and Kenneth F. Scheve Jr., "Interstate Competition and Welfare Policy," in *Welfare Reform,* ed. Schram and Beer, 21–41.

43. Richard M. Francis, "Predictions, Patterns and Policymaking: A Regional Study of Devolution," in *Welfare Reform,* ed. Schram and Beer, 180.

44. Allard, "Revisiting *Shapiro,*" 69. For example, New York set the percentage at 50 and Rhode Island at 70.

45. Judith Havemann, "Welfare Magnet Provision Blocked by Judge in California," *Washington Post,* April 5, 1997, A6; Robert Pear, "Judge Rules States

Can't Cut Welfare for New Residents," *New York Times,* October 14, 1997, A1, A20.

46. Linda Greenhouse, "Newcomers to States Win a Right to Equal Welfare," *New York Times,* May 18, 1999, A1, A16.

47. Sanford F. Schram, "Introduction," in *Welfare Reform,* ed. Schram and Beer, 3.

48. Hancock, *Hands to Work,* 153.

49. Linda Greenhouse, "Justices Reject Congress's Curbs on Welfare Suits: First Amendment Issue," *New York Times,* March 1, 2001, A1, A16.

50. "Free Speech for the Poor," *Boston Globe,* March 3, 2001, A14.

51. Isabel Sawhill et al., "Results to Date," in *Welfare Reform and Beyond,* ed. Sawhill et al., 9–19. This chapter contains a helpful series of charts summarizing data from the federal Department of Health and Human Services. Data collected through the beginning of 2002 indicate that thirty-four states reported increases in welfare enrollment in the most recent months surveyed therein, but that the total national level was practically unchanged. See also Robert Pear, "Federal Welfare Rolls Shrink, But Drop Is Smallest Since '94," *New York Times,* May 21, 2002, A12.

52. Thomas L. Gais et al., "Implementation of the Personal Responsibility Act of 1996," in *The New World of Welfare,* ed. Blank and Haskins, 37.

53. For historical comparisons, as well as a critique of and alternatives to official government measures of poverty, see Gary Burtless and Timothy M. Smeeding, "The Level, Trend and Composition of Poverty," in *Understanding Poverty,* ed. Danziger and Haveman, 27–68.

54. Ample tables of data, including detailed poverty statistics for each year, are available on the website of the Census Bureau at www.census.gov. For one analysis of the deeper significance of these trends, see Ray Boshara, "Poverty Is More Than a Matter of Income," *New York Times,* September 28, 2002, sec. 4, p. 13.

55. See, for example, Somimi Sengupta, "How Many Poor Children Is Too Many?" *New York Times,* July 8, 2001, sec. 4, p. 3.

56. 2000 Census Bureau statistics cited in David Hilfiker, *Urban Injustice: How Ghettos Happen* (New York: Seven Stories Press, 2002), xvii.

57. Based upon analysis of Census Bureau figures by the Children's Defense Fund as reported in Sam Dillon, "Report Finds Deep Poverty Is on the Rise," *New York Times,* April 30, 2003, A18.

58. Paul Offner, "Reducing Non-Marital Births," in *Welfare Reform and Beyond,* ed. Sawhill et al., 146. See esp. figure 1, which portrays the leveling off of such births in the mid-1990s. Further analysis of an even larger body of data appears in Cancian and Reed, "Changes in Family Structure," in *Understanding Poverty,* ed. Danziger and Haveman, 69–96.

59. Sanford F. Schram and Joe Soss, "Success Stories: Welfare Reform, Policy Discourse, and the Politics of Research," in *Lost Ground: Welfare Reform, Poverty, and Beyond,* ed. Randy Albelda and Ann Withorn (Cambridge, MA: South End Press, 2002), 69.

60. Ron Haskins and Wendell Primus, "Welfare Reform and Poverty," in *Welfare Reform and Beyond,* ed. Sawhill et al., 62.

61. Sawhill et al., "Results to Date," *Welfare Reform and Beyond,* ed. Sawhill et al., 14.

62. Douglas Besharov, "The Past and Future of Welfare Reform," *The Public Interest*, no. 150 (Winter 2003): 8.

63. Richard B. Freeman, "The Rising Tide Lifts . . . ?" in *Understanding Poverty*, ed. Danziger and Haveman, 123.

64. Besharov, "The Past and Present of Welfare Reform," 9.

65. Ibid., 20.

66. For example, Rebecca M. Blank cites EITC as one of the "government programs that assist poor families [that] have been more successful than many want to claim." See her impressive volume, *It Takes a Nation: A New Agenda for Fighting Poverty* (Princeton, NJ: Princeton University Press, 1997), 84. Further liberal commentary on EITC and related benefits for the working poor appears throughout *Making Work Pay: America After Welfare—A Reader from The American Prospect*, ed. Robert Kuttner (New York: The Free Press, 2002).

67. This point is demonstrated very clearly in Cammisa, *From Rhetoric to Reform*, 129.

68. Michael Massing, "Ending Poverty as We Know It," in *Making Work Pay*, ed. Kuttner, 21–37.

69. This prediction of Gary Burtless is quoted in Jeffrey L. Katz, "Welfare: Putting Recipients to Work Will Be the Toughest Job," *Congressional Quarterly Weekly Report*, July 8, 1995, 2005.

70. For example, the *Boston Globe* offered prominent coverage during 1999 to the release of: (1) a Commonwealth of Massachusetts survey of former recipients (Jordana Hart, "Ex-state Welfare Recipients Living Better, Survey Finds," April 17, 1999, A1, A6); (2) a combined federal report of results in twenty-one states (Laura Meckler, "Ex-welfare Recipients Faring Better, But Still Impoverished," May 12, 1999, A3); (3) a Government Accounting Office summary of welfare-to-work efforts in seventeen states (Judith Havemann, "Once Off Welfare, Most Work, Report Shows," May 27, 1999, A17); and (4) an Urban Institute survey of welfare leavers (Laura Meckler, "Families Leaving Welfare Still Have Trouble Meeting Basic Needs," November 12, 1999, A14).

71. For one example, see Reiko Hayashi, "Welfare Reform and Women's Wages," *Journal of Poverty* 3, no. 2 (1999): 1–19.

72. Ron Haskins, "Effects of Welfare Reform on Family Income and Poverty," in *The New World of Welfare*, ed. Blank and Haskins, 105.

73. Ibid., 128.

74. Ibid.

75. Pavetti, "Welfare Policy in Transition," 269.

76. Ibid.

77. Ibid.

78. Ibid., 271. These findings are confirmed by subsequent reports, such as the 2005 Urban Institute study, *Assessing the New Federalism: Eight Years Later*, ed. Golden et al., esp. part 1.

79. Kathryn Edin and Laura Lein, *Making Ends Meet: How Single Mothers Survive Welfare and Low-Wage Work* (New York: Russell Sage Foundation, 1997).

80. See chap. 4, "Making Ends Meet on a Welfare Check." Out of the 214 respondents, the sole woman who made ends meet on her benefits alone lived a lifestyle so frugal that her neighbors reported her to the authorities at the Department of

Social Services. She was accused of endangering her children by depriving them of adequate clothing (e.g., her son lacked a winter coat).

81. Michael Wiseman, "Food Stamps and Welfare Reform," in _Welfare Reform and Beyond,_ ed. Sawhill et al., 175–76.

82. Statistics reported in Elizabeth Reckler, "Millions Eligible for Food Stamps Aren't Applying," _New York Times,_ February 26, 2001, A1, A11.

83. Wiseman, "Food Stamps and Welfare Reform," 176.

84. Robert Greenstein and Jocelyn Guyer, "Supporting Work Through Medicaid and Food Stamps," in _The New World of Welfare,_ ed. Blank and Haskins, 352–57.

85. The study, titled "Losing Health Insurance: The Unintended Consequences of Welfare Reform," was conducted by an independent consumer group called Families USA and released May 13, 1999. Its findings are described in Robert Pear, "Study Links Medicaid Drop to Welfare Changes," _New York Times,_ May 14 1999, A8.

86. "Medicaid and the Torn Safety Net," _America,_ July 31, 1999, 3.

87. Alan Weil and John Holahan, "Health Insurance, Welfare, and Work," in _Welfare Reform and Beyond,_ ed. Sawhill et al., 184.

88. For more information regarding this consensus, as well as suggestions for Medicaid reform, see Greenstein and Guyer, "Supporting Work Through Medicaid and Food Stamps," esp. 336–46.

89. Weil and Feingold, "Introduction," in _Welfare Reform: The Next Act,_ ed. Weil and Feingold, xxi. The absolute number of child-only cases is actually down slightly in recent years, but the decline is much less steep than that of the overall caseload, hence the increase in relative percentage.

90. Nina Bernstein, "Side Effect of Welfare Law: The No-Parent Family," _New York Times,_ July 29, 2002, A1, A14.

91. This figure comes from an Urban Institute report summarized in the unsigned editorial, "Family Welfare," _Boston Globe,_ August 5, 2002, A10.

92. Census data reported and analyzed in Nina Bernstein, "Child-Only Cases Grow in Welfare," _New York Times,_ August 14, 2001, A1, A21.

93. Statistics from a variety of sources confirming the conclusions in this paragraph appear in Bernstein, "Side Effect of Welfare Law," _New York Times,_ August 14, 2001, A1, A14. Updated statistical analysis of child-only cases appears in Marianne P. Bitler et al., "Has Welfare Reform Affected Children's Living Arrangements?" _Focus_ (Bulletin of the Institute for Research on Poverty at the University of Wisconsin-Madison) 23, no. 2 (Summer 2004): 14–19.

94. This program description appears in each of the thirteen state reports, over three dozen occasional papers, and several series of bulletins and updates published by the project. See, for example, p. v in L. Jerome Gallagher et al., _One Year After Federal Reform: A Description of State Temporary Assistance for Needy Families (TANF) Decisions as of October 1997._ Occasional Paper 6 (Washington, DC: Assessing the New Federalism Project of Urban Institute, June 1998). The Project also maintains an impressive and free web-based State Database that allows users to select their own variables, to customize cross-tabulated searches, and to analyze longitudinal data (for the years 1993 to present) regarding over eight hundred indicators of state welfare policies and family well-being across all fifty states. It is accessed (as of 3 July 2006) at www.urban.org/Content/Research/NewFederalism/StateFocus/StateFocus.htm. It includes a Welfare Rules Database that summarizes the content of state legislation, caseworker manuals, and other state

regulations. Among its sources of regularly updated information are the National Survey of America's Families and the National Conference of State Legislatures.

95. For one instance in the series where this purpose is stated, see Gretchen G. Kirby et al., *Income Support and Social Services for Low-Income People in Massachusetts* (Washington, DC: Assessing the New Federalism Project of Urban Institute, December 1997), iv.

96. This anonymous quotation appears in Robert Pear, "State Welfare Chiefs Ask for More U.S. Guidance," *New York Times,* September 10, 1996, A16.

97. Rebecca M. Blank and Lucie Schmidt, "Work, Wages, and Welfare," in *The New World of Welfare,* ed. Blank and Haskins, 70–102. A helpful chart summarizing these findings on state policies appears at 84–85.

98. Thomas Gais and R. Kent Weaver, "State Policy Choices Under Welfare Reform," in *Welfare Reform and Beyond,* ed. Sawhill et al., 33–40. The phrases cited immediately above in this paragraph appear on 33–35, including Table 1 on 34.

99. Pavetti, "Welfare Policy in Transition," 246.

100. Gais and Weaver, "State Policy Choices," 34 (see Table 1).

101. Ibid., 37–38.

102. Pamela Winston, *Welfare Policymaking in the States: The Devil in Devolution* (Washington, DC: Georgetown University Press, 2002).

103. Linda F. Crowell, "Welfare Reform: Reforming Welfare or Reforming Families?" *Families in Society: The Journal of Contemporary Human Services* 82, no. 2 (March–April 2001): 157. Some of these seven states, along with a handful of others, already featured some elements of county administration even before the 1990s.

104. Nathan, "The Newest New Federalism for Welfare," 5.

105. The four-part *New York Times* series consisted of: Alan Finder, "Evidence Is Scant That Workfare Leads to Full-Time Jobs," April 12, 1998, A1, A26; Steven Greenhouse, "Many Participants in Workfare Take the Place of City Workers," April 13, 1998, A1, A28; Rachel L. Swarns, "Mothers Poised for Workfare Face Acute Lack of Day Care," April 14, 1998, A1, A21; and Vivian S. Toy, "Tough Workfare Rules Used as Way to Cut Welfare Rolls," April 15, 1998, A1, A27.

106. Jason DeParle's initial long feature article ("Getting Opal Caples to Work," *New York Times Magazine,* August 24, 1997, 32–37, 47, 54, 59–61) at the time that cash assistance was in effect being phased out in Wisconsin was followed by his series of seven *New York Times* updates and detailed profiles of programs and families affected by them in Wisconsin during 1998 and 1999. The first in this series was "Wisconsin Welfare Experiment: Easy to Say, Not So Easy to Do," October 18, 1998, 1, 24. The last was "Bold Efforts Leave Much Unchanged for the Poor," December 30, 1999, A1, A12, A13. His reporting experience over these years contributed to DeParle's eventual, well-received volume, *American Dream: Three Women, Ten Kids and a Nation's Drive to End Welfare* (New York: Viking Penguin, 2004).

107. Details regarding Wisconsin's programs are based on information compiled from state reports and contained in the occasional paper from the nonpartisan Center for Economic Development, *Welfare Reform and Beyond: A Policy Update* (New York: Research and Policy Committee of the Center for Economic Development, 2002), 18.

108. These findings appear in Robert Pear, "Welfare Spending Shows Huge Shift," *New York Times,* October 13, 2003, A1, A10.

109. Maria Cancian and Daniel R. Meyer, "Economic Success among TANF Participants: How We Measure It Matters," *Focus* (Bulletin of the Institute for Research on Poverty at the University of Wisconsin-Madison) 23, no. 2 (Summer 2004): 9.

110. These statistics are based on Wisconsin state reports and appear in Francis Fox Piven, "Thompson's Easy Ride," *The Nation,* February 26, 2001, 11–14.

111. DeParle, "Bold Efforts Leave Much Unchanged," A12.

6

THE POLITICS AND ETHICS OF WELFARE REAUTHORIZATION

Previous chapters in this book focus either on policy history and analysis, on one hand, or on ethical concerns and church contributions to the welfare debate, on the other hand. In bringing our study of welfare policy up to the present, this chapter addresses both topics together. The major development we might have hoped to investigate in this final chapter turns out to be a nonevent, as the definitive review and reauthorization of the 1996 welfare law (due in 2002) has been delayed for nearly four years as of this writing and is not expected now until at least 2010. Nevertheless, the unfolding of welfare policy debates over these years occasions the following observations and reflections on the levels of politics and ethical concern.

THE POLITICS OF REAUTHORIZATION

Just as few observers could have predicted the sweeping, even radical nature of the welfare reform of the 1990s, no one expected the utter deadlock over welfare policy that we are experiencing in the first decade of the new millennium. The 1996 welfare reform law technically expired September 30, 2002. Unable to pass a definitive reauthorization bill, Congress maintained the status quo in TANF block grants and eligibility rules by passing a series of stopgap funding measures over the subsequent three and a half years. Through the early months of 2006 there were eleven such extensions. Most of these came on a quarterly basis, renewing TANF without significant alteration for three months at a time, although on two occasions Congress extended the life of current cash welfare arrangements in six-month increments.[1] Finally, in February 2006, with Washington's energies distracted by other pressing issues such as terrorism and the war in Iraq, the decision was made by congressional leaders working on the overdue 2006 budget reconciliation bill simply to fold TANF funding into the omnibus budget bills for the next several years. Thus, according to the terms of this funding allocation compromise, it is most likely that the welfare system will continue in its present form until the year 2010. Minor modifications in program rules, allowable under existing law at the discretion of the president and the federal Department of Health and Human Services, are still possible and would proceed by executive fiat of President George W. Bush or his successor. However, the main story regarding our nation's welfare system is that the arrangements originally scheduled to be reviewed after six years of experimentation have been extended to a decade now, and will likely be frozen in place without substantial review or alteration for several more years.

While congressional slowdowns and logjams surprise few Americans anymore, an analysis of the multiyear delay in reauthorizing welfare reveals fundamental causes beyond the partisan bickering that has held up so many spending bills and other pieces of important federal legislation in recent years. The root causes of the welfare stalemate also transcend the fact that America's response to terrorism and its preoccupation with the wars in Iraq and Afghanistan have commanded center stage in our national life from September 2001 to the present. The delay in reauthorizing welfare has not been primarily due to a lack of attention. Rather, Congress found itself stymied on the future of social policy because of the presence of sharply contrasting visions and competing proposals for the next steps regarding our nation's programs for low-income families.

One route Congress could follow was mapped out by President Bush. Starting in early 2002, Bush proposed a welfare reauthorization bill that included stricter work requirements (states would eventually have to comply with a 70 percent participation standard rather than the previous 50 percent), an increase in work hours per week required of participants (from thirty to forty), and a tighter definition of work activities (a prohibition on counting more than sixteen hours of attendance at school, job-training programs, or substance abuse treatment programs toward the minimum work hours). The Bush plan also included provisions for states to spend up to $350 million per year on abstinence-based sex education programs and marriage-promotion initiatives. States would operate these novel counseling and mentoring programs using a combination of funds diverted from the TANF block grants and additional federal matching funds. The basic TANF block grants to the states would remain at the same levels (about $17 billion), but no additional federal money would initially be set aside for child care under the Bush plan.[2]

On two occasions during Bush's first term, the House of Representatives passed versions of the president's welfare proposal: during the 107th Congress on May 16, 2002 (by a margin of 229 to 197) and during the 108th Congress on February 13, 2003 (by a margin of 230 to 192).[3] On both occasions, despite pushing his welfare agenda extraordinarily hard on Capitol

Hill, the president persuaded only a handful of Democrats to support his bill.[4] The pressure Bush exerted paid off mostly in enforcing strict party discipline among House Republicans. Key players in the triumph of the Bush bill over more moderate Democratic alternatives included then–Health and Human Services secretary Tommy G. Thompson and his assistant Wade F. Horn, who served as Bush's point men on the issue, as well as Representative Wally Herger, a California Republican who chaired the House Ways and Means Human Resources Subcommittee. Herger was the primary sponsor of the 2003 bill (labeled HR 4737) and used his considerable muscle to streamline the process by which the Bush welfare package passed the House. It did so in record time—with a vote on the floor of the House just nine days after the bill's introduction and without benefit of the customary markup process in the three committees that share jurisdiction over welfare.[5]

Senate Republicans, for their part, were not able to deliver the welfare reauthorization issue to President Bush for a number of reasons. Early in Bush's first term, the razor-thin Republican majority in the Senate was upended by the May 2001 defection of Senator Jim Jeffords of Vermont, who quit the GOP abruptly and announced his intention to vote thereafter with the Senate Democrats, giving them the narrow majority. This transfer of control over the apparatus of the upper chamber disrupted the progress of many pieces of Republican-sponsored legislation, including welfare reauthorization. For their part, the Democrats were unable to parlay their temporary control of the Senate into a workable compromise on welfare. In fact, the leader of the short-lived Democratic majority in the Senate, Tom Daschle of South Dakota, came to be vilified by many liberal Democrats for his welfare strategy. He was accused of vacillating and delaying the progress of a potential welfare bill shortly before the election, perhaps in the hope of striking a more favorable compromise in a potentially more Democratic Congress in 2003.[6] Instead, Daschle's gamble turned out to be a losing wager, as Republicans regained control of the Senate after the 2002 midterm elections and increased the margin of their majority in the 2004 election that unseated Daschle himself along with several other prominent Senate Democrats.

But several features of the landscape of the Senate proved a deterrent to a quick Bush victory despite growing Republican strength in the chamber. Despite holding majorities, the Republicans could not overcome complicated Senate procedural rules that allow the minority party to block or delay action indefinitely, so long as they can muster a requisite forty votes. In addition, perhaps because of the electoral dynamic of statewide election of senators, the Senate perennially tends to attract and retain more centrist members than the House, and many of the most moderate Republicans in the Senate harbored serious reservations about the Bush welfare plan. Some of these moderates sit on the Senate Finance Committee, a key body that reviews all welfare proposals before they can proceed to the Senate floor. Charles E. Grassley, the Iowa Republican who assumed the chair of the

Finance Committee when the Republicans regained control of the Senate after the November 2002 elections, has a solid reputation as a conciliator and has repeatedly agreed to slow down divisive versions of welfare legislation, even those he personally supports. However, even more consequential than the irenic style of Chairman Grassley has been the resolve of Olympia J. Snowe (R-ME) to shape the welfare bill to her liking. For Snowe, this entails sharply increased federal commitments to subsidize child care for mothers making the transition from welfare to work, as well as more lenient and flexible provisions than appear in the Bush proposal regarding work requirements and how they may be fulfilled. Revealing a key concern that motivates her advocacy of alternative welfare plans, Senator Snowe frequently cites the statistic that only 15 percent of income-eligible children receive child care subsidies.[7]

It was, in fact, Senator Snowe who played the pivotal role in bringing welfare reauthorization at last to the Senate floor, the closest it has yet come to passage. In September 2003 the Senate Finance Committee was considering a version of a welfare bill that closely matched what the House had passed earlier in the year; the differences would surely have been worked out through compromise in conference committee and sent on to the White House for certain approval. With the eight Democrats on the committee voting against the package, Snowe agreed at last to side with her eight fellow Republicans to allow the bill to advance to the full Senate. However, she did not reverse her earlier position of blocking the bill until she garnered significant concessions. Snowe's vote to approve the measure was conditioned upon receiving a promise that she would be able to offer an amendment to the final version of the bill to add $5 to $6 billion for child care, on top of the $1 billion that had already been added by the Senate Finance Committee to the original Bush proposal and the House bill.[8] The deal eventually fell apart anyway, at least partially because the Senate version had pared down Bush's forty-hour work requirement to thirty-four hours and added more exceptions on work rules than hard-liners were in the end willing to countenance.

The next time a version of welfare reauthorization reached the Senate floor, in March 2004, a similar compromise measure (one that included all the child care funding Snowe had supported) received a stunning 78–20 vote of initial approval.[9] However, it was soon bogged down with demands on the part of Senate Democrats for so many amendments and side deals (including one to raise the minimum wage from $5.15 to $7 per hour) that the compromise once again proved to be too unpalatable for the Republican majority to accept. The welfare bill was shelved on April 1, 2004 after the Republican leadership failed to muster the sixty votes needed to limit debate on the bill.[10] No welfare proposal again progressed as far as those described above, and the February 2006 decision to roll TANF funding into successive budget bills without substantial program review or changes until 2010 reflects general frustration with this congressional deadlock.

In retrospect, many of the vicissitudes of recent welfare legislative proposals evidence electioneering tactics rather than sincere attempts to improve social policy. Neither side in recent debates is immune from charges that its welfare posturing amounts to thinly veiled ploys for favorable attention and repeated attempts to use welfare as a wedge issue amidst a hotly contested electoral landscape. Conversely, perhaps the most sincere actors to tread onto the national welfare policy stage in recent years have been the governors of the fifty states. The National Governors' Association, in a March 2004 letter to Congress, made an eloquent case for the advantages of definitive action on welfare policy. Displaying a seriousness of purpose that has often eluded the House and Senate as they have flirted for years with giving President Bush constantly shifting portions of what he proposed on welfare policy, the governors made a bipartisan appeal to stop the endless bickering and settle on an agreeable compromise. The governors' letter advocated a five-year reauthorization of TANF that would be more stable than the recent status quo of frequent short-term funding extensions, for it would "provide states with the predictability needed for continued success of welfare reform initiatives across the country."[11] In this, the National Governors' Association was reprising its constructive role in the 1996 round of welfare reform, making solid arguments regarding the practicalities of social policy, of which legislators on the national scene often seem to lose sight. One of these practical details is the need for states to plan well in advance for future budget cycles, especially in the new era of devolution.

However much we might admire the forthrightness of the nation's governors and their measured impatience with the political process in Washington, it is also important to consider the argument that further postponement and continued indeterminacy may prove preferable to a quick but inadequate resolution to the ongoing welfare policy struggle. Simply to acquiesce to all aspects of President Bush's blueprint on social policy for the sake of expediency would have constituted an abdication of responsibility on the part of those who, for reasons of principle, have opposed Bush's brand of "compassionate conservatism," whether in Congress or beyond, whether among Democrats or within the president's own party. Indeed, a significant subplot of the welfare reauthorization saga has been the test of wills among Republicans themselves, most notably in the U.S. Senate. Within the ranks of the GOP, support for many aspects of Bush's agenda has waxed and waned according to the vicissitudes of events such as the president's failed campaign to privatize Social Security and the many setbacks in the war in Iraq. Party discipline eroded as the White House continued its losing streak. The ultimate failure to enact the full Bush welfare plan may be chalked up to the unwillingness of congressional Republicans to close ranks behind a president who turned out to be surprisingly vulnerable even after winning a second term in office, albeit in a second consecutive electoral photo finish. The fact that thirty-one Senate Republicans defied Bush's instructions in the aforementioned March 2004 showdown on a welfare bill signaled the limits of the president's support on Capitol Hill, at least on domestic issues.[12] The February 2006 decision to put off definitive action on welfare until much later makes eminent sense in light of these political considerations.

To this point, the present chapter has focused on the fate of the Bush proposal, but there are other ways of organizing this narrative of the reauthorization process. The events from 2002 to 2006 may also be portrayed as a function of competing visions of the future of social policy. Those with serious doubts about the workability and desirability of President Bush's version of compassionate conservatism seek to broaden the picture considerably. Rather than zeroing in on stricter enforcement of the personal responsibility agenda, they tend to focus on such social responsibilities as enhancing government's role in the tasks of making work available and making work pay for those attempting the transition from welfare to work. These alternative voices emphasize concern about the practicalities of life in a nation whose low-income families are experiencing sharply diminished access to welfare benefits. This set of concerns has provided the motivation for those who oppose parts or all of the Bush proposal from within the Republican Party—most prominently Olympia Snowe in her insistence on substantially increased child care funding and more generous provisions for meeting work requirements. These same apprehensions stand behind the numerous Democratic bills and amendments submitted to Congress that were routinely steamrolled off the agenda by the Republican congressional majority.

Because the next section of this chapter shifts from the politics to the ethics of reauthorization, these last observations supply something of a conceptual bridge. In light of the elements of the Bush proposal for welfare reauthorization, and against the background of what we saw in chapter 5 regarding the implementation and effects of the 1996 welfare reform so far, what ethical judgments may we reach regarding a desirable future for American welfare policy?

ONGOING ETHICAL CONCERNS REGARDING WELFARE POLICY

Elsewhere, in an exploration of relevant issues that appeared in the early months of the reauthorization debates, I have outlined the most important ethical concerns that arise from the standpoint of Christian social ethics in viewing the likely shape of welfare reauthorization.[13] This section updates and extends that analysis by examining six interrelated aspects of the current discussion: (1) the TANF funding mechanism; (2) work participation requirements; (3) eligibility rules, including time limits, sanctions, and exemptions; (4) marriage promotion programs and the family cap; (5) work-support programs ancillary to TANF; and (6) the imposition of disproportionate burdens upon particular demographic groups. In each case, we will examine ethical aspects of the status quo in federal welfare policy as well as possible alternatives. In doing so, we will return to the framework of Catholic social teaching introduced in chapters 1 and 4.

The TANF Funding Mechanism

Serious calls for revising the basic structure of the TANF block grant system have been almost completely absent in political discourse, but weighty arguments proposing significant ethical reservations remain. The formula for dividing the annual federal contribution to states' welfare programs was set in 1995 as part of the bargaining that preceded the adoption of the 1996 legislation. It has not been adjusted since that time, and there appear to be no proposals on the table for updating the distribution of shares that go to each state. Probably for fear of opening up a Pandora's box of claims and counterclaims regarding which states deserve a larger share due to demographic shifts, politicians seem loathe to revisit the question and to consider reapportioning the fixed TANF funding pool.

Many grounds could be cited to support the case for reapportionment. High-growth states over time find themselves supporting a larger population with the same TANF block grant. States with rising unemployment and falling incomes (at least relative to other states) may discover that their share of the national welfare caseload has increased as more families within their borders slip below the poverty line than is occurring elsewhere. States that, for reasons beyond the control of public authorities, find themselves less readily able to move welfare recipients into work in the private sector and off the welfare rolls face a heavier demand for their capped share of federal block grants, while more successful states sit on excess TANF funding.

A key principle of Christian social ethics may be cited here in objection to the current arrangements for federal welfare spending. This is a deep-seated conviction, present in scripture, developed in patristic thought, and incorporated into various versions of Christian doctrines of creation and providence, among other topics, that God intends the material resources of this world to serve the actual human needs of all, not just the desires of a few. Chapter 1 surveyed the Roman Catholic discourse regarding this theme, with its development of concepts like the social character of property, the proper role of the state in promoting the common good, and the universal destination of material goods. Especially in the most recent documents of Catholic social teaching, this imperative constitutes a call for public efforts beyond privately administered charitable initiatives.[14] In a prosperous country like the United States, government has a positive and solemn duty to devote significant resources to the task of poverty alleviation. While there is room for reasonable disagreement regarding the size and extent of the welfare functions of a given state, it seems beyond dispute that it is right to expect a certain measure of equity and procedural fairness in the administration of funds that are set aside for public assistance to poor families. Equity entails that families facing similar difficulties and barriers to thriving are eligible to receive similar levels of assistance, regardless of the accidents of geography (that is, which states and local jurisdictions these families happen to inhabit within the national community).

The current system of TANF block grant funding offends against this principle of equity in the distribution of poor relief. Because it has no provision for adjusting the shares states receive over time, it perpetuates the problem (long a part of AFDC program administration, as we saw in chapter 2) of unequal access to public assistance. Our nation's welfare arrangements continue to feature high- and low-benefit states, and the TANF block grant system is interacting with ongoing economic trends to exacerbate state-to-state differentials whose historic roots are tainted with racial discrimination. While the field of political history reveals these disturbing facts, the discipline of ethics ventures the judgment that there ought to be a proportionate relationship between resources provided by our public authorities and the actual needs of people in all parts of the nation. To perpetuate a welfare system that fails to make provision for demographic shifts, caseload changes, and even the differential effects of economic recessions and business cycles on different parts of our nation amounts to systematic, even if unintentional, discrimination.

Even if it is unlikely to reverse the new style federalism of the 1996 welfare law or to reinstate the principle of entitlement to federal welfare assistance, the reauthorization process could be an occasion to redress the many ways in which the TANF program is unresponsive to actual human needs. Unfortunately, little concern has been expressed so far regarding the size and structure of the block grants to the states. Public discourse around the reauthorization seems to suggest that most observers are satisfied with a system that locks into place a rigid formula of fixed and capped spending commitments to alleviate poverty. Indeed, the actual financial commitment falls every year, as the effects of inflation eat into the real value of the federal share of welfare spending, regardless of the level of spending on the part of the states.[15] The reauthorization debate has unfortunately so far ignored the need for adjustments that would make the block grant system more responsive to actual human needs.

Work Participation Requirements

This is another item on the reauthorization agenda that, at least from an ethical perspective, represents a missed opportunity for rethinking a problematic aspect of recent welfare reforms. As chapter 3 described in detail, the 1996 welfare law gave states wide leeway to develop their own welfare-to-work programs, but this unprecedented freedom to experiment without federal oversight was conditioned upon a set of strict requirements. In order to qualify for their full federal block grant, states had to meet a minimum work participation rate for their welfare caseloads. Since 2002, the required rate has been 50 percent. Starting in February 2002, when it announced its initial welfare reauthorization proposal, the Bush administration has advocated for raising this rate to 70 percent, with the increase to be phased in over four years. Further, in the interest of getting tough on work, the Bush proposal sought to close various loopholes in work requirement enforcement. The standard for required work effort would rise from thirty to forty hours per week, now with no more than ten of those hours to be accounted for through education or job preparation activities as opposed to actual work in the private or public sectors.[16] Whereas states are allowed under the 1996 law to limit the work requirement to twenty hours per week for mothers with children under the age of six, the president's plan aimed at eliminating most existing state allowances for the needs of new mothers.[17]

It is hardly surprising that voices on the right would be eager to build on the perceived success of the 1996 law in further expanding its work-based approach to welfare. The questions that remain to be settled involve whether this path of strict work enforcement, however desirable it may be, turns out to be realistic and feasible, given the characteristics of the population it targets—mostly single mothers with young children to care for. The nation's governors quickly went on record with their assessment that this proposed ratcheting up of work requirements is patently unrealistic. The same month that Bush announced his plan for welfare reauthorization, the National Governors' Association, consisting of a majority of Republicans, announced its demurral. Citing their experience in implementing work-based welfare reform over the previous six years, the governors protested that work requirements should be eased, not tightened, as the nation updates the 1996 law.[18]

Within months, the governors had produced a study to demonstrate how impractical stricter work standards would be.[19] One of the major arguments against mandating higher standards was described in chapter 5, where we saw that states have so far relied on the caseload reduction credit to meet the rising work percentage requirements. We noted that since 1996, states have complied with the work rules by counting as the denominator in calculating work participation rates the gross number of welfare cases in the mid-1990s, when AFDC enrollment was at its historic high point. Only by receiving credit for the overall drop-off in the caseload have states met their quotas and avoided forfeiting large portions of their allotted block grants. Once this practice is discontinued, as the Bush proposal called for, few (or possibly no) states would meet a 50 percent work participation requirement, much less one of 70 percent. The governors said openly what all informed welfare policy observers acknowledge at least privately in moments of candor: that it is only by cooking the books that states have so far artificially met unrealistic work quotas.

Once again, policy history runs up against moral concerns, as principles drawn from theological ethics pass an unfavorable judgment regarding the drift of U.S. welfare policy. As our survey of welfare policy development in chapter 2 demonstrates, our nation has been moving for decades decidedly away from an income-maintenance rationale for its welfare programs and toward a work-enforcement approach. With the 1996 law, we moved definitively from a national policy based on work incentives to one based on work requirements. On the surface, this rationale can be defended for its congruence with a bundle of laudable values ambient in American culture, with its high regard for the work ethic. "Getting tough on welfare" makes for powerful campaign rhetoric, appealing to the senses of reciprocity ("those who receive should also give something back") and fairness ("many mothers successfully join the workforce, why cannot welfare mothers?") that play an important role in our political culture.

However, the insistence that practically all mothers, regardless of their life circumstances, enter the workforce on a forty-hour-per-week basis amounts to a simplistic and potentially dangerous mandate. To the empirical data upon which the nation's governors base their objections we can add moral arguments regarding the value of mothers spending at least the first months and perhaps years of the lives of their children primarily in the home. We saw in chapter 4 that the U.S. Catholic bishops, drawing upon previous theological reflection on family life, proposed detailed arguments along these lines in the welfare debates of the 1980s and 1990s. While maintaining a pro-work posture ("Those who can work ought to work," affirmed their 1995 document on welfare reform), the bishops provided some needed contextualization to work solutions to the welfare problem as proposed by hard-liners.[20] The bishops reminded us that such measures prove to be inadequate unless welfare recipients receive the transition assistance they need and thus encounter hope for real progress toward dignified and sustainable self-sufficiency. Without substantial job preparation and transitional help, single parents who expect to leave welfare through work are unlikely to escape poverty and will likely cycle back into dependency. Neither rapid entrance into the job market (the much-vaunted work-first strategy) nor public service employment (such as the workfare programs tried intermittently by a few states such as Wisconsin and cities such as New York) hold any promise as silver bullet solutions to the problems of low-income, single-parent families. As the bishops argue, and as other religious traditions attest, work is just one part of the overall fabric of social life. Arbitrary work rules and one-size-fits-all programs for single parents are simply punitive unless the larger social ecology of family life is acknowledged, accounted for, and supported in appropriate ways.

Under provisions of the original Bush proposal, even fewer families would have recourse to anything but work, no matter the challenges facing their lives that lead them to seek public assistance. They would surely be busier, but no better off, as single parents would possess even less time to nurture their children, complete their education, and upgrade their skills while working outside the home as increasingly required by law. In light of these practical concerns, proposals to raise work requirements across-the-board come up short on ethical grounds. In terms of the Catholic social teaching principles enumerated at the end of chapter 1, higher work requirements appear to conflict with the prohibition against placing people in impossible situations. Taking a stand against getting tougher on work for welfare mothers may not be a politically popular tactic. Nevertheless, it emerges as a moral imperative to ask some hard questions before we acquiesce in a national policy that imposes heavy burdens upon low-income families that some will find impossible to bear.

These concerns about the practicality as well as the ethics of enhanced work requirements turn out to be more than idle ruminations. The February 2006 agreement that extended the TANF system also accorded the executive branch new authority to set standards for the interpretation of work rules under which states are accountable to the federal Department of Health and Human Services. In late June 2006, the Bush administration announced its intention to enforce new uniform standards for the fulfillment of work requirements. These include stricter measures for compliance with federal expectations regarding the twelve categories of upper- and lower-tier activities that count as work preparation and work experience. Equally significant, new program rules henceforth discontinue the use of the caseload reduction credit, the bookkeeping technique that had artificially allowed states to claim inflated successes in moving former welfare recipients into work. Because the new denominator for calculating percentages of caseload success will shift from the high 1994 levels to the much lower 2005 levels, states will have a much more strenuous standard to meet, and many states are likely to forfeit significant percentages (perhaps as high as the upper limit of 21 percent) of their federal TANF grants under the new system of enforcement.[21] Although President Bush ultimately settled for half a loaf and did not succeed in raising the work requirement to 70 percent of the current caseload as his initial proposal sought, nevertheless work requirements are becoming far more stringent under the terms of these new rules.

Eligibility Rules: Time Limits, Sanctions, and Exemptions
Recall from the description of the 1996 welfare legislation in chapter 3 that, in a striking departure from previous AFDC policy, the law imposed a five-year lifetime limit on eligibility for federal welfare benefits. While states are free to provide such recipients with supplementary benefits from their own state revenues (a few generous states are doing so), they may also exercise the prerogative to impose shorter time limits. Starting in 2001, hundreds of thousands of families have hit the five-year federal time limit, and every subsequent year will witness more families for whom the welfare clock has expired.

Like time limits, sanctions are designed to motivate welfare clients to take proactive steps to comply with program rules such as job search and work participation requirements and eventually to leave the welfare system altogether. The usual penalty for noncompliance is a temporary and partial reduction of welfare benefits, although the full family sanction (the loss of a family's entire cash grant, at least for a time) is also employed in some states. Similar financial penalties have long been a feature of the welfare landscape, but the 1996 welfare law gave states unprecedented freedom to impose sanctions, including the experiments with Learnfare and Immuno-fare mentioned in chapter 3. We have already noted the major moral objections that arise in response to a welfare policy that assumes the worst about recipient families, namely that they constitute a class of people who, unlike the rest of society, respond only to the harshest of negative incentives (sticks rather than carrots).

It may well be that, by some calculus or other, certain families truly deserve these drastic punishments for their failure to cooperate with the terms of public assistance programs. Overly lenient program rules probably do send unfortunate messages and invite some recipients to take unfair advantage of the welfare system. However, consider two serious problems with sanctions as practiced in the new era of welfare policy. First, on the practical level, administrative mistakes are made on occasion, and they seem to come particularly frequently in welfare offices. While partial cutoffs of benefits may be a sustainable inconvenience, the full-family sanction, if erroneously imposed and not very quickly corrected, could become a life-threatening injustice. Untimely and unforeseen cutoffs of family income may cause eviction from rental housing, immediate homelessness, and resort to unreliable emergency services or to desperate measures such as borrowing money from loan sharks. Second, on a more philosophical level, full-family sanctions raise the ethical objection that public policies are punishing children for the behavior of their parents regarding both the cause of the imposition of the sanction and the aftermath. Children may find themselves victims of the unsavory arrangements for family financing that their desperate parents fall into: prostitution, drug running, and other illegal activities. Many other aspects of American welfare policy in this new era of uncompromising emphasis on personal responsibility are susceptible to this line of criticism, but none more obviously than punitive sanctions policies imposed by states.

While it is probably not the intention of any welfare reformer deliberately to harm children, nevertheless structuring a system around time limits and sanctions is an approach that fails to negotiate a reasonably adequate way around the "dual-client trap." This phrase describes the inextricable way in which punishing custodial parents, who arguably sometimes deserve such penalties, inevitably harms their children, who cannot be at fault in the same sense. The merits of this point win recognition across the political spectrum. Liberal economist Rebecca Blank identifies sanctions and time limits as "the most objectionable part of the 1996 legislation" because they are based on the false assumption that few recipients face insuperable barriers to employment and self-sufficiency.[22] Even the conservative analyst

Robert Rector of the Heritage Foundation, one of the most high-profile Washington-based advocates for the strict behavioral requirements of the 1996 law, appears to be backpedaling on this bundle of issues. In a 2001 essay he expressed serious doubts about the continuing usefulness of these limits, claiming that, although "time limits have played an enormous symbolic role in welfare reform, . . . it seems that the heyday for time limits as a major mechanism of reform has passed."[23]

On a theological level, several arguments could be mounted for scaling back the reliance on time limits and sanctions. Adherents to Catholic social teaching might well invoke the preferential option for the poor, one of the principles explicated in chapter 1. As we saw there, the option for the poor is a concept developed in the context of Latin American liberation theology but has been incorporated, albeit cautiously, into recent papal social documents and addresses.[24] Although we normally think of such an option for the poor being made by an individual or by voluntary groups such as churches, even governments might appear to be under an obligation not to go out of their way needlessly to make the lives of the poor more difficult, as sanctions and time limits arguably do.

Indeed, a potential remedy is already at hand, written into the same law that implemented these policy measures on a national basis. The 1996 welfare reform law allows each state to designate up to 20 percent of its caseload as exempt from the time limit. This provision is a welcome measure of mercy, but still it establishes a rather arbitrary mark that should be improved upon. In the interest of bringing greater rationality to the exemption, it should be extended to all those who meet objective qualifications according to carefully delineated categories of hardship. Otherwise, applicants for benefits will continue to engage in an odd game of one-downsmanship with each other, competing with one another for precious slots reserved for those least capable of self-sufficiency. We have already seen in chapter 5 how the Wellstone-Murray Family Violence Option has been extended to the states in recent years as an amendment to the 1996 law, allowing states to exempt women demonstrably at risk of domestic violence from the welfare time limits. Even without altering the framework of current welfare arrangements, more extensive exemptions from time limits could be granted to cover a variety of impediments to rapid progress toward employability, such as medical conditions, family crises, recessions, and other structural barriers and hardships.

It would be an egregious missed opportunity for legislators to overlook the need to abridge these punitive aspects of current welfare policy. This is especially so since there appears to be a growing consensus that time limits and sanctions are proving counterproductive in our era. The ethical high ground increasingly appears to belong to those who make the case for further categories of exemptions and less arbitrariness in granting exceptions to time limits and sanctions.

Marriage Promotion Programs and the Family Cap

Among the most important motivations behind the 1996 welfare law were concerns about family formation and reducing out-of-wedlock births. The very preamble to the law begins, "Marriage is the foundation of a success-ful society," and it goes on to laud "the formation and maintenance of two-parent families."[25] A subtext of the law is the theory that one shortcut to sharply reducing welfare dependency is to adopt public policies that encour-age stable family life within the context of traditional marriage. Yet most family-values conservatives were dissatisfied when the 1996 law turned out to be a rather feeble instrument for their preferred agenda. As we saw in chapter 3, most of the conservative mandates they preferred (such as teen-age mother exclusions and strict family caps) were rendered state options in the final legislative compromise. The pro-family rhetoric contained in the law was, by most accounts, reduced to mere window dressing and was not readily translated into aggressive policy on the part of the states. Conserv-atives like Robert Rector and Charles Murray pinned their hopes for a re-vival of the marriage promotion agenda on the reauthorization process.

The Bush administration sought to mollify such family-values conserva-tives. Its successive welfare proposals since February 2002 have all included unprecedented and ambitious initiatives along these lines. Hundreds of mil-lions of dollars would be earmarked for research and demonstration proj-ects in the interest of developing marriage promotion programs targeted at the low-income families most likely to receive welfare benefits. A key role would be played by state governments, which would serve as clearinghouses for the distribution of federal grants for such activities as pro-marriage ad-vertising campaigns and classroom-based education as well as pre-marriage counseling and weekend mentoring seminars to explain to eligible couples the virtues and advantages of marriage. Succeeding versions of the Bush welfare proposal and the reauthorization plan sponsored by House Repub-licans varied somewhat in detail, but funds earmarked for marriage promo-tion generally expanded as the plan displayed increasing appeal to Bush's conservative base in the months leading up to the 2004 election. Modest ini-tial suggestions for a $300 million program grew by 2004 to a more ambi-tious plan to commit approximately $1.5 billion over six years to various marriage promotion services.[26] The 2006 budget agreement that included welfare provisions to extend TANF funding for up to four more years au-thorized federal agencies to spend $150 million per year on marriage pro-motion and responsible fatherhood programs and grants.[27]

The initial publicity campaigns to announce these Bush proposals were greeted with a fair amount of scorn and derision, primarily on the part of liberals who branded it Bridefare and accused it of manipulative social engineering. A March 2002 *Boston Globe* editorial urged states to shun co-operation with this "federally funded version of the Bride of Franken-stein."[28] A less spirited op-ed in the *New York Times* a few months later offered concrete suggestions for better use of the funds. It contended that, instead of engaging in unproven experiments to overcome the reluctance of potential brides, government should use this money to offer a variety of tangible work supports and foster social and economic conditions that render marriages more attractive for the working poor.[29] Even the Committee for Economic Development, a nonpartisan research group that generally supports the Bush welfare reform proposal, warns against hasty public interventions in such sensitive personal matters as marriage behavior.

It surprised even more observers when Michael Tanner, a long-time critic of the old AFDC system and the liberals who supported it, began to speak out against this aspect of the Republican welfare plan, which he called derisively "a giant government program . . . [which] may have unintended negative consequences."[30] But Tanner's criticisms of marriage promotion turn out to be fully congruent with the agenda of his employer, the Cato Institute, a libertarian think tank that consistently espouses small-government approaches. Fiscal conservatives like Tanner are not always in sync with the priorities of social conservatives. The final sentence of Tanner's 2003 essay attacking the Bush proposal serves as a needed reminder that the right wing of the political spectrum does not speak with a single voice on this issue: "If liberals had introduced this costly big-government social experiment, conservatives would be outraged, and they would be right."[31]

Attempts to assess the moral significance of this issue in welfare reauthorization must grapple with the great complexity that characterizes all such interactions between government policy and such private behavior as decisions about marriage. On one hand, it is hard to disagree with the proposition that children fare better on all relevant developmental and educational indices in more stable households. A significant body of data supports the claims of pro-marriage voices regarding the human and social costs associated with the failure to form and sustain healthy marriages.[32] Indeed, proposals to reduce teen pregnancy and extramarital births and to increase the role of noncustodial fathers in the lives of their children hold the potential to resolve much of the welfare conundrum. On the other hand, simplistic approaches to family formation that are advocated on a narrowly moralistic basis will not only fail as pragmatic public policy, but appear ethically suspect as well. Encouraging couples to wed on an indiscriminate basis can end up being harmful, indeed potentially dangerous for women and children. After all, not all men who sire children are good candidates for responsible parenthood. For a variety of reasons, ranging from their personal qualities to their economic prospects and even histories of criminal activity, many such men do not make desirable husbands. It is wise to heed feminist voices that raise weighty concerns about the potential for abuse and violence in households that are hastily drawn together for extrinsic reasons, such as economic viability or in response to the pressure of a government-run mentoring program, rather than on the basis of genuine affection and the desire to forge a shared future regardless of the necessary sacrifices.

Feminists such as Gwendolyn Mink and the dozen contributors to an impressive 1999 volume of essays edited by Elizabeth Bounds, Pamela Brubaker, and Mary Hobgood offering critiques of welfare policy do us a great service by demonstrating the relationship between welfare rights and women's equality.[33] Welfare policies that make it difficult for a single mother to survive without a male breadwinner and policies that implicitly marginalize and stigmatize female-headed households harm women in the name of enforcing a set of social norms that are undeniably patriarchal.[34] It is certainly laudable to encourage stable marriages, but to enshrine in the public policies of a pluralistic society the principle that a low-income parent is to be punished for failure to live up to this noble ideal is frankly unjust. The preferences regarding family structure and behavior that we might pursue and advocate in our capacity as private citizens and religious individuals do not translate neatly and simply into public policy. In sum, as good a thing as a healthy marriage is, we should be wary of proposals that suggest that marriage is a suitable boundary between deserving and undeserving recipients of government assistance. Any artificial rehabilitation of the institution of marriage without substantial support for the concrete conditions that support family life is a half-measure that has no place in sound public policy.

A closely related issue in TANF reauthorization is the family cap. Recall from the account of the welfare reform debates of the mid-1990s in chapter 3 that this is the policy of denying to families already on welfare an increase in benefits upon the birth of an additional child. The family cap is one of several policies designed to discourage welfare recipiency by limiting access to welfare, in this case by effectively raising the cost of having a child while remaining on the welfare rolls. The 1996 law allowed all states for the first time to opt for implementing the family cap, and twenty-three states eventually did adopt some version of it. Much attention regarding the effectiveness of the family cap has been directed to the state of New Jersey, a pioneer in this policy by virtue of a federal waiver that allowed the state to experiment with the family cap well in advance of the 1996 welfare overhaul. Particular controversy has swirled around the findings of a Rutgers University study of the demographic effects of the family cap starting with its implementation in 1992. The state-commissioned study released its first report in December 1997, but Rutgers was forced to revise it in November 1998 in response to objections from critics who questioned its methods, disputed its conclusions, and demanded its retraction.[35] The controversies surrounding the policy and its results dragged on for years, culminating in a New Jersey State Supreme Court ruling in 2003 that the state is indeed entitled to continue the policy.[36]

Family caps are a sensitive topic for obvious reasons: they involve the reproductive decisions of low-income women and have implications for the rates at which families resort to abortion, a practice that the family cap appears to encourage. The Rutgers researchers reported these four findings in the first four years of family cap implementation in New Jersey: (1) twenty-five thousand children were denied benefits under this law; (2) many women cited the family cap as a reason not to have children; (3) fourteen thousand fewer births than would have been expected among the target population of low-income women took place, at least partially because of the law; and (4) the number of abortions among the target group was fourteen hundred higher than would have been expected in the absence of a family cap policy. The report calls the latter item "a small but nontrivial effect of the family cap on the abortion rate."[37] The findings galvanized opposition to family caps on the part of anti-abortion forces, including many Catholics and evangelicals, as well as from feminists concerned about the reproductive freedom of low-income women.

As might be expected, the family cap has been a major focus of concern for the Catholic community regarding welfare reform. The U.S. bishops lobbied hard against the cap in Washington in the mid-1990s and subsequently in many state capitals once the devolution of policy shifted the welfare debates to the state level, particularly with regard to state options such as family caps. Opposition to the family cap is still a major feature of all the literature on welfare reform emanating from official Catholic sources.[38] It is a particularly poignant illustration of the principle regarding "not placing people in impossible situations" as developed in chapter 1 and also emerges as a prime example of an "absolute moral prohibition on policy" as we saw in chapter 4. Also noteworthy is the way this issue brings together, however uneasily, socially conservative Christians and secular feminists, who generally oppose the family cap as an infringement of the reproductive rights of single women, and pits them against right-wing supporters of the 1996 law that promoted (or at least permitted) the family cap.[39] It is quite revealing to see various versions of family values agendas clashing over disputed aspects of a specific policy that holds serious implications for the well-being of America's families.

The ethical issues surrounding family caps are numerous and may be summarized by a series of questions that remain open-ended: Should a state government seek to influence the reproductive behavior of its citizens by means of stipulations on benefits that target certain families? What assumptions regarding moral anthropology are reflected in support for such a policy? Even if it is deemed acceptable to intend to influence the decisions of women to bear children who will likely add to the welfare caseload, is the family cap morally objectionable on other grounds? Is it relevant to consider the various indirect ways the family cap harms the innocent children who are born into this situation (of being ineligible for welfare benefits)? How should public policy makers account for the additional effect of encouraging abortions, especially in a nation so deeply divided on this issue? In short, may we justify the conclusion that the family cap is simply too blunt an instrument for the purposes it seeks to serve?

Like proposals for marriage promotion, the family cap is likely to remain an extremely divisive and sensitive social policy issue. Clear-cut answers to these questions are likely to remain elusive for years to come, as no broad consensus appears to be developing regarding the wisdom of adopting these policies. There are good reasons behind the qualms many experience when they consider these strategies for reducing the welfare rolls. Against this background of deep ambivalence on the part of many observers, perhaps the very least we may hope for is that the ethical aspects of these neuralgic public policy choices not be overlooked on the welfare reauthorization agenda. While we may all greet with enthusiasm the modest recent progress against teen pregnancy, abortion, and extramarital births in our nation, it remains a matter of dispute whether we act ethically when we adopt public policies that encourage such social trends, whether welcome or not, by sharply restricting the options and resources of low-income women and their families.[40]

Work-Support Programs Ancillary to TANF: Addressing the Plight of the Working Poor in America

While cheerleaders for the welfare reform of 1996 are eager to point to declining caseloads and a handful of social indicators signaling modest successes for low-income Americans in the past decade, by any fair accounting, progress against poverty in our nation has been insufficient. By way of illustration, Census Bureau reports for 2003 and 2004 reveal an increase in the number of Americans living below the poverty line despite a sustained (albeit sluggish) economic recovery. Approximately thirty-six million people, nearly one in eight Americans, find themselves in poverty, and most of them live in families with at least one working adult. Child poverty increased by 11 percent from the beginning of 2001 to the end of 2003, evidence that stagnant and even declining earnings in the lower half of the income distribution are hitting hardest those who are most vulnerable.[41]

Among our nation's chief responses to persistent poverty is a package of assorted benefits and services that are often considered ancillary to cash welfare benefits, although in some cases the size of these programs actually dwarfs current TANF expenditures. Previous chapters have provided occasions to investigate certain aspects of this patchwork of federal and state programs, including food stamps, Medicaid, EITC, subsidized child care, housing assistance, and an array of other interventions and services. Building upon the analysis above, this section identifies key ethical issues regarding the way these programs interact with the welfare system, particularly with respect to new concerns about the well-being of the working poor.

Perhaps the most important and disturbing trend has been an astonishing decline in the rate at which low-income families eligible for these benefits are actually applying for and receiving them. As detailed in chapter 5, this peculiarity is especially pronounced in the food stamp program, where sharp reductions in enrollment over the past decade could in no way be attributed to reduced need. The 30 percent decline in what is called the take-up rate came to be attributed to a number of complex factors, including the perpetuation of misinformation regarding the continued eligibility for food stamps of families transitioning off TANF. A certain share of blame may be laid upon state social services offices, which too often diverted applicants to private charitable agencies or sought to discourage potential applicants from receiving benefits in order to comply with federal pressure to lower error rates in eligibility assessment.[42] In any case, on the level of ethical judgments, there is no excuse for subjecting poor families to humiliations and hassles as they seek to secure rightful benefits. Obvious remedies for these injustices would include establishing appropriate information campaigns to alert leaver families of continuing eligibility, streamlining application procedures, and setting up more convenient one-stop social service offices. More fundamentally, federal program rules should never be arranged so that states experience incentives to trim the food stamp rolls or benefits through diversion strategies as they do currently. The attempted reauthorization process in Washington has so far overlooked the ethical imperatives associated with making this vital resource more accessible to working poor families who qualify.

Chapter 5 details a similar story of erosion in coverage within the Medicaid program. Medicaid enrollment fell steeply in the late 1990s, despite provisions in the 1996 welfare law that guaranteed continuing health insurance coverage for those leaving welfare for work—both transitional coverage and continuing Medicaid eligibility for low-income working single parents who meet a means test. For reasons that have proven difficult to uncover, far too many former welfare families who are fully eligible for medical benefits are joining the ranks of the forty-five million or so Americans who lack health insurance. Here the story is complicated by the recent addition of a new category of health care coverage, the State Children's Health Insurance Programs (SCHIPs). In describing the introduction of SCHIPs, chapter 5 notes how they are partially funded by federal grants, but are so insufficiently promoted by the financially strapped states that tens of billions of available federal dollars annually go untapped and forfeited while millions of children remain uninsured.[43] As is the case with food stamps, there is a continuing need to rationalize policy administration so as to eliminate perverse incentives for states to discourage applications from eligible segments of the population. Potential remedies include simplifying Medicaid eligibility rules, the definitive de-linking of welfare and Medicaid benefits, better publicizing efforts, and more effective outreach to low-income people, especially poor children, who lack health insurance.[44]

Similar stories could be told regarding child care subsidies, public housing assistance, and the Earned Income Tax Credit. As is the case with food stamps and Medicaid, millions of families eligible for these types of cash or in-kind benefits are not receiving them. This distressing situation persists for a number of reasons, including lack of information, poor program administration, deliberate strategies of diversion practiced by social service staff, and the desire of potential applicants to avoid the stigma and hassle that often accompany receipt of benefits. In order to benefit from programs (such as housing and day care subsidies) that are not categorical entitlements, applicants often find themselves on long waiting lists. Each of these causes of benefit denial or deferment raises serious ethical concern regarding the way our nation's system of assistance to low-income citizens operates in ways that frustrate the very purposes of these programs. Even the most benign interpretation, namely that declining participation rates and rising refusal and diversion rates are due mostly to unintentional effects regarding complex interactions among various programs and their eligibility criteria, fall short. Perpetuating administrative practices that deny crucial benefits to those most in need is a serious and indefensible violation of the intent of public policy. The prevalence and persistence of these disturbing trends at this particular moment in our nation's history occasions the posing of some profound questions regarding the significance of these benefit programs and our national commitment to assisting low-income families.

The claim that these benefits should flow more freely can be supported in two ways. The first is to view antipoverty programs against the historical context in which they were founded, largely stemming from the New Deal and its effort to institutionalize the social rights of citizenship. The American welfare state of the twentieth century, while never as ambitious in scale or scope as its European cousins, sought to assist those who had been dealt a difficult hand in life. The welfare provisions of the Social Security Act of 1935, as well as subsequent legislation that expanded the original ADC program, were fashioned to protect the most vulnerable (especially children) from the ravages of utter destitution when they found themselves in families with no regular breadwinner. From this perspective, facilitating the flow of benefits in cash or in-kind programs is a matter of continuing the commitment to cushion our nation's most vulnerable families against severe hardship. Because welfare is part of a safety net for families in exceptional circumstances, the argument runs, it should remain available and unencumbered by unreasonable barriers that block access to those eligible for benefits.

But even for those observers whose enthusiasm for the American welfare state is quite limited and who remain opposed to the principle of income entitlements, a second rationale for supporting these antipoverty programs today is readily available. Food stamps, Medicaid, EITC, child care subsidies, and similar benefit programs are increasingly functioning as work supports, allowing low-income Americans to survive amidst job markets and economic conditions that are often frankly inhospitable. Those who rely upon these means-tested benefits are not members of some deviant class outside the mainstream of social life, being warehoused by a government upon which they are utterly dependent. Recipients are ordinary working Americans whose salaries happen not to meet all the material needs of their families. They find themselves eligible for cash or in-kind benefits that help them in their economic struggles by supplementing their inadequate salaries. In an age of globalization, with corporate outsourcing and international job competition exerting downward pressure on prevailing wages at the lower rungs of the U.S. job market, it is not surprising to see millions of Americans, members of proud and respectable families, taking advantage of such benefits. This is particularly true of those who apply for EITC, a work-support program that operates through the income tax system. This entire category of benefits deserves praise for the several functions it performs—at once encouraging work exits from welfare, assisting poor families once they leave the rolls, and buoying the earnings of families who have never entered the welfare system.

The opening years of this millennium have already witnessed numerous voices seeking to redefine government's role in the economy. From the right wing of the political spectrum come enthusiastic calls for establishing an opportunity society or even an ownership society that would promote and enable successful entrepreneurship and risk taking as the privileged means of upward economic mobility. While the outlines of this proposed project are still far from clear, it is not hard to locate within these broad parameters a continued role for work-support programs. Even within the terms of a vision that places a premium on the ideal of independent families relying on entrepreneurial skill for a sufficient income, it is impossible to ignore the reality that many families are not particularly good candidates for absolute self-sufficiency. For a variety of reasons pertaining to family structure, limited job prospects, and barriers to employment such as skill deficits and even simple bad luck, a significant percentage of America's families will never find themselves close to the top tiers of the proposed ownership society. How should public policy account for these ordinary families? Rather than engaging in the fool's errand of dreaming up a completely new system of adequate income supports, we would do well to avoid such a reinventing of the wheel and instead recognize the vital role of our existing work-support programs. Regardless of the stigma that may be attached to them in certain policy circles, work supports are proven means to make the lofty goals being discussed both possible and plausible even for low-wage workers. From this perspective, it makes eminent sense for our economic and political systems to promote the continuation and even enhancement of effective programs like food stamps, Medicaid, EITC, housing assistance, and child care subsidies.

A number of recent works have called attention to the importance of our nation's system of work supports, and some of these portrayals of the vital role played by social programs have attracted considerable public attention. Most prominent is Barbara Ehrenreich's *Nickel and Dimed: On (Not) Getting By in America*, a 2001 best seller consisting of a first-hand account of the author's struggles to make ends meet on the subpoverty wages faced by millions of low-skilled Americans.[45] A similar chronicle of the challenges facing several families locked into the lower echelons of the labor market is David K. Shipler's *The Working Poor: Invisible in America*.[46] Also winning wide acclaim is Jason DeParle's *American Dream: Three Women, Ten Kids, and a Nation's Drive to End Welfare,* a 2004 volume that explicitly addresses the aftermath of the 1996 welfare reform. All three of these exemplify a genre pioneered by journalist Jonathan Kozol, whose several volumes on poverty and social issues in America are nonfiction portrayals of people, neighborhoods, and entire social systems that seek to describe social problems rather than to propose detailed solutions for them.[47] In these accounts, and dozens of others that provide thick descriptions of contemporary American life, both scholarly and more journalistic in nature, a dual focus generally pervades the work. The first aspect often concerns the phenomenon of personal resolve and resiliency in the face of hardship. In this body of literature, we find often repeated the insight that in the face of dire situations, determination and personal motivation count for more than we might expect. If all we know about the welfare poor or the working poor concerns the disadvantages and barriers to success that they face, then we are in danger of underestimating the ability of these hard-pressed but tenacious people to overcome long odds to survive and even to succeed.

The second aspect commonly treated in these works brings us back to the reflections above regarding the role of government policy and public benefits in making possible even modest measures of success. In short, the working poor cannot magically lift themselves up by their bootstraps without systematic public commitments to support their personal efforts. It is patently unrealistic to expect heroic individual exertion to undo the cumulative effects of powerful historical and economic forces, some of them global in extent, that hinder the progress of millions of people in our affluent society. Whether in pursuit of the minimal goal of survival or the more ambitious goal of gaining a foothold in the more secure segment of the job market, the working poor in America truly are at the mercy of public policy decision makers. Emblematic in this regard are the protagonists of DeParle's volume cited above—three African American women from Milwaukee who relied intermittently and for various reasons upon welfare benefits throughout the 1990s but who barely had an inkling of the sea change playing out in Washington policy circles at the time. The very lives of some of the children featured in DeParle's account were possibly saved by the last-minute deal that in 1996 guaranteed Medicaid benefits to families exiting the welfare rolls, but the mothers of these children remained completely oblivious to this, indeed to all congressional wheeling and dealing. While the swings within debates over the adoption of more restrictive or more generous work-support policies may bring shifting measures of satisfaction to politicians or think-tank-based researchers, the outcomes of these same debates often determine the margins between success and failure for millions of working poor families.

Discussions of the plight of the working poor in contemporary America have a marked tendency quickly to open up much broader questions regarding the role of government in addressing poverty. It is almost impossible to maintain a narrow focus on program details when such enormous questions about the fundamental philosophy behind social policy loom in the background. To what extent is it possible or desirable to roll back the New Deal, as some propose today? Does the general strategy of privatization, perhaps in tandem with some version of compassionate conservatism, constitute an adequate substitute for the social functions fulfilled for decades by the welfare state, our complex of safety net arrangements that lately appear to be in the process of being dismantled?

It is obviously impossible to address all these questions in a way that is simultaneously satisfactory to observers on all parts of the political spectrum. However, all can surely agree with at least this assertion: proposals to offer systematic and adequate assistance to the working poor have a curious way of challenging many assumptions and much conventional wisdom about the future of social programs. On the sheer level of political symbolism, the plight of low-income working families is hard to overlook with impunity. By definition, the working poor are not those who can somehow be conceptually separated from mainstream America, but rather are people who clearly play by the rules and work hard. Indeed, they often log much longer hours, albeit in low-wage work positions, than many of those who enjoy far greater affluence. In the very act of taking advantage of the work supports discussed above, the working poor demonstrate that they are seeking not handouts, but a hand up, in other words, not something for nothing, but rather reasonable supplementation of their own work efforts. Indeed, services such as subsidized child care and health insurance provide the very conditions that make their work effort possible. The social contribution of members of these families by means of work effort cannot be denied, as they ask in return for more of the means to a decent livelihood than labor markets alone are currently providing. In doing so, they in no way offend the cultural norm of reciprocity, a staple value within American political culture by which we seek to match social contribution with rewards deserved, requested, and received.

Their status as contributors to society renders the claims of the working poor credible and even urgent as social priorities. As David Shipler contends, "the term 'working poor' should be an oxymoron" because no one in America should be poor if they work reasonably assiduously.[48] Now that TANF, with its work requirements and time limits, has replaced AFDC, with its open-ended entitlements and the associated perception that it perpetuated long-term dependency, it is possible to argue that the welfare poor have been ushered across the moral boundary that formerly separated them from the working poor. Logically, a work-based welfare system should attract no stigma at all. If this argument regarding subtle shifts in American opinion is convincing, it means that recipients of public assistance are now capable of commanding greater public sympathy and social recognition by virtue of their work effort and their attachment to the workforce. With ambitious welfare reform in the rearview mirror, we are at last in a position to move forward with the constructive task of creating better life prospects for all our low-income citizens, leaving behind the stigmas and resentments that have for generations held them back from social progress.

Social policy observer Mary Jo Bane mounted exactly this argument in 1999, at a time when the success of the 1996 law in reducing the national welfare caseload by nearly half was just coming into focus.[49] Now that politicians are no longer able credibly to capitalize on fears of a marginalized welfare underclass and resentment of the expensive interventions government makes to address their needs, our political system can perhaps move forward and address the practical issues regarding the advancement of the working poor. The authors of a proposal called "Reforming Welfare Reform," which appeared in the progressive journal *The American Prospect* in 2001, were on the same page as Bane, expressing the hope that the reauthorization process would enact productive measures to assist the working poor. They ventured this sweeping pronouncement: "The reauthorization debate represents a historic opportunity to reframe a set of policies outside the welfare system designed to end working poverty as we know it."[50] Now that welfare caseloads have been reduced so dramatically in the work-based welfare system of our new millennium, a truly ethical approach to welfare reform reauthorization will turn wholeheartedly to the task of reducing poverty among those families that send adults daily into the workplace but still need assistance to make ends meet. Work-support programs should be enlarged, better coordinated, and made more accessible so that working poor families have a more reasonable opportunity to earn living wages and live in financial security.

The Imposition of Disproportionate Burdens upon Particular Demographic Groups

While the section immediately above spoke with hope regarding progress into the mainstream of American life for a large group of the working poor, this section calls attention to the alarming plight of smaller cohorts who are not likely to be as fortunate. Since 1996, welfare reform has spelled serious hardship for members of particular demographic groups, and the reauthorization process as it has developed so far appears unlikely to relieve the disproportionate burdens that have accrued to these unfortunate people.

Concerns about concentrated hardship turn out to be the flip side of what is usually portrayed as the great accomplishment of the 1996 law, which succeeded in moving approximately two million families off the welfare rolls. A roughly equal number, however, remain in the welfare system, left behind by various disadvantages that block their route out of welfare, including barriers to employment and stable marriage. The dairy analogy of "skimming the cream off the top" is often invoked in describing the dynamic by which some families succeed and others fail to transition out of welfare. The most fortunate (the cream of the crop by virtue of greater skills, job readiness, or other factors) relinquish their status as welfare families, leaving behind the others to wallow in the stigma of failure. What is sometimes overlooked is the way that this dynamic tends to concentrate in the remaining pool of welfare recipients certain personal and demographic characteristics. In previous chapters we have had occasion to note the tendency of single mothers with such problems as depression, drug addiction, and a history of abuse to populate the welfare rolls in disproportionate numbers.

Paying close attention to the ethnic identity of those thus left behind also reveals much about the issues of stigma and hardship associated with dependence on the welfare system. In surveying the history of American welfare policy in chapter 2, we note the persistence of what might be called a racial overlay in the administration and perception of welfare programs in America. The strategy of coloring the face of welfare black has in the past allowed opponents of expanded social programs to use welfare spending as a wedge issue, often appealing to racial stereotypes by means of coded language. Martin Gilens, Jill Quadagno, and other scholars of American political culture provide abundant documentation that racial stigma has played a major role in retarding the scope of public assistance in our nation's history, despite the persistence of substantial public support for the general principle that government should undertake sizable antipoverty efforts.[51]

Is it the case, then, that the representation of racial minorities has become more concentrated in the pool of welfare recipients? Although such trends are difficult to ascertain with precision, using government data compiled during the first seven years of welfare reform, researcher Douglas Besharov found ample evidence to support this claim. Over a span of years when the overall welfare caseload declined 60 percent nationally, Besharov calculates that "the number of white families on welfare showed the steepest decline, falling by 63 percent, while the number of black families on welfare fell by 52 percent, and the number of Hispanic families by 44 percent, with immigration presumably countering what would have been a larger decline."[52] Since whites were the only group to exceed the overall rate at which families departed the welfare rolls, it is obvious that the remaining families still receiving welfare represent an even higher concentration of ethnic minorities than before. Welfare reform had the effect of sorting out recipients in various ways, but it has unfortunately functioned so as to exacerbate the way blacks and Hispanics are overrepresented in the welfare system. White families seem to have been able to parlay a variety of aggregate advantages (perhaps in educational attainment, job readiness, and ability to land jobs through the operation of social networks) in ways that minorities were not able to match. It is unclear what changes in the welfare system might address this disturbing trend, but awareness of these realities should undoubtedly inform the reauthorization process.

The brief mention of immigrants receiving welfare in the quote from Besharov just above raises further concerns about an even smaller and more defined group that maintains some contact with the welfare system. With all the restrictions on benefits under the 1996 law, it is quite rare for immigrant families to be eligible for welfare, but there are some exceptions. Among them are the Hmong tribal people, refugees from Southeast Asia who arrived in the United States in the past three decades. Because they suffered so severely due to American involvement in their region during the Vietnam War era (they were allies of U.S. military forces in several key theaters of operation), thousands of Hmong refugees received very favorable treatment from the federal government, including eligibility for social benefits denied even to other refugees and asylees. With extremely limited job prospects and rather constricted social networks to fall back upon, single-parent families in this immigrant group are especially vulnerable to cutoffs in TANF and other benefits. Many advocates for the Hmong have expressed dire concern about the effects on this struggling community of the sweeping welfare law of 1996, with its rationale of getting tough on recipients, including the few immigrants eligible for benefits.[53]

A larger but equally definable group affected by welfare reform is the community of Native Americans. No ethnic group in the United States has suffered more from the effects of poverty, unemployment, and economic isolation than members of Native American tribes, whether or not they live on Indian reservations. A particularly high percentage of Native Americans has depended for decades upon a range of government benefits, including SSI, food stamps, and welfare payments. As a result, real hardship was expected by tribal communities and families as the restrictive welfare law of 1996 was phased in. One early study predicted that, because Native Americans are among our nation's "poorest populations and those most severely limited in employment opportunities, . . . the effects of welfare reform may be greatest on the native people of this country."[54]

A seldom noticed part of the welfare reform law of 1996, section 412, offered tribes the novel option of running their own welfare programs, separate from the programs of the states in which reservations are located. Tribal governments exercising this option to design and operate their own TANF services would enjoy a greater, indeed unprecedented measure of "authority and flexibility to self-administer welfare policies on their reservations." Unfortunately, the measure failed to provide "adequate financial and technical resources to exercise these responsibilities effectively."[55] The major lacuna in the law is the lack of any federal funding for program support costs, such as the funds necessary to build program infrastructure and to hire caseworkers. In the absence of provisions for start-up money, few tribes found it within their reach to take advantage of this otherwise inviting offer. One early report recounted: "Of the 557 federally recognized Indian tribes, 11 have applied for approval to run welfare programs . . . [and these] are generally smaller and have less poverty than other tribes."[56] Another study recounted a range of five possible models by which tribes might administer welfare programs in conjunction with states or subcontractors, but concluded that financial constraints were so severe that tribal options were ultimately hardly expanded beyond what they had previously been.[57]

The instinct to offer special status to tribal entities is a good one, as it allows Native American groups to take advantage of the beneficial aspects of devolution, including the power to tailor welfare services to fit their own unique problems and circumstances. This is especially important in light of the cultural and geographic distance that generally separates the tribes from the rest of American life. Thus, it is rather unfortunate that this initiative turned out to be a nonstarter. Among the ethical priorities prominent in the reauthorization process should be special attention to the needs of Native Americans and other ethnic groups for whom welfare reform has come at a very high price in terms of disruptions and deprivations for their most vulnerable families.

Because Native Americans inhabit the most economically depressed sections of our nation, the hardship that falls on them when social policy becomes more restrictive is obvious. But it does not take much imagination to extrapolate from the plight of Indian reservations to a broader picture of the geography of poverty in America. In urban ghetto neighborhoods, in farm communities struggling with job loss, in rust-belt towns experiencing capital flight—wherever poverty is concentrated—there will be particular groups who suffer disproportionately from the effects of welfare reform. Whether we construe the notion of demographic groups narrowly (as in the case of Native Americans or Hmong tribal peoples) or broadly (to include less clearly definable groups, such as the undereducated or chronically ill single parents), it is impossible to deny that getting tough with welfare recipients has imposed particularly onerous burdens on identifiable segments of our national population. Those who play a role in reauthorizing the welfare legislation should pay careful attention to the harms already imposed and should not squander the opportunity to alleviate undue burdens upon needy families wherever possible.

PUBLIC CHURCH CONTRIBUTIONS TO SOCIAL POLICY:
PRESENT AND FUTURE

All Americans have a stake in seeing the ethical issues outlined above sorted out, debated, and adequately addressed in the welfare reauthorization process. Even those with no direct regular contact with the welfare system or means-tested benefits of any sort have an interest in a fair resolution of these questions, ranging as they do from relatively small details of program administration to larger, quasi-philosophical questions about the purpose and extent of our nation's commitment to alleviating the multiple hardships facing low-income families.

The future of antipoverty efforts is an especially prominent concern for members of religious communities, which have historically exercised great solicitude for the poorest members of American society. Robert Bellah and the other authors of the classic work *Habits of the Heart* reaffirm an indisputable observation about the special role played by religious congregations in America. Within a highly individualistic and market-based cultural context, they serve as "communities of memory," worthy of the title "a haven in a heartless world," or as one person interviewed for Bellah's volume phrased it, a primary locus where we expect to find "the value of caring about people."[58] While members (and especially leaders) of churches, mosques, synagogues, and other religious institutions occasionally go public with advocacy relating to a wide range of public issues, in no area have public church efforts been more prominent than on issues of social justice, including the budgetary priorities and poverty alleviation efforts of state and national government.

In speaking out of their faith traditions and on behalf of their congregations, religious leaders addressing issues of public policy must tread a very narrow path through some potentially hazardous thickets. They must engage in advocacy within the strictures of the American tradition of institutional separation of church and state, as enshrined in the First Amendment of the U.S. Constitution and subsequent interpretations of constitutional law. While religious voices enjoy a legal right to issue practically any type of utterance they like, it is advisable to shape all discourse through certain unspoken canons of civility and toleration. Harshly judgmental expressions of opinion regarding policy matters where honest disagreements among people of good will are likely will soon become counterproductive, garnering more resentment than new support. The most welcome and effective religious voices will be those that are always mindful that they cast their public policy advice into a pluralistic environment and that other perspectives are legitimate and deserve to be taken seriously. The slide towards a confessional politics of intolerance and condemnation that some detect in recent American public life is not a healthy sign.

On the other hand, religious communities and their leaders should not be overly timid in their advocacy in support of values that are deeply rooted in their traditions. There will always be a place for prophetic voices in our public life. To make due allowances for the situation of moral pluralism does not preclude vigorous action for social change, even through activism that proceeds in the full-throated voice of robust, particularistic religious identity. It would constitute an inexcusable dereliction of responsibility for inheritors of religious traditions to set aside the social wisdom contained in their sacred texts and theological doctrines in the name of a bland social harmony, or in the interest of not offending rigid secularists who are comfortable only with privatized varieties of faith. To relegate faith to the private sphere is to eviscerate much of its very essence. In sum, when one considers the matter of how faith should inform political activity, a key concern is to develop an appropriate style of public engagement. It is imperative to strike a felicitous balance between fidelity to one's religious identity and faith convictions, on one hand, and sensitivity to the opinions of other members of our pluralistic society, on the other hand, as religious communities carry forward their public policy involvements.

These general comments on the necessity and possibilities of public church activity provide a counterpoint to the foregoing analysis of the U.S. Catholic bishops' advocacy of certain positions regarding American social policy in general, and welfare reform in recent decades, in particular. In chapter 4 we recount the bishops' articulation of a series of principles, derived from universal Catholic social teaching, with relevance to contemporary welfare debates. Needless to say, these principles are still quite relevant in the stalled reauthorization process about a decade later. The moral priorities the bishops spoke of in the 1990s tend to be quite general in nature, identifying broad concerns that should shape social policy rather than specifying highly detailed courses of governmental action. The underlying methodology of the bishops is clear: they start with long-standing church teachings about the importance of making vigorous efforts on behalf of the poor and about concern for the common good. They then adapt these general principles and values to the American scene, accounting for the distinctive features of American political culture and the specific policy challenges facing our nation at a given moment. Their documents seek to articulate a vision of how socially responsible welfare policy should proceed.

When we look at how the bishops have addressed welfare reauthorization, we discern an unmistakable continuity with their previous efforts in advocating for an ethical approach to updating our nation's welfare system. The Office of Social Development and World Peace, a department of the Bishops' Conference whose work is described in chapter 4, has continued its distinctive brand of activity that seeks to contribute to the welfare debate. Posted on its website between November 2001 and April 2006 are twenty-eight advocacy documents regarding welfare reform.[59] Some are addressed to government officials, such as key leaders of Congress, others to fellow Catholic activists, inviting them to reflect on the principles and priorities contained in these updates and action alerts as they fashion their own advocacy efforts. On the two occasions (April 11, 2002 and February 10, 2005) when representatives of the Bishops' Conference testified on Capitol Hill regarding TANF reauthorization, the full text of this testimony was posted on the same website. The twenty-eight documents posted during the reauthorization period make frequent reference to the key documents on welfare reform that came from the Bishops' Conference and Catholic Charities USA during the previous round of welfare debates. Typically, the more recent letters and updates comment on proposed features of pending legislative bills (such as revised work requirements and additional funding for child care subsidies), but they draw from the same material regarding the principles behind their judgments about desirable policy. Among the major priorities in reauthorization identified by the voice of the bishops are increased access to benefits for immigrants, greater fairness in funding work supports such as food stamps, and continued opposition to the family cap.

Those seeking a fuller picture of Catholic advocacy should investigate additional Catholic voices that are particularly active in the ongoing debates over welfare policy. Some of these objects of study would be organs of the official church, such as the state Catholic Conferences that now operate in a majority of state capitals and serve as the mouthpieces and lobbying arms of the Catholic dioceses within that jurisdiction. Other relevant voices are quasi-official in nature; an excellent example is the impressive welfare lobbying initiative of Network, a national social justice organization founded and maintained by members of religious orders of women in the United States.[60] Harder to identify but also vitally important are numerous organized as well as informal efforts on the part of lay Catholics to influence or to enact welfare policy in such a way that the outcome is as humane as possible, given the constraints.

Obviously, bishops, clerics, and members of religious orders are not the only leaders or social activists in the Catholic Church. They are merely the most easily identifiable and the most frequently conspicuous. We may never know the extent of innumerable heroic efforts on the part of social workers, social services administrators, legislators, and other lay activists, motivated by faith convictions and Catholic social principles, to soften the potentially punitive aspects of welfare legislation through broad-based initiatives throughout the country. Though generally lacking in official ecclesial status and nearly impossible to track and enumerate, such lay activism is gradually coming to occupy its rightful but long-delayed place as the center of gravity of Catholic social action.[61] Through hands-on initiatives in their workplaces, neighborhoods, and beyond, socially responsible lay Catholics routinely put into practice the principles of Catholic social teaching in ways that few observers fully recognize. Although the institutional church still struggles to acknowledge this as ecclesial activity per se, such grassroots work that forms or applies public policies is as worthy of the moniker "social justice ministry" as the writing and promulgation of pastoral letters and encyclicals.[62] Indeed, in an intriguing twist upon conventional wisdom, a careful study of the history of Catholic social thought reveals that the roots of what is called social Catholicism developed from such lay social action, particularly in parts of western Europe at the dawn of the industrial age. It was only when such grassroots work for social justice trickled up to the levels of bishops and popes in the late nineteenth century that the genre of social encyclicals was launched. The magisterium (that is, the official teaching authority of the Roman Catholic Church) was actually a reluctant latecomer to the social gospel.[63]

This description of Catholic efforts to soften the harsh effects of welfare reform runs the risk of becoming misleading if it appears overly sanguine. A look at two sobering facts is all that is required to balance the picture and remind us of the daunting challenges ahead. First, it is still true that, up to the present, Catholic input into the welfare reform process can point to no major legislative victories. The general drift of the stalled reauthorization debate offers little encouragement either. Recent welfare-related documents from the Bishops' Conference are generally of the damage control variety. In both tone and substance, they communicate a certain measure of resignation, satisfied to aim at winning minor concessions in what is likely to be a disappointing eventual reauthorization outcome.

A second disturbing item is something that most observers of public life today readily call to mind whenever the terms "Catholic Church" and "well-being of children" are mentioned in close juxtaposition. The child abuse scandal that has rocked the Catholic Church in the United States has cast a long shadow. Starting with the January 2002 revelations that the Boston archdiocese attempted for decades to cover up clergy sex abuse in a systematic way, the scandal has left the church reeling. The fallout from these revelations of betrayed trust—including embarrassing details of malfeasance on the part of priests and negligence on the part of bishops in practically every U.S. diocese, thousands of lawsuits and expensive settlements, bankruptcies of several diocese, and belated adoption of controversial Church policies for child protection—is staggering and still unfolding. It is fair to say that no aspect of church life is unaffected by the depth and shock of these revelations.

In a masterful essay that concludes an extraordinary reference work titled *Modern Catholic Social Teaching,* Jesuit scholar John Coleman engages in some informed prognostication regarding the future of Catholic social thought. Coleman calls attention to the many challenges and contexts that relate to the task of "bringing the tradition forward into the future."[64] These include new currents of thought and such new social realities as globalization and enhanced religious pluralism—all of which affect the ability of the Catholic Church to share its social teaching broadly in the wider society. If the same essay were written today, it would have no choice but to include copious coverage of the abuse scandal, as this has been by far the most dramatic and relevant development to unfold since the essay was penned.[65] While it is impossible to assess or quantify its full effects, it is beyond dispute that the scandal has seriously damaged the credibility of the Catholic Church. Because of its diminished stature in the eyes of American society, the church is tragically finding itself unable to respond to pivotal public developments.

It is not hard to compile a list of such missed opportunities for effective social action and teaching even in the few years since the scandal broke. Perhaps the most agonizing instance involved the aftermath of Hurricane Katrina, the great storm that devastated so much of the Gulf Coast after making landfall near New Orleans on August 29, 2005. Overcoming the inadequate levee system and flooding vulnerable neighborhoods in New Orleans, a disproportionate number of them populated primarily by low-income African Americans, Katrina raised deeply troubling social questions as surely as she raised the water level in coastal Louisiana and Mississippi. These questions linger long after the worst of the flood damage has been cleaned up and the rebuilding commenced. How did we for so long tolerate such severe residential segregation and neglected infrastructure, a combination with deadly results for so many? Why were federal and local emergency management systems so callous toward the plight of the poor, who possessed neither the automobiles nor the credit cards that evacuation planners assumed were available to all? How can we make certain that future crises will not reveal such belated and inadequate allocation of resources to assist our neediest citizens at key moments when our national community is tested?

New Orleans is a city featuring a large and ethnically diverse Catholic population, as well as a traditionally high profile for the Catholic Church and its affiliated institutions. If Church leaders were operating from a position of full strength, the plight of the city and its poor citizens who lost lives and property in the Katrina catastrophe would have provided a rare opportunity for profound reflection on social justice. This prime teaching moment may have allowed the church to serve as a key venue for unprecedented conversations about budgetary priorities, racial discrimination, corrupt governance practices, and other relevant aspects of American social life and public policy. If the Church had not relinquished so much of its credibility regarding social issues in recent years, post-Katrina discourse could have matured into a true and sustained act of discernment about needed structural reforms and justice issues rather than an ephemeral and inconclusive exercise in hand-wringing. But because the constructive role of the Catholic community as a public church was so compromised, an important potential source of moral leadership remained relatively silent, and the national dialogue on the lessons to be learned from the Katrina episode was truncated.

This forfeiture of credibility is probably most severe when the Church ventures to speak about topics concerning children and families. We can only speculate precisely what this means for future Church advocacy on welfare reform. To what extent has the Church's voice already been muted by preoccupation with the scandal? Would a more ambitious and public campaign against ethically objectionable aspects of welfare reauthorization proposals have been possible and likely had the scandal not broken in 2002, the same year that the legislation was introduced? Should the Church seriously study the possibility of taking bold symbolic actions (such as ritual apologies and more convincing efforts to support and heal survivors of abuse) in an effort to atone for its errors? Should the Church perhaps now consider a lower profile for clerical figures and promote lay leaders as the primary spokespersons for the social policies it wishes to advocate?

An honest engagement with each of these questions enables us to fashion a way forward. In order to forge a constructive future for effective advocacy on public policy, the Catholic Church in the United States will need to turn a corner and somehow improve the way it is perceived. It will find itself unable to exert any significant influence on future welfare legislation unless it allays suspicion that it is capable of being tragically callous to the well-being of children and families. If it is able somehow to leap this towering hurdle and win a new and favorable hearing, only then can it reoccupy its former place as a credible advocate for the least among us. Only then can this important community of memory speak out effectively regarding issues of urgent moral concern, including the struggles of the often-forgotten poorest families in America.

NOTES

1. One of the six-month extensions was agreed to on a bipartisan basis in September 2004 in order to prevent a potential program shutdown. A three-month extension passed during that month would have expired during the Christmas recess and just several weeks after the November 2004 election. The prospect of gridlock in a lame-duck Congress, amidst exacerbated uncertainty regarding the likely shape of the next Congress and the prospect of changeover at the White House, prompted the longer-than-usual extension in this case. See Jim Abrams, "Congress Gives Up on Broader Highway, Welfare Bills," *Boston Globe,* October 1, 2004, A20.

2. For full details of the initial Bush proposal, as well as comparisons with other legislative plans of Republicans and Democrats, see Anjetta McQueen, "Bush's Bipartisan Welfare Proposal Paves Way for Congressional Action," *CQ Weekly,* March 2, 2002, 590–91. A summary of provisions of the slightly altered Bush plan announced early in the next Congress appears in Richard W. Stevenson, "Bush Urges Congress to Extend Welfare Law, with Changes," *New York Times,* January 5, 2003, A19.

3. Amy Goldstein and Juliet Eilperin, "House Passes GOP Welfare Bill: Tougher Work Rules, Fund to Promote Marriage Included," *Washington Post,* February14, 2003, A4.

4. Amy Goldstein, "Bush Presses Lawmakers to Back Welfare Changes," *Washington Post,* January 15, 2003, A4; Stevenson, "Bush Urges Congress," A19.

5. Anjetta McQueen, "Welfare Overhaul Points Up Intra-Party Differences," *CQ Weekly,* May 18, 2002, 1299–1302.

6. For coverage of the dramatic Senate events regarding welfare in the fall of 2002, see the frequent and detailed updates in *CQ Weekly* (the successor publication to *Congressional Quarterly Weekly Report*). On the obstructionist role played by Daschle in particular, see David Nather, "Fifty Senators Push for Welfare Overhaul, But That May Not Be Enough," *CQ Weekly,* September 14, 2002, 2348.

7. For commentary on the significance of Senator Snowe's advocacy of increases in federal child care subsidies during this legislative battle, see the editorial, "Smarter Welfare Reform," *New York Times,* March 27, 2004, A28.

8. Robert Pear, "Bill on Changes in Welfare Advances to Full Senate," *New York Times,* September 11, 2003, A16.

9. Mark Sherman, "Senate Welfare Bill Raises Child Care Funds," *Boston Globe,* March 31, 2004, A4.

10. Robert Pear, "Senate, Torn by Minimum Wage, Shelves Major Welfare Bill," *New York Times,* April 2, 2004, A12.
11. Governors' letter quoted in Robert Pear, "Governors Ask for Extension of Welfare Law," *New York Times,* April 1, 2004, A19.
12. The aforementioned 78–20 vote added $6 billion in child care funding to the Republican-sponsored Senate welfare bill, endorsing Olympia Snowe's plan over that of Bush. For details, see Robert Pear, "Senate Increases Child Care Funds in Welfare Bill," *New York Times,* March 31, 2004, A1, A17.
13. Thomas Massaro, SJ, "United States Welfare Policy in the New Millennium: Catholic Perspectives on What American Society Has Learned About Low-Income Families," *Journal of the Society of Christian Ethics* 23, no. 2 (2003): 87–118.
14. Among the numerous citations from documents of Catholic social teaching that could be offered on this point are *Mater et magistra,* 119–52, and *Gaudium et spes,* 69–71.
15. The actual value of the fixed $16.5 billion pool of TANF grants shared annually by the states declined by over 12 percent in real terms from 1996 to 2002 and continues to decrease with annual inflation rates hovering around 3 percent in recent years. These funds are not indexed for inflation, nor are states required to enact cost-of-living adjustments in the welfare benefit levels they set, as is the case for Social Security benefits. See Isabel V. Sawhill et al., "Problems and Issues for Reauthorization," in *Welfare Reform and Beyond,* ed. Sawhill et al., 21.
16. For an overview of the work requirement stipulations in the original Bush proposal, see Robin Toner and Robert Pear, "Bush's Plan on Welfare Law Increases Work Requirements," *New York Times,* February 26, 2002, A16.
17. A spirited opinion piece objecting to Bush's proposed elimination of state exemptions for mothers of young children appeared in the summer of 2003 from the dean of Brandeis University's Heller School for Social Policy and Management. See Shonkoff, "Connecting the Dots for Poor Children," *Boston Globe,* July 24, 2003, A11.
18. Robert Pear, "Governors Want Congress to Ease Welfare Work Rules," *New York Times,* February 24, 2002, 18.
19. Robert Pear, "Study by Governors Calls Bush Welfare Plan Unworkable," *New York Times,*April 4, 2002, A14.
20. United States Catholic Conference, "Moral Principles and Policy Priorities on Welfare Reform," 676.
21. Robert Pear, "New Rules Force States to Limit Welfare Rolls," *New York Times,* June 28, 2006, A1, A17; Kevin Freking, "States Brace for Stricter Welfare Work Requirements," *Boston Globe,* June 28, 2006, A3. For further descriptions of the potential hardships caused by these new work rules, see the series of timely studies posted on the website of the Center on Budget and Policy Priorities, especially Mark Greenberg and Sharon Parrott, "Summary of TANF Work Participation Provisions in the Budget Reconciliation Bill" (January 18, 2006) at www.cbpp.org/1-18-06tanf.htm (accessed June 30, 2006).
22. Rebecca Blank and Ron Haskins, "Welfare Reform: An Agenda for Reauthorization," in *The New World of Welfare,* ed. Blank and Haskins, 24.
23. Robert Rector, "Comment on State Sanctions and Time Limits," in *The New World of Welfare,* ed. Blank and Haskins, 267.

24. See, for example, John Paul II's *Sollicitudo rei socialis,* 42.
25. Text of Public Law 104-93, Title I, sec.101. Found in *U.S. Statutes at Large,* vol. 110, part 3, p. 2110.
26. Robert Pear and David D. Kirkpatrick, "Bush Plans $1.5 Billion for Promotion of Marriage," *New York Times,* January 14, 2004, A1, A16.
27. Pear, "New Rules," A17.
28. "Bush's Family Plan," *Boston Globe,* March 4, 2002, A14. A later satirical essay making similar points is Barbara Ehrenreich, "Let Them Eat Wedding Cake," *New York Times,* July 11, 2004, sec. 4, p. 13.
29. Frank Furstenberg, "What a Good Marriage Can't Do," *New York Times,* August 13, 2002, A21.
30. Michael Tanner, "Wedded to Poverty," *New York Times,* July 29, 2003, A27.
31. Ibid.
32. A comprehensive list of studies documenting impressive correlations of positive childhood outcomes and related social indicators with two-parent families appears in Murray, "Family Formation," in *The New World of Welfare,* ed. Blank and Haskins, 138–39.
33. Elizabeth M. Bounds, Pamela K. Brubaker, and Mary E. Hobgood, eds., *Welfare Policy: Feminist Critiques* (Cleveland, OH: Pilgrim Press, 1999).
34. Gwendolyn Mink, *Welfare's End* (Ithaca, NY: Cornell University Press, 1998), esp. chaps. 1, 4, and 5. See also the several related essays in *Whose Welfare?* ed. Gwendolyn Mink (Ithaca, NY: Cornell University Press, 1999).
35. On these developments, see Tamar Lewis, "Report Tying Abortion to Welfare Is Rejected," *New York Times,* June 8, 1998, A18; Barbara Fitzgerald, "Welfare Cap in New Jersey Raised Abortion Rate, Study Finds," *Boston Globe,* June 9, 1998, A3.
36. David Kocienewski, "New Jersey's Justices Uphold Cap on Aid to Mothers on Welfare," *New York Times,* August 5, 2003, A17.
37. Jennifer Preston, "With New Jersey Family Cap, Births Fall and Abortions Rise," *New York Times,* November 3, 1998, A29.
38. On the national level, materials posted since 2002 on the website of the United States Conference of Catholic Bishops regarding welfare reauthorization invariably highlight opposition to family caps. See www.nccbuscc.org/sdwp/national/welfare2.htm for frequently updated lists of relevant advocacy documents. One emblematic printed report from a prominent local Catholic source voicing opposition to the family cap is Catholic Charities of the Archdiocese of Boston, *Children First: An Illustrative Profile of How the Children and Families of Catholic Charities Are Coping with Welfare Reform in Massachusetts* (Boston: Catholic Charities of the Archdiocese of Boston, December 8, 2000).
39. On page 19 of their coauthored introduction to *Welfare Policy: Feminist Critiques,* Bounds, Brubaker, and Hobgood list the family cap as among the aspects of welfare policy they oppose. Gwendolyn Mink (*Welfare's End,* 70) also strongly opposes the family cap.
40. See, for example, the analysis of recent research by the Alan Guttmacher Institute that appears in Nina Bernstein, "Teenage Rate of Pregnancy Drops in U.S.," *New York Times,* February 20, 2004, A14.
41. See the Census Bureau website www.census.gov for these and other relevant statistics. One particularly poignant attempt to synthesize the lessons of a recent

Census Bureau report appears in the unsigned editorial, "Economic Reality Bites," *New York Times,* August 28, 2004, A26.

42. For further analysis regarding these trends and explanations for them, see Michael Wiseman, "Food Stamps and Welfare," in *Welfare Reform and Beyond,* ed. Sawhill et al., 173–80.

43. Robert Greenstein and Jocelyn Guyer, "Supporting Work Through Medicaid and Food Stamps," in *The New World of Welfare,* ed. Blank and Haskins, 336–46.

44. These proposals are discussed in Alan Weil and John Holahan, "Health Insurance, Welfare and Work," in *Welfare Reform and Beyond,* ed. Sawhill et al., 181–88.

45. Barbara Ehrenreich, *Nickel and Dimed: On (Not) Getting By in America* (New York: Henry Holt and Co., 2001).

46. David K. Shipler, *The Working Poor: Invisible in America* (New York: Alfred A. Knopf, 2004).

47. Of perhaps most relevance to the issues regarding welfare reform is Jonathan Kozol, *Amazing Grace: The Lives of Children and the Conscience of a Nation* (New York: Crown Publishers, 1995).

48. Shipler, *The Working Poor,* ix.

49. Mary Jo Bane, "Poverty, Welfare and the Role of Churches," *America,* December 4, 1999, 8–11.

50. Jared Bernstein and Mark Greenberg, "Reforming Welfare Reform," *The American Prospect,* January 1–15, 2001, 11.

51. Gilens, *Why Americans Hate Welfare,* esp. chaps. 3 and 7; Quadagno, *The Color of Welfare,* chap. 5.

52. Besharov, "The Past and Future of Welfare Reform," 6.

53. See, for example, Neubeck and Cazenave, *Welfare Racism,* 198. Extensive information about the special challenges facing Hmong in the United States appears at www.hmongnet.org.

54. Layne K. Stomwall et al., "The Implications of 'Welfare Reform' for American Indian Families and Communities," *Journal of Poverty* 2, no. 4 (1998): 2.

55. Shanta Pandey et al., "Promise of Welfare Reform: Development Through Devolution on Indian Reservations," *Journal of Poverty* 3, no. 4 (1999): 38.

56. Pam Belluck, "Tribes' New Power Over Welfare May Come at Too High a Price," *New York Times,* September 9 1997, A1, A20.

57. Pandey et al., "Promise of Welfare Reform," 47.

58. Robert Bellah et al., *Habits of the Heart: Individualism and Commitment in American Life* (New York: Harper and Row, 1985). The cited phrases appear on pp. 237, 224, and 228, respectively.

59. All twenty-eight documents appear at www.nccbuscc.org/sdwp/national/welfare2.htm (accessed 1 Sept. 2005).

60. See the numerous welfare policy materials available at www.networklobby.org/.

61. One organization that serves as a clearinghouse for information on lay social activism of this type is the National Center for the Laity based in Chicago. Information on this group, including its periodic newsletter, "Initiatives: In Support of Christians in the World," is available at www.catholiclabor.org/NCL.htm.

62. An encouraging recognition of the importance of such lay activity appears in a 1998 Bishops' Conference document, "Everyday Christianity: To Hunger and Thirst for Justice," *Origins* 28, no. 24 (November 26, 1998): 413–18.

63. These points are amplified in Thomas Bokenkotter, *Church and Revolution: Catholics in the Struggle for Democracy and Social Justice* (New York: Image Books of Doubleday, 1998).

64. John Coleman, SJ, "The Future of Catholic Social Thought," in *Modern Catholic Social Teaching: Commentaries and Interpretations,* ed. Himes et al. (Washington, DC: Georgetown University Press, 2005), 532.

65. Despite its 2005 publication date, the contents of this reference volume generally do not reflect developments after 2001.

Bibliography

Abramovitz, Mimi. *Regulating the Lives of Women: Social Welfare Policies from Colonial Times to the Present.* Boston: South End Press, 1988.

Abrams, Jim. "Congress Gives Up on Broader Highway, Welfare Bills." *Boston Globe,* October 1, 2004, A20.

Albelda, Randy, and Ann Withorn, eds. *Lost Ground: Welfare Reform, Poverty, and Beyond.* Cambridge, MA: South End Press, 2002.

Allard, Scott W. "Revisiting *Shapiro:* Welfare Magnets and State Residency Requirements in the 1990s." In *Welfare Reform: A Race to the Bottom?* ed. Sanford F. Schram and Samuel H. Beer, 61–81. Washington, DC: Woodrow Wilson Center Press, 1999.

Alvarez, Lizette. "In New Retreat, Senate Restores Food Stamps for Legal Immigrants." *New York Times,* May 13, 1998, A1, A18.

"Appropriations: GOP Leaders Pull out of Deal." *Congressional Quarterly Weekly Report,* November 1, 1997, 2688.

Aquinas, St. Thomas. *Summa Theologiae,* English Blackfriars ed. 60 vols. New York: McGraw-Hill Book Co., 1966.

Aristotle. *Politics.* Book I. In *Basic Works of Aristotle,* ed. and with an introduction by Richard McKeon, 1127–146. New York: Random House, 1941.

Associated Press. "Georgia Threat to Cut Welfare Seen to Boost Vaccinations." *Boston Globe,* July 15, 2000, A4.

Association of the Bar of the City of New York. "Report and Recommendations on HR 4, 'The Personal Responsibility Act of 1995.'" *Record of the Association of the Bar of the City of New York* 50 (June 1995): 493–521.

Avila, Charles. *Ownership: Early Christian Teaching.* Maryknoll, NY: Orbis Books, 1983.

Baker, Peter. "Virginia Targets Welfare Moms in Effort to Track Down Absentee Dads." *Washington Post,* July 31, 1995, A1, A12.

Bane, Mary Jo. "Poverty, Welfare and the Role of Churches." *America,* December 4, 1999, 8–11.

———. "Stand By for Casualties." *New York Times,* November 10, 1996, sec. 4, p. 13.

———, Brent Coffin, and Ronald Thiemann, eds. *Who Will Provide? The Changing Role of Religion in American Social Welfare.* Boulder, CO: Westview Press, 2000.

———, and David T. Ellwood, eds. *Welfare Realities: From Rhetoric to Reform.* Cambridge, MA: Harvard University Press, 1994.

———, and Lawrence M. Mead. *Lifting Up the Poor: A Dialogue on Religion, Poverty and Welfare Reform.* Washington, DC: Brookings Institution Press, 2003.

Banfield, Edward. *The Unheavenly City Revisited.* Boston: Little, Brown and Co., 1974.

Bassuk, Ellen L., et al. "The Characteristics and Needs of Sheltered Homeless and Low-Income Housed Mothers." *Journal of the American Medical Association* 276, no. 8 (August 29, 1996): 640–46.

Bellah, Robert, et al. *Habits of the Heart: Individualism and Commitment in American Life.* New York: Harper and Row, 1985.

Belluck, Pam. "Tribes' New Power Over Welfare May Come at Too High a Price." *New York Times,* September 9, 1997, A1, A20.

Bernstein, Jared, and Mark Greenberg. "Reforming Welfare Reform." *The American Prospect,* January 1–15, 2001, 10–16.

Bernstein, Nina. "Child-Only Cases Grow in Welfare." *New York Times,* August 14, 2001, A1, A21.

———. "Side Effect of Welfare Law: The No-Parent Family." *New York Times,* July 29, 2002, A1, A14.

———. "Teenage Rate of Pregnancy Drops in U.S." *New York Times,* February 20, 2004, A14.

Berrick, Jill Duerr. *Faces of Poverty: Portraits of Women and Children on Welfare.* New York: Oxford University Press, 1995.

Besharov, Douglas. "The Past and Future of Welfare Reform." *The Public Interest,* no. 150 (Winter 2003): 4–21.

Bitler, Marianne P., et al. "Has Welfare Reform Affected Children's Living Arrangements?" *Focus* (Bulletin of the Institute for Research on Poverty at the University of Wisconsin-Madison) 23, no. 2 (summer 2004): 14–19.

Black, Amy E., Douglas L. Koopman, and David K. Ryden. *Of Little Faith: The Politics of George W. Bush's Faith-Based Initiatives.* Washington, DC: Georgetown University Press, 2004.

Blank, Rebecca M. "The Employment Strategy: Public Policies to Increase Work and Earnings." In *Confronting Poverty: Prescriptions for Change,* ed. Sheldon Danziger, Gary D. Sandefur, and Daniel H. Weinberg, 168–204. Cambridge, MA: Harvard University Press, 1994.

———. *It Takes a Nation: A New Agenda for Fighting Poverty.* Princeton, NJ: Princeton University Press, 1997.

———, and Ron Haskins. "Welfare Reform: An Agenda for Reauthorization." In *The New World of Welfare,* ed. Rebecca M. Blank and Ron Haskins, 3–32. Washington, DC: Brookings Institution Press, 2001.

———, and Ron Haskins, eds. *The New World of Welfare.* Washington, DC: Brookings Institution Press, 2001.

———, and Lucie Schmidt. "Work, Wages, and Welfare." In *The New World of Welfare,* ed. Rebecca M. Blank and Ron Haskins, 70–102. Washington, DC: Brookings Institution Press, 2001.

Bokenkotter, Thomas. *Church and Revolution: Catholics in the Struggle for Democracy and Social Justice.* New York: Image Books of Doubleday, 1998.

Boshara, Ray. "Poverty Is More Than a Matter of Income." *New York Times,* September 28, 2002, sec. 4, p. 13.

Boulding, Kenneth E. "The Boundaries of Social Policy." *Social Work* 12, no. 1 (1967): 3–11.

Bounds, Elizabeth, Pamela K. Brubaker, and Mary E. Hobgood, eds. *Welfare Policy: Feminist Critiques.* Cleveland, OH: Pilgrim Press, 1999.

Bumiller, Elisabeth. "Bush Says $2 Billion Went to Religious Charities in '04." *New York Times,* March 2, 2005, A17.

———. "Bush Urges More Money for Religious Charities." *New York Times,* March 10, 2006, A16.

Burtless, Gary. "The Effect of Reform on Employment, Earnings and Income." In *Welfare Policy for the 1990s,* ed. Phoebe H. Cottingham and David T. Ellwood, 103–45. Cambridge, MA: Harvard University Press, 1989.

———, and Timothy M. Smeeding. "The Level, Trend and Composition of Poverty." In *Understanding Poverty,* ed. Sheldon H. Danziger and Robert H. Haveman, 27–68. Cambridge, MA: Harvard University Press, 2001.

"Bush's Family Plan." *Boston Globe,* March 4, 2002, A14.

Califano, Joseph A., Jr. "To Reform Welfare, Treat Drug Abuse." *Washington Post,* September 18, 2002, A29.

———. "Welfare's Drug Connection." *New York Times,* August 24, 1996, 23.

Cammisa, Anne Marie. *From Rhetoric to Reform: Welfare Policy in American Politics.* Boulder, CO: Westview Press of HarperCollins, 1998.

Cancian, Maria, and Daniel R. Meyer. "Economic Success Among TANF Participants: How We Measure It Matters." *Focus* (Bulletin of the Institute for Research on Poverty at the University of Wisconsin-Madison) 23, no. 2 (Summer 2004): 9–13.

———, and Deborah Reed. "Changes in Family Structure: Implications for Poverty and Related Policy." In *Understanding Poverty,* ed. Sheldon H. Danziger and Robert H. Haveman, 69–96. Cambridge, MA: Harvard University Press, 2001.

Carley, Michael, and Donna Hardina. "Going to the Source: AFDC Recipients' Perspectives on Their Unemployment." *Journal of Poverty* 3, no. 3 (1999): 53–70.

Carney, Dana. "GOP Casts a Kinder Eye on 'Huddled Masses': Lawmakers, Candidates Are Backing Away from Immigration Crackdown of the Mid-90s." *Congressional Quarterly Weekly Report,* May 15, 1999, 1127–29.

Catholic Bishops of the Pacific Northwest. "The Columbia River Watershed: Caring for Creation and the Common Good." *Origins* 30, no. 38 (March 8, 2001): 609–19.

Catholic Bishops of the South. *Voices and Choices: A Pastoral Message on Justice in the Workplace from the Catholic Bishops of the South.* Cincinnati, OH: St. Anthony Messenger Press, 2000.

Catholic Charities of the Archdiocese of Boston. *Children First: An Illustrative Profile of How the Children and Families of Catholic Charities Are Coping with Welfare Reform in Massachusetts.* Boston: Catholic Charities of the Archdiocese of Boston, December 8, 2000.

Catholic Charities USA. *Transforming the Welfare System: A Position Paper of Catholic Charities USA.* Alexandria, VA: Catholic Charities USA, January 24, 1994.

Center for Economic Development. *Welfare Reform and Beyond: A Policy Update.* New York: Research and Policy Committee of the Center for Economic Development, 2002.

Center for Public Justice. *A Guide to Charitable Choice: The Rules of Section 104 of the 1996 Federal Welfare Law Governing State Cooperation with Faith-Based Social-Service Providers.* Washington, DC: Center for Public Justice, January 1997.

Center on Budget and Policy Priorities. *Urban Institute Study Confirms That Welfare Bills Would Increase Child Poverty.* Washington, DC: Center on Budget and Policy Priorities, July 26, 1996.

Chaves, Mark. "Religious Congregations and Welfare Reform: Assessing the Potential." In *Can Charitable Choice Work? Covering Religion's Impact on Urban Affairs and Social Services,* ed. Andrew Walsh, 121–39. Hartford, CT: Leonard E. Greenberg Center for the Study of Religion in Public Life at Trinity College, 2001.

Clymer, Adam. "Filter Aid to Poor Through Churches, Bush Urges." *New York Times,* July 23, 1999, A1, A10.

Coleman, John, SJ. "Development of Church Social Teaching." In *Readings in Moral Theology No. 5: Official Catholic Social Teaching,* ed. Charles E. Curran and Richard A. McCormick, SJ, 169–87. New York: Paulist Press, 1986.

———. "The Future of Catholic Social Thought." In *Modern Catholic Social Teaching: Commentaries and Interpretations,* ed. Kenneth R. Himes et al., 522–44. Washington, DC: Georgetown University Press, 2005.

Conlan, Timothy. *New Federalism: Intergovernmental Reform from Nixon to Reagan.* Washington, DC: Brookings Institution, 1988.

Copperman, Adam, and Juliet Elperin. "House to Vote on Church Programs: Bill Will Allow Hiring Based on Beliefs." *Washington Post,* May 8, 2003, A29.

Cottingham, Phoebe H., and David T. Ellwood, eds. *Welfare Policy for the 1990s.* Cambridge, MA: Harvard University Press, 1999.

Crowell, Linda F. "Welfare Reform: Reforming Welfare or Reforming Families?" *Families in Society: The Journal of Contemporary Human Services* 82, no. 2 (March–April 2001): 157–64.

Cuniff, Ruth. "Big Bad Welfare." *The Progressive* 58 (August 1994): 20.

Curran, Charles E. *Directions in Catholic Social Ethics.* Notre Dame, IN: University of Notre Dame Press, 1985.

Danziger, Sheldon H., and Robert H. Haveman, eds. *Understanding Poverty.* Cambridge, MA: Harvard University Press, 2001.

———, Gary D. Sandefur, and Daniel H. Weinberg, eds. *Confronting Poverty: Prescriptions for Change.* Cambridge, MA: Harvard University Press, 1994.

De La Cruz, Donna. "20 Held After Protest on NYC Welfare Policy." *Boston Globe,* December 8, 1999, A9.

DeParle, Jason. "Aid from an Enemy of the Welfare State." *New York Times,* January 28, 1996, sec. 4, p. 4.

———. *American Dream: Three Women, Ten Kids, and a Nation's Drive to End Welfare.* New York: Viking Penguin, 2004.

———. "Bold Efforts Leave Much Unchanged for the Poor." *New York Times,* December 30, 1999, A1, A12, A13.

———. "Getting Opal Caples to Work." *New York Times Magazine,* August 24, 1997, 32–37, 47, 54, 59–61.

———. "Wisconsin Welfare Experiment: Easy to Say, Not So Easy to Do." *New York Times,* October 18, 1998, 1, 24.

Dewar, Helen. "Senate Bill to Aid Charities Retooled." *Washington Post,* March 28, 2003, A15.

Dillon, Sam. "Report Finds Deep Poverty Is on the Rise." *New York Times,* April 30, 2003, A18.

Dionne, E.J., Jr. *Community Works: The Revival of Civil Society in America.* Washington, DC: Brookings Institution Press, 1998.

Dorr, Donal. *Option for the Poor: A Hundred Years of Catholic Social Teaching.* Maryknoll, NY: Orbis Books, 1992.

Dugger, Celia. "Backlog Threatens Immigrants Seeking Citizenship." *New York Times,* March 7, 1997, A1, A26.

Eagleson, John, and Philip Scharper, eds. *Puebla and Beyond: Documentation and Commentary.* Maryknoll, NY: Orbis Books, 1979.

Eckholm, Erik. "For the Neediest of the Needy, Welfare Reforms Still Fall Short, Study Says." *New York Times,* May 15, 2006, A19.

"Economic Reality Bites." *New York Times,* August 28, 2004, A26.

Edelman, Marian Wright. *Families in Peril: An Agenda for Social Change.* Cambridge, MA: Harvard University Press, 1987.

Edin, Kathryn, and Laura Lein. *Making Ends Meet: How Single Mothers Survive Welfare and Low-Wage Work.* New York: Russell Sage Foundation, 1997.

Ehrenreich, Barbara. "Let Them Eat Wedding Cake." *New York Times,* July 11, 2004, sec. 4, p. 13.

———. *Nickel and Dimed: On (Not) Getting By in America.* New York: Henry Holt and Co., 2001.

Ellis, Ralph D. *Ethical Foundations for Policy Analysis.* Washington, DC: Georgetown University Press, 1998.

Ellwood, David T. *Poor Support: Poverty in the American Family.* New York: Basic Books, 1988.

Elshtain, Jean Bethke. "Single Motherhood: Response to Iris Marion Young." *Dissent* (spring 1994): 267–69.

Esping-Andersen, Gosta. *The Three Worlds of Welfare Capitalism.* Princeton, NJ: Princeton University Press, 1990.

"Faith-Based Initiative to Get Push: Bush to Implement Parts of Proposal." *Washington Post,* August 31, 2002, A22.

"Family Welfare." *Boston Globe,* August 5, 2002, A10.

Feingold, Kenneth, and Sarah Staveteig. "Race, Ethnicity, and Welfare Reform." In *Welfare Reform: The Next Act,* ed. Alan Weil and Kenneth Feingold, 203–19. Washington, DC: Urban Institute Press, 2002.

Field, Kelly. "Immigrants' Benefits Revisited." *CQ Weekly,* February 15, 2003, 399.

Finder, Alan. "Evidence Is Scant That Workfare Leads to Full-Time Jobs." *New York Times,* April 12, 1998, A1, A26.

Fitzgerald, Barbara. "Welfare Cap in New Jersey Raised Abortion Rate, Study Finds." *Boston Globe,* June 9, 1998, A3.

Fix, Michael, and Ron Haskins. "Welfare Benefits for Non-Citizens." In *Welfare Reform and Beyond: The Future of the Safety Net,* ed. Isabel V. Sawhill et al., 205–12. Washington, DC: Brookings Institution Press, 2002.

Fleming, Julia. "The Right to Reputation and the Preferential Option for the Poor." *Journal of the Society of Christian Ethics* 24, no. 1 (Spring–Summer 2004): 73–87.

Florida Conference of Catholic Bishops. "Promoting Meaningful Welfare Reform." *Origins* 24, no. 37 (March 2, 1995): 609–12.

Fornicola, Jo Renee, Mary C. Segers, and Paul Weber, eds. *Faith-Based Initiatives and the Bush Administration: The Good, the Bad, and the Ugly.* New York: Rowman and Littlefield Publishers, 2003.

Francis, Richard M. "Predictions, Patterns, and Policymaking: A Regional Study of Devolution." In *Welfare Reform: A Race to the Bottom?* ed. Sanford F. Schram and Samuel H. Beer, 177–94. Washington, DC: Woodrow Wilson Center Press, 1999.

Fraser, Nancy. "Women, Welfare and the Politics of Need Interpretation." In *Unruly Practices: Power, Discourse and Gender in Contemporary Social Theory*, 144–60. Minneapolis, MN: University of Minnesota Press, 1989.

"Free Speech for the Poor." *Boston Globe*, March 3, 2001, A14.

Freeman, Richard B. "The Rising Tide Lifts . . . ?" In *Understanding Poverty*, ed. Sheldon H. Danziger and Robert H. Haveman, 97–126. Cambridge, MA: Harvard University Press, 2001.

Freking, Kevin. "States Brace for Stricter Welfare Work Requirements." *Boston Globe*, June 28, 2006, A3.

Freudenheim, Milt. "Charities Say Government Cuts Would Jeopardize Their Ability to Help the Needy." *New York Times*, February 5, 1996, B8.

Friedman, Donna Haig, et al. *After Welfare Reform: Trends in Poverty and Emergency Service Use in Massachusetts*. Boston: Center for Social Policy, John W. McCormack Institute of Public Affairs at the University of Massachusetts at Boston, June 2001.

Fujiwara, Lynn H. "Asian Immigrant Communities and the Racial Politics of Welfare Reform." In *Whose Welfare?* ed. Gwendolyn Mink, 100–31. Ithaca, NY: Cornell University Press, 1999.

Furstenberg, Frank. "What a Good Marriage Can't Do." *New York Times*, August 13, 2002, A21.

Gaillardetz, Richard R. "The Ecclesiological Foundations of Modern Catholic Social Teaching." In *Modern Catholic Social Teaching: Commentaries and Interpretations*, ed. Kenneth R. Himes, O.F.M. et al., 72–98. Washington, DC: Georgetown University Press, 2005.

Gais, Thomas, and R. Kent Weaver. "State Policy Choices Under Welfare Reform." In *Welfare Reform and Beyond: The Future of the Safety Net*, ed. Isabel V. Sawhill et al., 33–40. Washington, DC: Brookings Institution Press, 2002.

Gais, Thomas L., et al. "Implementation of the Personal Responsibility Act of 1996." In *The New World of Welfare*, ed. Rebecca M. Blank and Ron Haskins, 35–69. Washington, DC: Brookings Institution Press, 2001.

Gallagher, L. Jerome, et al. *One Year After Federal Reform: A Description of State Temporary Assistance for Needy Families (TANF) Decisions as of October 1997: Occasional Paper Number 6*. Washington, DC: Assessing the New Federalism Project of Urban Institute, June 1998.

Gans, Herbert J. *The War Against the Poor: The Underclass and Antipoverty Policy*. New York: HarperCollins Publishers, 1995.

Gilder, George. "End Welfare Reform as We Know It." *American Spectator* (June 1995): 26.

Gilens, Martin. *Why Americans Hate Welfare: Race, Media and the Politics of Antipoverty Policy*. Chicago: University of Chicago Press, 1999.

Gingrich, Newt. *To Renew America*. New York: HarperCollins Publishers, 1995.

Glendon, Mary Ann. *Rights Talk: The Impoverishment of Political Discourse*. New York: Macmillan, 1991.

Golden, Olivia A., et al. *Assessing the New Federalism: Eight Years Later*. Washington, DC: Urban Institute, 2005.

Golden, Tim. "If Immigrants Lose U.S. Aid, Local Budgets May Feel Pain." *New York Times*, July 29, 1996, A1, A12.

Goldstein, Amy. "Bush Presses Lawmakers to Back Welfare Changes." *Washington Post*, January 15, 2003, A4.

Goldstein, Amy, and Juliet Eilperin. "House Passes GOP Welfare Bill: Tougher Work Rules, Fund to Promote Marriage Included." *Washington Post,* February 14, 2003, A4.

Goodman, John C. "Welfare Privatization." *Wall Street Journal,* May 28, 1996, A18.

———. "Why Not Abolish the Welfare State?" *Common Sense* 2 (Winter 1995): 63–72.

Goodstein, Laurie. "Churches Are Wary of Government Aid to Assist the Needy." *New York Times,* October 17, 2000, A1, A25.

———. "Religious Groups See Larger Role in Welfare." *New York Times,* December 14, 1997, 39.

Gordon, Linda. *Pitied but Not Entitled: Single Mothers and the History of Welfare 1890–1935.* New York: The Free Press, 1994.

Greenberg, Anna. "Doing Whose Work? Faith-Based Organizations and Government Partnerships." In *Who Will Provide? The Changing Role of Religion in American Social Welfare,* ed. Mary Jo Bane, Brent Coffin, and Ronald Thiemann, 178–97. Boulder, CO: Westview Press, 2000.

Greenberg, Mark, and Sharon Parrott. "Summary of TANF Work Participation Provisions in the Budget Reconciliation Bill." Washington, DC: Center for Budget and Policy Priorities, January 18, 2006. Available at www.cbpp.org/1-18-06tanf .htm (accessed 30 June 2006).

Greenhouse, Linda. "Justices Reject Congress's Curbs on Welfare Suits: First Amendment Issue." *New York Times,* March 1, 2001, A1, A16.

———. "Newcomers to States Win a Right to Equal Welfare." *New York Times,* May 18, 1999, A1, A16.

Greenhouse, Steven. "Many Participants in Workfare Take the Place of City Workers." April 13, A1, A28.

———. "Nonprofit and Religious Groups to Fight Workfare in N.Y." *New York Times,* July 24, 1997, A1, A24.

Greenstein, Robert, and Jocelyn Guyer. "Supporting Work Through Medicaid and Food Stamps." In *The New World of Welfare,* ed. Rebecca M. Blank and Ron Haskins, 335–68. Washington, DC: Brookings Institution Press, 2001.

Gueron, Judith M., and Edward Pauly. *From Welfare to Work.* With Cameran M. Lougy. New York: Russell Sage Foundation, 1991.

Hancock, LynNell. *Hands to Work: The Stories of Three Families Racing the Welfare Clock.* New York: HarperCollins Publishers, 2002.

Handler, Joel F. *The Poverty of Welfare Reform.* New Haven, CT: Yale University Press, 1995.

Hart, Jordana. "Ex-state Welfare Recipients Living Better, Survey Finds." *Boston Globe,* April 17, 1999, A1, A6.

Hartiocollis, Anemona. "Experiment on Truancy Advances: Attendance Is Tied to Welfare Benefits." *New York Times,* September 12, 1997, A35.

Haskins, Ron. "Effects of Welfare Reform on Family Income and Poverty." In *The New World of Welfare,* ed. Rebecca M. Blank and Ron Haskins, 103–36. Washington, DC: Brookings Institution Press, 2001.

———, and Wendell Primus. "Welfare Reform and Poverty." In *Welfare Reform and Beyond: The Future of the Safety Net,* ed. Isabel V. Sawhill et al., 59–70. Washington, DC: Brookings Institution Press, 2002.

Havemann, Judith. "Once Off Welfare, Most Work, Report Shows." *Boston Globe,* May 27, 1999, A17.

———. "Republicans Steadfast on Welfare Overhaul." *Washington Post,* November 23, 1996, A4.

———. "Welfare Magnet Provision Blocked by Judge in California." *Washington Post,* April 5, 1997, A6.

———, and Barbara Vobjeda. "A $21 B Plan to Cushion the Poor." *Washington Post,* February 5, 1997, A6.

Hayashi, Reiko. "Welfare Reform and Women's Wages." *Journal of Poverty* 3, no. 2 (1999): 1–19.

Hernandez, Raymond. "Clinton's Stance on Workfare Alienates Her Liberal Allies." *New York Times,* May 22, 2002, A24.

Hicks, Alexander. *Social Democracy and Welfare Capitalism: A Century of Income Security Politics.* Ithaca, NY: Cornell University Press, 1999.

Hilfiker, David. *Urban Injustice: How Ghettos Happen.* New York: Seven Stories Press, 2002.

Himes, Kenneth R., et al., eds. *Modern Catholic Social Teaching: Commentaries and Interpretations.* Washington, DC: Georgetown University Press, 2005.

Himmelfarb, Gertrude. *The De-moralization of Society: From Victorian Virtues to Modern Values.* New York: Alfred A. Knopf, 1995.

Hollenbach, David, SJ. *Claims in Conflict: Retrieving and Renewing the Catholic Human Rights Tradition.* New York: Paulist Press, 1979.

———. *The Common Good and Christian Ethics.* New York: Cambridge University Press, 2002.

Holmes, Stephen A. "Public Cost of Teen-Age Pregnancy Is Put at $7 Billion This Year." *New York Times,* June 13, 1996, A19.

Holy See of the Roman Catholic Church. "Charter of the Rights of the Family." *Origins* 13, no. 27 (December 15, 1983): 461–64.

Hoover, Dennis R. "Charitable Choice and the New Religious Center." *Religion in the News* (Spring 2000): 4–7, 26.

———. "The Faith-Based Initiative Re-ups." *Religion in the News* (Spring 2005): 18–20.

Hughes, Mark Alan. "Welfare Dust Bowl." *Washington Post,* September 25, 1995, A23.

Institute for Family Studies at Marquette University. *The New Consensus on Family and Welfare.* Washington, DC: American Enterprise Institute for Public Policy Research, 1987.

Jenks, Christopher, and Kathryn Edin. "Do Poor Women Have a Right to Bear Children?" *The American Prospect,* no. 20 (1995): 43–52.

Jenks, Christopher, and Paul E. Peterson, eds. *The Urban Underclass.* Washington, DC: Brookings Institution, 1991.

Jeter, Jon. "Welfare Plan Rebuffed by Maryland Clerics." *Washington Post,* December 12, 1996, A1, A24.

———, and Judith Havemann. "Rural Poor May Seek Greener Pastures: Welfare Recipients Face Relocation as a Result of Work Rules." *Washington Post,* October 14, 1996, A1, A18.

"John Engler, Welfare Maverick." *New York Times,* March 21, 1996, A24.

John Paul II. *Familiaris Consortio: Papal Exhortation on the Family.* Washington, DC: USCC Office of Publishing and Promotion Services, 1981.

———. "Redemptor Hominis." *Origins* 8, no. 40 (March 22, 1979): 625–44.

Johnson, Dirk. "Wisconsin Welfare Effort on School Is a Failure, Study Says." *New York Times,* May 19, 1996, 20.

Katz, Jeffrey L. "Welfare: After 60 Years, Most Control Is Passing to States." *Congressional Quarterly Weekly Report,* August 3, 1996, 2190–96.

———. "Welfare Overhaul Law." *Congressional Quarterly Weekly Report,* September 21, 1996, 2696–2705.

———. "Welfare: Putting Recipients to Work Will Be the Toughest Job." *Congressional Quarterly Weekly Report,* July 8, 1995, 2001–05.

Katz, Michael B. *The Price of Citizenship: Redefining the American Welfare State.* New York: Henry Holt and Co., 2001.

———. *The Undeserving Poor: From the War on Poverty to the War on Welfare.* New York: Pantheon Books, 1989.

Kaus, Mickey. "How the GOP Discredits Welfare Reform." *Washington Post,* April 25, 1997, A27.

Keigher, Sharon M. "America's Most Cruel Xenophobia." *Health and Social Work* 22, no. 3 (August 1997): 232–37.

Kilborn, Peter. "Little-Noticed Cut Imperils Safety Net for the Poor." *New York Times,* September 22, 1996, 1, 16.

———. "Unlearned, Unhealthy, and Mostly Uninsured." *New York Times,* August 5, 1997, A10.

Kingdon, John W. *Agendas, Alternatives and Public Policies.* New York: Harper-Collins Publishers, 1984.

Kirby, Gretchen G., et al. *Income Support and Social Services for Low-Income People in Massachusetts.* Washington, DC: Assessing the New Federalism Project of the Urban Institute, December 1997.

Kirchoff, Sue. "Some Benefits for Immigrants Won't Lapse." *Washington Post,* May 3, 1997, A11.

Kocienewski, David. "New Jersey's Justices Uphold Cap on Aid to Mothers on Welfare." *New York Times,* August 5, 2003, A17.

Kozol, Jonathan. *Amazing Grace: The Lives of Children and the Conscience of a Nation.* New York: Crown Publishers, 1995.

Kurz, Demie. "Women, Welfare and Domestic Violence." In *Whose Welfare?* ed. Gwendolyn Mink, 132–51. Ithaca, NY: Cornell University Press, 1999.

Kuttner, Robert. *The Economic Illusion: False Choices Between Prosperity and Social Justice.* Boston: Houghton Mifflin Co., 1984.

———, ed. *Making Work Pay: America After Welfare—A Reader from The American Prospect.* New York: The Free Press, 2002.

Laarman, Rev. Peter. "An Insult to the Poor." *Sojourners,* May–June 1998, 37.

Land, Philip S., SJ. *Shaping Welfare Consensus: U.S. Catholic Bishops' Contribution.* Washington, DC: Center of Concern, 1988.

Lerman, Robert I. "Child-Support Policies." In *Welfare Policies for the 1990s,* ed. Phoebe H. Cottingham and David T. Ellwood, 219–46. Cambridge, MA: Harvard University Press, 1999.

Levy, Clifford. "In Mayor's Race, Clash on Workfare and Immigrant's Suicide." *New York Times,* February 23, 1997, 34.

Lewin, Tamar. "Cut Down on Out-of-Wedlock Births, Win Cash." *New York Times,* September 24, 2000, sec. 4, p. 5.

———. "Report Tying Abortion to Welfare Is Rejected." *New York Times,* June 8, 1998, A18.

Lewis, Oscar. *The Children of Sanchez.* New York: Random House, 1961.

Luker, Kristin. *Dubious Conceptions: The Politics of Teenage Pregnancy.* Cambridge, MA: Harvard University Press, 1996.

Mare, Robert D., and Christopher Winship. "Socioeconomic Change and the Decline of Marriage for Blacks and Whites." In *The Urban Underclass,* ed. Christopher Jencks and Paul E. Peterson, 175–202. Washington, DC: Brookings Institution, 1991.

Maritain, Jacques. *Man and the State.* Chicago: University of Chicago Press, 1951.

Marshall, Nichola L. "The Welfare Reform Act of 1996: Political Compromise or Panacea for Welfare Dependency?" *Georgetown Journal on Fighting Poverty* 4, no. 2 (Spring 1997): 333–45.

Marshall, T. H. "Citizenship and Social Class." In *Citizenship and Social Class,* ed. Tom Bottomore, 3–51. London: Pluto Press, 1992.

———. *Social Policy in the Twentieth Century.* 3rd rev. ed. London: Hutchison and Co., 1970.

Massaro, Thomas J., SJ. *Catholic Social Teaching and United States Welfare Reform.* Collegeville, MN: Liturgical Press, 1998.

———. "United States Welfare Policy in the New Millennium: Catholic Perspectives on What American Society Has Learned About Low-Income Families." *Journal of the Society of Christian Ethics* 23, no. 2 (2003): 87–118.

———, and Thomas A. Shannon, eds. *American Catholic Social Teaching.* Collegeville, MN: Liturgical Press, 2002.

Massing, Michael. "Ending Poverty as We Know It." In *Making Work Pay: America After Welfare: A Reader from The American Prospect,* ed. Robert Kuttner, 21–37. New York: The Free Press, 2002.

McFate, Katherine. *Making Welfare Work: The Principles of Constructive Welfare Reform.* Washington, DC: Joint Center for Political and Economic Studies, 1995.

McQueen, Anjetta. "Bush's Bipartisan Welfare Proposal Paves Way for Congressional Action." *CQ Weekly,* March 2, 2002, 590–91.

———. "Welfare Overhaul Points Up Intra-Party Differences." *CQ Weekly,* May 18, 2002, 1299–1302.

Mead, Lawrence M. *Beyond Entitlement: The Social Obligations of Citizenship.* New York: The Free Press, 1986.

———. *The New Politics of Poverty: The Nonworking Poor in America.* New York: Basic Books, 1992.

———. "The Politics of Conservative Welfare Reform." In *The New World of Welfare,* ed. Rebecca M. Blank and Ron Haskins, 201–20. Washington, DC: Brookings Institution Press, 2001.

———. "The Poverty Debate and Human Nature." In *Welfare in America: Christian Perspectives on a Policy in Crisis,* ed. Stanley W. Carlson-Theis and James W. Skillen, 209–42. Grand Rapids, MI: William B. Eerdmans Publishing Co., 1996.

———, ed. *The New Paternalism: Supervisory Approaches to Poverty.* Washington, DC: Brookings Institution Press, 1997.

Meckler, Laura. "Ex-welfare Recipients Faring Better, But Still Impoverished." *Boston Globe,* May 12, 1999, A3.

———. "Families Leaving Welfare Still Have Trouble Meeting Basic Needs." *Boston Globe,* November 12, 1999, A14.

"Medicaid and the Torn Safety Net." *America,* July 31, 1999, 3.

"Mental Illness and Welfare Reform." *Boston Globe,* September 9, 1998, A18.

Mich, Marvin L. Krier. *Catholic Social Teaching and Movements.* Mystic, CT: Twenty-Third Publications, 1998.

Mink, Gwendolyn. *Welfare's End.* Ithaca, NY: Cornell University Press, 1998.

———, ed. *Whose Welfare?* Ithaca, NY: Cornell University Press, 1999.

Mitchell, Allison. "Greater Poverty Toll Is Seen in Welfare Bill." *New York Times,* November 10, 1995, A27.

Moore, Stephen, ed. *Restoring the Dream: The Bold New Plan by House Republicans.* New York: Times Books of Random House, 1995.

Moynihan, Daniel Patrick. "The Big Lie of 1996." *New York Times,* January 28, 1997, A13.

———. "Welfare Reform: Serving America's Children." *Teacher's College Record* 90 (spring 1989): 337–41.

Mullahy, John, and Barbara L. Wolfe. "Health Policies for the Non-elderly Poor." In *Understanding Poverty,* ed. Sheldon H. Danziger and Robert H. Haveman, 278–313. Cambridge, MA: Harvard University Press, 2001.

Murray, Charles. "Family Formation." In *The New World of Welfare,* ed. Rebecca M. Blank and Ron Haskins, 137–68. Washington, DC: Brookings Institution Press, 2001.

———. *Losing Ground: American Social Policy 1950–1980.* New York: Basic Books, 1984.

———. "What To Do About Welfare." *Commentary* 98 (December 1994): 26–34.

Murray, John Courtney, SJ. "Leo XIII: Two Concepts of Government." *Theological Studies* 14 (1953): 551–63.

———. *We Hold These Truths: Catholic Reflections on the American Proposition.* New York: Sheed and Ward, 1960.

Nakashima, Ellen. "Learnfare Starts off Slowly in Virginia." *Washington Post,* February 12, 1996, D1, D5.

Nathan, Richard P. "The Newest New Federalism for Welfare: Where Are We Now and Where Are We Headed?" In *Rockefeller Reports.* Albany, NY: Nelson A. Rockefeller Institute of Government, October 30, 1997.

———. "Will the Underclass Always Be with Us?" *Society* 24, no. 3 (March–April 1987): 57–62.

Nather, David. "Fifty Senators Push for Welfare Overhaul, But That May Not Be Enough." *CQ Weekly,* September 14, 2002, 2348.

———. "Funding of Faith-Based Groups Spurs New Civil Rights Debate." *CQ Weekly,* June 10, 2000, 1385–87.

Neubeck, Kenneth J., and Noel A. Cazenave. *Welfare Racism: Playing the Race Card Against America's Poor.* New York: Routledge, 2001.

Novarro, Mireya. "Teen-Age Mothers Viewed as Abused Prey of Older Men." *New York Times,* May 19, 1996, 1, 18.

O'Brien, David J., and Thomas A. Shannon, eds. *Catholic Social Thought: The Documentary Heritage.* Maryknoll, NY: Orbis Books, 1992.

Offner, Paul. "Reducing Non-marital Births." In *Welfare Reform and Beyond: The Future of the Safety Net,* ed. Isabel V. Sawhill et al., 145–59. Washington, DC: Brookings Institution Press, 2002.

Olasky, Marvin. *Renewing American Compassion: How Compassion for the Needy Can Turn Ordinary Citizens into Heroes.* New York: The Free Press, 1996.

———. *The Tragedy of American Compassion.* Washington, DC: Regnery Gateway, 1992.

Page, Benjamin I., and Robert Y. Shapiro. *The Rational Public: Fifty Years of Trends in Americans' Policy Preferences.* Chicago: University of Chicago Press, 1992.

Pandey, Shanta, et al. "Promise of Welfare Reform: Development Through Devolution on Indian Reservations." *Journal of Poverty* 3, no. 4 (1999): 37–61.

Parrott, Sharon. *How Much Do We Spend on Welfare?* Washington, DC: Center on Budget and Policy Priorities, August 4, 1995.

Patterson, James T. *America's Struggle Against Poverty 1900–1980*. Cambridge, MA: Harvard University Press, 1981.

Pavetti, Ladonna A. "Helping the Hard-to-Employ." In *Welfare Reform and Beyond: The Future of the Safety Net,* ed. Isabel V. Sawhill et al., 135–42. Washington, DC: Brookings Institution Press, 2002.

———. "Welfare Policy in Transition: Redefining the Social Contract for Poor Citizen Families with Children and for Immigrants." In *Understanding Poverty,* ed. Sheldon H. Danziger and Robert H. Haveman, 229–77. Cambridge, MA: Harvard University Press, 2001.

———, and Dan Bloom. "State Sanctions and Time Limits." In *The New World of Welfare,* ed. Rebecca Blank and Ron Haskins, 245–69. Washington, DC: Brookings Institution Press, 2001.

Pear, Robert. "Actions by States Hold Keys to Welfare Law's Future." *New York Times,* October 1, 1996, A22.

———. "Bill on Changes in Welfare Advances to Full Senate." *New York Times,* September 11, 2003, A16.

———. "Clinton Considers Moves to Soften Cuts in Welfare." *New York Times,* November 27, 1996, A1, A19.

———. "Clinton Will Seek Tax Breaks to Ease Paths off Welfare." *New York Times,* January 28, 1997, A1, A12.

———. "Federal Welfare Rolls Shrink, But Drop Is Smallest Since '94." *New York Times,* May 21, 2002, A12.

———. "40 States Forfeit Health Care Funds for Poor Children." *New York Times,* September 24, 2000, 1, 26.

———. "Governors Ask for Extension of Welfare Law." *New York Times,* April 1, 2004, A19.

———. "Governors Want Congress to Ease Welfare Work Rules." *New York Times,* February 24, 2002, 18.

———. "Judge Rules States Can't Cut Welfare for New Residents." *New York Times,* October 14, 1997, A1, A20.

———. "New Rules Force States to Limit Welfare Rolls." *New York Times,* June 28, 2006, A1, A17.

———. "Senate Increases Child Care Funds in Welfare Bill." *New York Times,* March 31, 2004, A1, A17.

———. "Senate, Torn by Minimum Wage, Shelves Major Welfare Bill." *New York Times,* April 2, 2004, A12.

———. "Senate Votes to Deny Most Federal Benefits to Legal Immigrants Who Are Not Citizens." *New York Times,* July 20, 1996, 9.

———. "State Welfare Chiefs Ask for More U.S. Guidance." *New York Times,* September 10, 1996, A16.

———. "States Forfeit Unspent U.S. Money for Child Health Insurance." *New York Times,* October 14, 2002, A15.

———. "Study by Governors Calls Bush Welfare Plan Unworkable." *New York Times,* April 4, 2002, A14.

———. "Study Finds Children's Aid Goes to Adults." *New York Times,* August 8, 2002, A1, A19.

———. "Study Links Medicaid Drop to Welfare Changes." *New York Times,* May 14, 1999, A8.

———. "Welfare Spending Shows Huge Shift." *New York Times,* October 13, 2003, A1, A10.

———, and David D. Kirkpatrick. "Bush Plans $1.5 Billion for Promotion of Marriage." *New York Times,* January 14, 2004, A1, A16.

Peck, Jamie. *Workfare States.* New York: Guilford Press, 2001.

"The Personal Responsibility and Work Opportunity Reconciliation Act of 1996." *U.S. Statutes at Large* 110 (1997): 2105–2355.

Peterson, Paul E. *The Price of Federalism.* Washington, DC: Brookings Institution, 1995.

Piven, Francis Fox. "Thompson's Easy Ride." *The Nation,* February 26, 2001, 11–14.

———, and Richard A. Cloward. *Regulating the Poor: The Functions of Public Welfare.* Updated ed. New York: Vintage Books of Random House, 1993.

Polanyi, Karl. *The Great Transformation: The Political and Economic Origins of Our Time.* Boston: Beacon Press, 1944.

Pollack, Harold, and Peter Reuter. "Myths About Drugs and Welfare." *Washington Post,* October 1, 2002, A21.

Preston, Jennifer. "With New Jersey Family Cap, Births Fall and Abortions Rise." *New York Times,* November 3, 1998, A29.

"Provisions of the Welfare Bill." *Congressional Quarterly Weekly Report,* August 3, 1996, 2193.

Quadagno, Jill. *The Color of Welfare: How Racism Undermined the War on Poverty.* New York: Oxford University Press, 1994.

Rabinovitz, Jonathan. "Welfare Cuts for Truancy Are Stalled: Task Force in Hartford Finds Problems in Plan." *New York Times,* May 7, 1996, B1, B4.

Rawls, John. *A Theory of Justice.* Cambridge, MA: Harvard University Press, 1971.

Reckler, Elizabeth. "Millions Eligible for Food Stamps Aren't Applying." *New York Times,* February 26, 2001, A1, A11.

Rector, Robert. "Comment on State Sanctions and Time Limits." In *The New World of Welfare,* ed. Rebecca M. Blank and Ron Haskins, 264–69. Washington, DC: Brookings Institution Press, 2001.

Rector, Robert, and William F. Lauber. *America's Failed $5.4 Trillion War on Poverty.* Washington, DC: The Heritage Foundation, 1995.

Reischauer, Robert D. "The Welfare Reform Legislation: Directions for the Future." In *Welfare Policy for the 1990s,* ed. Phoebe H. Cottingham and David T. Ellwood, 10–40. Cambridge, MA: Harvard University Press, 1999.

———. "Welfare Reform: Will Consensus Be Enough?" *Brookings Review* 5 (Summer 1987): 3–8.

———, and R. Kent Weaver. "Financing Welfare: Are Block Grants the Answer?" In *Looking Before We Leap,* ed. R. Kent Weaver and William T. Dickens, 13–26. Washington, DC: Brookings Institution, 1995.

Ribadeneira, Diego. "With Eye on Funds, Focus Turns from Pantry to Workplace." *Boston Globe,* December 1, 1998, B1, B4.

Ricard, Bishop John. "Factors of Genuine Welfare Reform." *Origins* 24, no. 34 (February 9, 1995): 564–66.

———. "A Shifting, Churning Economy." *Origins* 24, no. 12 ((September 7, 1995): 199–200.

Rich, Michael J. *Federal Policymaking and the Poor: National Goals, Local Choices and Distributional Outcomes.* Princeton, NJ: Princeton University Press, 1993.

Roberts, Dorothy. "Welfare's Ban on Poor Motherhood." In *Whose Welfare?* ed. Gwendolyn Mink, 152–67. Ithaca, NY: Cornell University Press, 1999.

Rogers, Melissa. "Charitable Choice: A Threat to Religion." *Sojourners,* July–Aug. 1998, 28–30.

Rom, Mark Carl, Paul E. Peterson, and Kenneth F. Scheve Jr. "Interstate Competition and Welfare Policy." In *Welfare Reform: A Race to the Bottom?* ed. Sanford F. Schram and Samuel H. Beer, 21–41. Washington, DC: Woodrow Wilson Center Press, 1999.

Rowan, Carl T. "Back to State's Rights." *Washington Post,* November 5, 1995, C7.

Ryan, John A. *Distributive Justice: The Rights and Wrongs of Our Present Distribution of Wealth.* New York: Macmillan Co., 1925.

———. *A Living Wage: Its Ethical and Economic Aspects.* New York: Macmillan Co., 1912.

Sargent, Hilary. "Sit-In at State House Urges Reprieve of Benefit Cutoff." *Boston Globe,* December 1, 1998, B4.

Sawhill, Isabel V., et al. "Problems and Issues for Reauthorization." In *Welfare Reform and Beyond: The Future of the Safety Net,* ed. Isabel V. Sawhill et al., 20–29. Washington, DC: Brookings Institution, 2002.

———. "Results to Date." In *Welfare Reform and Beyond: The Future of the Safety Net,* ed. Isabel V. Sawhill et al., 9–19.Washington, D.C.: Brookings Institution, 2002.

———et al., eds. *Welfare Reform and Beyond: The Future of the Safety Net.* Washington, DC: Brookings Institution, 2002.

Schorr, Lisbeth B. *Common Purpose: Strengthening Families and Neighborhoods to Rebuild America.* New York: Anchor Books of Doubleday, 1997.

———. "What Works: Applying What We Already Know About Successful Social Policy." *The American Prospect,* no. 13 (1993): 43–54.

Schram, Sanford F. *After Welfare: The Culture of Postindustrial Social Policy.* New York: New York University Press, 2000.

Schram, Sanford F., and Samuel H. Beer, eds. *Welfare Reform: A Race to the Bottom?* Baltimore: Johns Hopkins University Press, 1998.

———, and Joe Soss. "Success Stories: Welfare Reform, Policy Discourse, and the Politics of Research." In *Lost Ground: Welfare Reform, Poverty, and Beyond,* ed. Randy Albelda and Ann Withorn, 57–78. Cambridge, MA: South End Press, 2002.

Schwartz, Joel. *Fighting Poverty with Virtue: Moral Reform and America's Urban Poor 1825–2000.* Bloomington: Indiana University Press, 2000.

Sengupta, Somini. "How Many Poor Children Is Too Many?" *New York Times,* July 8, 2001, sec. 4, p. 3.

Sexton, Joe. "Dependency's Double Edge." *New York Times,* November 9, 1997, 37.

———. "The Trickle-Up Economy: Poor Neighborhoods Fear a Disaster If Welfare Is Cut." *New York Times,* February 8, 1996, B1, B9.

Shapiro, Joseph P. "Can Churches Save America?" *U.S. News and World Report,* September 9, 1996, 46–51.

———. "Marvin Olasky's Appeal: A Golden Age of Charity." *U.S. News and World Report,* September 9, 1996, 52–53.

Sherman, Mark. "Senate Welfare Bill Raises Child Care Funds." *Boston Globe,* March 31, 2004, A4.

Shipler, David K. *The Working Poor: Invisible in America.* New York: Alfred A. Knopf, 2004.

Shklar, Judith. *American Citizenship: The Quest for Inclusion.* Cambridge, MA: Harvard University Press, 1991.

Shonkoff, Jack P. "Connecting the Dots for Poor Children." *Boston Globe,* July 24, 2003, A11.

Skocpol, Theda. *Protecting Soldiers and Mothers: The Political Origins of Social Policy in the United States.* Cambridge, MA: Harvard University Press, 1992.

"Smarter Welfare Reform." *New York Times,* March 27, 2004, A28.

"Spelling the End of Welfare as We Know It." *New York Times,* August 4, 1996, sec. 4, p. 3.

Steinfels, Peter. "As Government Aid Evaporates, How Will Religious and Charity Organizations Hold Up as a Safety Net for the Poor, the Sick and the Elderly?" *New York Times,* October 28, 1995, 11.

Stevenson, Richard W. "Bush Urges Congress to Extend Welfare Law, with Changes." *New York Times,* January 5, 2003, A19.

———. "Rules Eased on Financing Social Work." *New York Times,* September 23, 2003, A20.

Stolberg, Sheryl Gay. "Senate Passes Version of Religion Initiative." *New York Times,* April 10, 2003, A18.

Stomwall, Layne K., et al. "The Implications of 'Welfare Reform' for American Indian Families and Communities." *Journal of Poverty* 2, no. 4 (1998): 1–15.

Super, David A., et al. *The New Welfare Law.* Washington, DC: Center on Budget and Policy Priorities, August 14, 1996.

Swarns, Rachel L. "Mothers Poised for Workfare Face Acute Lack of Day Care." April 14, 1998, A1, A21.

Swindell, Bill. "Faith-Based Offices an End Run Around Languishing Legislation." *CQ Weekly,* November 2, 2002, 2861–62.

Tanner, Michael. "Ending Welfare as We Know It." *Policy Analysis,* no. 212 (July 7, 1994): 1–33.

———. "Wedded to Poverty." *New York Times,* July 29, 2003, A27.

Toner, Robin. "Rallies in Capital Protest Bush Welfare Proposals." *New York Times,* March 6, 2002, A17.

———, and Robert Pear. "Bush's Plan on Welfare Law Increases Work Requirements." *New York Times,* February 26, 2002, A16.

Toy, Vivian. "Tough Workfare Rules Used as Way to Cut Welfare Rolls." April 15, 1998, A1, A27.

———. "Welfare Offices Issue 6000 Emergency Checks." *New York Times,* November, 28, 1996, B14.

Tropman, John E. *The Catholic Ethic in American Society: An Exploration of Values.* San Francisco: Jossey-Bass Publishers, 1995.

———. *The Catholic Ethic and the Spirit of Community.* Washington, DC: Georgetown University Press, 2002.

———. *Does America Hate the Poor? The Other American Dilemma.* Westport, CT: Praeger Publishers, 1988.

Tufts University Center on Hunger, Poverty, and Nutrition Policy. *Statement on Key Welfare Reform Issues: The Empirical Evidence.* Medford, MA: Tufts University Center on Hunger, Poverty, and Nutrition Policy, 1995.

United States Bishops. "Everyday Christianity: To Hunger and Thirst for Justice." *Origins* 28, no. 24 (November 26, 1998): 413–18.

United States Catholic Conference. *Economic Justice for All.* Washington, DC: USCC Office of Publishing and Promotion Services, 1986.

———. "Moral Principles and Policy Priorities for Welfare Reform: A Statement of the Administrative Board of the U.S.C.C." *Origins* 24, no. 41 (March 30, 1995): 673–77.

———. *Putting Children and Families First: The Challenge for Our Church, Nation and World.* Washington, DC: USCC Office of Publishing and Promotion Services, 1992.

———. "U.S.C.C. Statement on Political Responsibility." *Origins* 25, no. 22 (November 16, 1995): 369, 371–83.

United States Congress. House. Committee on Ways and Means. Subcommittee on Human Resources. *Family Support Act of 1988: Hearings Before the Subcommittee on Human Resources.* 103rd Cong., 2nd sess., March 15, 1994. Washington, DC: General Printing Office, 1994.

Vobjeda, Barbara, and Judith Havemann. "Governors Seek Changes in Welfare Reform Law." *Washington Post,* February 1, 1997, A1, A12.

Walzer, Michael. "Socializing the Welfare State." In *Democracy and the Welfare State,* ed. Amy Gutman, 13–26. Princeton, NJ: Princeton University Press, 1988.

———. *Spheres of Justice: A Defense of Pluralism and Equality.* New York: Basic Books, 1993.

Wattenberg, Ben J. *Values Matter Most.* New York: The Free Press, 1995.

Weaver, R. Kent. *Ending Welfare as We Know It.* Washington, DC: Brookings Institution Press, 2000.

Weaver, R. Kent, and William T. Dickens, eds. *Looking Before We Leap: Social Science and Welfare Reform.* Washington, DC: Brookings Institution, 1995.

———, Robert Y. Shapiro, and Lawrence R. Jacobs. "Public Opinion on Welfare Reform: A Mandate for What?" In *Looking Before We Leap: Social Science and Welfare Reform,* ed. R. Kent Weaver and William T. Dickens, 109–28. Washington, DC: Brookings Institution, 1995.

Weigel, George. "The Virtues of Freedom: *Centesimus Annus.*" In *Building the Free Society: Democracy, Capitalism and Catholic Social Teaching,* ed. George Weigel and Robert Royal, 207–23. Grand Rapids, MI: William B. Eerdmans Press, 1993.

Weil, Alan, and Kenneth Feingold, eds. *Welfare Reform: The Next Act.* Washington, DC: Urban Institute Press, 2002.

———, and John Holahan. "Health Insurance, Welfare, and Work." In *Welfare Reform and Beyond: The Future of the Safety Net,* ed. Isabel V. Sawhill et al., 181–88. Washington, DC: Brookings Institution Press, 2002.

Weiner, David. "Missing the Boat on Charitable Choice." *Religion in the News* (June 1998): 8–9.

Weir, Margaret. "Urban Poverty and Defensive Localism." *Dissent* (Summer 1994): 337–42.

White House Office of the Press Secretary. *Executive Order: Establishment of White House Office of Faith-Based and Community Initiatives.* Washington, DC, January 29, 2001.

Will, George F. *Statecraft as Soulcraft: What Government Does.* New York: Simon and Schuster, 1983.

Wilson, William Julius. *The Declining Significance of Race: Blacks and Changing American Institutions.* Chicago: University of Chicago Press, 1978.

———. *The Truly Disadvantaged: The Inner City, the Underclass, and Public Policy.* Chicago: University of Chicago Press, 1987.

———. *When Work Disappears: The World of the New Urban Poor.* New York: Albert A. Knopf, 1996.

Winston, Pamela. *Welfare Policymaking in the States: The Devil in Devolution.* Washington, DC: Georgetown University Press, 2002.

Wiseman, Michael. "Food Stamps and Welfare Reform." In *Welfare Reform and Beyond: The Future of the Safety Net,* ed. Sawhill et al. 173–80. Washington, DC: Brookings Institution Press, 2002.

Wolk, James L., and Sandra Schmahl. "Child Support Enforcement: The Ignored Component of Welfare Reform." *Families in Society: The Journal of Contemporary Human Services* 80, no. 5 (September–October 1999): 526–30.

Wong, Doris Sue. "Learning-Disabled Welfare Recipients Lose Ruling." *Boston Globe,* August, 27, 1998, E8.

———. "Suit Says Welfare Slights the Disabled." *Boston Globe,* August 12, 1998, B1, B6.

Young, Iris Marion. "Making Single Motherhood Normal." *Dissent* (Winter 1994): 88–93.

Zedlewski, Sheila R., et al. *Potential Effects of Congressional Welfare Reform on Family Incomes.* Washington, DC: Urban Institute, 1996.

———, and Pamela Loprest. "Will TANF Work for the Most Disadvantaged Families?" In *The New World of Welfare,* ed. Rebecca M. Blank and Ron Haskins, 311–34. Washington, DC: Brookings Institution Press, 2001.

INDEX

Abramovitz, Mimi, 51
ADC. *See* Aid to Dependent Children
AFDC. *See* Aid to Families with
    Dependent Children
African Americans
    child poverty among, 163
    discrimination against in welfare
        policies, 59–60
Aid to Dependent Children (ADC),
    52, 57–58, 60
Aid to Families with Dependent
    Children (AFDC)
    conservative criticism of, 61–62
    matching grants, calls for
        replacement of, 79–80
    Medicaid benefits and, 104–5
    the "permanent crisis" of,
        55–61
    racism in, 60
    replacement of, 1 (*see also* welfare
        reform)
Amendments to the Social Security
    Act of 1962, 57
*American Dream: Three Women, Ten
    Kids, and a Nation's Drive to
    End Welfare* (DeParle), 209–10
American Enterprise Institute for
    Public Policy Research, 141n7
American political culture, 47–48,
    57–59
Americans United for Separation of
    Church and State, 74n58
Amnesty International, 16
Aquinas, St. Thomas, 18, 21–22, 24
Archer, Bill, 181n4
Aristotle, 18, 24
Ashcroft, John, 65–66
Australia, 26

Balanced Budget Amendment,
    100
Bane, Mary Jo, 131, 157, 212
Banfield, Edward, 109n22
Bellah, Robert, 215–16
Bennett, William J., 147n57
Berger, Peter, 44n57
Berrick, Jill Duerr, 113n67
Besharov, Douglas, 165, 213
Bhargava, Deepak, 158
bishops, contributions to Catholic
    social teaching by, 10
Bishops' Conference. *See* United
    States Conference of Catholic
    Bishops
Blank, Rebecca M., 185n66, 200
block grants, 79–84, 195–96
Bloom, Dan, 108n15
Boulding, Kenneth, 36
Bounds, Elizabeth, 204, 223n39
Bridefare, 202
Brookings Institution, 80, 176
Brubaker, Pamela, 204, 223n39
Burke, Edmund, 44n57
Burtless, Gary, 167
Bush, George H. W., 125
Bush, George W., 1, 67–70, 190–91,
    193–94
Bush administration
    marriage promotion programs
        proposed by, 202
    welfare reauthorization proposals
        of, 190–91, 193–94
    work requirement proposals of,
        197–99

Califano, Joseph A., Jr., 144–45n39
Cammisa, Anne Marie, 55

Walesa, Lech, 10
Wall Street Journal, 63
Walzer, Michael, 64
War on Poverty, 128
wealth, moral guidelines for the use of,
  23. *See also* distributive justice;
  property
Weaver, R. Kent, 55, 176–77
Weir, Margaret, 83–84
welfare
  Catholic social teaching on (*see*
    United States Conference of
    Catholic Bishops)
  charitable and faith-based
    organizations, role of, 61–70
    (*see also* charitable
    organizations; faith-based
    organizations)
  convictions assumed to shape, 48
  of the future, political spectrum
    regarding, 1–3
  historical roots of, 49–52
  illegitimacy and, data regarding,
    95–97
  indispensable role of government in,
    65
  moral boundaries and posturing
    associated with, 57–58
  the New Deal and its legacy, 52–55
  the "permanent crisis" of AFDC,
    55–61
  program goals, issue of, 56–58
  race and racism associated with,
    59–60
  recidivism and "spell dynamics,"
    studies of, 131
  social control, as a means of, 51
  stigma attached to, 37–38, 54, 58
  subpoverty benefit levels, state
    comparisons revealing,
    71–72n21
  in the United States, limits of,
    37–38
  universalism and, 36–37
  See also Aid to Families with
    Dependent Children
welfare cycling, 131
welfare magnets, 159–60
welfare mothers. *See* single motherhood

Welfare Policymaking in the States
  (Winston), 177
welfare reform, 77–78, 105–6
  absolute moral prohibitions and,
    133–35, 205
  agenda of, 1
  anti-illegitimacy measures in, 94–97
  block-granting, 79–84
  Catholic social teaching on (*see*
    United States Conference of
    Catholic Bishops)
  charitable choice as part of, 65–70
  child nutrition programs, 104
  child-support enforcement associated
    with, 97–98
  documents of the Catholic Church
    on, 125–27
  employment and, barriers to,
    130–33
  ethical issues raised by
    reauthorization (*see* ethics of
    welfare policy)
  faith-based organizations, role of (*see*
    faith-based organizations)
  federal assistance to child care
    services, 103–4
  food stamps, 102–3
  guidelines for evaluating, 33–40,
    80–82, 127–41
  implementation of (*see* implementing
    welfare reform)
  incentives without reductionism,
    need for, 135–38
  Learnfare, 99–100
  legal immigrants and (*see*
    immigrants)
  Medicaid and, 104–5
  outcomes of (*see* implementing
    welfare reform)
  the politics of, 61
  poverty and dependency, relative
    priority of reducing, 127–30
  public opinion and, 48–49
  resistance to, 158–59
  single mothers and (*see* single
    motherhood)
  Social Services Block Grants, 105
  stigma and social marginalization,
    need to avoid, 138–40